FREEDOM'S

FREEDOM'S WEB

Student Activism in an Age of Cultural Diversity

ROBERT A. RHOADS

The Johns Hopkins
University Press
Baltimore and
London

© 1998 The Johns Hopkins University Press
All rights reserved. Published 1998
Printed in the United States of America on acid-free paper
9 8 7 6 5 4 3 2 1

The Johns Hopkins University Press
2715 North Charles Street
Baltimore, Maryland 21218-4319
The Johns Hopkins Press Ltd., London
www.press.jhu.edu

Library of Congress Cataloging-in-Publication Data will be found at the end
    of this book.
A catalog record for this book is available from the British Library.

ISBN 0-8018-5887-9

contents

PREFACE & ACKNOWLEDGMENTS

In this book I seek to make sense of a major form of student activism of the 1990s—student demonstrations organized around multiculturalism and identity politics. The phrase "student demonstrations" refers to *visible public protests organized by students to call attention to a particular concern or set of concerns*. For example, the mid- to late-1980s saw a significant number of student demonstrations organized around the anti-apartheid movement and institutional divestment. Shantytowns popped up on campuses around the country as students used highly visible protests to raise public awareness of human suffering in South Africa. Of course, the decade of the 1960s is the period many of us reflect upon when we think of student demonstrations. It was during this decade that students most vividly expressed the power of student passion and protest.

There is much evidence to suggest that in the 1990s there has been an increase in student demonstrations and campus unrest in comparison to the climate that prevailed in the two preceding decades. Furthermore, while the 1960s are likely to remain the high-water mark of student protest, today's student demonstrators remind us that campus protest is something more than a 1960s phenomenon. We know, for example, that even in the earliest days of Harvard and Yale, students often protested the quality of food as well as their treatment at the hands of their tutors. Student protests continued to erupt from time to time as American higher education expanded into the frontier and issues as far ranging as pedagogical style to control over the extracurricular and sporting life surfaced at one college or another. Because history is important in understanding the contemporary context, the historical background of student protests will be discussed in greater detail in chapter 2.

While student protest is as old as American higher education itself, it is particularly the decade of the 1960s that speaks to the actions of contemporary student activists. The democratic concerns of the 1960s, which launched major campus movements against social inequality, limited student rights, and American imperialism, in many ways have resurfaced among today's most vociferous students. No, we are not reliving the 1960s all over again, and this book makes no such claim. However, understanding the decade of the 1960s is helpful in making sense of the contemporary student concern with identity politics, which was arguably born of the "decade of unrest." That we may understand today's students by relating their struggles to the past is part of what the phrase "freedom's web" is intended to capture.

But "freedom's web" also alludes to another quality of contemporary student activism. And that is that, despite what is predominantly a multifarious movement with seemingly few connections among the African Americans, Asian Americans, Chicanos, gays, and women who lead the majority of campus protests of the 1990s (often including the support of progressive White allies), there are sophisticated sources of common ground that connect many of these students. This is the other theme that the metaphor "freedom's web" seeks to uncover. In particular, the final chapter (chapter 8) highlights this quality of contemporary student activism as the notion of "collective consciousness" is examined.

Thus, the intent of this book is to explore student activism as a form of multicultural expression revolving around issues of social justice and equality. Campus unrest of the 1990s may be seen as democracy playing itself out in the truest sense, as marginalized peoples seek at this moment in history a fair chance to achieve social, political, and economic opportunity. To capture the identity struggles revealed through the many examples of contemporary student unrest, five case studies were selected: the 1993 Chicano studies movement at UCLA, the Mills College strike of 1990, the 1993–96 American Indian protests at Michigan State University, gay liberation activities at Pennsylvania State University from 1991 to 1993, and African American protests at Rutgers University in 1995. While these cases all involved at least two site visits as a means to gather archival and interview data, a sixth case is introduced in chapter 8 that primarily involved the use of the Internet as a means to gather data. This case is the Free Burma Coalition centered at the University of Wisconsin; it is used to highlight the emerging role of advanced technology in creating activist communities and in reframing the identities of today's, and perhaps tomorrow's, student activists.

Method

Case studies offer insights that other methods cannot easily obtain. For example, in the early 1970s Alexander Astin, Helen Astin, Alan Bayer, and Ann Bisconti used case study research to contextualize their national findings of student involvement in campus protests.[1] Their national survey revealed three dominant themes of student unrest during the 1969–70 academic year: racial unrest, demonstrations centered on academic and student life, and protests of American military policy. Through their use of three purposely selected cases (representing each type of protest identified in the larger analysis), Astin and colleagues were able to provide, in addition to a chronology of events, a depth of understanding about key aspects of the organizational context (setting), key issues contributing to student unrest, the relevant cast of characters involved in a specific protest movement, and institutional changes resulting from student protest. Mayer Zald and Michael Berger offered support for situating analyses of social movements within organizational contexts when they suggested that organizations are primary vehicles for social change.[2]

In a manner similar to Astin's strategy, case studies are used in this research project as a means to identify common connections cutting across contemporary campus unrest. The project therefore seeks to build bridges among what appear as islands of student protest. Simply put, the book explores the philosophical and utilitarian webs uniting contemporary student activists to one another and to the past (primarily the 1960s). "Freedom's web" is thus woven across the contemporary American landscape as well as across generations. The image of the web captures the importance of solidarity. As the students fighting as members of the Free Burma Coalition are quick to point out, "A thousand spiders can tie down a lion."

The central goal of this study is to advance a phenomenological understanding of contemporary student activism. The basic stance of phenomenologists such as Edmund Husserl, Maurice Merleau-Ponty, and Alfred Schutz[3] is that social science tends to take for granted the experiences of humans acting, doing, or creating, as if the meaning of human activity is self-evident. Instead, a phenomenological approach suggests an interrogation of human behavior, the situating of human activity not simply as a means to some higher-level ends, but as part of a process of creating meaning. Schutz criticized traditional social science research for taking the existence of humans and their interactions for granted as though, "I can understand the other and his acts and he can understand me and my doings."[4] Instead, Schutz argued that there is much complexity and meaning in the basic elements of social life that needs to be rigorously explored. Schutz did not reject "science" as a means for understanding human behavior. He simply sought a more phenomenon-oriented approach to social science research, one that focused on the meaning and significance social experience held for participants. Hence, from a phenomenological standpoint, human actions such as participating in campus demonstrations need to be interpreted for the meaning that such activities hold for students' lives. The question according to Schutz is "How is it possible that man accomplishes meaningful acts?"[5]

In order to conduct phenomenological research, one must be clear about the kind of phenomenon to be studied. In the case of this project, the primary concern is identifying the nature of student demonstration (as a form of activism) as it is revealed on contemporary college and university campuses. Therefore, specific cases must be identified in order to conduct appropriate analysis. The early challenge in framing the study then was to select representative cases that might yield understandings of contemporary student activism as a social movement. A first step in developing a helpful sample of cases was to get some idea of the terrain of student activism in the 1990s. This was accomplished through an analysis of reported incidents of student activism as described in national and regional newspapers such as the *New York Times* and the *Chronicle of Higher Education*. After an extensive search, over two hundred major incidents of student activism were identified. These incidents were then analyzed to identify possible themes. The vast majority of campus incidents (over 50 percent) were associated with racial and ethnic struggle, women's concerns, or gay rights activities and represent what recent scholars have described both affectionately and pejoratively as "cultural wars," "campus wars," "multicultural unrest," or "identity politics." The majority of the remaining examples of student activism concerned campus funding/tuition concerns, governance issues, world affairs, and environmental causes.

Each site was visited at least two times within a two-year time frame.[6] The overall study was conducted over a six-year span (1992–97) and three of the cases were retrospective in nature (Mills College, UCLA, and Rutgers). The first visit involved establishing initial contact and identifying key informants. Although some interviews occurred during the initial visit, the majority of interviews were conducted during the second site visit and after greater familiarity with the specific case of student activism had been achieved. Students who had already graduated were contacted through their alumni office and many were interviewed over the telephone. Whenever possible, alumni were interviewed face-to-face.

Data were collected using formal and informal interviews, open-ended surveys, participant observation, the use of key informants, document analysis, and the interpretation of artifacts. Data collection followed the basic strategies suggested in the work of Yvonna Lincoln and Egon Guba when they described "naturalistic inquiry."[7] Lincoln and Guba argued that the naturalistic paradigm strongly leans toward qualitative methods because they are more flexible in addressing multiple realities, offer greater insight into the transaction between the inquirer and the object(s) of study, and make assessing the mitigating role of the inquirer easier. From their perspective, the researcher is far from a mere bystander, and instead actively engages research participants in the social construction of meaning, a philosophical stance akin to that adopted by Peter Berger and Thomas Luckmann in their seminal work *The Social Construction of Reality.*[8]

In all, 101 formal interviews and 9 informal interviews were conducted. Formal interviews were tape recorded and transcribed verbatim. These interviews typically lasted anywhere from one to two hours in length. Data from informal interviews, which tended to be much shorter in duration, were recorded through the use of hand notes. The principal documents used as a source of data were letters, memos, newspaper articles, editorials, and students' class papers and journals related to their involvement in activities such as political organizing or volunteer work. In terms of artifacts, various films and audio recordings about student activism and campus demonstrations were collected and analyzed.

Interpretation of the data involved coming to terms with the meanings campus constituents gave to various student actions and their organizing in general. In analyzing the data, content analysis was employed as a means to identify key themes. The following research questions helped to guide the analysis: What meaning do students give to their participation in campus demonstrations? And, What significance does multicultural student protest have for understanding the collegiate experience during the 1990s? Member checks were employed by sharing initial drafts of the case studies with students and faculty who provided feedback for subsequent rewrites.[9]

I thank the following Michigan State University graduate students for their assistance in collecting data for this book: Kayton Carter, Julio Martinez, Anthony Gutierrez, Matthew Helm, and Scott Dixon. I also wish to acknowledge the financial support of MSU's College of Education and the Center for the Study of Advanced Learning Systems (ALS), headed by Kathryn Moore. Thanks also to William Tierney, Philip Altbach, Paul Rogat Loeb, and Arthur Levine for their helpful comments. I am grateful to Jacqueline Wehmueller and Marie Blanchard for their exceptional editorial assistance. And finally, I thank my father, Freeman Rhoads, for his support over the years.

FREEDOM'S
WEB

chapter one

PASSION AND PROTEST
ON CAMPUS

In the early years of the 1960s, thousands of college students spent their summers in the South as they worked to advance the civil rights of the American Negro. These were the youthful idealists of the age who believed that the American dream was for everyone, regardless of race. They felt strongly that Blacks should have civil and social equality with Whites and they were willing to risk life and limb to contribute to this just cause.

Many of the predominantly middle-class students who ventured south found their experience to be an astounding cultural contrast to what they had come to know on the campuses of Michigan, Harvard, Oberlin, and Stanford, just to name a few of the institutions from which their pilgrimage originated. Civil rights work brought them into contact with Black activists and organizational leaders such as Bob Moses, James Forman, and Julian Bond. From these individuals, college students across the country learned the ways of resistance and the role of civil disobedience in forging social change in the old South.[1]

One of the more significant civil rights projects was the voter registration drive in Mississippi during the summer of 1964. Over one thousand college students worked to help register Negro voters and begin what amounted to the largest voters' rights campaign in Mississippi's repressive history. The summer project helped thousands to officially register, as Mississippi was dragged kicking and screaming into the twentieth century. The students' efforts were not without dire consequences, however, and by the time the school bells at Princeton University and Reed

College began to chime in early September, four volunteers were dead, eighty others had been badly beaten, and sixty-seven homes and churches had been burned or bombed.[2]

The close of Freedom Summer stimulated a growing interest in human rights, and within the ivy walls of American colleges and universities the democratic pulse beat with a passion and verve never before witnessed. Armed with the tools of civil disobedience and a spirit radicalized by witnessing the American dream betrayed, thousands of college students committed themselves to transforming campuses into sites of social and political change. For the remainder of the decade, the American college campus would become the central stage for the drama of democracy's ebb and flow, as the struggle of Blacks became a movement of African Americans characterized by Stokely Carmichael as the rising tide of "Black Power."[3]

In addition to the Civil Rights Movement, other social movements were beginning to get played out on the campuses of such places as the University of California at Berkeley, the University of Wisconsin, and Howard University. At these institutions, as well as at countless others, students fought for greater freedom and an end to administrative intrusion supported in previous generations by a philosophy of *in loco parentis*. Under the banner of the "Free Speech Movement," students argued for and in most cases won increased rights and freedom of expression, which in turn contributed to a rising tide of student resistance against the war in Southeast Asia. As the decade progressed, armies of students burned their military induction cards, the American flag, and occasionally some herbal substances as they came to reject a modern-day version of manifest destiny known to them as "American imperialism." Together, these students and the complex movements of which they were a part initiated a student-led march toward increased democracy as freedom's web was beginning to be spun.

As the decade moved inexorably closer to the 1970s, other social movements also became influential in campus life inasmuch as many began to see the Civil Rights Movement as excluding the concerns of women and homosexuals. This perspective is reflected in the work of Cherríe Moraga: "Major missing elements of the Civil Rights Movement . . . were consciousness and activism around specifically female and sexual concerns."[4] The rise of the Women's Movement and Gay Liberation during the late sixties addressed some of the shortcomings of a civil rights struggle that had failed to unite the multitude of groups denied justice and equality within U.S. society.[5] As the pulse of the movements of the sixties slowly weakened, the Women's Movement and Gay Liberation mounted enough strength to survive the political apathy that followed the decade of unrest. By the close of the 1960s, women's groups existed in over forty U.S. cities, including large urban areas such as Chicago and San Francisco, but also were found in university towns such as New Haven as well as more conservative areas like New Orleans, Durham, Iowa City, and Minneapolis. Ten years later, women's liberation organizations had expanded to such a degree that there were an estimated fifty such groups in New York City, thirty-five in San Francisco, thirty in Chicago, and twenty-five in Boston.[6] Civil rights organizations were proving inadequate to the needs of women, and increasingly that need was met by women-centered political associations and activities.

Adding to the liberatory struggles of the late 1960s and the 1970s was the Gay Liberation Movement, which stormed into the 1970s on the strength of the Stonewall Riots in Greenwich Village in 1969.[7] In 1974, gay liberation won a vote of confidence from the American Psychiatric Association when "homosexuality" was removed from the Diagnostic and Statistical Manual–II (DSM-II) as a form of mental illness and many homosexuals began to identify as lesbian, gay, or bisexual. The change in psychological interpretation had a significant impact on campus life, wherein college counselors, faculty, and administrators were forced to rethink their attitudes and develop more affirming policies and practices toward lesbian, gay, and bisexual students.

During the early and mid 1960s, the Civil Rights Movement was associated primarily with the plight of Blacks and their struggle for equal rights and freedom. However, Blacks were not alone in this quest for justice, and as the decade progressed other groups also forged their way into the American consciousness. By the end of the decade, diverse groups such as Mexican Americans and Chicanos were beginning to assert their sense of racial pride and national identity. Nationalistic beliefs associated with La Raza and Chicanismo took firm root on college campuses in the western region of the country and documents such as *El Plan de Santa Barbara* served as the founding tenets for the Movimiento Estudiantil Chicano de Aztlan, the powerful Chicano student group simply known as MEChA.[8] The Civil Rights Movement, which at one time had been centered on Black struggle, began to take on a much more diffuse quality. Thus, as the decade of the 1960s progressed, groups such as Chicanos, gays, and women became vitally concerned with achieving equal rights and liberty and found the college campus to be an attractive setting for organizing political activities. These campus activists, often described as the "New Left," were democratic dreamers whose "radical" social philosophy was represented by a belief that all people regardless of race, gender, or sexual orientation had the right to be treated as equals.

As Freedom Summer gave way to the Summer of Love, which gave way to the assassination of Martin Luther King Jr. and its eventful aftermath, the decade of unrest exploded in May of 1970 as the anger and turmoil of youthful resistance boiled over. With the U.S. invasion of Cambodia, renewed energy was injected into student demonstrators around the country. Nowhere was this more evident than in a little sleepy town in northern Ohio.

In the spring of 1970 Leigh Herington was a graduate student at Kent State University, where he also worked as assistant sports information director. Herington had served in the U.S. Army for ten months before being discharged because of an eye injury. His experience in the army and his knowledge of weaponry contributed to the shock he felt as he stood alongside the public information officer (PIO) for the National Guard as they observed from a knoll a student confrontation with the Ohio National Guard. He recalled the tragedy:

> We watched this bizarre scene of military men trying to push these
> kids around a very large area of the Commons. That didn't make much
> sense to me. It appeared that some of the kids were having a lot of fun,
> although there was tear gas going off. I felt it was a serious confronta-
> tion, but many people there did not grasp the significance and impor-
> tance of what was happening. At any rate, we watched the guardsmen
> go across the campus and up over behind Taylor Hall where we lost
> sight of them. When they came back up, we saw them come up to the
> top of the hill and we saw them turn and kneel. We then heard the firing
> and saw smoke. I looked at the PIO and said, "Isn't that dangerous to
> fire blanks that close?" He turned to me and said, "To my knowledge,
> no blank ammunition has been issued." Having been in the military,
> it nearly knocked me over that they were using live ammunition. My
> second response was, "Wouldn't it be dangerous to shoot live ammuni-
> tion over their heads?" And the next thing I saw were the ambulances.
> I actually never got to the site because I knew I was going to be needed
> up in the News Service.[9]

And Scott Bills offered his account of what happened at Kent State: "They fired for thirteen seconds and expended, by most accounts, sixty-one rounds of ammunition. It was 12:25 P.M. Four students were killed and nine were wounded."[10] Ten days later, Philip Gibbs and James Green were killed by police gunfire at Jackson State College and thus joined Allison Krause, Jeffrey Miller, Sandra Scheuer, and William Schroeder of Kent State University as casualties of a new kind of war situated on their own country's soil. While Kent State and Jackson State were hardly the meccas of student activism during the decade of the 1960s, they soon became the symbols of youthful rebellion against authoritarianism as a generation of antiestablishmentarianism was crowned.

Launched by the campus killings and the U.S. invasion of Cambodia, thousands of students at hundreds of colleges and universities around the country simultaneously stormed Old Mains, legislative buildings, courthouses, and other architectural manifestations of the "establishment" in what amounted to the single largest student protest movement in the history of the country.[11] While the Civil Rights Movement had launched a momentous wave of student activism, it was the Peace Movement that closed the door on the decade of campus unrest.

After Kent State and Jackson State and the countless other campuses where students demonstrated against the war, the student ethos began to change. At first, the difference was hardly noticeable, but by the mid-seventies seemingly overnight a new generation of students had arrived on the American campus scene. No one is quite sure what happened. Maybe the few most committed activists who tended to generate the passion of protest simply burned out or graduated and got on with their lives. By the mid-1970s the economy had slowed down and perhaps students had more to worry about than "equality and justice for all." Or perhaps, as Arthur Levine conjectured, their dreams and heroes simply died.[12] After all, the 1960s witnessed the tragic deaths of Martin Luther King Jr., Malcolm X, John F. Kennedy, and Bobby Kennedy. These were inspirational leaders who connected with the youth of the day. It seems no great stretch of the imagination to conclude that the loss of such leaders eventually would contribute to a form of political malaise.

Although identifying the complex forces that were at work is a hit and miss proposition, the effects were far more obvious. The students of the mid to late 1970s went off to college and, as Levine noted in his work, they never really felt like "real" college students. Many longed to feel the excitement of the previous decade but efforts to recapture the passion through campus organizing were often treated by fellow students as mimicry, and student activists were looked down upon as 1960s wanna-be's. Instead of campus wars over policies and politics, the vast majority of students of the mid to late 1970s waged their battle against polyester and embraced political apathy. And although the previous generation was noted for student drug use, the reality is that the late 1970s marked the peak use of marijuana among college students. If the students of the 1970s were to take anything from the 1960s, Timothy Leary's call to "turn on" and "drop out" seemed most appealing.

Reaganomics became the defining theme of the early 1980s as disco began to be erased from our short-term memories by something known as "New Wave" and then "Progressive" music and "Rap." The music was arguably as exciting as the sixties, but the students did not seem to be. Media images of "Yuppies" (Young Urban Professionals) in pursuit of the good life in weekly television series such as *Thirty Something* became the theme of the day as advertisers, movie makers, and commercial executives sought to cash in on the Baby Boomers, who by now had passed from the days of youthful poverty to adulthood, financial stability, and family responsibility. As the 1980s rolled on, student activism became a distant memory. It seemed that the campus would never again be the place of intellectual and political vitality so passionately embraced by the liberal and progressive students of the past.

On April 4, 1985, a group of Columbia University students blockaded the entrance to Hamilton Hall, the main administration building, and demanded that the university withdraw its investments from South Africa. In the process, these students helped to rekindle the flames of the Civil Rights Movement. Over the next few years, the Divestment Movement gained momentum as shantytowns appeared on campuses around the country and students felt a renewed sense of commitment to something bigger than their own lives.[13]

What followed the student demonstrations organized around divestment in South Africa is the focus of this book. The Divestment Movement, which was fairly successful at hundreds of colleges and universities, ignited interest in student direct action; a new campus movement was in the making. With historical roots in the civil rights struggle of the 1960s, there appeared a more multiplicitous expression of social justice and equality for all. Moving beyond the rhetoric of "equal participation," the activist students of the 1990s demanded something more. They sought to renew the sixties New Left project of participatory democracy; it was no longer adequate simply to be present in organizational life—all people, including those previously denied a voice, ought to have the opportunity to contribute to a more inclusive vision of democracy. These students believed that "the basic meaning of democracy is the rule of the people. Only when everyone participates in making and carrying out decisions can we be sure that the people do, in fact, rule."[14]

One by one, diverse racial and ethnic student groups, gays, and women sat in, taught in, took back, closed down, bombed, fasted, marched, and rallied and in general attempted to push their agenda into the realm of public consciousness. Clearly the United States was not reliving the 1960s, but something indeed was stirring on the American college campus. After nearly two decades of relative silence and a heavy dose of careerism and political apathy, passion once again flowed in the hearts and souls of students—at least in some of them. Certainly, career-minded students still prevailed. And, for sure, the "slacker" image of Generation X portrayed in films such as *Reality Bites* applied to many. However, amid what is easily the most diverse population of college students in U.S. history there has emerged a sizeable population of activists concerned with campus and social change who organized around what can be defined as "multiculturalism." The influence of multiculturalism on contemporary students, the central focus of this work, has also been described by Arthur Levine and Jeanette Cureton, who argue that traditional student political groups largely have been replaced by what they term "support/advocacy" groups, which have their roots in the Black student associations of the 1960s.[15] As Levine and Cureton point out, the growth of student groups committed to race, ethnicity, gender, sexual orientation, and disability concerns dramatically increased over the 1970s and 1980s. Thus, as the 1990s opened, thousands of student groups committed to a variety of equity concerns were in position to make their voices heard. No wonder that Levine and Cureton's study found multiculturalism to be the number one source of student unrest in the 1990s (a finding confirmed by the research undergirding this book).

Thus, for many students, the dream of freedom and justice for all has been recharged and the Civil Rights Movement has been resuscitated in the form of the Multicultural Student Movement of the 1990s. Meta Mendel-Reyes captured a bit of this movement in her book *Reclaiming Democracy*:

> The stereotype of the apathetic "Generation X," so-called by everyone except its own members, ignores the reappearance of participatory politics on campus such as the nationwide demonstrations that followed the passage of California's anti-immigrant Proposition 187, in 1994. Swarthmore College students formed the multiracial Coalition Against Xenophobia (CAX), which led hundreds of Philadelphia-area students, and a few community members and faculty, on an exuberant march around the Liberty Bell on a very cold and rainy December

afternoon. Although these protests received a few seconds of television coverage and a newspaper article here or there, brief glimpses of young activists engaged in nonviolent protest cannot compete with the image of participatory politics that dominates nineties political culture: the self-indulgent or gun wielding sixties "rebels."[16]

The point here is that, for a variety of reasons, few in the media have attached any significance to contemporary student activism. Perhaps it is more beneficial to those who make such decisions to portray students as self-indulgent and apathetic or to cast them in the larger-than-life shadow of the activists of the 1960s.

What is fairly obvious is that few in today's society even acknowledge that student activists populate many of our most famous and not so famous institutions of higher learning. Maybe the issues are not as exciting as the Peace Movement, the Free Speech Movement, or the Civil Rights Movement. Multiculturalism and cultural diversity suggest by their definitions a certain degree of cultural diffusion (a decentering of culture). And yet these new democratic dreamers, despite their diversity, have strong connections through the philosophical and idealistic visions they hold. It is an age of cultural diversity, and building and maintaining communications across the many student groups challenge their ability to successfully unite their causes. Nonetheless, modest connections have been made and a new movement of student activism is upon us.

The Contemporary Context

As the last decade of the twentieth century opened, student demonstrations were once again visible on many U.S. campuses. Nowhere was the power of direct action more vivid than in the spring of 1990 on the campus of a small liberal arts college nestled in the hills of west Oakland. The Mills College student strike epitomized the power of the student body to influence campus policies and to bring social issues into the public's consciousness. The board of trustees had made the decision to become a coeducational institution, leaving behind 138 years of tradition as an all-women's college. But the decision never came to fruition, due to the passionate protests of the women of Mills. Shannon McMackin, a senior in the spring of 1990, spoke at a commencement ceremony that marked the culmination of the most eventful period in her young life as the battle to maintain what to her was a "dear tradition" had been waged and won. "Emotion is not a weak quality. It's passion. And passion more than logic leads to change." McMackin's speech took place on the grounds of Toyan Meadow, the grassy lawn separating the main administration building from the student union, at the precise place where she had stood only two weeks before as she heard the announcement of the college's president that Mills was going to become coed. Her shock had been captured on film and sent around the country as an expression of the anguish of the Mills College women. But, on graduation day, McMackin's face glowed with the pride of victory, of fighting for what she and her fellow students believed was right.

Two years later, Timothy Jones (a pseudonym) spoke to a gathering of students at Pennsylvania State University. The event was part of National Coming Out Day and Timothy was there to share his coming-out experiences with an audience of roughly two hundred students. "Lesbian, gay, and bisexual people have two choices: come out or stay in your closet and continue hating yourself. Coming out is better than hating yourself. . . . It's about celebrating yourself." Timothy was one of the leaders of the Lesbian, Gay, and Bisexual Student Alliance (LGBSA). He and other members of LGBSA led a group of students as they applied ongoing pressure to institutional leaders to add a sexual orientation clause to the university's official statement of nondiscrimination. The students had organized a variety of public events and had held open meetings to challenge the university's policy. One of the key events they planned was a takeover of the president's office. This demonstration never came to fruition, in that the fear they struck in the board of trustees when members got wind of the students' plan was enough to convince them to approve the clause. The students' passion and commitment served as reminders to everyone that there are times when doing the right thing can be so persuasive that mountains can be moved, even in conservative Happy Valley.

A year later, on the campus of the University of California at Los Angeles, Marcos Aguilar began a hunger strike along with five other students and one faculty member as they demanded the creation of a Chicano studies department. For over twenty years, UCLA had halfheartedly supported a Chicano studies interdepartmental program only to see its viability called into question on an almost yearly basis. Chicana and Chicano students felt that the program needed to be strengthened and that granting it departmental status with the authority to hire and promote its own faculty was a way to ensure its survival. Some two weeks before the hunger strike, Marcos Aguilar had been among the ninety students and community members arrested for their participation in a sit-in at the UCLA Faculty Center. The arrests and the treatment they received at the hands of the university and Los Angeles Police Department only served to increase their commitment to the movement. These students saw Chicano studies as a link between an elite institution and a city comprised of the largest Mexican American population in the country. Building a strong Chicano studies department was not simply a battle over who decides curricular matters. Their fight was part of a larger effort to improve the place of Chicanas and Chicanos in American society and to help them connect to a rich culture and history.

The actions of Shannon McMackin, Timothy Jones, Marcos Aguilar, and their many student peers have put colleges and universities on alert that student activism is once again alive and well. The Mills College strike of 1990 was followed a few years later by additional student demonstrations as students took direct action to pressure the college to diversify its faculty. By this time, members of the administration had become somewhat exasperated with the present-day students. As one high-ranking official remarked, "Now today, they are protesting for diversifying the faculty. They want us to hire more faculty of color. I'm up to my neck in student activism."

No sooner had the ink dried on Penn State's new more inclusive statement of nondiscrimination than lesbian, gay, and bisexual students started their next political battle. They had two targets in mind: the unequal treatment of lesbian, gay, and bisexual students by the university's ROTC program, and the lack of university benefits provided to partners of lesbian, gay, and bisexual faculty and staff.

And in 1993 when the César Chávez Center for Instruction in Chicana and Chicano Studies was created and given the authority to hire and promote five full-time faculty, UCLA had gone a long way toward stabilizing the program. But problems still endured, and three years later the program continued to struggle as the position of department chair had become a revolving door. Activists who had organized the hunger strike pondered whether they had given up too much when they agreed to end the two-week-long fast. A few students contemplated renewed efforts to foster community support and spur the faculty and administration into a concerted effort to bolster the program. Only time would tell whether their thoughts would be converted to action.

"Martyrs for Multiculturalism" was the *Newsweek* headline that described the case of UCLA and Chicano studies.[17] The article hinted at the "balkanization" of the academy to which programs such as Chicano studies are believed by most conservatives and some liberals to contribute. Yet, for the multiracial protesters who took over the UCLA Faculty

Center, life in the United States was already "balkanized" by a variety of institutional forces that had long privileged one group at the exclusion of others. For the student demonstrators at UCLA, multiculturalism was not an additional source of division. Quite the contrary: It was viewed as a positive force in creating greater inclusion, and legitimizing Chicano studies was one step in this broad democratic project. For the UCLA student protesters, their struggle was a matter of creating a space for Chicanos in the curriculum and within the university's power structure. Should these students and countless other multicultural supporters around the country be blamed for contributing to the "culture wars," as so many writers would have Americans to believe?[18] Ronald Takaki offers a cogent response to such charges:

> As our diversity is increasingly recognized today, it is accompanied by even more defensive denial, grim jeremiads of the Allan Blooms about the "closing of the American mind," and demagogic urgings of the Patrick Buchanans to take back "our cities, our culture, and our country." But who, in this case, are "we"? Such a backlash is defining our diversity as a "cultural war," a conflict between "us" and "them." Reflecting a traditional Eurocentrism that remains culturally hegemonic, this resistance is what is really driving the "disuniting of America."[19]

If indeed the struggle at UCLA over curricular representation was part of an ongoing cultural war, it certainly had not been started by a group of multiracial twenty-somethings.

When one examines the case of UCLA along with those of Penn State, Mills College, and countless other examples in which identity politics are at the center of campus conflict, it becomes clear that the effort to build a more democratic society forms the heart of a campus movement committed to multiculturalism. The fact that large numbers of Americans see such efforts as divisive reflects the reality that many in our society are comfortable with current curricular and institutional structures that are far from inclusive. The status quo looks pretty good from a privileged vantage point! The sad reality is that many Americans are resistant of any effort to build a truly participatory and inclusive society. A clear example was the significant resistance from the Right to combine voter registration with driver's registration. Apparently, such a system would make voting too accessible.

While the Divestment Movement of the 1980s has played a key role in igniting contemporary student activism, other forces are involved as well. For example, many of today's generation of students are the offspring of the activists of the 1960s and reflect a thirty-year cycle of children of activists dating back to the 1930s, the 1960s, and then the 1990s. One might expect a similar phase of increased student activism in the 2020s. Another force perhaps has been the backlash against the conservatism of the Reagan years. Arguably, there has been a reemergence of more liberal-minded thinking among some of today's youth. In fact, data from the Cooperative Institutional Research Program (CIRP) headed by UCLA's Higher Education Research Institute reveals that while the students of the late 1980s tended to report less interest in politics than their 1960s predecessors, they also reported a higher rate of involvement in organized demonstrations. As Eric Dey, Alexander Astin, and William Korn conclude, "These trends suggest that there is a rapidly expanding number of American college students who are dissatisfied with the status quo and with traditional political methods of bringing about social change."[20]

The students of the 1990s are a long way from becoming the "New," New Left. The reality is that the vast majority of incoming students in the early 1990s continued to be "middle of the road" in terms of their political perspectives.[21] Nonetheless, many have moved beyond the apathy that so characterized much of the 1970s and 1980s. Julie Batz, an alumna of Mills College who assisted students as a facilitator during the strike of 1990, offered the following explanation of the changing student zeitgeist: "When I was at Mills in the late 1980s, student activism was beginning to be stirred by the divestment movement and apartheid in South Africa. All that was emerging in the late 1980s and it kind of introduced a whole new generation of student activists." And Jorge Mancillas, a professor at the University of California at Los Angeles who participated in the Chicano studies hunger strike of 1993, offered a similar assessment: "I really sense a mood shift among students in this country that leads me to believe that the Chicano studies movement is one small step in a larger social movement that's gonna unfold over the years. . . . It was a small part in a larger process which hasn't unfolded fully yet." The unfolding of the social movement alluded to by Mancillas seemed most evident in the spring of 1996.

Spring of 1996

On March 14, 1996, college students around the country joined in what was known as "National Day of Action." Thousands of students participated in rallies, pickets, teach-ins, vigils, and marches in defense of access to education, immigrants' rights, and affirmative action and in opposition to what activists described as a toxic atmosphere toward students, people of color, and lesbian, gay, and bisexual people. Students pointed to H.R. 2128, which could overturn decades of Supreme Court rulings on affirmative action, anti-immigrant and affirmative action legislation in states such as California, threats to higher education in the form of proposed cuts to the Department of Education and Americorps, and various state initiatives aimed at limiting the rights of lesbian, gay, and bisexual people, as evidence of the widespread intolerance and xenophobia. Using electronic mail to get the word out, the Center for Campus Organizing in Cambridge, Massachusetts, played a pivotal role in what turned out to be a highly successful day of action and a follow-up "Week of Action" (March 27–April 2). The demonstrations were also promoted by Four Winds Student Movement in Los Angeles, the University of California Student Association, and the Democratic Socialists of America, among other supportive organizations.

Perhaps it was mere coincidence that March 14 also marked the 113th anniversary of the death of Karl Marx, whose life many of these students seemed to look to for revolutionary inspiration. Or perhaps the date had been selected for that very reason. No matter the rationale, National Day of Action was an exclamation that the decade of the 1990s had become something different from the two preceding decades and that activism was alive and well among contemporary college students. March 14, 1996, served as a call to students around the country that what was needed most was a return of social and political consciousness to American college campuses. The spring of 1996 offered many examples of student response to this call.

In Corvallis, Oregon, students marched on the campus of Oregon State University demonstrating against a series of racist incidents that had occurred on the campus, including defacing of Anita Hill posters with racial slurs. Despite there being fewer than two hundred Black students at OSU, the march drew anywhere from fourteen hundred to two thousand participants including representatives from the Black Student Union, the Mexican American and Chicano student organization (MEChA), and the Oregon Public Employees Union.

One day earlier, students from the University of California at San Diego held a demonstration aimed at defeating the anti–affirmative-action legislation being pushed through the California legislative process, some of which already had been adopted by the University of California system. Their efforts were part of a larger state-wide plan of action as students took to the offensive in countering hostility directed at minorities disguised in the form of the California Civil Rights Initiative. Approximately three hundred students participated in a march that ended when eighteen students were arrested for overtaking the intersection at La Jolla Village Drive in San Diego. "I'm doing this because I think people need to find out what's going on," stated UC San Diego undergraduate president Naomi Falk as she was handcuffed and pushed into a police van. "I hope a lot of people are paying attention." Earlier in the day, Greg Akili of the San Diego Equal Opportunity Coalition spoke to a crowd of about seven hundred, which was described by the administration as the most emotional and militant protest in fifteen years. "Say no to these attempts to dictate that we can only have one kind of society with one kind of people," shouted Akili.[22]

Campus organizations around the country joined their UC San Diego and OSU peers. Students from several D.C. colleges and universities, including Howard University and George Washington University, combined forces to lead a demonstration at House Republican leader Newt Gingrich's Washington apartment in protest of what they perceived as unfair scapegoating of minorities and immigrants. Students from the Coalition for Economic Justice at the University of North Carolina at Chapel Hill held a speak-out on campus and mini-demonstrations at several places in Chapel Hill, including the office of Jesse Helms. Members of MIT's Committee for Social Justice, Mujeres Latinas, Hunger Action Group, Amnesty International, and South-Asian American Students organized a week of consciousness raising culminating in a rally aimed at countering racism, homophobia, sexism, and anti-immigration sentiment.

Students at the University of New Mexico arranged a meeting with President Richard Peck to discuss the spiraling tuition increases at the university and the impact on low-income families throughout the state. President Peck became incensed and according to students told them that they lacked an appreciation for the division of labor on the campus. Students also reported that as Peck left the meeting he offered one last word of advice: "You go to classes. We make policy." Apparently, the lessons of the 1960s had been lost on some institutional leaders. In response, students from the Progressive Student Alliance (PSA) erected a shanty on the lawn in front of the administration building as an expression of free speech meant to depict the widening gap between tuition and the income of New Mexican residents. Within hours campus police arrived at the shanty and ordered students to tear it down. The students refused and two were arrested. The following day about 150 students attended a rally to organize students for a board of regents meeting that would take place later the same day. A PSA member spoke for the group and expressed two demands: (1) that the regents honor a student referendum on tuition increases to be held on April 10 and (2) that all students involved in recent campus protests be given amnesty. The regents did not respond to the students and refused to negotiate with future PSA representatives. Ultimately, fourteen additional students were arrested and faced criminal charges. The administration repeatedly maintained a hardline stance and saw the running of the university as their domain and not the province of students.

Also, in the spring of 1996, approximately one hundred Columbia University students occupied Hamilton Hall and demanded that President George Rupp institute a department of ethnic studies. About fifty additional students rallied outside. The demonstrations at Hamilton Hall were signs of support for four other students who had entered the tenth day of a hunger strike. Five days later and after at least a dozen arrests, students walked out of Hamilton Hall arm in arm chanting "What do we want? Ethnic Studies! When do we want it? Now!" And, "The students united will never be defeated!" Later in the same day, the two-week-long hunger strike ended after extensive negotiations in which a compromise position was reached: The university agreed to commit to the creation of a Latino and Asian American studies program with the help of a blue ribbon panel to search for qualified faculty. This was short of the students' vision of a department of ethnic studies. Their dissatisfaction was expressed in the Ethnic Studies Manifesto they soon released:

> We believe that Columbia University's recent commitment to the establishment of Asian American and Latino Studies programs is shortsighted and naive. We call on the administrative and intellectual leadership of Columbia to acknowledge that the future development of curricular, theoretical, methodological, and practical contributions of Ethnic Studies can only be nurtured and sustained by the creation of a Department of Ethnic Studies. . . . Only with departmental status can such fields of study be insured centrality in the curriculum. Only with a department will Columbia be able to attract leading scholars and ensure that tenure be evaluated internally and not subject to the politics of other departments. . . . Only a Department of Ethnic Studies will insure Columbia's place at the forefront of academia.

The events of the spring of 1996 highlight a number of issues around which students organized. But other concerns have also contributed to campus unrest throughout the nineties. For example, the decade got off with a big bang with the help of the women at Mills College, who had a model to follow in the actions of the students of Gallaudet College, where at the close of the 1980s students successfully replaced their newly hired president with another, who like themselves was hearing impaired. Identity concerns, however, were not the only theme as countless causes drew student ire. For example, around the country students at hundreds of colleges and universities held candlelight vigils and demonstrations throughout the decade demanding the retrial of death-row inmate Mumia Abu-Jamal, sentenced for the 1981 killing of a Philadelphia police officer despite the conflicting testimony of key witnesses. In 1991, students at the University of Michigan, Wayne State University, UCLA, University of California at Davis, and Columbia University, just to name a few, held protests against U.S. involvement in the Persian Gulf War. In 1993, students at Yale, Brandeis, Columbia, Harvard, Stanford, Wesleyan, Brown, the University of Cincinnati, the University of Washington, and the University of Virginia held rallies to express their outrage over the global community's inability to end the atrocities in Bosnia. City University of New York students organized multiple rallies throughout the 1990s to protest ongoing tuition hikes. At the University of Texas students held demonstrations and teach-ins to protest the elimination of minority-based fellowships and scholarships. The students rejected Chancellor William Cunningham and President Robert Berdahl's rationale that the Fifth Circuit Court's decision in the Hopwood case forced the university to take proactive steps to eliminate minority support. Instead, the students sought an alternative to what they perceived as the wholesale abandonment of affirmative action programs. In 1996, graduate teaching assistants at Yale initiated a semester-ending strike when they refused to turn in student grades as part of their effort to improve labor conditions for TAs. In an episode that brought to mind the Rodney King beating, students at the Claremont Colleges protested the mistreatment of illegal immigrants at the hands of the Riverside sheriff's department. And finally, through student boycotts, activists at Harvard University effectively scuttled a $1 million contract between the university and Pepsi because of the company's ties to the repressive military regime in Burma.

While liberal and progressive agendas obviously have attracted the greatest percentage of campus demonstrations, conservative issues have also drawn student activists. Key conservative concerns throughout the decade have included support for the war with Iraq, anti-abortion demonstrations at campus health clinics, support for the creation of White student unions at campuses such as the University of Florida, and student protests in opposition to gay rights as evidenced by the emergence of student organizations such as STRAIGHT at Penn State University (*S*tudents *R*einforcing *A*dherence *i*n the *G*eneral *H*eterosexual *T*radition).

Clearly, campus unrest has become somewhat common throughout the 1990s. But unlike the 1960s, in which there were three major unifying themes that gave greater national coherence to student demonstrations, the nature of unrest in the 1990s, despite activities such as National Day of Action, has appeared far more fragmented. There is, however, one fiber loosely connecting many but certainly not all examples of contemporary campus unrest—the struggles of students from marginalized groups and their supporters who seek to elevate diverse communities and cultures. Theirs is a struggle often described as identity politics.

Identity Politics and Democratic Struggle

The Wellesley College commencement ceremony of 1969 marked a momentous occasion in the school's nearly one-hundred-year history. For the first time ever, the students had gained the right to have a student speak at commencement. The speaker the students selected addressed the campus unrest so pervasive during her years in college.

> Every protest, every dissent, whether it's an individual academic paper or a Founder's parking lot demonstration, is unabashedly an attempt to forge an identity in this particular age. That attempt at forging for many of us over the past four years has meant coming to terms with our humanness. . . . There's a strange conservative strain that goes through a lot of New Left, collegiate protest that I find intriguing because it harkens back to the old virtues, the fulfillment of original ideals. It is a very unique American experience. It is such a great adventure. If the experiment in human living doesn't work in this country, in this age, it's not going to work anywhere.[23]

Of course, the "great adventure" this student alluded to is that of democracy itself. Her words conveyed the idea of democracy as a utopian experiment in participatory decision making. This is why the cacophony heard throughout American society and especially on our college campuses is in many ways democracy playing its own tune. The strain of voices we hear also represents the identity struggles of various groups whose ability to participate in this noble experiment in human living historically has been limited.

As the first ever student speaker at the Wellesley College commencement ceremonies, Hillary Rodham was writing history both for the students of the school as well as for women around the country who dreamed of playing integral roles in this great adventure. Twenty-one years later, the women of Mills College followed the footsteps of those who had blazed a cultural trail and opened new frontiers for them. In the spring of 1990, Mills College women fought to preserve the advances they had achieved as women. They held to a deep conviction that there was a great need and benefit in preserving women's space within the larger landscape that is American higher education. Their struggle was about much more than merely keeping men out; it was about women's education and the place of women in a society that has been largely male dominated. The Mills College strike of 1990 represented the struggle of women to define their own lives as "womyn" by preserving public spaces where a womynist identity could be fostered.

Identity also lay at the heart of the student struggle at Rutgers University when a multiracial group led by African American students protested racist comments made by President Francis Lawrence. For African American students at the university, their fight with Lawrence was more than a battle of words; it was a battle over the right and responsibility to create images of what it means to be an African American in the United States. For many on the New Brunswick campus, it seemed as though history was repeating itself. On April 4, 1968, the assassination of Martin Luther King Jr. had sent tremors across that campus. Nearly thirty years later, shock waves from those same tremors were felt among an African American student population that once again felt betrayed by the White power structure. A notice published by Black student organizations back in 1968 might as well have been released once again: "We black people have reached a breaking point. We shall not tolerate this racism any longer. This system must be changed whether with white help or without it."[24]

When students at UCLA demanded a Chicano studies program with full departmental standing, they were trying to erase years of marginality that had come to define the lives of Mexican Americans in the United States. In situating Chicano culture and history as legitimate subjects of inquiry, these students were in a very real sense claiming their own rights to full and equal participation in the great adventure. Their struggle was the fulfillment of the early work of Chicano activists of the late 1960s who first proposed the idea of Chicano studies as part of *El Plan de Santa Barbara*. UCLA historian Juan Gómez-Quiñones discussed the relevance of the Santa Barbara conference:

> In the area of struggle for higher education for Mexican students and the development of Chicano studies programs, the 1969 Santa Barbara conference and the Plan de Santa Barbara reflected a major attempt to provide conceptual cohesion, to develop common guidelines, and to consolidate past gains and prepare the ground for future ones [gains]. . . . Eventually, programs were established at many campuses, and as such they represented a net gain; but these programs were shaped and directed according to the rules of the university game.[25]

The "university game" of limiting ethnic studies programs such as Chicano studies to nondepartmental status was in part what Gómez-Quiñones alluded to and what so aggravated student activists at UCLA in the early 1990s. In the end, the students chose to reject the university's rules and play by a set of their own.

The democratic challenge of including diverse voices in a more participatory form of decision making echoes the work of C. Wright Mills and his critique of the American power structure. In *The Power Elite*,[26] Mills argues that the key decisions shaping this country rest in the hands of a few men situated within government, industry, and the military. It was the work of Mills as much as any social philosopher that shaped the writing of the Port Huron Statement in 1962, which served as the guiding document for the Students for a Democratic Society (SDS). As James Miller explained, "The intellectuals of the New Left felt no compulsion to search for a substitute proletariat—a class destined by the hidden hand of economic development to hasten the dawn of universal human freedom. . . . The guiding influence remained C. Wright Mills—not Karl Marx."[27]

The influence of both SDS and the Port Huron Statement on the American political scene and on campus life should not be underestimated. Again, Miller is helpful: "This statement is one of the pivotal documents in post-war American history. Its publication was crucial in catapulting SDS to national prominence. It also helped to popularize an idea that would exercise a profound influence over the radical politics of the next decade: the idea of 'participatory democracy.' This idea came to define the New Left of the Sixties, as countless young people put democracy to the test."[28]

In his autobiography, Tom Hayden, one of the authors of the Port

Huron Statement, highlighted several of the fundamental characteristics of participatory democracy:

- that decision-making of basic social consequence be carried on by public groupings;
- that politics be seen positively, as the art of collectively creating an acceptable pattern of social relations;
- that politics has the function of bringing people out of isolation and into community, thus being a necessary, though not sufficient, means of finding meaning in personal life;
- that the political order should serve to clarify problems in a way instrumental to their solution; it should provide outlets for the expression of personal grievance and aspiration; opposing views should be organized so as to illuminate choices and facilitate the attainment of goals.[29]

Drawing on a term coined by Mills, the statement challenged the "New Left" to "awaken its allies, and by beginning the process towards peace, civil rights and labor struggles, reinsert theory and idealism where too often reign confusion and political barter."[30] The document closed by suggesting that if it appears that SDSers "seek the unattainable, then let it be known that we do so to avoid the unimaginable."

In the 1990s, SDS no longer led campus activists who dreamt of a more participatory form of democracy. As an official organization, they had long since faded from the campus scene. In many ways, however, key elements of the Port Huron Statement lived on through the Multicultural Student Movement and the quest by contemporary students to achieve greater inclusion.

There is, of course, another interpretation of today's campus unrest and the identity politics that get played out on an almost daily basis. For many traditionalists, both conservative and liberal, identity politics mark the decline of the canon and the rich traditions of an education which once sought to ground students in a common experience. The common experience was rooted in the philosophical ideals represented by Western culture. For conservative writers such as Dinesh D'Souza,[31] multiculturalism is not about democracy—it is about chaos and fragmentation, despite research suggesting otherwise. For example, Alexander Astin reported that campus commitment to diversity and multiculturalism has a positive effect on racial understanding. As Astin explained, "The fact that a strong emphasis on diversity enhances the student's commitment to promoting racial understanding is of special interest, given that some critics have alleged that emphasizing issues of race and multiculturalism tends to exacerbate racial tensions on the campus. Quite the opposite seems to be the case."[32] And Sylvia Hurtado offers a similar finding when she notes that "data support the notion that an institutional commitment to diversity can substantially improve minority and, to some extent, white student perceptions of race relations on campus."[33] The point here is that progressive-minded institutions which demonstrate a serious commitment to multiculturalism may avoid some of the tension arising when minority students and women have to take issues of diversifying the campus environment into their own hands. In other words, multicultural protesters should not be seen as the source of tension; a lack of institutional diversity is more likely the culprit.

Despite Astin's and Hurtado's findings of the benefits of multiculturalism, students, from D'Souza's perspective, have been spurred on by faculty too deeply embedded in the relativism of multiculturalism, deconstructionism, poststructuralism, postmodernism, feminism, Marxism, gay/lesbian studies, and ethnic studies. According to the traditionalists, many of today's faculty are part of a "conspiratorial group of academic barbarians marching under various profane banners . . . storming the barricades of Truth, Reason, Beauty, Western Civilization, and other capitalized self-evidently 'transcendental' or 'universal' Values."[34] Thus, the enemy for conservatives such as D'Souza, William Bennett, and Lynn Chaney are the left-leaning professors like Juan Gómez-Quiñones and Jorge Mancillas, who have not only spurred today's students on but have actually gotten their hands dirty in the process.

Western thought has much to teach today's students. But, at the same time, it must be recognized that not all of what Western civilization represents has been beneficial to the quest for equality and social justice. Western thinking has brought us the enslavement of indigenous peoples of Africa, the near annihilation of North American Indians, the atom bomb, and the Holocaust, just to mention a few of the cataclysmic ideas and actions. As Audre Lorde pointed out, much of Western thinking conditions people to see things in terms of simple oppositions such as good versus bad, dominant versus subordinate, up versus down, superior versus inferior: "In a society where the good is defined in terms of profit rather than in terms of human need, there must always be some group of people who, through systematized oppression, can be made to feel surplus, to occupy the place of the dehumanized inferior. Within this society, that group is made up of Black and Third World people, working-class people, older people, and women."[35] It is systematized oppression enacted through a variety of postsecondary educational mechanisms such as control of the curriculum, decisions about educational access, the governance and regulation of campus life, and the allocation of resources that as a whole profoundly affects the lives of the dehumanized in this society. Tearing down and replacing such mechanisms therefore is part of a larger project and is at the heart of the democratic struggle witnessed on today's college and university campuses.

But resistance to multiculturalism is not limited to the Right. Attacks also derive from liberal-leaning social critics who have grown impatient and mistrustful of what they see on today's campuses. Perhaps the most astute criticism derives from Todd Gitlin, who, interestingly enough, was one of the young leftists contributing to the rise of SDS back in the early 1960s. Now a professor at New York University, Gitlin has adopted more of a centrist position in his criticism of identity politics and multiculturalism. While Gitlin assuredly agrees with the democratic vision of equality and justice for all, he sees identity politics as a detour and a new kind of orthodoxy enforced through institutional policies: "Claims about the diversity of the human condition that made much good sense (and wreaked much havoc) in their origins have, over time, hardened into an orthodoxy that, with drearily uniform slogans, elevates diversity—that is, fragmentation—to religious heights. The new identity orthodoxy is more than a cultural tropism encouraged by a passion for community; it is enforced by laws and administrative regulations."[36] Gitlin goes on to argue that nowhere is such enforcement more powerful than on college and university campuses. "On campus, today's obsession with difference is distinguished, too, by the haughtiness of the tribes and the scope of their intellectual claims. Many exponents of identity politics are fundamentalists—in the language of the academy, 'essentialists'—and the belief in essential group differences easily swerves toward a belief in superiority."[37]

Gitlin maintains that the pervasiveness of identity politics is a driving force in the breakup of the Left. The proliferation of identity groups not only has contributed to fragmentation within academe, but according to Gitlin, is responsible for a lack of "commons" among the Left. But the research undergirding *Freedom's Web* suggests that the "separate political standing" that Gitlin ascribes to identity groups is not nearly so "separate" as he believes it to be. The identity politics described throughout this book is hardly the unbridgeable domain of isolationism Gitlin and others rightfully fear. The problem they see may be more a matter of an attribution error than of the actuality of culturally diverse others who have supposedly closed the door to communication with White males and any other human manifestation of power and privilege. As this book reveals, even the most strident students of today's "culture wars" are more than willing to join arms with other freedom fighters — that is, if we understand freedom as the right of all people to share in the construction of meaning in their lives, including their educational lives. Perhaps the "common dreams" that Gitlin speaks of as part of the vision of the Left are not so distant after all but hidden in the daily muck of misunderstanding. Instead of seeing multiculturalism as the "vexatious balkanization of America," we may be far better off, as Takaki argues, "responding to our diversity as an opportunity to open American minds."[38]

No matter what one's political persuasion, it is hard to argue with the notion that multiculturalism represents in a very real sense a revolutionary change in American campus life: Even the conservative-leaning Nathan Glazer acknowledged not so wryly that "we are all multiculturalists now."[39] In case study research focused on the goal of creating community in higher education, Irving Spitzberg and Virginia Thorndike discussed a number of multicultural initiatives under way in the late 1980s.[40] Soon thereafter, Arthur Levine and Jeanette Cureton described the multicultural movement as "the quiet revolution," and reported that 34 percent of all colleges and universities have a multicultural general education requirement.[41] Although many multicultural initiatives have been enacted without campus uproar, in numerous cases efforts to restructure campus life around diversity and multiculturalism have been intensely debated and resisted. The examples of student activism and campus conflict discussed in this book suggest that the movement may not be so quiet after all.

One should not be surprised that colleges and universities highlight the cultural tension inherent throughout our society. Because education plays such a key role in fostering and enhancing a democratic citizenry, as John Dewey's[42] work reminds us, it is reasonable to expect that many of the social tensions of the democratic adventure will be apparent in campus life.[43] After all, "The educational system is . . . of central importance in determining who will be able to participate fully and meaningfully in our democratic society."[44] The fact that schooling in general is a central target of political and cultural conflict is hardly anything new to democracy's struggle. For example, in his analysis of the antebellum reform movement of the 1800s, Ronald Walters highlighted how education became the target of efforts to influence the nature of the American citizenry:

> School reform, however, played equally well to the darker moods of the middle-class men and women. Since the eighteenth century Americans had fretted over what would become of the republic if its people declined in virtue. That appeared to be happening—politics fell into the hands of the demagogues; foreigners and paupers made the cities unpleasant and threatening for respectable folk. Schools were the answer. In [Horace] Mann's words, they were the means for decent Americans to "free ourselves from the low-minded and the vicious; not by their expatriation, but by their elevation." Education would teach good behavior and make the dangerous classes trustworthy.[45]

In the 1990s, one might wonder if multiculturalists had become the new "low-minded and vicious" bringing down ivory towered cities on the hill, while the William Bennetts of American society sought to elevate the "dangerous classes" by teaching them from his very own book of virtues. One cannot help but wonder what college and university curricula might resemble if not for the identity politicians who take issue with the long history of ethnocentrism undergirding traditional views of higher learning.

In his book *Generation at the Crossroads*, Paul Loeb wrote about identity politics and contemporary students: "Organizing around common racial or sexual identity can anchor students in common experience and history. It can help them challenge the myths that all Americans begin with equal chances. It can unearth the pain of wanting to succeed while knowing that it might mean having to leave behind family, friends, and community."[46] Loeb went on to warn, however, that an exclusionary form of student identity politics, in which Blacks only speak to Blacks, or Puerto Ricans only speak to Spanish-speaking students, is damaging to the democratic vision. When student interaction is limited to intragroup conversations, how can social transformation requiring real communication be achieved? Organizing around cultural identities may be necessary for social change, but identities nonetheless ought to remain a flexible space that enables border crossing and dialogue across differences.[47]

The problem is that underrepresented students who turn to one another for sources of support are often characterized by the majority as adopting isolationist behaviors. Few accuse White students who eat together in the school's cafeteria of being segregationists, but as soon as a group of African American or Mexican American students take their meals together, a conspiracy of some sort must be under way. The reality is that research has shown that students from underrepresented groups often look for "safe spaces," which may be thought of as social networks connecting members of the same cultural group. Group identification on the part of underrepresented minorities does not necessarily suggest an inability or lack of desire to communicate cross-culturally, although majority students may interpret their behavior in this manner.[48]

Constructing identities around one's cultural background ought not be the end of social struggle. It is a simplistic and an essentialist form of logic to see identity as autonomous and exclusionary, as if we are not interwoven into some larger and highly interactive social matrix. For Peter McLaren, democracy should not be seen as a "seamless, smooth or always harmonious" project. Forming identities around diversity is not the goal, but rather "diversity must be affirmed within a politics of cultural criticism and a commitment to social justice."[49] In other words, students need to recognize that cultural differences do exist and that such differences contribute a great deal to the kinds of social experiences they have. At the same time, cultural differences must not be positioned as barriers to building connections in the larger struggle for social justice.

The struggle for identity should be seen as a piece of the complex democratic project—a starting point from which to battle for social justice and equality. The argument here reflects in part Gitlin's apprehension that identity politics (and the intellectual work of cultural studies as a discipline) may be seen as an end in itself. The problem, as Gitlin argues, is that social change external to the campus and beyond the reach of esoteric intellectualism may not occur.[50] While this is indeed something to fear, we cannot underestimate the power of the university and of education in general to shape tomorrow's citizens and leaders. The point is that social change does take place within the context of higher learning, but it may not be the kind of immediate change individuals such as Gitlin call for as part of advancing a democratic agenda. Clearly, the university should not be removed from the struggle for advancing democracy, but neither should it be situated as the sole or primary agent of democratic change.

One Final Thought

In advancing a discussion of contemporary student activism, it is helpful to point to another key aspect of campus unrest—the role of the media in calling attention to student demonstrations and in identifying what issues or events receive public attention (and thus become part of our collective consciousness). This has been a problem throughout the years: "It would not be stretching the point to suggest that the mass media significantly perpetuate and escalate various local conflicts both through their accurate reporting and their frequently error-filled, highly selective perspectives. One comes increasingly to respond to what was said about what was said than to what actually was said and in what context."[51]

Furthermore, it is not only what the media highlights that has relevance; what they choose to ignore is also important. Without the media coverage of campus life in the 1960s would we have the same impressions we have today of that generation? Who can ever forget the scenes at Kent State flashed across the nation via television? But why are the scenes at Jackson State less ingrained in people's memories? What images do we hold of those killings? And is there perhaps racism in the media that makes it less likely for events such as Jackson State, which involved the killing of two Black students, to be less a part of our consciousness? Does racism contribute to the lack of media coverage of today's multicultural unrest? And what about homophobia? Where has the media coverage been for all the National Coming Out Day celebrations and gay pride rallies over the past ten to fifteen years? In many ways, lesbian, gay, and bisexual students have been the most persistent student activists in recent years, and yet rarely are images of their struggle presented to a national audience.

How can one ever forget the police car surrounded by students during the free speech demonstrations at Berkeley? People throughout this country still recall the clips of the antiwar demonstrations and the images of long-haired college students burning draft cards at universities such as Wisconsin and Columbia. These memories were brought to us by ABC and Harry Reasoner, NBC and Chet Huntley and David Brinkley, and, of course, the trusted voice of Walter Cronkite of CBS. What would we recall of the 1960s were it not for television?

At the same time, little national attention was given to SDSers and the Weathermen at Penn State, and so their involvement is not etched in our national consciousness. SUNY Buffalo also had its share of student activism and campus unrest in the 1960s and yet the school is seldom mentioned as an "activist" campus.[52] Yet, for those who endured the tension and conflict at Penn State and SUNY Buffalo, it was quite real.

In *The Campus War: A Sympathetic Look at the University in Agony*, John Searle offers a telling example of the relevance of the media. He tells the story of attending a speech given by Noam Chomsky on the war in Vietnam and how at the end of it a student stood up and explained in an exasperated tone that the whole thing had been a waste of time: "Because no one had summoned the television crews. Without the presence of TV it simply did not count."[53] While one may disagree with the premise of Searle's look at campus unrest, in which he sees the Left and the Right exploiting television by introducing theatrics and in the end "all at the expense of the university,"[54] it is hard to dispute his premise about the importance of the media in creating a stage for both the Left and the Right.

What is real? Is history real if it is not captured by television or the newspapers? How is meaning created and what is the role of the media? These are questions that leave us wanting and at times reflecting on the simpler days of a bygone era. As Jean Baudrillard argued, "We live in a world where there is more and more information, and less and less meaning."[55] What meaning does student activism hold for us today? And where is the media throughout it all? What role does the media play in student activism and efforts to create meaning and a collective sense of consciousness? These are questions we should keep in the back of our minds as we explore student activism in the 1990s.

The university is a place where knowledge is created, and because knowledge is clearly political, as Michel Foucault's[56] work so pointedly reveals, then the university is necessarily a site where identity politics will undoubtedly unfold. From such a perspective, student activism is not to be taken as a sign that the university is in agony, but instead may be seen as an example of a plurality of voices struggling to be heard. Thus, the central point of this book is rather straightforward: If we can learn to stand the strains of passion, we might understand the pain underlying their expression.

chapter two

HISTORICAL WEBS OF
CONNECTION

Revisiting the 1960s

The Multicultural Student Movement of the 1990s reflects both the changing face of the American college student and the general nature of student culture as it has evolved over the years. A salient feature of student culture is activism (obviously, apathy is present as well!), and student understandings of the 1960s shape many of the cultural norms associated with campus protest and demonstration. The fact that student activists of the 1990s often turn to the 1960s as a resource for making sense of their present-day lives reminds us of how important the past can be in the construction of meaning.

But the influence of the 1960s extends far beyond the passage of cultural norms over the course of time. Arguably, the issues that framed the social concerns of students of the sixties have resurfaced. In their commitment to educational and social equity and the opportunity to shape campus life, we once again are witnessing a resurgence of civil rights concerns and a push for more participatory forms of institutional governance. That the contemporary student movement may pale in comparison to the activities of the "decade of unrest" is no reason to ignore the significant, albeit less far-reaching, efforts of the students of the 1990s.

With the shadow of the 1960s lingering over contemporary students, it is hardly surprising that the decade is often reflected in the thoughts and actions of contemporary student activists. For example, a student at Rutgers University discussed African American student resistance in the 1990s and its connection to the 1960s: "I think there was some sort of connection to the 1960s, but I think it was difficult for people to correlate what was going on in the 1990s with, say, the Vietnam protests. I'm sure the people who protested in the sixties against the war felt the same kind of sadness and anger because it was their friends who were coming back maimed or killed." This student went on to point out that the 1995 spring demonstrations at Rutgers had more than an emotional connection to the sixties: "The ironic part is that the spring protests marked the twentieth anniversary of the pullout from Saigon . . . so there was just so much of a connection between events. . . . One of the first teach-ins on the Vietnam War was here on campus."

A student at UCLA involved in the 1993 Chicano studies movement also connected the contemporary movement to a previous generation's battles: "It was rather obvious to us that we needed to have classes about our own history at the university. We never received such information in high school. To some of us it was just obvious that we needed to have those classes. It wasn't so obvious to us at first that we needed to have a major. We started to become aware of the fact that without a program the classes would start to disappear. Our fear was that the social movement from which those classes came would eventually be ignored or forgotten. So our goal was not only to preserve those classes but to preserve the spirit of the movement of the sixties and seventies, which had institutionalized Chicano studies at UCLA." Perhaps there is much truth in the simple assertion that "the past often informs the present." Or so historians would like us to believe.

When social analysts reflect back on the history of student activism in the United States, as the contemporary student activists discussed in this book often do, they too turn to the decade of the 1960s. The fondness for which this decade is remembered is revealed in the thoughts of the student activists who lived through that time. For example, Bill Arthrell was among the crowd of about two thousand students on the afternoon of May 4, 1970, and later was one of twenty-five students indicted by the Ohio grand jury charged with investigating the Kent State shootings. He recalled the charges brought against him and the significance of his generation's struggle.

> Still the war went on. Still I was indicted. We approached a collective
> of radical lawyers in downtown Pittsburgh. Like many others of my
> generation, my feelings about Kent State were inseparable from the
> Vietnam War. Rennie Davis had called us the "most important gen-
> eration in American history." We were not only the largest, but also
> probably the only generation that had such a sense of itself and its own

mission that it fashioned a revolution in that image. College students, high school kids, disenchanted hippies, even disillusioned GI's. Had all America been young in 1970, we would have been the spearhead of a revolution instead of the object of repression. But America wasn't young. It was old men sending young men off to war. It was old corporations looking for new foreign markets. It was a generational gap that pitted "The Times They Are A-Changing" against "America right or wrong."[1]

The fondness of remembrances past sometimes clouds the truth. But whose truth is it anyway? For Bill Arthrell and other Kent State students such as Ruth Gibson, who chaired the Kent Committee to end the Vietnam War, the truth they came to know was the violence that took the lives of their fellow students. Their vision inspired by that truth never came to fruition. Gibson reflected on where she had hoped the movement would go:

> I was just absolutely sure that within five to ten years the student movement would become a much broader social movement, one that would encompass many elements and would be stronger and more explicitly socialist. I thought that the movement would unite all the dissident elements—blacks, Mexican-Americans, workers, etcetera—and was just going to topple the government. The government could no longer relate to or express the will of the people. It was an oppressor, a tyrant government; how could it stand?[2]

Perhaps the broad student movement seen in Gibson's vision is the contemporary Multicultural Student Movement, which arguably has been many decades in the making.

In Todd Gitlin's *The Sixties: Years of Hope, Days of Rage* he provides a personal account of the decade of unrest and offers testimony to the power of history and the intersection of common struggles: "Life is always lived in common, whatever rugged individualists may think, but in the Sixties it seemed especially true that History with a capital H had come down to earth, either interfering with life or making it possible; and that within History, or threaded through it, people were living with a supercharged density: lives were bound up with one another, making claims on one another, drawing one another into the common project."[3]

Unquestionably, history has much to reveal about the nature of student unrest and the movements forged on college and university campuses of the 1990s. And although people's remembrances always seem to turn to the 1960s, as with Gitlin's fond memories of his experiences as a leader of SDS (Students for a Democratic Society), the reality is that campus activism is as old as Harvard itself. American student activism in retrospect reveals a rich history of student life and cultural manifestations of student resistance over issues as mundane as the quality of the school cafeteria's butter to matters as serious as war.

The Early Years

From the nation's earliest days, following the founding of Harvard in 1636, William and Mary in 1698, and Yale in 1701, students have from time to time offered a variety of forms of protest out of dissatisfaction with the institutions that sought to educate them through strict religious and social norms and where "discipline and piety" reigned.[4] In its early days, students at Harvard protested the restrictive disciplinary codes punitively enforced by President Leonard Hoar, accounts of which include at least one known whipping of a student.[5] A few years later, also at Harvard, students drew the ire of President Charles Chauncy, who attacked them in a letter to the school's overseers for their long hair and generally unruly behavior.[6]

At Yale, students complained vehemently about the custom of ranking students in classes based on their fathers' social position, and they effectively convinced President Naphtali Daggett in 1767 to list students in the more acceptable alphabetical manner.[7] At both Harvard and Yale, animosity evolved between the students and their tutors, who struggled to enforce strict rules against "card playing" and "tavern going" while students often responded with disorderly protests described as "riots."[8] The resistance of students toward the established academic norms of their tutors, professors, and school administrators had not changed much at Yale a hundred years later when Lyman Bagg recalled his four years as an undergraduate and the heavy emphasis on the social aspects of the "Yale experience":

> The boy who comes to college with the deliberate intention of shirking every possible study is hardly to be considered a very admirable character, but I think he is less to be pitied than the one who goes through the four years, digging and grinding for a stand [a good grade], existing all unconscious of the peculiar and delightful life about him, and graduating in as utter ignorance of its philosophy as if he had never left his paternal roof-tree.[9]

The attitude of Bagg and many other students of the mid to late nineteenth century reflected a popular poster of the day: "Don't Let Your Studies Interfere with Your Education." It was this kind of pervasive attitude that led Christopher Jencks and David Riesman to argue nearly a century later that student social life and obtaining the proper credentials had displaced serious academic pursuits.[10]

As the American frontier expanded, Harvard and Yale were no longer alone in facing student resistance and discontent. During the early years at the University of Virginia, the sons of southern aristocrats were antagonized by professors who tried to maintain strict academic standards, so much so that pistols were occasionally carried to the classroom by students to keep professors in their place.[11] While colleges attempted to socialize students to the values and behaviors of a gentrified class, students oftentimes turned to their own pleasures in the form of drinking, athletics, and secret societies. An entire way of life was forming through student interactions and it would eventually gain enough strength to compete and at times overtake the relevance of the academic component created by the faculty and administration.[12] Student culture might have been born at Harvard and Yale but it prospered at colleges and universities on the frontier as well.

Student culture was not always about resisting education through tavern going or card playing. For instance, it was student initiative that led to the first literary and debate clubs, which represented a counter-pedagogy to the more traditional and painfully didactic recitation: "The recitation was not a discussion group in the twentieth-century sense; it was utterly alien to the spirit of Socratic byplay. Rather it was an oral quiz, nearly an hour in length, held five times per week throughout the academic year."[13] Often it was the students themselves who sought out more stimulating and "relevant" learning. When Jewish students found themselves excluded from elite social clubs and fraternities at eastern schools such as Yale, they formed their own social organizations, placing heavy emphasis on scholarship and academic achievement. As Dan Oren explains, "Finding their social development restrained by the undergraduate caste system, [Jewish students] turned to intellectual pursuits to sublimate their energies."[14]

Despite the best-laid plans of the faculty and administration, students have found a multitude of ways to subvert the higher learning enterprise. Over the years a number of scholars have examined the collegiate experience from the perspective of student culture,[15] defined by Howard Becker as "a shared way of looking at one's world and acting in it."[16]

From this perspective, student activism may be understood as an aspect of student culture, in that activists often have a shared vision of the social world and a commitment to action through organized demonstrations (oftentimes described as "direct action").

In the mid to late 1800s students began to pay greater attention to sports as a form of extracurricular activity, though few could have ever imagined the huge crowd attracted by the first intercollegiate football game played between Rutgers and Princeton in the fall of 1869. Sports, as a central element of student culture, became so popular and distracting that colleges and universities began to focus much of their attention on gaining official control over collegiate athletics. In 1860, the faculty at Harvard banned the annual football meeting between freshmen and sophomores, an event that had come to be known as "Bloody Monday" because of its ferociousness. Once again, students turned to demonstration to voice their displeasure with what they perceived as an intrusion into student life.

> Harvard sophomores showed their abhorrence of the faculty edict by conducting an elaborate funeral and burial of football. The new freshmen, 136 strong, looked on as a procession marched slowly through town, led by a pair of mourners performing on muffled drums. Behind them were four spade bearers, and six pall bearers carrying a six-foot coffin on their shoulders. The rest of the sophomore class, wearing torn shirts and trousers reminiscent of past battles, followed in full ranks.[17]

Although student resistance to administrative control of their sporting life would continue for the next sixty years or so, in the end intercollegiate sports became a mainstay of collegiate life and the province of college and university administrators. Of course, we know where all of this has led, and today college football and basketball coaches are some of the most powerful and highest paid individuals on campus, often raking in salaries many times that of the presidents whose signatures endorse their checks. It seems hard to believe that the original collegiate coaches were simply student volunteers.

Disputes over the control of college athletics continued well into the twentieth century, but it was not until the 1930s that American higher education truly witnessed the dawn of widespread student activism.[18] With the founding of the American Student Union in 1935, over twenty thousand socialists, communists, and liberals were united under one banner and for the first time in American politics formed a significant body of left-leaning students. The strength of the American Student Union highlighted the growing discontent among U.S. college students that was manifested in April of 1934 when 25,000 students around the country took an antiwar pledge. The movement grew more powerful the following year as 185,000 students were counted as participants in antiwar demonstrations. Clearly, the peace movement of the 1930s was the dominant theme of the day; a survey of the times indicated that roughly 40 percent of students would refuse to participate if drafted to fight in a war.[19]

Politically speaking, the 1930s marked a turn to the left, as scores of students spurred on by the Great Depression of 1929 turned to radical, socialist ideas.[20] The Communist Party in America was an especially important influence on their political and economic ideologies. Evidence suggests that a majority of students favored a constitutional revision enabling more people to live comfortably at the expense of individual property rights.[21] Relatedly, by the close of the decade, the Young Communist League claimed more than 22,000 members.[22] Not too surprisingly, the majority of college students of the 1930s tended to support Franklin Delano Roosevelt and his New Deal. The students of the 1930s, like Roosevelt, saw little reason to support the status quo and sought to transform American society around a liberal philosophy. In Roosevelt they found an ally, and his "Four Freedoms" speech delivered in early January of 1941 captured much of their sentiment:

> In the future days which we seek to make secure, we look forward to a world founded upon four essential human freedoms. The first is freedom of speech and expression—everywhere in the world. The second is freedom of every person to worship God in his own way—everywhere in the world. The third is freedom from want, which, translated into world terms, means economic understanding which will secure to every nation a healthy peacetime life for its inhabitants—everywhere in the world. The fourth is freedom from fear, which, translated into world terms means a world-wide reduction of armaments to such a point and in such a thorough fashion that no nation will be in a position to commit an act of physical aggression against any neighbor—anywhere in the world.[23]

With Roosevelt offering inspiration for world peace and an end to poverty, campus radicals and liberals not only engaged in massive peace demonstrations but also organized a free speech movement comparable in size and scope to that of the 1960s.

While the 1930s was perhaps the first decade in U.S. history specifically remembered for high levels of student activism, no decade has created more interest in student unrest than that of the 1960s. In terms of activism, both on campus and off, the 1960s has become the standard-bearer by which all other decades are compared.

The Inevitable Comparison

Discussions of the current generation of students and their activism are difficult to hold without resorting to comparisons of student activism of the 1960s. What is difficult to ascertain is a fairly accurate gauge of the level of student involvement, either in the 1960s or the 1990s. Although the research strategy undergirding this book is not designed to assess the amount of activism, the question of level of involvement is nonetheless one to be considered. At first, one might think it preposterous to even attempt such a comparison. After all, no decade has witnessed the level of student activism that the 1960s did. One might also conclude that because of perceptions of the 1960s, or even misperceptions, contemporary student activism may be significant and yet be all but ignored because it pales in comparison to its predecessor. But what does the data tell us?

Richard Peterson examined the extent of student involvement in campus protest for the academic year 1964–1965 by surveying the deans of students at a thousand colleges and universities. Peterson's survey focused on "organized protest," which he defined as "the existence of a group of reasonably like-minded students which sought in collective manner to make its opposition to some existing situation known to the appropriate authorities."[24] The study, which had a response rate of 85 percent, revealed that civil rights attracted the greatest attention among student activists, with 38 percent of the deans reporting protests related to such matters. What is interesting in terms of evaluating the extent of student activism is that in most cases, especially at two-year and smaller private colleges and even at most state universities, student activism was reported as being quite insignificant, indeed virtually nonexistent. Instead, activism tended to appear at the larger research universities, such as the University of California at Berkeley and the University of Wisconsin. Peterson reasoned that the twin themes of powerlessness and loss of identity on the part of students at larger schools may contribute to their turning to organized protest as a form of empowerment and identification. An obvious weakness of Peterson's study is that it is based simply on the perceptions of deans. While the study's method perhaps lent itself to underestimation, or perhaps overestimation in rare cases, the overall findings more than suggest that student activism was not as high during the mid 1960s as fond memories often imply.

Perhaps we have focused too much attention on some of the images conveyed by the media and superimposed the happenings at Berkeley, Columbia, and Kent State across all colleges and universities. As a result, we are left with an inflated sense of the degree of student activism during this time period. Seymour Martin Lipset and Philip Altbach argued this very point: "The scope of the American student 'revolution' has been greatly exaggerated by the mass media, which have seized upon dramatic forms of student political activity and have devoted substantial attention to them."[25]

The idea that leftist radicals were in the process of taking over American colleges and universities may have been a reflection of either conservative rhetoric intended to strengthen the fortress of traditionalism or leftist fabrication designed to improve the negotiating positions of groups like SDS (Students for a Democratic Society). The *National Guardian*, a leading left-wing newspaper in the mid 1960s, estimated that there were only about twelve thousand members of all the "new left" organizations in the U.S. and that SDS could only claim twenty thousand members and supporters.[26] And Peterson's study revealed that out of 849 deans who responded, only 6 reported that more than 5 percent of the student body was comprised of students associated with the "new student left."[27] Furthermore, Peterson extrapolated that at only about 10 percent of all four-year colleges in the country did more than 3 percent of the student body have ties to leftist student organizations. The idea that student revolutionaries were taking over American college campuses was far from a reality.

Other studies of student activism in the 1960s also are revealing. One study reported that 18 percent of students had participated in different forms of campus demonstrations,[28] which is a rather large figure but perhaps not nearly as high as the percentage of present-day forty-five- to sixty-year-olds who are likely to report having been involved in campus demonstrations during their college years in the 1960s. It may be too difficult to admit to having been a college student during "the decade of unrest" and not having participated in student demonstrations of some kind. One can almost imagine the reaction of a contemporary teenage son or daughter upon hearing that mom or dad failed to participate in one of the largest social movements of the century. "How uncool can you be!" The reality is that activist movements, including those of the

1960s, are almost always a minority phenomenon in that the vast majority of students tend to be largely uninterested.[29]

In a telling study conducted by Leonard Baird in 1965,[30] students were asked to check which of the following they had participated in: (1) organizing a college political group or campaign; (2) working actively in an off-campus political organization; (3) working actively in a student movement to change institutional rules, procedures, or policies; (4) initiating or organizing a student movement to change institutional rules, procedures, or policies; (5) participating in one or more demonstrations for some political or social goal, such as civil rights, free speech for students, states' rights. The survey was administered to twenty-nine colleges and universities and obtained data from 2,295 men and 2,834 women (the study had a 43 percent response rate). Baird characterized any student who checked three or more statements as an "activist," a student who checked one or two as a "moderate activist," and a student who did not check any was termed a "non-activist." In all, Baird found that only 2.7 percent of the men and 2.5 percent of the women were "activists" (as he defined the term). Approximately a quarter of the students fit the "moderate activist" category (21.6 percent of the men and 24.5 percent of the women). Astonishingly, 75.7 percent of the men and 73.0 percent of the women fit into the category of "non-activists." Baird's findings reinforce the idea that widespread activism in the 1960s was more myth than reality. His study also offers support to the theory that student activism of the 1960s likely was centered at certain campuses and involved a group of highly committed students who were far from the majority within the local student population.

If the decade of the sixties has been somewhat overrated as a period of unending campus turmoil and unrest, what is one to make of the 1990s? There are a number of indications that passion and protest have indeed returned to many campuses around the country. For example, there is much evidence to suggest that student volunteerism increased throughout the late 1980s and into the early 1990s.[31] Volunteerism, although obviously not the same as political activism, nonetheless provides evidence of an increasing social consciousness. The growth in the early 1990s of campus volunteer organizations such as Campus Compact, which by the early part of the decade had recruited over 250 campuses (over 600 by 1998), and Campus Outreach Opportunity League (COOL), which was working with more than 600 colleges by 1992, provides additional support.[32] The sense that students of the early 1990s were exhibiting a renewed commitment to community and social concerns led Arthur

Levine and Deborah Hirsch to describe a new wave of volunteerism on American college campuses and to predict a wave of activism to follow: "Our research indicates that every period of student unrest has been preceded by a rise in student volunteerism and social engagement. The seeds of future unrest were apparent in our interviews."[33] Additional support comes from the environmental movement. For example, the first national student environmental conference, called Threshold, attracted over two thousand students to the campus of the University of North Carolina, Chapel Hill, in 1989. The next year, seven thousand students attended the event at the University of Illinois, Urbana-Champaign.[34] Paul Loeb offers rich qualitative evidence of a high level of commitment to political and social change among many contemporary students, but as he explains in his book, their efforts may be drowned out by even higher levels of student apathy.[35]

There have been a few large-scale data gathering efforts to assess student activism. For example, research from the UCLA Higher Education Research Institute (HERI) headed by Alexander Astin revealed that 37 percent of incoming freshmen in 1989 reported that they had participated in a demonstration of some kind the year before going to college.[36] Three years later the figure was even higher, at 40 percent.[37] Contrast these figures with the 15.5 and 16.3 percent indicated back in 1966 and 1967, years which are believed to be near the peak period of American student activism.[38] Obviously, what a student does during his or her senior year in high school may or may not get enacted on the college campus. The general point of the HERI data is that they indicate the potential for a rising tide of involvement in demonstration among college students. One question that these data cannot answer is whether or not students of 1966 or 1967 interpreted the meaning of the term *demonstration* in a manner akin to contemporary students responding to a similar question. It is conceivable, for example, that a student of the 1990s might classify refusing to drink Pepsi as a form of political demonstration against the company's involvement in Burma. By the same token, a student at Berkeley or San Francisco State in the late 1960s might not consider a student gathering a "demonstration" unless at least one police officer arrived on the scene.

In addition to the HERI findings, in the mid 1990s Levine and Cureton conducted an extensive study of U.S. campuses and noted that 93 percent of the colleges and universities they visited had experienced student unrest within the previous two years.[39] Based on surveys of undergraduates conducted in 1969, 1976, and 1993, Levine and Cureton also report the following: In 1969, 28 percent of undergraduates reported participating in a demonstration; in 1976, that figure had dropped to 19 percent; by 1993 the percent involved in demonstrations had risen to 25 percent, only a few percentage points from the level reported in 1969.

Whatever the actual number of students involved, it can still be said that the 1960s was certainly the greatest age of student activism this country has ever witnessed. The decade was a period of monumental political and social change, and American college students reflected the transformation of the larger society, and, in some cases, were themselves catalysts for social change. On the other hand, contemporary students are often cast as apathetic, when in fact many are just the opposite. How many students may be classified as "uninvolved" and how many are likely to fit an "activist" category is difficult to ascertain. What is clear is that various groups of students have once again turned to direct action as a means of political and cultural expression. And regardless of their overall size, their issues and concerns have relevance to understanding contemporary student culture.

While today's generation of student activists is difficult to compare to previous generations in terms of size, there are, however, similar social and political orientations that form a web of connection across these two decades. Because of their strong ideological affiliation with the 1960s, it is helpful to review the decade of unrest as a way of making sense of contemporary students as they forge new movements.

Campus Unrest in the 1960s

The activism of the 1960s was in many ways born of student involvement in civil rights demonstrations and out of a concern for racial equality. The year many look to in identifying the birth of campus unrest is 1961. That year "must be seen primarily as the year during which students became deeply involved in positive action on behalf of the Negro."[40] Through their participation in the civil rights struggle, primarily in the South but throughout other parts of the country as well, students learned skills and strategies of resistance and in turn used their knowledge of direct action and resistance on the college campus, which they viewed as another arena for their struggle against racial hatred and inequality.[41]

The 1960s burst upon the scene and campus life began to rage at a pitch never before imagined. It was a decade dramatically unlike its predecessor: While the students of the 1950s had been characterized as the "silent generation," students of the early 1960s made it clear that they would be silent no longer. Irving Howe commented on this unique period in the history of collegiate life: "After a decade of torpor, in which petty caution dominated academic life, the campus became again what in part—but only in part—it should always be: a place of intellectual opposition and political controversy."[42] And Frederick Obear reflected on the connective fibers that launched student protest:

> Evolution of student protest during the decade of the sixties was extremely rapid. Beginning with the inheritance of quietism, students came awake politically to fight segregation and racial injustice in the South. The escalation of the war in Vietnam had the effect of broadening their concern; the resultant draft calls added self-interested motives for political action to the existing idealism. Events at Berkeley showed how activist techniques could be applied to campus reform. The three strands, race relations, peace, and educational reform, became gradually fused together in a movement based largely on the campuses: a movement which has come to be called the New Left.[43]

Obear is correct when he identifies three primary themes of campus activism as race relations (the Civil Rights Movement), peace (the Peace Movement), and educational reform (the Free Speech Movement). These issues often merged as student organizers sought to strengthen the power of their demonstrations and as media depictions generally confused the mosaic of student activists and their intentions. In what follows, each of these significant movements is explored.

The Civil Rights Movement

The Civil Rights Movement originating in the 1950s is arguably the principal source of student activism of the subsequent decade. Following the Supreme Court's 1954 desegregation decision (Brown vs. Board of Education), two student groups emerged committed to social and economic equality: the Student Nonviolent Coordinating Committee (SNCC) and the Congress of Racial Equality (CORE). From the early 1960s on, these groups played a major role in student activism and campus organizing for civil rights.

> Both organizations, the first [SNCC] operating primarily in the South and the other [CORE] more concentrated in the North, came to accept civil disobedience against unjust laws as the most effective way of gaining the supremely moral end of equal rights. Although only a small minority of students were willing to engage in acts of civil disobedi-

ence, there can be little doubt that the overwhelming majority of the academic community, both student and faculty, agreed with the objectives of these groups, and admired their courage in risking jail to fight for equal rights.[44]

In January of 1960 four Black students from North Carolina Agricultural and Technical College (North Carolina A & T) were arrested for a sit-in at a local drugstore lunch counter that refused to serve Negroes. In the next few weeks, Black students from colleges throughout North Carolina followed suit. Students from Winston-Salem Teachers College, North Carolina College, Fayetteville Teachers College, Johnson C. Smith University, Barber-Scotia College, Elizabeth City Teachers College, Kittrell College, Shaw University, Friendship Junior College, and St. Augustine College were arrested for illegal sit-ins. This form of civil disobedience soon spread to Virginia, where Black students from Hampton Institute, Virginia State University, and Virginia State College followed the lead of their student peers from North Carolina A & T. Soon thereafter, students from Fisk University in Tennessee organized sit-ins. Then Black students from Alabama State College followed as they staged a sit-in in Montgomery.[45]

For many Black students, the price of social revolution was severe. In February of 1968, three students at South Carolina State College were shot to death by police during a student demonstration. In May of 1969, a North Carolina A & T student was killed in a shootout between students and police. One year later, two students were killed at Jackson State as Mississippi highway patrolmen fired into a crowd of student demonstrators. And finally, two students were killed as sheriff's deputies reclaimed Southern University's administration building, which Black students had occupied to call attention to the university's discriminatory racial policies.[46]

The North Carolina sit-ins marked a pivotal point in the Civil Rights Movement as students and activists discovered the power of direct action through civil disobedience, and the next few years in the South were marked by freedom rides, boycotts, sit-ins, marches, and picket lines. Liberal-minded White students joined the efforts of fellow Black students as the movement began to gain recognition in the mainstream of American culture. The tactics successful in the South were soon embraced by northern students. As Durward Long noted, "Student activists had discovered the weapons with which institutional racism could be fought in America."[47] The Civil Rights Movement stirred "as nothing else could, the moral imagination of young people in the United States. Here, they felt, was an issue unclouded by ambiguity, an issue demanding and allowing a full-hearted response. Shaken out of complacency and into disturbance, stirred by the lunch counter sit-ins and the Freedom Rides, American students began to organize themselves as an important auxiliary in the battle for Negro freedom."[48]

As the decade progressed, the civil rights struggle moved from one of Negroes or Blacks seeking integration to one of Blacks or African Americans committed to nationalism. The shift in how Black struggle was framed by its leaders was captured most poignantly by the idea of "Black Power," the subject of a speech given by SNCC leader Stokely Carmichael at the University of California at Berkeley on November 19, 1966.

> Now we are engaged in a psychological struggle in this country and that struggle is whether or not black people have the right to use words they want to use without white people giving their sanction to it. We maintain, whether they like it or not, we gon' use the word "black power" and let them address themselves to that. We are not gonna wait for white people to sanction black power. We're tired of waiting. Every time black people move in this country, they're forced to defend their position before they move. It's time that the people who're supposed to be defending their position do that. That's white people. They ought to start defending themselves, as to why they have oppressed and exploited us.[49]

As the focus shifted from integration to nationalism and Blacks sought to make their own contributions to emancipation, the role of White student leaders and demonstrators became less influential. "The change was also due in part to the rapidly increasing intellectual base to the Black Power movement which gave it more dynamism and helped to increase its unity. The writings of Eldridge Cleaver, Kenneth Clark, Stokely Carmichael, and Frantz Fanon gave blacks an ideological structure."[50]

Perhaps no single campus demonstration captured the evolution of the Black civil rights struggle and the growing relevance of Black Power better than the actions of students at Howard University as they conducted their sit-in at the administration building in the spring of 1968. By this time, organizations such as CORE and SNCC had converted to all-Black memberships and antisegregationist ideology was giving way to Black nationalism. The Black Panther Party had inspired Black students around the country, and Howard University was no exception, forming a local Black Power Committee (BPC). Along with the Student Rights

Organization (SRO), which had first organized in 1964 immediately following the Free Speech Movement at Berkeley, BPC made for a powerful voice in Howard's day-to-day affairs.[51]

Despite the growth of student-led political organizations such as SRO and BPC, the administration at Howard and in particular President James M. Nabrit Jr. turned a deaf ear to many of the students' complaints about campus policies. To the administration, student protests and disruptions were unacceptable behavior for a Howard University student whose status at the institution was a privilege and not a right. The university's statement on student behavior made this perfectly clear: "Attendance at Howard University is a privilege, in order to protect its standards of scholarship and character, the University reserves the right, and the student code concedes to the University the right, to deny admissions to and to request the withdrawal of any student at any time and for any reason deemed sufficient to the University."[52] Such statements notwithstanding, students engaged in a variety of demonstrations reflective of their positions on Black struggle in America. For example, they successfully heckled General Lewis Hershey as he attempted to present a discussion at the university: "America is a Black man's true battleground," yelled one of the students as about forty others rushed the stage and forced the general to end his discussion and leave the podium.[53]

During a period of almost four years, students and the administration repeatedly clashed, with little progress made by students. Time and time again, Howard's administration took an authoritarian stance and offered a punitive response. The one exception was a sit-in at the president's office in which the students demanded an end to compulsory ROTC participation. On this occasion President Nabrit gave in and allowed a student leader—Ewart Brown—to mediate the crisis. In the end, Nabrit agreed to end the compulsory requirements of the ROTC program.

Tension at Howard reached a peak in the spring of 1968 when students united under a new organization known as Ujamma (Swahili for "togetherness") made new demands aimed at creating a truly Black university. Student agitation was sparked in part by the shootings at South Carolina State College, where state highway patrolmen in Orangeburg had fired into a group of students and killed three and wounded thirty others. Reflecting both a sense of respect and rage, Ujamma's list of demands were called the "Orangeburg Ultimatum."[54]

Stirred by the deaths at Orangeburg and the fact that Howard's administration had sent out letters to thirty-nine students ordering them to appear before a judicial board for previous demonstrations, the students held a rally on March 19 that culminated in a sit-in led by Ewart Brown and Ujamma members. Several hundred students entered the main administration building while hundreds more congregated outside. In a short time, the administration vacated the building and declared the campus closed for the day. Two days later Dr. Kenneth Clark and three other members of the Howard board of trustees entered discussions with the students, while President Nebrit was conspicuous by his absence. The students had sixteen demands, but perhaps the most important pertained to Howard's becoming a Black university and to students' being given greater say in campus policies. The following morning additional meetings were held and eventually an agreement was reached. Student representation would be included on all campus committees that dealt with student-related matters and the university would move to enact an Afro-American orientation to its curriculum.

The impact of the student unrest at Howard was felt for years to come as it paralleled the larger struggle of African Americans in U.S. society. As Lawrence de Graaf explained, "In four years the dominant attitude at Howard changed from one of preoccupation with white middle-class values and indifference to the 'Negro Revolt' and the role of the university in it to a rejection of such values and to direct action to make Howard more relevant to blacks in their quest for identity and power."[55]

By the late 1960s, Black student protests came to overshadow other forms of student activism both "in its frequency and intensity."[56] The Civil Rights Movement born of the 1950s had moved beyond its innocence and had gained increasing levels of influence in American society. It is hard to disagree with the assessment that the Multicultural Student Movement of the 1990s owes much of its success to the civil rights activities of the 1960s.

The Free Speech Movement

The Free Speech Movement arose out of student discontent at the University of California at Berkeley. The events of 1964 and 1965 became in many ways the defining moment of a relatively young university, and to this day, for better or worse, Berkeley is the first university many think of when they consider student activism and campus unrest. Civil rights activists along with other political groups such as Friends of SNCC, Young Democrats, Young Republicans, and various socialist organizations made the Berkeley campus a hotbed of political discussion and controversy. As long as the groups did not recruit members on campus, they were welcome to share their views. Advocacy and political organizing would not be tolerated, although clearly this fine line was often violated.[57]

In the fall of 1964, the university administration decided to enforce the line drawn between speech and advocacy. They designated the strip of sidewalk separating the campus from the city of Berkeley as the line of demarcation. Bancroft Way, the traditional place for student tables and organizing could no longer be used for such purposes. It did not take long, however, for the students to convince the university to reconsider its position, as they effectively argued that there is little difference between what gets defined as "speech" and that which is defined as "advocacy." Furthermore, the students argued that such distinctions were next to impossible to enforce and would lead to arbitrary and capricious action on the part of the university. The administration coalesced on the advocacy point but refused to permit the collection of monies for organizing purposes. This infuriated many of the student leaders, who, armed with civil disobedience tactics, launched a counteroffensive. Student groups intentionally collected organizational funds specifically to challenge the university's new enforcement. Eventually, several students were charged and brought before the dean of men. When the offending students arrived in Sproul Hall, the main administration building at Berkeley, they were accompanied by another three hundred or more who demanded to be charged as well. This effectively ended any punitive action on the part of the administration.

The university looked to a different strategy to enforce student behavior and turned to strong-arm tactics by calling in police, to be positioned along Bancroft Way. It did not take long for the students to gain a meeting with then President Clark Kerr and achieve a withdrawal of the extra police force. According to Nathan Glazer, a professor at Berkeley at the time, the movement at this point, which was quickly becoming the "Free Speech Movement," came under the principal direction of the civil rights activists and lost some of its right-wing support when "questionably legal activities (like sitting-in at Sproul Hall)" began to take place.[58]

Once again, it seemed as if the students had won the battle. However, the university raised a new issue. If the university was going to allow advocacy and organizing (through recruitment), then it at least ought to be able to restrict such activities to the legal realm, meaning that any efforts to organize activities such as civil disobedience would not be permitted. Thus the university announced that any advocacy or organizing using illegal tactics would be punishable under university policy.

Everything came to a head as students reoccupied Sproul Hall, accompanied by the singing of Joan Baez, who by now had joined in support of their cause. The day was December 2, 1964. The next day the university called in the police and began carrying out about eight hundred students. A day later a strike of graduate teaching assistants was launched. Faculty involvement, present to varying degrees all along, came to the forefront as a group of liberal professors offered a resolution in support of political activity on campus but only with provisions for time, place, and manner so as to not interfere with the academic enterprise. The Free Speech Movement (FSM), as the group was now officially known, supported the resolution and pushed for its immediate passage. On December 8 the faculty voted to pass the resolution and also demanded that responsibility for student disciplinary action related to political activity be placed completely in the hands of the faculty. Their frustration with the administration's handling of matters was evident.

Not all of the faculty at Berkeley were supportive of the Free Speech Movement and student political activity. Nathan Glazer conveyed the cynicism with which some viewed the movement:

> Those of us who watched the Free Speech Movement (FSM) daily set up its loud-speakers on the steps of the administration building to denounce the president, the chancellor, the newspapers, the Regents, the faculty, and the structure and organization of society in general and universities in particular, could only admire the public-relations skill exhibited in the choice of a name for the student movement. Life, however, is not so simple as to present us with a classic free speech issue on the shores of San Francisco Bay.[59]

For Glazer, what occurred at Berkeley was clearly the outgrowth of the Civil Rights Movement and what students had learned of civil disobedience as it was enacted in the South. Acts of civil disobedience were commonplace in 1963 as students from Berkeley, San Francisco State, and elsewhere had sit-ins, shop-ins, and sleep-ins as part of their effort to pressure Bay-area businesses to hire Black workers. But in Glazer's mind, students were out of control: "The fact that the state of California has a law banning discrimination in employment and a commission devoted to ending discrimination in employment seemed to leave the demonstrators unmoved. Indeed, they often insisted that they themselves rather than the state agency should police the agreements they had won from employers." However, as the students came to realize, agencies were lethargic, and direct action tended to produce immediate results. Social justice was served in the students' minds, although Glazer obviously disagreed:

"Was the Bay Area Mississippi, it was asked, that actions had to be taken which destroyed businesses when there was legal redress for the wrongs that the students believed existed?"[60]

Despite the views of Glazer and other less liberal faculty at Berkeley, the majority of professors were sympathetic to the students' cause. In fact, as Philip Selznick pointed out, the faculty passed a resolution that largely supported the position of the free speech demonstrators by a seven to one vote. "Almost everyone disliked the administration's policy, and most were now determined to say so." Selznick went on to argue that there was more than administrative ineptness involved in agitating the students to such levels: "Arbitrary administrative action lay at the base of the controversy, and was fuel to its flames at every step. These matters bear closely on the charge that somehow 'law and order' went down the drain at Berkeley."[61]

The Free Speech Movement was highly effective in achieving student voice and in pushing the university to embrace more liberal policies. The stirrings at Berkeley marked a new day in student activism: "By the end of 1964, the students at Berkeley had proved that they had the power to initiate change, and that their direct action techniques would work outside the South. To some, the possibilities seemed limitless."[62]

As the free speech demonstrations at Berkeley wound down, similar protests surfaced at other campuses around the country and often were played out as part of a general concern for students' rights. Although few of these campuses experienced the degree of tension evidenced at Berkeley, the protests nonetheless proved vexing to administrators used to near complete control over the American college student.

The fight for freedom of speech and student rights was waged at the same time that U.S. involvement in Vietnam was escalating, and soon demands for an end to the war drew the attention of campus activists: "The war in Vietnam was taking more and more U.S. servicemen, and protest against it mounted proportionately."[63] With free speech victories in hand, students felt greater compulsion than ever to voice their views on the war through campus demonstration. Protest became a driving force in expressing what student activists saw as an expansionist agenda aimed at Southeast Asia.

The Peace Movement

Campus recruiters and the military industrial complex were quickly becoming the targets of student ire as antiwar sentiment grew during the latter half of the 1960s. Student demonstrations targeted representatives of the armed services and the CIA, who used college campuses as recruiting sites. During the 1967–68 academic year, demonstrations involving physical obstruction of recruiters took place at Brown, Williams, Stanford, Harvard, Pennsylvania, and Oberlin, and at state universities such as Colorado and Illinois. Dow Chemical also drew the anger and attention of students who targeted the company because of its production of napalm.[64]

In the spring of 1966 students at the University of Wisconsin were led by SDS in occupying a corridor outside of the registrar's office to express their dissatisfaction with the administration's cooperation with the local Selective Service Board. The following year students orchestrated protests of campus visitations by Dow and the CIA.[65] In the fall of 1967 students at Indiana University protested the "University's war-complicity in providing space for Dow," which resulted in violence and the arrest of twenty-three students.[66] And at Penn State University student protests erupted in the fall of 1968, transforming what had been largely a sleepy central Pennsylvania campus: "A change in campus attitudes towards authority had taken place, in part because the national political system had proven to be unresponsive to calls for change." The students at Penn State were divided between the "doves" on the left and the "hawks" on the right. This became most apparent when in the spring of 1969 "a half-dozen SDSers stormed into the HUB [Hetzel Union Building] in April to harass military recruiters and tear up their literature. Several hawkish students then beat up the radicals."[67]

Rick Kowall, a student from Alabama, expressed the sentiment of many of the students of the day as he addressed his local draft board: "You cannot begin to eliminate warfare by allowing yourself to participate in an organization dedicated to waging it. It was for that reason that I returned my draft card to this board in November 1968, knowing that I would willfully refuse to report for that induction, and knowing that the probable penalty for such an act would be arrest and imprisonment."[68]

Although campus unrest was evident at less well known state universities such as SUNY Buffalo and Kent State, the larger more prestigious schools such as Berkeley and Wisconsin received much of the media attention. Indeed, it was only after four students lay dead on the ground that the media attended to student antiwar demonstrations that had been growing increasingly intense at Kent State. The deaths there and, next, at Jackson State sent shock waves around the country and set off nationwide protests as over four million students at some 1,350 colleges and universities protested the massacres and the invasion of Cambodia.[69]

Soon after the deaths at Kent State, students and faculty at Michigan State University marched to President Clifton Wharton's office in the main administration building chanting "On strike—shut it down! 1, 2, 3, 4,—we don't want your fucking war! 5, 6, 7, 8—we don't want your fascist state!" With smaller student groups interrupting classes and recruiting more students for the rapidly escalating demonstration, eventually some three thousand students surrounded the Hannah Administration Building and demanded that the Michigan State president pay tribute to the four slain Kent State students and urge President Nixon to withdraw troops from Cambodia.[70]

The Peace Movement gained strength throughout the 1960s, but it was often mired in confusion with a parallel counterculture movement described by some as the "free love" movement. The confusion was most apparent in the Bay area of San Francisco, where throngs of hippies and activists often collected on the same grounds but not necessarily for the same reasons.

While the hippies made Golden Gate Park their home, they were a somewhat different blend of a youthful and not so youthful cultural enclave occupying space across the bay from their Berkeley cousins. The hippies often were recognized by their long hair, beads, flowery shirts and dresses, sandals, and faded bell-bottoms. Turning on to marijuana and LSD as they tuned in to the music of Jerry Garcia and the Grateful Dead, the hippies were about dropping out and rejecting the society that their parents had helped to create. This was not the intent of the activist-oriented youth from Berkeley and San Francisco State, who envisioned a new society founded on participatory democracy and freedom. Together, the hippies and the activists played and listened to music, read poetry, and got high. Some youth were active members in both movements, moving in and out of the two enclaves and thus adding to their somewhat amorphous quality. Every now and then one could spot the diehard activists by their work boots and drab clothes, as well as by the handful of pamphlets they frequently passed around. While the activists dreamed of restructuring society, the hippies chose instead to create their own world of "sex, drugs, and rock-n-roll," which all came together in the Summer of Love in 1967 when hippies from around the country were drawn to a little corner of San Francisco known simply as Haight-Ashbury. "For the first time, surrounded by fellow freaks, it dawned on the hippies that their ruling fantasy might really be correct, that the evolutionary tides might really be flowing in their direction. Perhaps it was a consequence of all the LSD, but from the Love Pageant on, a naive optimism permeated the Haight, combined with a mystical faith that whatever was needed would be provided." And for a while it was. But questions loomed on the horizon: "What if we're all wrong?" asked Allen Ginsberg as he basked in the sunlight of the "Gathering of the Tribes for the First Human Be-In" in Golden Gate Park and listened to Timothy Leary lead a crowd in chanting "turn on, tune in, drop out."[71]

Inspired by the 1950s Beat Generation and the literary likes of Jack Kerouac, whose classic work *On the Road* reflected a countercultural call to a "live and love for today" mentality, the hippies were a stark ideological contrast to the activists who still held to utopian dreams. The hippies chose to reject the norms of a society, which more and more resembled William Whyte's *The Organization Man* and Max Weber's "iron cage of humanity," while the activists hoped to reshape social life around idealistic visions of freedom, equality, and justice for all. What brought them together from time to time was their deep resentment of the America that they were set to inherit and the opportunity to fashion a rapidly expanding counterculture through music, art, drugs, and political and sexual freedom.

The Summer of Love passed into fall. The end of the 1960s, the decade of unrest, was coming to a close. In a few years, a new generation of youth and students would appear on the scene. The counterculture movement that compelled the hippies of the 1960s, like the jeans they wore, soon faded away along with the idealism of the student activists. In turn, the 1970s ushered in a different mix of youth culture that rarely seemed very "counter" and which, akin to the child in the shadows of the favored son, struggled for its own sense of identity.

Making Sense of the 1960s

There are many explanations as to why the 1960s witnessed such an incredible rise in student activism. Clark Kerr argues that the volatility of students and youth culture is one explanation as to why the 1960s exhibited significant campus unrest.[72] After all, the period was one of great social upheaval, and students were an effective barometer of the tension existing throughout the larger society. Research by Eric Dey on undergraduate political attitudes tends to confirm the notion that students mirror the larger social context.[73] But to simply conclude that the 1960s represents the ultimate example of youthful rebellion fails to take into account that many of these students came from liberal families who were likely to support their son's or daughter's involvement in social and political issues.[74] One might easily conclude that the student activists of liberal-minded parents could hardly be seen as "rebellious."

Herbert Moller offers a demographic explanation when he argues that periods of revolutionary social change from the sixteenth century onward reflect the increased size of corresponding youth cohorts: "In any community the presence of a large number of adolescents and young adults influences the temper of life; and the greater the proportion of young people the greater the likelihood of cultural and political change."[75] Add to Moller's analysis the general observation that adolescents and young adults, particularly in collegiate settings, pay significant attention to developing a philosophical and political orientation,[76] and a powerful mix is formed. Keep in mind, of course, that the 1960s represents the decade in which the first surge of the baby boomers came of age and headed off to college. The combination of the moratorium of college life and the challenge of their serious-minded struggle for identity in conjunction with an increased cohort size may have been too volatile a mix for any society to endure.

Other theorists suggest a more institutional theory: that major universities became overly enamored with research at the expense of student concern and that as a consequence student dissatisfaction grew.[77] As the "multiversity" prospered throughout the 1960s, students became mere numbers in a tuition-driven quest by faculty for reduced teaching loads and the use of graduate teaching assistants became a primary means of instruction.[78] Lipset and Altbach point out that this was true more of the larger state universities than of smaller private colleges, a point that studies of student satisfaction as well as national profiles of institutional characteristics tend to support.[79] They also maintain that at large state universities such as Berkeley, the unstable social structure may have induced in students a heightened tension and awareness of institutional inequities. The larger and most successful state universities resemble in many ways the nouveaux riches "who constantly worry about their status and who seek evidence that they have really arrived."[80] The result is not only heavy competition among faculty and students but also a general attitude of having to prove oneself in order to move up in the academic world. The more established and mostly Eastern elite privates such as Harvard, Yale, and Princeton do not have to contend with external opinions about their quality or place in American higher education, in that their position has already largely been secured. Indeed, many of their faculty are former graduates and have come to fully embrace the traditions of these elite institutions. A degree of homogeneity exists at such schools and lends itself to agreement and hence limits conflict.

In addition to the argument that faculty culture may be more homogeneous at elite private schools, and thus less prone to conflict, there is the fact that the student body itself tends to be much more heterogeneous at the larger state universities.[81] As social theory tends to demonstrate, heterogeneity is more likely to lead to conflict and unrest as diverse perspectives are brought into contact with one another.[82] Although there may be exceptions, Lipset and Altbach's thesis of heterogeneity and size as major contributing factors to campus unrest is plausible. Peterson's[83] study of student protest also tends to support the notion that much of the activism of the 1960s was centered at the larger, more prestigious colleges and universities and that student protest was largely nonexistent at teachers colleges, technical institutes, and less academically oriented denominational colleges.

Other explanations have been offered as well. Liberalized or progressive parenting is another rationale often heard. "Too much freedom and too little responsibility" is the accusation that followed the children of the 1940s and early 1950s as they were ushered off to college. Perhaps they took Erik Erikson's "moratorium" (a period marked by youthful exuberance and forgiveness for one's mistakes) to heart as they searched for the kind of person they desired to become and found a rebel in the closet. But this theory has a hard time explaining why student activism of the 1960s faded away as the decade of the 1970s progressed. The assumption is that students of the 1970s were also raised under the more liberalized child rearing ideas of the likes of Dr. Spock (not the one with pointed ears!). As C. Vann Woodward aptly explained: "Presumably, there were as many permissive or authoritarian parents, as many Oedipus-complexes or red-diaper babies, as many strong fathers or ineffectual fathers, and as many 'psychosocial moratoriums' after 1970 as there were before."[84]

For whatever reason and most likely a combination of many, the passion and protest of the 1960s gave way to the more acquiescent decade of the 1970s. The deaths at Jackson State and Kent State in 1970 and subsequent mass demonstrations against the U.S. advance into Cambodia signified both the peak of student activism as well as a tolling of the bell announcing the end of a unique and dramatic period in American history. As Daniel Foss and Ralph Larkin explain in their discussion of the "dissident youth movement of the 1960s":

It was during this period that the processes which define the existence of a social movement—intensification of social conflict, reinterpretation of social reality, and redefinition of the self—ceased to be mutually reinforcing. . . . The end of the decade saw the movement develop a number of divergent thrusts. This divergence, had the movement not exhausted itself, might have foreshadowed a broadening and deepening of revolt, rather than its end. But as it happened, each thrust itself represented a path to accommodation or to encapsulation of dissidence.[85]

After the Cambodian demonstrations, campus life in general began to reflect once again the kind of silence that had not been seen since the 1950s. As our country and our students passed through the 1970s and early 1980s, generally speaking, student protests and calls for direct action were minimal by comparison to the previous decade. Bell-bottomed, tie-dyed-T-shirt-wearing, long-haired students were still on campus and turning on to marijuana at rates higher than ever before, but concerns about social and political issues did not seem as strong. Maybe the end of the Vietnam War marked some sort of culmination for student activists. Or perhaps many of the principal instigators simply graduated and got on with their lives. Maybe career concerns became central as the economy slowed and the job market tightened. Or possibly passion just seeped out of campus life like it does from a relationship sometimes. Whatever the explanation, American society reached a calm in its voyage through time's endless sea. For the American college campus and the many faculty and administrators who survived the decade of unrest, the straits of tranquillity could not have come a minute too soon.

There are many questions about the longevity of what students actually accomplished during the 1960s, especially in terms of influencing college and university governance. All one has to do is look around today's colleges and universities and witness the repeated mistakes evidenced by exclusionary decision making by presidents and boards of trustees, by mid- and senior-level administrators, and by faculty in the classrooms. One cannot help but wonder if our memories are too short. Glazer may have been quite prophetic when he wrote more than twenty-five years ago that "it could turn out, that in the end, it is rather easier to change the world than the university."[86] Maybe this is what the students of the 1970s and 1980s learned from their predecessors—that despite the incredible commitment and efforts of the previous decade's students, the university would inevitably return to its roots in authoritarianism.

The Acquiescence of the 1970s

With the end of the Vietnam War in sight and administrative concessions to student free speech and student rights seemingly won on many of the larger campus fronts, student social and political interests fell into a kind of slumber as the pursuit of more individualistic goals took precedence for the vast majority. The 1970s was a decade for rebels without a cause, who often turned to marijuana as an outlet for their drowsy discontent. The students were still concerned about the social good, but the passion that flowed in the 1960s was missing in action. This was the decade of polyester, the Bee Gees, Donna Summer, John Travolta, Saturday Night Fever, Saturday Night Live, and Saturday night specials. But disco was not the only game in town; musicians and groups such as Bob Marley, the Clash, and the Sex Pistols offered serious challenges to musical and entertainment norms. As Bob Dylan had warned a decade before, "The times they are a-changin'," and in the 1970s they certainly did.

The 1970s was also a period of recession, as many of the economic support structures such as the steel and automotive industries began to crumble. Professional careers were no longer a sure thing for the college educated, and competition for lucrative opportunities reached a ferocious peak. Computer science majors were told that they had to have a 3.5 grade point average or better to be considered by most reputable companies. Such claims seemed to fly in the face of the supposed technology boom and the need for people with computer skills. "If there is a shortage of computer people, then why do I have to have near perfect academic credentials?" asked computer science majors of the mid-seventies. Education majors heard similar stories of unemployed teachers whose grades and volunteer experiences were insufficient to earn them that first teaching assignment, or even an interview. Consequently, students tended to adopt one of three philosophies about their undergraduate education. One philosophy was to demand near perfection of oneself. Get all A's and join all the right organizations. The other extreme was to "just get by." Get a degree and have some fun in the process. Worry about jobs later. After all, what good would worrying do now? And if college took a few more years than four—"What's the big deal?" John Belushi's character Bluto in the movie *Animal House* provided inspiration to many of these students. Who can ever forget his memorable line as he pondered expulsion from Faber College: "Seven years of college down the drain." A third orientation fell somewhere between the "perfectionist" and the "partier." These students wanted to do well in school, but at the same time they recognized that there was more to college than knocking oneself out just to get a job. Many of these students sought the intrinsic rewards of college life and furthered their education through postbaccalaureate work. Their common refrain was "Well, if I can't get a job, I might as well go to graduate school."

The notion that students of the 1970s tended to withdraw from social and political issues is hardly surprising. After all, these students had witnessed the U.S. involvement in a war that in the end made little sense even to the die-hard hawks. The 1970s was the decade that brought the Watergate fiasco, in which an entire generation of youth witnessed the president of their own country breaking the law and getting away with it. As Arthur Levine notes in his book *When Dreams and Heroes Died*, the decade was a period of tremendous pessimism, as revealed by student thoughts he collected in his research of college and university life: government doesn't give a damn; all politicians are crooks; Nixon was like all of us, only he got caught; Nixon was a victim, that's all; and I don't trust government as far as I can throw the capitol building.[87] It was a decade in which the ends justified just about any means, and the ends seemed to be in line with personal success rather than the common good. With all that the students of the 1970s witnessed, it is hard to find fault with their logic.

The students of the 1970s were also saddened to a degree by a belief in what they might have missed during the 1960s. Whether or not the memories were part myth, these students reflected fondly on their generational predecessors. Levine speaks of his research and interactions with students of the 1970s, who surprised him by their allusions to the students of the 1960s and a near mythical fondness for their generational forbears. As one student told him: "We're not real college kids like the people who went to school in the 1960s."[88] It seemed as though the students of the 1970s could never achieve what the previous generation had accomplished in forging social change, so why even try? And besides, what was there in terms of political and social issues that was worthy of passion and protest? While campus life calmed down, one wondered if student unrest was simply asleep, or worse yet, dead. Ralph Turner warned that student dissatisfaction was only festering: "Disillusionment with higher education and approval of disruption persist as a dimension of broader political orientations beneath the surface calm."[89] As the decade of the 1980s progressed, the surface calm was penetrated by student agitation with antidemocratic forces in South Africa and apartheid's economic support from U.S. colleges and universities.

Divestment and the 1980s

If there was one significant issue that served as a catalyst for contemporary student activism, it was the Divestment Movement of the 1980s. Around the country, students organized demonstrations in an effort to force colleges and universities to end their economic investments in South Africa. This movement became particularly powerful during the mid 1980s as political activity by Blacks in South Africa increased to such a point that the South African government declared a state of emergency. As state repression expanded in scope and intensity, so did worldwide media coverage, which in turn inspired concerned students around the world.

The Divestment Movement in the United States began at schools such as Columbia University, where in 1981 the Coalition for a Free South Africa (CFSA) formed from the university's Black Student Organization.[90] At first their mission was primarily educational as they planned forums, discussions, and provided informational leaflets on the social, economic, and political circumstances of Blacks in South Africa as well as the investments their university had made in South African corporations. Early efforts to convince President Michael Sovern failed, but students nonetheless continued to work within the system: "CFSA spent two more years in committees, negotiations, forums, marches, vigils, debates, petitions, and even a two-week hunger strike, during which they unsuccessfully sought to meet with the trustees."[91] After President Sovern openly criticized their rallies and marches and refused to meet with the students, they decided to take more serious action.

On April 4, 1985, Columbia students blockaded the entrance to Hamilton Hall and demanded that the university withdraw its investments.[92] The actions at Columbia set off a chain reaction that reached many of the smaller and remote campuses such as Clarkson College in Potsdam, New York, where students constructed shantytowns as a symbol of the living conditions South African Blacks faced under the oppression of apartheid.

There were other issues in the 1980s. For example, numerous protests took place against the CIA and its involvement in Central America. A common tactic was to establish picket lines or blockades when CIA recruiters were scheduled for campus visits. Students at Brown University disrupted a CIA career information session by staging a mock citizen's arrest as they cited the CIA's violations of domestic and international laws for mining the harbors of another country.[93]

Although other issues surfaced from time to time, concerns associated with South Africa shaped the tenor of campus activism in the mid and late 1980s and paved the way for direct action in the 1990s. In their analysis of the post-1960s transformation, Philip Altbach and Robert Cohen posit, "It can be argued that the 1980s have been a kind of transitional period between the extraordinary quiet of the 1970s to a more active period in the future."[94] The Divestment Movement may have been more than merely a transitional stage; it likely has been the major contributor to the eventual multicultural unrest that would come to signify the 1990s. In many ways, the racial unrest uncovered by divestment activities lit the match to the multicultural fires of the 1990s. One case in point was the divestment movement at Dartmouth.

It was in January of 1986 on the campus of Dartmouth that a group of right-wing students (many of whom were staff writers for the conservative *Dartmouth Review*) attacked and dismantled shanties that had been constructed in protest against investments in South Africa. The *Review* was quick to praise the dismantling of Dartmouth's shantytown and in fact opined that the actions should have been taken earlier. An angry reaction was stirred among many of the African American students, in part because the attacks had occurred on the birthday of Martin Luther King Jr. African American students soon proceeded to occupy the main administration building. The demonstration ended some thirty hours later when college officials agreed to hold a day-long teach-in to confront the pervasive racism at Dartmouth.[95] In a matter of thirty hours, student activism had shifted on one campus from an issue of divestment to one of racism and concerns tied to multiculturalism.

Another factor that, along with the Divestment Movement, served as a stimulus to unite members of various minority groups was the growing influence of conservatism throughout the 1980s. It was the decade of Reaganomics, and conservatism anesthetized the collective consciousness of an entire society. Sure there was resistance. And certainly some students continued to campaign for equal rights, liberty, participatory democracy, and a variety of idealized visions extending beyond their own well-being. But conservatism was pervasive and especially damaging to minority communities such as African Americans.

Virtually all of the major indicators of the well-being of the African-American community showed that it was in a state of crisis. The social fabric of the community, which had been weakened in the 1970s by some general conservative trends, was torn further apart in the 1980s by long-term unemployment and underemployment, low wage jobs, reduced real income, smaller college participation rates, increased deterioration in the quality of elementary and secondary education, increased impoverishment of the youth, reduction of health and social services, a drop in the accessibility of decent housing, and a general increase in anxiety and insecurity.[96]

The declining outlook for prosperity among African Americans as well as among other racial groups such as Chicanos and American Indians contributed to a growing sense of intragroup solidarity and in the end fostered the rising tide of identity politics characteristic of the 1990s.

A sense of solidarity was also being forged among various groups of gays and women. Scores of progressive-minded college women took to the streets as "Take Back the Night" marches became a common occurrence. And "coming-out" rallies and gay pride events grew prevalent as lesbian, gay, and bisexual students sought to combat the tide of eighties conservatism that labeled them as "deviants" or as "abominations in the eyes of God." As powerful as conservative economic policies had become, Christian fundamentalism and conservative social attitudes claimed ground as well. As a result, throughout the 1980s, right-wing forces at times thwarted gay liberation efforts and the struggle for women's reproductive rights.

Thus, when we look back on the 1980s, especially the close of the decade, we get a sense of the increasing levels of resentment and hostility among underrepresented groups and women. The ideals and goals envisioned during the decade of unrest had been supplanted by conservative economic, political, and social policies shaping the country throughout the second half of the 1970s and into the 1980s. The question that remains is what will be remembered of campus life from the 1990s? What is to be written about the defining concerns of the contemporary generation of activists?

The Roots of the Multicultural Student Movement

The Civil Rights Movement of the 1960s, which was originally focused on the struggle for equality of the American Negro, lost much of its steam in the early 1970s. The movement did not end, but arguably it lost its preeminence as the nation's central political and social concern.

At the same time, cultural diffusion led to the expansion of parallel movements encompassing a variety of diverse groups traditionally marginalized within U.S. society, including American Indians and Mexican Americans. Like African Americans, these groups also fought for their rightful place within U.S. society.

As the major movements of the decade of the 1960s faded from view, a multitude of causes came to the forefront, creating a cultural mosaic of diverse concerns. The late 1960s and early 1970s marked a pivotal point in the emergence of Chicano nationalism, but the movement's power swayed during a decade and a half of political and social conservatism. Through efforts largely inspired by the life and death of César Chávez, the spirit of La Raza, born of the 1960s, was resurrected at UCLA, where students organized to achieve departmental status for Chicano studies. In the mid 1990s, American Indian students at Michigan State University relived the anger and pain of the Trail of Tears as they waged a new battle with governmental manipulation and betrayal. Unlike many of their recent ancestors, who felt that they had little recourse but to give in to a structure overwhelmingly large and powerful, the Native students at Michigan State turned to direct action as they waged a battle with Governor John Engler over preservation of the state's Indian tuition waiver program. But the Multicultural Student Movement of the 1990s is not entirely centered on racial struggle; gay liberation and women's liberation also contribute. As the most obvious manifestations of campus unrest were fading over two decades ago, the Women's Movement and its impact on the American campus was gaining strength. Like the Women's Movement, the Gay Liberation Movement also picked up steam in the 1970s and 1980s, and whereas many students were unconcerned with political and cultural issues, lesbian, gay, and bisexual students around the country made "coming out" a public spectacle intended both to create awareness of the oppression they had experienced as well as to send notice to a homophobic society that they were not going to take it anymore.

History clearly is influential in the lives of the contemporary multicultural student activists discussed in this work. It is from the decade of the 1960s and to a lesser degree the early 1970s that today's students draw much of their knowledge of direct action. African Americans, American Indians, Chicanos, Asian Americans, gays, and women, among others, all are indebted to the freedom struggles central to the 1960s. These groups and individuals are the generational brothers and sisters of the students of the decade of unrest and exist across the broad landscape of U.S. social life as a kind of democratic diaspora waiting to be united. And it was the Divestment Movement of the 1980s, a movement itself rooted in a concern for racial equality and freedom, that inspired the Multicultural Student Movement as students once again came to envision the possibilities of social change and the power of committed and organized groups.

chapter three

"IMMIGRANTS IN OUR OWN LAND"

The Chicano Studies

Movement at UCLA

The history of Chicano studies at the University of California at Los Angeles is one of marginality. From its founding in 1973, the program has limped along on a shoestring budget and halfhearted administrative and faculty support. The death bells have tolled several times along the way—first, in 1988 when the faculty senate, supposedly out of a concern for the quality of students' educational experiences, recommended disestablishment. The bells tolled again only two years later when the administration suspended new admissions. But with each threat of extermination has arisen student and community support. This was true again in 1992 and 1993 when the program faced what was its most dire circumstances, as a sharpened scythe took direct aim at Chicano studies.

Dr. Charles Young had been hired as the chancellor of UCLA in 1968 after serving for several years as an assistant chancellor. Prior to his employment at UCLA, he had worked under the University of California at Berkeley president, Clark Kerr. Young was certainly no stranger to dealing with student activists and was known among his peers as a man of deep convictions. Throughout his tenure as chancellor he had been fairly supportive of Chicano studies as an interdepartmental program but was resistant to elevating its status within the curricular structure of the university. He had long argued that support for the program among students and faculty was limited and that therefore an interdepartmental program made sense. Young also maintained that locating Chicano studies across multiple disciplines such as sociology, political science, and history enabled Chicano scholarship to have a greater impact on the overall UCLA curriculum and student learning.

Many Chicano faculty and students disagreed with Young's stance toward the program. For example, Jorge Mancillas, an assistant professor of biology at UCLA's medical school and a key player in the Chicano studies movement at UCLA, was a staunch opponent of Young's position: "The most reasonable-sounding argument the chancellor made was that he wants students in all the conventional departments to be exposed to the field of Chicana/o Studies—and that could best be achieved without a separate department." However, as Mancillas went on to point out, "If you teach at a university, as I do, you realize how hollow that argument is. Courses in Chicano studies must be organized, staffed and taught by a specific department; existing departments have shown very little interest in the subject. Those who volunteer to teach in the (current interdepartmental) program find their efforts perceived as a sort of volunteerism or community service, not as part of their academic responsibilities. Their home departments see it as time away from their 'real responsibilities.'"[1]

No one can realistically deny that interdepartmental programs survive at the whim of the primary departments with which the faculty identify. As long as faculty salaries and promotion and tenure decisions rest with home departments such as sociology, Chicano studies would continue to reside on the margins of scholarship and knowledge production. For a community that has long struggled for equal rights and dignity within U.S. society as well as within academic life, placing the core of their culture on the curricular margins can hardly be seen as empowering. This was the stance of many UCLA students who during the Chicano studies movement identified with organizations such as MEChA (Movimiento Estudiantil Chicano de Aztlan) and Conscious Students of Color (CSC), the two groups that led the struggle against the administration's reluctant support.

The plight of Chicano studies at UCLA in many ways represents the ongoing struggle between emerging multicultural paradigms and longstanding academic disciplines, which represent the dominant knowledge structures of the academy. Multiculturalism seeks to alter traditional educational structures that have either intentionally or unintentionally imposed a common culture on a pluralist society and in the end have served to silence those with non-European cultural roots.[2] It is from a multicultural framework that one can make sense of the cultural conflict that was faced by student groups such as MEChA and Conscious Students of Color as they sought to create a more expansive curriculum.

Students such as Minnie Ferguson, Bonnie Chavez, and Marcos Aguilar, three of the chief proponents of Chicano studies among students at UCLA in 1993, offered resistance and embraced political struggle as an avenue for both campus and social change. Ferguson reflected on why she and others supported an autonomous Chicano studies program: "We saw it as a cultural center where the community could come in with problems. . . . And the center would help the community to do research to solve their problems. . . . We want a place where people can get the kind of service that a university is supposed to provide. What's really important is educating our students. By that I mean not schooling them but truly educating them on their roots, on who they are. They need to graduate from the university and be more than just a doctor for the establishment. They need to go back to their communities and service our people. It's basically an issue of education versus schooling. What UCLA offers is schooling. They train you. They train you to do things that this society needs in order for the status quo to continue. We wanted a department of Chicana/o studies to be something more than that." Ferguson's perspective reflected the early motto of the Chicano Student Movement in Southern California as it evolved during the late 1960s and early 1970s: "Of the community, for the community."[3]

Bonnie Chavez found it appalling that a university in a city where at least a third of the population is Mexican American does not have a Chicano studies department: "Other U.C. campuses have Chicano studies departments. There's no excuse for us not to have one."[4] Marcos Aguilar offered similar arguments when he pointed to the need to have the culture and history of Mexican Americans taught in college classrooms. At first, Aguilar thought that simply having a program was enough. However, as he learned more about the curricular structure of universities such as UCLA and as he came to understand the academic norms of faculty life, he soon realized that a department of Chicano studies was the only way to insure its survival and proper place within academe. Thus, for Ferguson, Chavez, and Aguilar, Chicano studies was seen as a space within the overall curriculum dedicated to the ideas and beliefs that framed their identity as Chicanos.

"You can't teach ideas out of people," lamented the character David Stiver in Richard Vasquez's novel *Chicano*.[5] What David Stiver came to recognize is what so many educators have failed to understand: Cultural identity is at the core of how people experience education, and the core of the ideas related to cultural identity will not simply fade away. The ultimate irony of course for Chicanos is that it is upon the land of their ancestors that they now have become the outsiders and it is within the cultural context of schooling that their status as second-class citizens takes its toll.[6] In his poem entitled "Immigrants in Our Own Land," Jimmy Santiago Baca reflected on the struggles of Chicanos in the United States.

> We came here to get away from false promises,
> from dictators in our neighborhoods,
> who wore blue suits and broke our doors down
> when they wanted, arrested us when they felt like,
> swinging clubs and shooting guns as they pleased.
> But it's no different here. It's all concentrated.
> The doctors don't care, our bodies decay,
> our minds deteriorate, we learn nothing of value.
> Our lives don't get better, we go down quick.[7]

The desire to alter the social circumstances that have led so many Chicanos to the level of hopelessness evident in Baca's poem was the driving force in motivating the Chicano students at the University of California at Los Angeles to demand the elevation of Chicano studies to departmental status. Tired of their cultural narratives being denied relevancy within the classroom, the students saw no alternative but to demand a permanent place within the curricular structure of the university. They, like Ernesto Galarzo in his classic autobiography *Barrio Boy*, wanted to be able to share their heritage, to debate their heroes and heroines. "She [Ernesto's mother] refused to decide for me whether Abraham Lincoln was as great as Benito Juarez, or George Washington braver than the priest Don Miguel Hidalgo. At school there was no opportunity to settle these questions because nobody seemed to know about Juarez or Hidalgo; at least they were never mentioned and there were no pictures of them on the walls."[8]

Sources of Tension

In April of 1990, students from MEChA held a demonstration in support of Chicano studies during which they demanded a meeting with Chancellor Young, who only a few months prior had approved the suspension of new admissions to the program. A month later, the United Community and Labor Alliance was formed from members of the Los

Angeles community who supported Chicano studies. Latino members from Los Angeles businesses, trade unions, and volunteer organizations gladly joined the alliance. Mothers of East LA, One Stop Immigration, Janitors for Justice, and the Farm Workers Union all stepped forward to support the movement. Students believed that community support would be a key factor in pressuring Young to reconsider the structure for Chicano studies. In addition to the students, professors Juan Gómez-Quiñones, Jorge Mancillas, and David Hayes-Bautista were instrumental in the formation of the alliance. Gómez-Quiñones had long been a supporter of Chicano studies and was renowned for his historical work on Chicano politics and activism. He commented on the role of the alliance: "The United Community and Labor Alliance was the key community group in supporting the development of Chicano studies at UCLA and in supporting the hunger strike. Without the Alliance, the movement wouldn't have had the community support it had."

As a result of pressure from MEChA, support from the United Community and Labor Alliance, and faculty apprehension, the administration decided to amend its decision to suspend enrollment and agreed to look into the issue in greater detail. The result was the formation of a special committee in the winter of 1991 whose task it was to evaluate Chicano studies and recommend the best administrative structure for the program. Over the course of the next several months, the committee met on many occasions to deliberate and debate various administrative and curricular considerations. However, when the time came to make a recommendation, they could not reach agreement. Seven members voted for the immediate creation of a Chicano studies department. Four members voted to strengthen Chicano studies as an interdepartmental program (IDP) and then review its status in three years to determine the possibility of the program's becoming a department. Three members of the committee voted to retain Chicano studies permanently as an interdepartmental program. Thus, eleven of the fourteen members indicated a desire for the program to be advanced toward departmental status (seven right away and four in the near future). Despite strong support for departmental standing, the administration interpreted the split decision as a lack of commitment to the program and chose to retain Chicano studies as an interdepartmental program. Once again, MEChA and the United Community and Labor Alliance voiced their displeasure over the administration's decision and what they perceived to be a lack of serious commitment to Chicano studies.

In the spring of 1991, a group of Latino faculty in collaboration with

MEChA and the community alliance began work to develop a proposal for a department. The general thinking at the time was that a concrete proposal as evidence of faculty support might convince Chancellor Young to consider what was in effect becoming a fairly strong Chicano studies movement. In January of 1992, twelve faculty submitted the proposal to the administration. A faculty member who helped to develop the proposal reflected on the issues at the time: "And so this stuff had been simmering for two or three years and we actually wrote a proposal for a department—the faculty did. . . . We wrote it in a very short period of time. We hadn't done the homework to really get it passed. It was a good proposal but it was responding a lot to political pressure from students. The students were organized. They were fairly nationalistic in their views about this thing. This was supposed to be Chicano studies for Chicanos."

As a hurried response to student and community pressure, the proposal lacked the kind of research and detail so often needed for curricular change to win approval. Several faculty recognized the unlikeliness of the proposal's succeeding, for not only did it lack extensive research, the administration knew of the pressure student groups such as MEChA had been applying to faculty affiliated with the Chicano studies program. "No one in the administration was going to support the proposal," explained one faculty member. "It was responding to student pressure. The administration and the academic side felt very strongly that they didn't want to institutionalize a program like this in response to student pressure. They were very nervous about whether there was enough faculty support even though there was a group of us who wrote the proposal."

While Chancellor Young weighed the matter, the Council on Undergraduate Education (a committee of the academic senate) offered formal support for departmental status, as did the departments of history, Spanish, and economics. Finally, a year and three months after the proposal was first submitted, Chancellor Young announced his refusal to establish Chicano studies as a department. The day was Wednesday, April 28, 1993. Young reiterated his earlier position: The present structure as an interdepartmental program was well suited for bringing diverse faculty from around the campus together to research and teach Chicano studies. The university's commitment to the program "was never in question," maintained Young. "The only question was what structure would be most effective."[9]

Letters from the UCLA Ethnic Staff and Faculty Association (ESFA), the Latino Legislative Caucus of the State of California, State

Senator Art Torres, California Assemblymember Richard G. Polanco, and U.S. House Representative Lucille Roybal-Allard, among others, pleaded with UCLA officials and the chancellor to reconsider. ESFA, for example, was appalled at the authoritarian stance of the administration: "ESFA looks forward to a continuing discussion of these issues and hopes for the eventual establishment of a relationship with the university's top administrative team which is devoid of the present autocratic arrogance and is based more on equality and mutual respect." Vivién Bonzo, co-chair of the United Community and Labor Alliance and a businesswoman within the Los Angeles community, denounced Young's decision as "characteristic of the failure of the UC system to respond to the needs of the ethnic communities."[10] Furthermore, Bonzo felt that the chancellor's decision was rather ill-timed, given the fact that on the same day of the announcement many Chicano students were attending the funeral of the farmworker leader César Chávez. Others wondered whether Young had planned his announcement for when students were away from the campus as a means to reduce campus tension. Regardless of Young's intentions, Bonzo expected that Chávez's death would stir increased activism within the UCLA Chicano community.

Although resistance to the program's status as a department often was linked to structural arguments (interdepartmental status was argued to be more beneficial for the entire campus community) and budgetary concerns (the administration contended that times were rough financially), many within the Chicano student community saw the administration's arguments as a smoke screen for the real issue: a lack of respect for and sensitivity to Chicano students and their cultural and political concerns. For Chicano students at UCLA, rejecting Chicano studies as an academic department was akin to rejecting their community as a legitimate expression of American culture and identity. In an opinion piece published in the *Los Angeles Times*, Saul Sarabia, editor of UCLA's Chicano, Latino, and Native American newsmagazine, captured the prevailing sentiments among the students:

> Within UCLA—and academia in general—Latinos have had few weapons to ensure that the study of the Latino community is not left to the whims of individual professors who may be, at best, uninterested or, at worst, ignorant. It is fitting, then, that the challenge to ivory-tower norms is unfolding at UCLA. The chancellor's decision not to establish a Chicano studies department was another collective slap in the

face of the Latino community, because it comes at a time when Latinos are increasingly recognizing that their history, contributions and large numbers do not translate into power and self-determination.[11]

Despite valid arguments that interdepartmental status offers the opportunity for faculty to communicate Chicano scholarship across traditional disciplines, there are many weaknesses to such an arrangement. One of the serious problems is that faculty with dual responsibilities in their primary department and in Chicano studies often are put in a bind. Ultimately, the primary department, which is almost always a traditional academic discipline, controls the purse strings and oversees the promotion and tenure process. The traditional department therefore influences faculty behavior to a much greater degree. Efforts to give Chicano studies a voice in new hirings in departments such as sociology or history are perceived as bread crumbs with little substance. Juan Gómez-Quiñones, who teaches a Chicano history course and is a full professor in the history department, indicated that shared arrangements give departments a veto over hirings. Thus, an exceptional scholar of Chicano politics applying for a position in Chicano studies and political science could in the end be rejected by the political science department. Gómez-Quiñones found such a structure unacceptable: "We figure the matter is not satisfactorily dealt with. For us, satisfaction would be getting a department." David Lopez, who was the acting director of Chicano studies at the time of Young's announcement, described the idea of joint hiring as "a consolation prize" that will prove inadequate and frighten away potential new professors.[12]

The Students Respond

On May 11, 1993, nearly two weeks after Young's official rejection of Chicano studies as a department, a group of about two hundred students mainly belonging to Conscious Students of Color, a multiracial student organization, marched across the Westwood campus to the Faculty Center, where half of the demonstrators proceeded to enter the building to initiate a sit-in. While the group strongly supported departmental status for Chicano studies, the target of the Faculty Center demonstration was a proposed budget cut to the Chicano Studies Library. Marcos Aguilar, who by this time had been deposed from MEChA for his militant stance and unwavering commitment to Chicano studies, participated with other members of a group known as Danzantes Azteca Cuauhtemoc (also called the Aztec Dancers). The Danzantes were known for favoring indigenous rituals as part of their commitment to embracing Chicano identity and culture. They also tended to be more militant in their political strategies and sought to develop a Chicano studies program that stressed the historic roots of northern Aztlan culture—the region that now comprises California, Arizona, and New Mexico. Northern Aztlan had been annexed by the United States following the end of the Mexican-American War through the formal signing of the Treaty of Guadalupe Hidalgo in 1848. The treaty reflected in part what Gómez-Quiñones described in his book *Roots of Chicano Politics, 1600–1940* as "Anglo Saxon chauvinism," reflected most poignantly by the belief in manifest destiny.[13]

Aguilar was part of a group of over ninety students who were arrested inside the Faculty Center and who eventually were charged with doing about $30,000 to $40,000 worth of damage to furniture, windows, and art work inside the facility. Aguilar acknowledged that a few students did the damage but that the LAPD also may have caused some breakage when they forced their way into a back room of the center to which the protesters had retreated. Various accounts tend to support the contention that a few students caused the damages and that their actions reflected a high degree of anger and frustration.

Three to four hours after arriving at between 8 to 9 P.M., approximately two hundred police officers from various LA-area police departments began hauling out over ninety students, who were then taken to local jails for booking, a process that extended into the early morning hours. Male protesters were taken to the LA County Jail. Women were removed to the Sybil Brand Institute. Both groups of students were stripped and cavity searched. This was a traumatic experience for many who had never so much as cheated on an exam before. The anger that had driven them to participate in the Faculty Center demonstration simmered during their time in jail and in the end was fueled by the general treatment they received at the hands of their own university and the LAPD.

In the spring of 1993, Bert Cueva was a senior majoring in Chicano studies and political science. She was actively involved in the student organizing to promote Chicano studies as a department and participated in the protest at the Faculty Center. She commented on the mood of the students: "I think that the students were already frustrated with the administration. Especially with Chancellor Young. They had gotten so much rhetoric about what he would and wouldn't do that it was like the students were pushed over the edge. I also think the students went in unprepared. Initially, it was supposed to be a sit-in. But it ended up being more like a takeover of the Faculty Center. I think a couple of people lost control and other people kind of followed. And that's where you saw a lot of destruction of paintings and some of the glass."

The day after the protest at the Faculty Center, Chicano students and their multiracial supporters continued their efforts to overturn Chancellor Young's decision. On this occasion, a crowd of more than six hundred students rallied in front of Royce Hall as they demanded Young's reversal. Cueva, one of the organizers of the Faculty Center demonstration, explained that the students regretted Tuesday's violence but nonetheless were committed to protesting Young's position on Chicano studies. Cueva felt that by denying departmental status to the program, UCLA continued to reinforce a "Eurocentric academic perspective" that denigrates the many rich cultures of the state of California. The chancellor was out of the country but Vice Chancellor Rich responded by pointing out that the protests would not lead Young to reverse his decision. "That decision has been made," she adamantly stated.[14]

Following the arrest of the students at the Faculty Center, there were a number of campus demonstrations demanding that charges be dropped. School was in session until June 6 and students as well as faculty wondered if the administration's plan would simply be to wait the students out as summer break rapidly approached. Over the next two weeks there were a number of demonstrations, some of which attracted nearly five thousand students and community members. The protesters demanded three things. First, they wanted the administration to renounce a 10 percent budget cut that had been planned for all ethnic and gender studies programs. Second, the students wanted the Chicano studies program elevated to departmental status. And third, they demanded that all charges against the ninety-some students arrested at the Faculty Center be dropped.

With a sense of urgency in the air, the students sought to increase pressure on the administration. Jorge Mancillas recalled the rapid pace with which the movement gathered steam: "There was a sense that the students would soon be going home, and then it would be over. So, we discussed ways to give the issue urgency, and the idea of a hunger strike was mentioned. On the 17th of May there was a meeting of students to plan the next step. At that point some of the students decided to take part in a hunger strike that would start the next day—May 18th." But Mancillas believed more planning was needed to effectively carry out a strike and so he persuaded the students to wait another week. In the meantime, there were important issues to be resolved. "I remember talking to the students who were planning to participate in the hunger strike and I told them that it was a mistake to plan it overnight—that they had to have a physical examination. They had to know what they were going to drink, and how they were going to conduct their hunger strike. Where they were going to set up. Where they were going to stay throughout it. They had to bring it to the attention of the press, and there had to be some preparation, some organization before going on with this."

Moved by the students' unwavering commitment, Mancillas offered to participate in the hunger strike as long as they agreed to follow his suggestions. A deal was struck and a series of meetings were held culminating with a medical examination at the community clinic the day before the strike was set to begin.

A Community's Struggle

Vivién Bonzo was one of the key community leaders who supported Chicano studies as a department. She and her family had been proprietors on Olvera Street since the 1920s. In 1993, some seventy years after her grandmother opened the first family business, she was the proud owner of La Golondrina Restaurant. Bonzo expressed pride in her Latina identity and felt a strong sense of indebtedness to her grandmother for the love she conveyed for her heritage: "She was a very strong believer in Mexican culture. She helped establish things like the Cinco de Mayo celebrations [Mexican Independence Day] here in Los Angeles. . . . She initiated a number of Mexican traditions in our restaurant on Olvera Street, like Las Posadas, the Blessing of the Animals, and different activities that were done specifically to promote Mexican culture. I'm very proud of my heritage and very aware of it." As a sign of her commitment to Mexican culture, Bonzo runs two galleries specializing in Latin art. "I think all my life I'll be surrounded by things Latin and Latin people. I like that."

Through her involvement to preserve Olvera Street, Bonzo came in contact with a variety of activists who later recruited her support for the Chicano studies movement at UCLA. For Bonzo, the involvement of the community was a central part of the movement, in that it confirmed in her own mind that the issues were larger than simply what courses and majors are offered at a university. She discussed the alliance and its vision: "I was involved in a group called the United Community and Labor Alliance. That was the name we chose for a group of interested members of the community who were brought together by friends, students, and professors concerned about the status of Chicano studies at UCLA. It had a long-term vision of establishing a department. It was much more substantive than symbolic."

Several legislators around the state also came out in support of the movement. State Senator Tom Hayden was one who saw the significance of UCLA's adopting a formal Chicano studies department. In an editorial published in the *Chronicle of Higher Education*, Hayden commented on the relevance of both multiculturalism and Chicano studies:

> I happen to favor multiculturalism as a means of researching and restoring what has been lost or suppressed in history, although a danger always exists of creating separatist enclaves instead of richer understanding of the human condition. But UCLA, which has been a battlefield in the multicultural wars, has particular reason to take Chicano studies seriously. The institution has been a predominantly white academy in the largest center of Chicano-Mexican-Latino culture in the United States. Today only 1.4 percent of its full professors are Latino, along with 17 percent of its undergraduates, while the Los Angeles public-school population is 65 percent Latino. Clearly, a public university like UCLA needed to do more to serve *all* of the city, not just west L.A.[15]

Perhaps it was fitting that one of the leading student activists of the 1960s and a co-author of the Port Huron Statement, the guiding document of Students for a Democratic Society (SDS), would surface in the middle of what contemporary student activists perceived as a vitally important democratic issue. After all, the kind of participatory democracy put forth by the Port Huron Statement ought to include the nature of what colleges and universities offer to students in the form of the curriculum.

In a city with one of the largest and fastest growing Mexican American populations it would be a tremendously positive step for one of California's elite public institutions to elevate Chicano studies to departmental status. Hayden was not alone in recognizing the significance of such a step. Another major supporter was State Senator Art Torres (D-Los Angeles), who persuaded the legislature to postpone spending over $800,000 on additions to UCLA's law school. "It's no longer just an academic question. It has become a symbol across the state that even this chancellor is unable to realize," explained Torres after a lengthy meeting with Young. Despite the efforts of Torres, the chancellor later stated that he had not changed his mind and still believed that Chicano studies should remain an interdepartmental program. Young also complained about being held hostage by legislative leverage by Torres and others. "I don't see myself responding to that kind of action," explained Young as he addressed questions of budgetary threats.[16]

It made perfect sense to student leaders such as Marcos Aguilar, Minnie Ferguson, Bonnie Chavez, and Bert Cueva that the entire community take on what they and many others perceived as an elitist institution that continued to contribute to the marginality of Mexican Americans. While there were many conflicts among student leaders, this was one area where they had near unanimous agreement. Aguilar, for example, stressed the role of the community and supported the efforts of individuals such as Vivién Bonzo, whose reputation within the business community brought greater credibility to the movement. And Cueva reinforced Aguilar's view of the role of the community: "I'd have to say that the community involvement was definitely key because it held the administration accountable."

The Hunger Strike

On Tuesday, May 25, the Chicano studies movement took a new turn as six students and Jorge Mancillas began a hunger strike and vowed to get a promise from the chancellor or die trying. In tents pitched just outside the main administration building, Mancillas commented on the meaning of the hunger strike: "This is not a symbolic act. This is not a political statement. Either we get a department of Chicano studies or you will see us die before your eyes." Chancellor Young responded by stating that the university would do everything in its power to protect the health and welfare of the protesters.[17]

At first, sixteen students indicated they would participate in the hunger strike. But as the date selected to launch the strike quickly approached, that number dropped to seven, and then six when one student had to drop out at the last minute because of a case of bronchitis. Thus the hunger strike began on May 25 and included Marcos Aguilar, a senior, Cindy Montañez, a first-year student, along with her sixteen-year-old sister Norma from San Fernando High School, Balvina Collazo, a sophomore, María Lara, a senior, and Joaquín Ochoa, a junior. Thus two men (Aguilar and Ochoa) and four women (Collazo, Lara, and the Montañez sisters) made up the group of hunger strikers. They, of course, were joined by Mancillas, who lived up to his promise. Paztel Mireles, the spiritual advisor to the Danzantes Azteca, also fasted, although he chose to remain in the background. Interestingly enough, all six students were born in Mexico and had come to the United States at different points in their lives. Also, all six students had the complete support of their families and thus hardly represented the image so often suggested of student activists as adolescents and young adults rebelling against parental values.

State Senators Hayden and Torres sent letters on behalf of the hunger strikers to urge President Bill Clinton and Governor Pete Wilson to intervene. In the letter addressed to Wilson they argued that "the difference of whether to create a Chicano studies department, versus a program, are now revealed as a deeper question of the role of the University in honoring the quest for Chicano identity. We believe the hunger strikers are serious when several of them express a willingness to die to prove how much this matter means to them. They clearly feel that they have no alternative to this course in the face of an administration which has been perennially cold to their aspirations. This is an issue they rightfully feel has been a matter of frustration for over two decades." In the letter to President Clinton, Hayden and Torres wrote, "We have spoken out on this issue. We have visited the campus. We have introduced budget language to encourage UCLA officials to take seriously the need for a UCLA Chicano studies department. But these are slow and tedious processes and meanwhile a human and educational tragedy of immense proportions is drawing closer." The authors ended their letter to President Clinton with a plea: "We therefore respectfully ask you to place this issue in an urgent moral context by communicating your feelings to UCLA Chancellor Charles Young and to the hunger strikers and their families."

Initially, the hunger strike was not fully supported by all members of the Chicano community. Some even tried to talk the students out of the strategy, even after they had already initiated the strike. During the first week of the hunger strike, for example, a community leader who requested anonymity tried to convince the students to end their fast. This individual recalled being pulled aside by several others from the community and asked to try to talk the students out of the strike. They were concerned for their lives because few saw Chancellor Young giving in to this kind of pressure. "Can't you get these folks to stop? Isn't there something you can do?" they pleaded. "I remember I actually went inside the tent and tried to talk to one of the strikers and it was like, you know, it was the wrong thing to do. They were already set in their minds to hold the strike until they got what they wanted. So that was the last time I tried."

Faculty also had doubts about whether or not a hunger strike was the appropriate strategy. As one professor explained, "The decision to be a hunger striker is one of saying you're going to make enormous sacrifice. You're willing to starve yourself for a cause. It's a very individual decision." This faculty member went on to suggest that perhaps the goal of gaining departmental status for Chicano studies was not important enough for such a serious and historically significant practice. "There were people who felt that a hunger strike to create an academic unit was questionable—that to use a hunger strike to fight for an academic unit in a university was problematic. César Chávez went on a hunger strike to fight for the basic survival of very poor people. So the whole idea of a hunger strike in an elite institution such as UCLA for an elite group of students was very problematic to some people."

Despite mixed feelings about the strike within the Chicano community, there were few who openly admitted their ambivalence; they did not want to undermine the serious action the students had taken. Any doubts or questions about the strike as a strategy were pretty much kept in the background and not shared with the media. And regardless of disagreements over strategy, most within the Chicano community wanted the same outcome—departmental status for Chicano studies.

As public outpourings from individuals such as Torres, Hayden, and actor Edward James Olmos came forth, pressure on the administration increased. Nevertheless, the hunger strike wore on and little resolution seemed likely, at least after the first several days. For Mancillas, health was quickly becoming a concern: "It was strange because physically I felt very weak. By the end of the strike I couldn't walk. . . . I wasn't in very good shape. . . . By the third day I was getting weak enough that they decided to put me in a wheelchair, but I was still walking [from time to time] on the seventh day. It was on the twelfth day that I really couldn't walk anymore. I was just too weak." One thing that surprised Mancillas was the fact that his mind stayed relatively sharp. He attributed this to the incredible support he and the other hunger strikers received. "With all the attention focused on us, it was an energizing effect to see thousands of people come through the camp and be so supportive."

In an interview conducted after the strike, Mancillas reflected on being asked by Chancellor Young four years prior to participate in a committee charged with determining the best structure for the Chicano studies program. "The chancellor promised that whatever the committee decided, he would do. But after many weeks of research and deliberation, the committee recommended that a separate department of Chicano studies be created at UCLA and the chancellor ignored our recommendation." It was impossible for Mancillas and the other six hunger strikers to see Young's decision as anything but unacceptable. How could a major public university situated within a city in which Latinos account for 40 percent of the population reject their culture and history as legitimate sources of knowledge and inquiry? After all, Los Angeles was founded by Mexicans in the late 1700s and was part of the southwestern region of North America that had belonged to Mexico for over three hundred years prior to being annexed to the United States.[18] "Annexed"? That was a clever term to many of the Chicano student nationalists who tended to think of the annexation of the Southwest more in terms of U.S. expansionism. The anger that led to the violence at the Faculty Center and which often shaped the words and tone of Chicano political discourse was deeply rooted in a sense among students such as Marcos Aguilar, Cindy and Norma Montañez, Balvina Collazo, María Lara, and Joaquín Ochoa that they had become immigrants in their own land.

The students who decided to participate in the hunger strike were some of the most strident supporters of Chicano studies and were not necessarily reflective of the general movement. The hunger strikers were identified by one faculty member as more of the nationalist-oriented students and did not represent the broad-based coalition epitomized by the Conscious Students of Color, which had led the demonstration at the Faculty Center. The hunger strikers, as one faculty member suggested, did not have full support of the rest of the movement: "Although the hunger strike was really the thing that broke the administration to do something, to really change the face of Chicano studies on this campus, it was something that really was not well supported by a lot of students, by a lot of faculty."

Questions about the appropriateness of a hunger strike and whether a group of nationalistic students should represent the movement highlight some of the inner tensions within the struggle to departmentalize Chicano studies. Despite the need for solidarity and the need to create a unified front, there was, as in most communities and cultures, much that pulled at the connective fabric of the Chicano studies movement.

Inner Strains

The movement had many splinters and disagreements throughout the months leading up to the hunger strike and its ultimate resolution. Some felt that the hunger strikers had too much say in the negotiations with the university. After all, they were only seven voices out of many. A community leader talked about the tensions that surfaced around the hunger strikers: "A couple of the hunger strikers made it clear that they were putting their lives on the line and so whatever they wanted they should get. That was their attitude—that their opinion was worth much more than anybody else's."

As the days of the hunger strike wore on, there was an increasing level of stress, fatigue, and irritability, especially among the fasters but also among others within the community who were playing a variety of supportive roles. Tension between different members of the movement surfaced during their conversations as a sense that the administration might not modify its policy began to creep into people's thinking. As one community member explained, "People didn't feel glorious every-day," and sometimes, "They were fighting it out among each other." But underlying some of the strains within the movement were real differences associated with diverse political agendas.

Marcos Aguilar had been kicked out of MEChA for his militant stance and his conviction that the organization's primary role and vision ought to focus on the creation of a Chicano studies department at UCLA. His unwavering commitment to this vision alienated him from many of the moderate Mechistas (MEChA members) who tended to adopt more mainstream policies and less offensive political strategies. Much of Aguilar's vision for the organization was grounded in the political philosophy of the late 1960s when more radical tactics were often deployed. Once again, the influence of the 1960s as a source for contemporary multicultural struggle surfaced.

In 1969, the role and vision for the Chicano movement within higher education was first spelled out in the early drafts of a document entitled *El Plan de Santa Barbara*. A section of the document simply called "Manifesto" reads as follows:

> For all people, as with individuals, the time comes when they must reckon with their history. For the Chicano the present is a time of re-naissance, of renacimiento. Our people and our community, el barrio and la colonia, are expressing a new consciousness and a new resolve. Recognizing the historical tasks confronting our people and fully aware of the cost of human progress, we pledge our will to move. We will move forward toward our destiny as a people. We will move against those forces which have denied us freedom of expression and human dignity. Throughout history the quest for cultural expression and free-dom has taken the form of a struggle. Our struggle, tempered by the lessons of the American past, is an historical reality.[19]

The document explained that the word *Chicano*, which in the past had been a pejorative and class-bound term, was to be the root source of identity for Mexican Americans. "The widespread use of the term Chicano today signals a rebirth of pride and confidence. 'Chicano' simply embodies an ancient truth: that man is never closer to his true self as when he is close to his community."[20] For Aguilar, Chicano struggle must therefore involve cultural work to reconnect with a distant past that had begun to be erased some two hundred years earlier through U.S. expansionism. His call for a spirit of nationalism, born of the late 1960s, and organized around Chicano identity, was too extreme to other Mechistas, many of whom saw the organization as both a social club and a political association.

One of the challenges presented by *El Plan de Santa Barbara* is the creation of "a curriculum program and an academic major relevant to the Chicano cultural and historical experience in America."[21] As the primary student group charged with campus organizing for Chicano renacimiento, MEChA organizations necessarily ought to have as one of their central goals the creation of Chicano studies programs. Furthermore, MEChA is charged by the Santa Barbara plan to be the leader of campus reform and is warned about building coalitions with groups that are markedly stronger. This was a concern of some of the Mechistas at UCLA in 1993 when Conscious Students of Color (CSC) organized their multiracial demonstration at the Faculty Center. For MEChA, coalitions present a perilous terrain through which they must carefully navigate, for there are implications for Chicano struggle: How can the rightful empowerment of Chicanos take place with help from non-Chicanos? Their concern was similar to that expressed by Blacks in the latter half of the 1960s as many broke away from their progressive White allies. This is the kind of identity divisiveness among progressive and left-wing groups that concerned Todd Gitlin in *The Twilight of Common Dreams*:

> The cultivation of difference is nothing new, but the sheer profusion of identities that claim separate political standing today is unprecedented. And here is perhaps the strangest novelty in the current situation: that the ensemble of group recognitions should take up so much of the energy of what passes for the Left. It is often for good reason that differences have multiplied, making their claims, exposing the fraudulence of the universalist claims of the past. . . . But what is a Left if it is not, plausibly at least, the voice of a whole people? For the Left as for the rest of America, the question is not whether to recognize the multiplicity of American groups, the variety of American communities, the disparity of American experiences. Those exist as long as people think

they exist. The question is one of proportion. What is a Left without a commons, even a hypothetical one? If there is no people, but only peoples, there is no Left.[22]

While Gitlin's concern about the "cultivation of difference" (or "over-cultivation" in his mind) certainly is a legitimate concern, the reality at UCLA is that students were able to forge a common movement through the use of identity politics, and not, as Gitlin tends to believe, in spite of such tactics.

When CSC took up the issue of Chicano studies and the threat of budget cuts to the Chicano Studies Library, it served as a wake-up call to many in MEChA. Milo Alvarez, a student with a long history of involvement in MEChA, spoke about what was happening: "At that time MEChA leadership was weak. . . . Most of the leaders were doing things like organizing social gatherings and drinking beer, instead of paying attention to the real issues that were going on. It wasn't until Conscious Students of Color hijacked our issue that conflict started to develop within MEChA." Alvarez went on to note that some of the younger Mechistas took over and started running the organization because they were dissatisfied with the lack of political orientation of the group.

There was another significant strain within the Chicano studies movement. From the early days of the Chicano movement throughout the United States there has been a lack of recognition of the unique experiences and contributions of Chicanas. As Cherríe Moraga has pointed out in her work, there has been much resistance to aligning Chicano struggle with a womanist agenda and thus a lack of recognition of the intersections between race and gender.[23] Concerns about the role of women and the unwillingness of MEChA leaders to align themselves with the Conscious Students of Color led several women from MEChA to become actively involved in political activities with CSC. In some ways, what the women of MEChA were expressing through the desire to enter into solidarity with CSC was their own empowerment as Chicanas.

UCLA English professor Sonia Sadlivar-Hull recognized some of the gender issues as she discussed the Chicano studies movement: "I really want to emphasize the role of the women students during the hunger strike and the subsequent curriculum discussions. During all of the negotiations, it was the women students who insisted on saying Chicano and Chicana studies and not just subsuming women's issues under the masculine O. Spanish is a romance language. It's very androcentric. Very sexist. So the women have been instrumental." And Bert Cueva discussed how gender issues got played out within MEChA. "Even within MEChA, our Chicana/Chicano base, we had a big division that was based on gender. There was a sector of Mechistas who wanted a strong program and department that was going to work with issues related to gender and issues regarding sexuality. And there was another constituency that just couldn't understand the importance of including women and advocated for, I guess, a traditional Chicano studies department, which a lot of us didn't want. Those type of divisions were also very apparent at the faculty level. So it was from the top to the bottom and bottom up; it wasn't just in the student sector."

A group of Mechistas, along with Chicanas who had distanced themselves from MEChA, stressed the need for a women's perspective to be part of the development of Chicano studies, and, in fact, were the first to propose "Chicana and Chicano Studies" as the name of the department they hoped to create. But even within this group of female students there was tension about the role of women in the movement. Several of the women who embraced indigenous ideals and rituals, such as the members of the Aztec Dancers, which included Minnie Ferguson, stressed more traditional roles for women. From their perspective, it was perfectly acceptable if women chose to take a supportive role instead of heading the movement. For these Chicanas, the goal is for women to *have such choices*. Others, such as Bert Cueva, tended to adopt a more liberal feminist viewpoint and saw a need for women to lead the movement and erase the stereotypes of women as behind-the-scene supporters.

Thus the tension within the Chicano studies movement was both political and gender related. It was political in that MEChA saw issues related to Chicano studies as their domain and the multiracial Conscious Students of Color had attempted to lead the struggle. For nationalistic-oriented Mechistas, the vision of La Raza involves self-empowerment, and non-Chicanos should not guide such efforts. Additionally, the most militant students, such as Marcos Aguilar, were too extreme in their political and cultural strategies for the more mainstream MEChA moderates. The tension revolving around gender issues related primarily to competing visions of what Chicano studies eventually ought to look like, with many of the women such as Minnie Ferguson aligning themselves with the more radical men, such as Aguilar, and demanding a department of Chicana and Chicano studies. At the same time, more traditional Mechistas were upset by what they perceived as the feminist encroachment upon the Chicano studies movement. And, of course, even within the Chicana movement there were disagreements about what constituted an empowering vision of womanhood. It was amid these competing visions of Chicano studies that the hunger strike emerged as the key event in creating a semblance of unity within the overall movement.

The Negotiations

For the first few days of the hunger strike, the group asked for a meeting with Chancellor Young. They wanted to hold discussions in order to make their position clear and to explain their vision of Chicano studies. Early requests were rejected by the chancellor, although eventually he agreed to hold an initial meeting. Young's reticence to talk with the students may have been overcome by an empowering march of students and community members that took place on Saturday, June 5. Demonstrators assembled at Placita Olvera and ended on the campus of UCLA at the site of the encampment in the Schoenberg Plaza across from Murphy Hall, the main administration building. A group of less than a hundred people began the march amid a cold spring rain. By the time they had reached the campus, some fifteen miles later, there were over one thousand protesters. Many involved in the Chicano studies movement considered the march the high point of the hunger strike. As much as anything else, this convinced the administration that the community was truly behind the cause and that it may be more expedient in the long run to at least hear their demands. Despite agreeing to meet with Chicano activists, Young was still concerned about the image of the university giving in to student pressure and the message it might send to future demonstrators.

The hunger strikers and various student representatives debated for nearly a full day as to who should meet with the administration. In part, they were not sure why they needed a meeting even though they had asked for one. By now they had made their demands clear. In fact, they were written on a large banner facing Murphy Hall: departmental status for Chicano studies, amnesty for all students involved in the Faculty Center demonstration, and full funding of all ethnic and gender studies programs. While they wanted to win concessions from the administration, they also feared that negotiations suggested a willingness to compromise. They did not want to send this message to the chancellor. He knew what their demands were. They simply wanted results.

A week had passed before the hunger strikers finally agreed they were ready to hold a meeting with the administration. They decided to send two faculty members and four students as representatives. Several students protested the idea of including faculty out of bitterness over what they saw as a lack of commitment among the faculty to Chicano studies. After all, these were the same people who were unable to agree upon a structure for Chicano studies, and whose lack of consensus Young had used as rationale for retaining Chicano studies as an interdepartmental program. To the hunger strikers, the faculty were part of the problem. Jorge Mancillas, however, convinced the students that faculty should be present and that there were a few who could be trusted.

Leo Estrada was one of the professors chosen to meet with the administration. Estrada reflected on the day he was called to meet with the strikers: "I was very quietly at home when I received a call asking me to come down to the campground because they wanted to talk to me. I think that's the way it was put. So I came onto the campus and walked into the tent. It was the first time I had seen the hunger strikers and by this time the camp had grown from a few tents to many with signs and flags and it was quite a scene." In one of the larger tents, Estrada met with the students, who were now being advised by four or five faculty members whom he recognized. They were consulting as a group when suddenly one of the students turned to him and said, "Would you go and represent us with the chancellor as one of the faculty members?" Estrada took a second and then responded with a resolute, "Yes." With that, Estrada became a key player in the negotiations and contributed mightily to ending the hunger strike. He reflected on the first meeting: "I remember walking into Murphy Hall with this group of people for a meeting that we were already about twenty minutes late for and I asked somebody what the agenda was and everybody kind of looked at me with confusion. We had spent so much time deciding who would go to the meetings that we never talked about our agenda."

Once inside the chancellor's office, Estrada decided to take the lead. It certainly would not be advisable to seem unprepared, so he got the meeting going. "I think you know we're here to represent the people who are outside and before going any further I think it is important just to reiterate why the hunger strike is going on." He then turned to a student named Christine Guzman and asked if she would review the demands for the chancellor. Guzman proceeded to discuss the issues in such a passionate and eloquent manner that the room became deathly silent. Estrada remembered the tone of her speech: "She was incredibly eloquent. She didn't just talk about it. She said it in a way that was both heartfelt and sincere and yet spoken with real strength. I don't know how else to say it. Just real strength." Estrada then asked each student to speak to Chancellor Young about the issues and why they were important to their lives.

One by one the students shared their own stories about how they had come to UCLA with high hopes only to face alienation. One student talked about being arrested at the Faculty Center and how humiliating the whole ordeal had been and how it threatened many of his educational and career goals. Nonetheless, this student was willing to let that stand if it meant achieving a Chicano studies department for his people. Finally, Steve Loza, the second professor asked to represent the students, simply stated that he was there to support the students. When all the students and Loza had finished speaking, Estrada then addressed the chancellor and asked him to give them a response. Estrada recalled the chancellor's reaction: "I feel like I've got a gun to my head and I refuse to negotiate under these circumstances and as far as I'm concerned there will never be a Chicano studies department at UCLA." Estrada found Young's tone to be adamant, cold, strong. At this point it became clear to Estrada that the chancellor resented being put in a defensive posture by the hunger strikers and he was not going to simply give in to the three demands as the student representatives had hoped.

In the days that followed, more people became involved in the negotiations and Young disappeared to his office as Scott Waugh, dean of social sciences, and Raymund Paredes, vice-chancellor for academic development, took primary responsibility for representing the administration's position. Paredes had been in the middle of debates about Chicano studies for years and was a supporter of a broad ethnic studies program that would include Chicano studies as an interdepartmental program. Paredes commented on some of his concerns: "One of the issues I raised in the early part of the discussions was should we have Chicano studies or should we have Latino studies instead? . . . My objection always to the notion of a Chicano studies department was that I thought the whole concept was regressive. I thought that before we decided on a Chicano studies department that one of the things we should talk about is ethnic studies and focus on comparative work. I thought that we might want to talk about cultural studies or American studies as a broader methodological approach."

Because of his resistance to Chicano studies as a department, Paredes found the hunger strike and the negotiations to be emotionally taxing in a way that few others could have understood. As the highest ranking Latino administrator at UCLA, he found himself vilified by students and the media. "I was probably the most outspoken person who challenged the position of the students and some of the faculty and because of my administrative position it probably increased the amount of resentment directed toward me. It was an awkward and unpleasant situation for me to be lined up with several UCLA administrators, none of whom was Latino, in a contentious environment fighting with Latino students, faculty, and community representatives. The whole situation lent itself to the image that I was the only Chicano who was against departmental status for Chicano studies. There was a lot of accusations that I was a sell out. The whole thing was very unpleasant for me."

In addition to faculty, administrators, and students, members from the Los Angeles Chicano community also began to attend the negotiations as individuals such as Vivién Bonzo came to play a role in the deliberations. Bonzo recalled being scolded by the hunger strikers. She had hoped that by being a little friendlier during the negotiations she could perhaps open up the dialogue and move past the rhetoric. However, she was advised not to be so amiable with the administration and that she should keep "a hard, cold, poker face." Bonzo also perceived that the administration lacked a sincere commitment to offer any substantive resolutions. "They offered dumb little things, like, 'We'll call the program César Chávez.' That's not enough if there's not the substance behind it. If you really don't have the intent, it doesn't matter what you call it." She remembered her frustration as well: "They were just trying to continue discussion just to show that they were doing something—that now they had moved into negotiations when it really wasn't like that at all."

Estrada became the moderator for every meeting and made it a habit of checking in with the hunger strikers prior to the negotiations to see if there was any new information. In his role as moderator, he found himself at times quite surprised by how prepared the students were; it seemed as though every time the administration came up with a legitimate reason as to why something could not be accomplished, the students had already anticipated that option and quickly responded with a reasonable counterargument. Although Estrada tended to side with the students' cause, he felt a need to come off as neutral as possible. "I would try and keep the discussion focused on the three major demands. As the students started to come up with new demands, I tried to find ways to keep them off the table unless they were related in some way to the original demands. If the administration tried to bring in things that were beyond the primary concern, I also tried to keep that off the table." The meetings tended to last anywhere from four to seven hours and Estrada usually ended them on a high note so that the next meeting might begin with a touch of optimism.

After three days of meetings the hunger strikers decided that they wanted to be part of the formal discussions. They feared that the faculty and community members representing them would not be as hard-line as they wanted them to be. Their participation altered the dynamics of the meetings and slowed the pace of the discussions. The momentum that had been gained was not completely lost but it was certainly stalled as the hunger strikers went through a period of emotional venting. Initial discussions on the part of the hunger strikers lasted nearly three hours as they explained their actions to the negotiating teams and community members in attendance. By this time, the number of observers in the room had grown to nearly thirty. The result was an extended session that lasted nearly twelve hours. And by now the hunger strike was into its twelfth day and tempers were growing shorter.

Eventually, the negotiations returned to the three demands. The demand for a department of Chicano studies hit numerous barriers as the administration raised all kinds of issues related to the formal procedures for curricular change. The students responded by pointing out how some of the barriers could be eliminated or alleviated. The demand that charges be dropped against the students arrested at the Faculty Canter was bogged down as UCLA's attorneys repeatedly explained that it was out of their hands and that the district attorney had to make that decision. In response, the students' lawyers argued that the DA could easily be influenced by the chancellor.

At the same time that negotiations were going on in the chancellor's office, other efforts were under way. A group of UCLA faculty led by Professor David Kaplan in the philosophy department developed the idea of a Chicano studies center that would be interdisciplinary and would have all the trappings of a department but would not be called a department. By avoiding the language of "department," Kaplan and his colleagues thought that perhaps the chancellor might approve their plan. The idea of a center enabled Young the opportunity to save face to a degree: He might not be seen as giving in to student pressure. This was an important point, as Young was already on record as stating that giving in to the student protesters was not part of his expectation. The plan was put on paper and pushed through the Council on Undergraduate Curriculum. The faculty then called an emergency session of the Academic Senate's Executive Committee, which reviewed and then approved the plan. Normally such administrative processes would take six months to a year, but this time approval was won in a matter of only three days. Estrada commented on what amounted to nothing short of a miracle: "The fact that they pulled it off in three days is amazing. First of all, coming up with the concept of this interdisciplinary center was in itself unique. There's no such thing. They made it up and they found something in the bylaws that made it possible and they created it out of the blue. They created a new structure that looked just like a department."

On the fifth day of negotiations (which was the second week of the hunger strike), the proposal developed by the faculty was offered to both sides to mull over. The plan called for the hiring of four full-time faculty committed to Chicano studies. The students wanted time to think about it. Was it a department or not? That was the question everyone debated for nearly twenty-four hours. Some argued that the new center was the same as a department but only lacked the title "department." Others complained that if it was equivalent to a department, then why not call it a department?

In keeping with an earlier decision in which he had promised the hunger strikers the final say, Estrada gathered everyone into a classroom away from the chancellor's office. On the chalkboard he outlined the three demands and how the administration had responded to each. The center proposed by the faculty was the equivalent of an academic department in many ways. The DA had agreed to drop all the charges and the records would be expunged so that the arrests would not show up on the students' records. There were some other matters related to the damages and an apology from the LAPD which were not resolved and most likely would not be. Funding for ethnic and gender studies would not be cut. "I showed each of the demands and how we had resolved each one of them. I went around the room and the community leaders for the most part said, 'You guys have won a great victory. It's time to end the hunger strike.'" Estrada was feeling positive about the approaching end that he could nearly envision. Finally, he could get back to his normal life. After everyone had offered their comments to the hunger strikers, Estrada said to the students, "We're going to leave you for the next few hours to make the final decision to accept or not accept because that was the deal."

Three hours later Estrada came back to the room and the students were talking about extending the strike. Also, they had added other demands to their original list. "They'd moved beyond the issues that were on the board and so we had a confrontation. I reminded them that we had started the process with three demands and that moving on to some of the things that they were talking about doing now—were things that I wouldn't support." Estrada threatened to walk away if the students insisted on pushing their new demands. To him, they were being unfair and they were not negotiating in good faith. He countered their arguments, "Your job is to make the decision on accepting or not accepting the deal as it was presented, as the commitment was made." The students became angry with Estrada and asked him to leave and give them more time to think. Two hours passed and Estrada once again returned. It was nine o'clock at night. "What's the answer?" he asked. The students responded, "We're gonna accept the deal but we're not gonna do it this evening. Tell the administration to go home because we want to have a news conference and we can't start a news conference at nine o'clock at night and get anybody here." They knew that if they could get the notice of the news conference out to the local media, they would get extended coverage and television play.

Estrada reflected on how the strike wound down: "So the deal was finally struck at about nine o'clock at night and I went up to the board and I erased what was there. I went around and shook everybody's hands and then I left. The next day they won their battle. They had a nice media thing and I basically just disappeared from the scene. They got their demands. They got the César Chávez Center. They got the charges against the students dropped. The hunger strike ended the next day and they had a celebration of breaking of the bread. And then it was over."

The Aftermath

It was on the fourteenth day that the hunger strike finally came to an end as the resolution was reached. Outside Murphy Hall chants of "Chicano power!" could be heard. Following the resolution, Chancellor Young was quoted as saying: "I'm glad it's over and I hope they get back to class and get back to their other activities and that we will have an opportunity to see this program become the great center, the great program, in Chicano studies we all want it to be." A number of the campus and community activists involved in the struggle spoke to a crowd of about four hundred people, many of whom waved Mexican flags. "Call it what you will, it is a department," declared Juan Jose Gutierrez, one of the community activists involved in the strike. "We did this to keep alive the flame that was ignited by César Chávez," Jorge Mancillas added as he positioned his weakened body in a wheelchair. "We continue his work for dignity and justice. This is just the first step." [24]

UCLA administrators made it clear, however, that the new César Chávez Center for Interdisciplinary Instruction in Chicana and Chicano Studies would not be an academic department and that the majority of professors would have joint appointments in other areas. There was still the fear, on the part of the administration, that without joint appointments, Chicano studies would become too politicized. Influence from other scholars around the campus was seen as a way of controlling for professorial and student politicization.[25]

Young maintained that the settlement provided little more than what the university was already willing to do without the hunger strike. The administration did, however, acknowledge that the changes might not have happened as fast. Young tried desperately to avoid the image that he had given in to pressure from Chicano activists or from State Senators Torres and Hayden, who had threatened budgetary reprisals against the university. Young responded to questions concerning the pressure from the two state senators: "I think anyone who knows me very well knows I don't take very well to threats. And especially threats from people who are using the public's money to try to tell us how we ought to run the university."[26]

Under the compromise, the Chicano studies program was to hire four new full-time professors in 1993–94 and two more the following academic year. The positions had already been set aside but the difference was that the primary identity of the new faculty would be in the Chicano studies center as opposed to one of the traditional academic disciplines. In fact, the new hires could if they so desired have all of their responsibilities tied to Chicano studies. The agreement also set aside funds for lectures and guest speakers from outside the university community. Another part of the settlement included dropping charges against eighty-four students cited for trespassing during the Faculty Center sit-in. More serious charges against the remaining students involved in the May 11 demonstration would also be dropped if restitution of $30,000 in damages was agreed upon.[27]

For many within the Chicano community at UCLA the resolution was a victory. In terms of the Chicano studies program, the opportunity for the César Chávez Center to hire its own faculty was key. As one professor with a history of involvement in the Chicano Studies Movement explained, "The key thing that defines departmental status is the ability to hire faculty and that's why creating the Chávez Center with faculty FTE was a victory and continues to be a victory."

The Larger Issues

The actions by the Chicano students at UCLA may be seen as part of the larger effort to rebuild their community by asserting the historical and cultural relevance of Mexican heritage. Many of today's Chicano students challenge politicians and university leaders to pay heed to their struggle and their rightful place in a multicultural democracy that has for years sought to silence them. As the idea of La Raza emerged throughout the 1960s, it has been rekindled by a new generation of activists who refuse to stand by as their culture is wiped away from history. In an article in the *Los Angeles Times*, Ralph Frammolino talked about today's Chicano college students: "Like their parents in the '60s and '70s, they call themselves Chicanos and are confronting officials with demonstrations, sit-ins, hunger strikes—and sometimes vandalism—to demand more respect for their culture and more faculty appointments for Latinos."[28] But unlike their parents who were more or less forced to assimilate through the policies and practices of mainstream education, today's students, Frammolino maintained, are used to a system that has shown a greater desire to accommodate the needs and cultural differences embraced by Chicanos. Thus the expectations students have of what institutions ought to be able to achieve have been raised. With higher expectations have come deeper disappointments, often at the hands of powerful individuals such as Chancellor Young.

But Chicano student activism also may be a response to the rising conservatism that advanced steadily during the Reagan-Bush years, and in California has become particularly insidious under Governor Pete Wilson. And more recently, Chicano students have witnessed attacks on affirmative action and immigrants enacted through legislation such as Propositions 187 and 209. Despite counterclaims by the Right that such efforts are really attempts to end "special privileges" and affirm "civil rights," the real issue seems more likely rooted in an isolationist xenophobia that often targets Mexicans and Mexican Americans throughout the state. The attacks on Mexican immigrants and Mexican Americans and often transposed to any Latino was clearly revealed in the beatings of border crossers by officers of the Los Angeles sheriff's department. Additionally, the LA uprising that followed the Rodney King beatings not only revealed the deep division between African Americans and Caucasians but also marked the clear division between Chicanos and Anglos. UC Berkeley Chicano studies professor Carlos Muñoz, a leader of the 1960s Chicano student movement, spoke about the LA riots and the response to the Rodney King verdict. Muñoz maintained that the riots represented a significant shift in race relations, which can no longer be framed simply as a Black and White issue. As he argued, the unrest demonstrated that there are "multitudes of Americans" and that "race also matters to Latinos." Muñoz also felt that the life and then the death of César Chávez had become increasingly influential to a new generation of Chicano students: "In my generation, César Chávez inspired us by his living example. And now the students of today are being inspired by his death."[29]

Leo Estrada saw the struggle of today's Chicano students as similar to what Blacks went through a decade or two earlier in their quest to connect to their African heritage. He described the struggle as a "search for their roots." For Estrada, and others, the challenge today's Chicano students face involves establishing a firm sense of cultural identity. What has emerged is the realization among many of the young that one's identity cannot be divorced from one's heritage. It is what some have described as "Chicanismo"—the idea of "cultural nationalism."[30] Juan Gómez-Quiñones described Chicanismo as "a radically political and ethnic populism" that challenged the "assumptions, politics, and principles of the established political leaders, organizations, and activity within and outside the community." He went on to write, "The emphasis of 'Chicanismo' upon dignity, self-worth, pride, uniqueness, and a feeling of cultural rebirth made it attractive to many Mexicans in a way that cut across class, regional, and generational lines . . . it emphasized Mexican cultural consciousness and heritage as well as pride in speaking Spanish."[31] Interest in the past and a commitment to community is evident in the rise of Mexican American student organizations such as MEChA, not just in California but across the country. Let us not forget that one of the original goals of MEChA, as suggested by *El Plan de Santa Barbara*, was to create a Chicano studies program at every California state university. What we see in many ways then is today's students returning to the identity politics that many of their parents embraced with the founding of such organizations in the late 1960s and corresponding to the growth and popularity of the philosophical ideals of Chicanismo and La Raza.

For State Senator Hayden, the Chicano studies movement at UCLA touched a flame in his own burning memories of the 1960s. On the Westwood campus he found kindred spirits engaged in the practice of participatory democracy as they fought to project their own voice into the curricular structures of the university. Interestingly enough, Hayden had met César Chávez two decades prior when he sought his support during the 1976 Democratic Party elections for a senate seat in California. In his autobiography he recalled meeting with Chávez, whom he described as "a thoughtful, utterly dedicated organizer whom I much admired." After a long conversation, Chávez offered Hayden some advice: "We've seen many candidates come and go. It would be a waste of time and money unless you build something lasting, like a machine. Not like Mayor Daley has, but a machine for people. That would interest us."[32] Now, nearly twenty years later, Hayden came to the support of the legacy of César Chávez.

Hayden astutely described what occurred at UCLA as a "struggle over cultural identity."[33] Clearly, this was the case. Inherent in such struggles are the possibility of change and the hope of a better and more inclusive tomorrow. This is captured in comments from community activist Vivién Bonzo: "I really think that Chicanos have had a difficult struggle throughout recent history in California and other states. First, in trying to assume an identity that somewhat evades them. Until more recently, with the onslaught of immigrants and the burgeoning Latino community . . . we didn't really have a good sense of what it is to be Mexican, at least in the very early years. I was fortunate to land here and so I got a really good sense of that. But a lot of people I know never did; they didn't really have a sense of Latino or Chicano identity. Nowadays, it is very different than it was twenty years ago or thirty years ago, when there wasn't such a strong identity with Mexicans and Latin things in general. So, Chicano studies becomes an important link in sort of filling in the blanks of people's struggles for an identity." And a student, Milo Alvarez, also noted the connection between Chicano studies and larger cultural concerns: "Chicano studies gives us intellectual space. . . . We're always fighting for our history and culture in an elitist institution such as UCLA. It's about empowering our people. . . . Basically, we are fighting for our own space in one of the most prestigious institutions in the United States."

The Chicano studies movement at UCLA revolved around issues of power: Who has the authority to define knowledge? Who gets to determine what constitutes legitimate forms of study? Who defines mainstream identities and marginal identities? Chicano students wanted Chicano history and culture to be as relevant as sociology, history, or political science, which have for decades been taught mostly by European Americans and focused primarily on European worldviews. As Refugio Rochín and Adaljiza Sosa-Riddell situated the problem in their treatment of Chicano studies and multiculturalism: "Why haven't [Chicano studies] scholars been recognized as important in higher education?" Rochín and Sosa-Riddell went on to point out:

Chicano studies professors . . . see critical linkages among race, gender, and socioeconomic conditions which other professors do not see. Today, the teachings and research in Chicano studies go well beyond the "celebration" of our differences and an appreciation of our similarities. Our curriculum is designed to educate students to challenge the status quo and the prevailing institutions and relationships of society. We want students to question conditions of poverty, discrimination, and inequality from different perspectives, from different community settings, and in terms of other languages, arts, and tasks.[34]

Rochín and Sosa-Riddell identified perhaps the principal source of tension and resistance to the legitimization of Chicano studies when they discussed its role in challenging the status quo. One might argue that it is the desire to preserve the traditional canon and all the benefits that it accrues for those who are part of the ruling class of knowledge brokers that prevents many institutional leaders and faculty from supporting new forms of knowledge construction such as Chicano studies. As Professor Sonia Saldivar-Hull explained, "If you look at UCLA, for example, the classes that are filling up are the classes in Women's Studies, Ethnic Studies, the nontraditional courses and there is a very basic power struggle going on here. In my department, English, for example, if students are not flocking to the courses on Chaucer and Shakespeare, modernist authors, and some American writers, perhaps these fields won't be funded. People won't be hired and there's very basic issues about power and demographics. People have a stake in keeping the traditional courses, keeping things the way it's always been. Why should they give up their power?" Saldivar-Hull saw no point in denying the politics of it all: "The difference between my courses and their courses is that I'm honest about the politics. Saying that Shakespeare or a course on Henry James is not political is quite naive. By refusing to name their politics, they're making a political statement. The first day of class I tell my students, we're going to study Chicano and Chicana literature. By the very fact that these authors have named themselves Chicano or Chicana, they've already articulated a partisan politics. So these texts definitely take sides. They will take a political stand and if you don't want to read that, if you think that you only want to look at a feminist structure of the text or aesthetics, you are in the wrong class. My class is one out of a hundred classes in English and they can choose one of the other classes. That always amuses them and very few students leave."

Standing on Academic Quicksand

How the struggle for Chicano studies will end at UCLA is still unclear. The César Chávez Center and the addition of full-time faculty lines has brought about some of the stability for which students and faculty had hoped. The program has improved in terms of its vitality. In 1993 there were only about thirteen students majoring in Chicano studies. Some three years after the strike and the creation of the César Chávez Center, there were about one hundred students with Chicano studies as a major and another sixty to seventy with a concentration. Additionally, nearly every Chicano studies course offered is filled immediately and students give every indication that if more courses were added they would be filled as well.

But problems still remain, and the center has gone through several department chairs, all of whom seem reluctant to commit their academic careers to a program in great flux and having such a contentious political history. The ultimate irony is that Raymund Paredes, vilified throughout the hunger strike, had to take his turn as acting chair of the program in 1996. Chicano and Chicana activists such as Marcos Aguilar and Minnie Ferguson cringe at the appointment of Paredes as acting chair, but the reality is that the position is one few have rushed to claim. For Paredes, the program must continue to grow. There is no other alternative. As he explained, "The reason this issue attracted so much attention in Los Angeles, California, and around the country is that people were taking the position that if UCLA, the largest and most prestigious public university in the community with the largest Chicano population, doesn't recognize us, doesn't validate us through a coordinated, well-developed academic program, then what does that say about our place in American society? That's what this controversy was all about. It became a symbolic struggle about empowerment, recognition, involvement in American culture and playing a significant role in higher education. And that's why Chicano studies at UCLA is such a hot potato because the Chicano community all over the United States recognizes how essential this program is."

The symbolic and political ramifications of the program may in part explain the tension that continues to revolve around the program, and which may serve to limit faculty commitment. Although five of the new faculty lines had been filled as of the fall of 1996, the search for a permanent chair continued. A few veterans of the UCLA faculty who keep a watchful eye on the center wonder if the new faculty are not "hedging their bets" by demanding a dual appointment in other more traditional disciplines. Their actions may contribute to the impression that the program is on shaky ground. There is fear that Chicano studies will become a stepping stone for new faculty on their way to more prestigious and established departments.

Frustration surfaces when these issues are discussed among Chicano faculty at UCLA. They are caught in the same institutional machine that made it difficult to create Chicano studies in the first place. In academe, power is linked to faculty status. And faculty status is tied to both tenure and rank, as well as the legitimacy of the discipline within which one works. Many believed that enabling the César Chávez Center to hire and promote its own faculty would offer the kind of power needed to develop the program further. While improvements have been made, the center still has a long way to go. Structurally, granting six faculty lines has solved part of the problem. However, there is a symbolic issue left to be resolved in terms of confronting the problem of a marginal identity, which, in turn, serves to limit faculty commitment. Certainly, presidents and chancellors can go a long way toward legitimizing marginalized programs, but as we have witnessed in the case of Chicano studies at UCLA, the leadership has already sent a message about the questionable value of the program despite the important victory of 1993.

chapter four

STRONG WOMEN,
PROUD WOMEN

The Mills College Strike

In 1852 the Benicia Seminary was founded in northern California to meet the educational needs of the daughters of well-to-do Protestant families living throughout the state. The city of Benicia, located on the north side of the Carquinez Strait, rivaled San Francisco as a leading California metropolis and served as the state's capital for a brief period from 1853 to 1854. The early pioneers of California wanted their daughters to have the benefits of an advanced education without sending them to far-away schools in the East. Many of the families had made their wealth as part of the California gold rush and resided in camp towns such as Rough and Ready, Park's Bar, Cache Creek, Charley's Ranch, Dry Town, and Sawyer's Bar. Other students came from families in more permanent cities such as San Francisco, Stockton, and Sacramento, and in the southern part of the state, from Los Angeles, Santa Barbara, and San Bernardino.[1]

From 1855 to 1865, Miss Mary Atkins, an 1845 graduate of Oberlin College, served with great devotion as principal of the Benicia school and was highly regarded by both the students and the trustees. In a history of Mills College, Rosalind Keep described the work of Mary Atkins: "Her work as a pioneer woman educator was arduous and exacting. She stood practically alone, carrying the responsibilities of the young academy with its rapidly increasing enrollment. She fashioned the warp and woof of the Benicia school in those early years, and wove her ideals into the very hearts and lives of the girls entrusted to her care."[2]

Whereas the majority of the newly founded seminaries and academies floundered in the 1850s, 1860s, and 1870s, the school at Benicia flourished. In 1865 Mary Atkins gave way to Cyrus Mills, who along with his wife Susan continued to build a western jewel of women's education. Enrollment grew so steadily that the school was forced to relocate to a tract of land in the foothills of what is now known as Alameda County. The new site for the college was nestled among fifty-five beautiful acres of hills, creeks, and trees. The alder trees so dominated the landscape that Cyrus Mills planned to name the new college "Alderwood." However, before he could christen the new school, a reporter had obtained an architect's copy of the building plans with "Mills" heading the documents. Early newspaper coverage hence referred to the school as "Mills College." The name stuck and Susan and Cyrus Mills, along with Mary Atkins, forever became etched in the founding and early development of Mills College.[3]

More than a century has passed since the Benicia school was relocated, but the beauty of the site that became Mills College remains to this day. Indeed, there is something remarkably hypnotic about the surroundings. Perhaps it is the calm setting amid swaying eucalyptus trees, or the flowing creek through the center of the campus that cuts along the banks of Prospect Hill descending from Lake Aliso and Pine Top. Or maybe it's the stark contrast between the city of Oakland and the trancelike quietude of a campus protected by oak, alder, and eucalyptus guardians on three sides and the Oakland Hills on the fourth. The city and the outside world are so distant as one relaxes on the grass of Toyon Meadow—the finely manicured lawn separating Mills Hall and the Student Union. The serenity of the campus makes it difficult to imagine the tension and rage that stirred the students in the spring of 1990.

The Winds of Change

Word of the possibility of Mills College becoming a coeducational institution had become widespread in the fall of 1989. Because of budgetary shortfalls, the board of trustees was seriously considering opening the college to men, thus ending the long tradition of Mills College as an all-women's institution. Part of the financial crisis had grown from the stock market failures of 1987, and some officials believed that the school's $72 million endowment could no longer effectively meet the operating costs of the college. Mills was about a third the size of other renowned women's colleges, such as Mount Holyoke and Wellesley, each with around two thousand students, and was having difficulty developing institutional strategies to keep pace with a rapidly changing society. Few questioned the quality of education women received at Mills, but the institution was reeling from the economic hard times of the late 1980s and there was little reason to believe that institutional viability would be dramatically improved in the 1990s. Dr. Mary Metz, the president of Mills College at the time of the crisis, expressed her view of the problem: "It's a great dilemma because of the evidence that attending women's colleges makes a difference in the lives of women. It has truly empowered women, and they've gone on to do greater things."[4] President Metz pointed out that nearly half the women in the 101st Congress and one-third of those on the boards of the thousand largest U.S. corporations had attended women's colleges. In contrast, she explained, study after study has shown that women are consistently ignored and more frequently interrupted in coeducational classes. Metz pointed out that women tend to excel in an atmosphere that is affirming. Such an atmosphere is easier to attain in a single-sex environment where men are not present to dominate class discussions.

Few would dispute Metz's claim that an all-women's education offered certain benefits for female learners. Research emerged during the 1980s and early 1990s that pointed to the effects of the "chilly classroom climate" for women in coeducational collegiate settings.[5] Other research has supported the general conclusion that college women do not receive the academic support needed to excel in a variety of fields, especially in the sciences, where male professors and students still dominate.[6]

Additionally, a whole body of research and theory has emerged over the past three decades offering insight into the different developmental journeys of women and men.[7] No work has been more significant than that of Carol Gilligan, who explored the "different voice" that women often bring to much of their psychosocial development. Gilligan revealed how women are more likely to emphasize relationships in weighing moral dilemmas. Her research challenged Lawrence Kohlberg's findings in which women were seen to be deficient because "relational ways of knowing" represented lower levels of moral reasoning in comparison to judgments based on an appeal to "justice."[8] Gilligan maintained that Kohlberg's model was based on a male worldview and thus could not adequately account for the experiences of women. As Gilligan and others such as Iris Marion Young argued, relational ways of knowing were not inferior to male-oriented justice perspectives; the differences simply reveal the complex ways that gender influences the development of the self.[9] From this body of predominantly feminist work, educators came to recognize the important relationship between gendered identities and the educational process. After years of failing to meet the educational needs of girls and women, research finally had made headway into understanding the diverse needs of female learners.

Many on the faculty at Mills College were keenly aware of the advantages of an all-women's education. They did not have to read the latest research on women's identity development or review relevant findings of educational attainment among female learners. Their lived experience informed them of the benefits on a daily basis. As one professor explained, "The students I have at Mills learn how to speak up in class. There aren't any men here to dominate the class. Whether they would or they wouldn't never becomes an issue. We could always debate whether they would actually dominate if they were here, but it never is an issue. All the talking is done by the women in the class and I think that's good. Hearing your own voice and developing confidence in speaking in front of groups in a supportive environment is key." And a second faculty member added, "There is a real strong cultural bias against women getting involved in math and science, and so a women's college provides an antidote to all of that. . . . Working at a women's college forces you to be more aware of what women are coming to college looking for in terms of leadership and in terms of . . . I don't want to say 'nurturance,' because that makes it sound like we're some sort of therapeutic institution, but encouragement of growth and an awareness of women's needs."

Despite strong support for women's education among the faculty of Mills College, many of the trustees and senior administrators found the financial imperatives too pressing. As President Metz explained, "We all believe in Mills' mission of being a liberal arts college for women. But the question we're having to face as we look at the twenty-first century is whether we can compete as a single-sex institution."[10] Robert Anderson, a professor of anthropology at Mills and the father of three daughters who had attended Mills, saw the move toward coeducational status as inevitable. "I see virtually no alternative to becoming coed. I think the economic reasons are compelling." Like Metz, he too saw the benefits of an all-women's college. "I think we produce stronger and more successful women in an environment that is aware of their special needs and the intense discrimination they have experienced in our society."[11]

In response to pressing economic concerns, the college formed three committees composed of faculty, staff, students, and alumnae to examine three possible options for Mills. One option was to downsize. Instead of envisioning the problem as a matter of increasing the revenue, the college could view it as one of cutting expenses by reducing staff and support services, for example. Option two was to expand enrollment by increasing recruitment efforts and upgrading specific programs within the college. Possible targets for enhancements were the graduate program and programs for nontraditional students, often described as "resumers" by the Mills College community. The third option was to expand enrollment by becoming a coeducational institution. All three committees were to be guided by a consulting firm hired to help shape the future of Mills.

Going coed was the choice of the chair of the board of trustees Warren Hellman, who gained the support of President Metz. Hellman had hired the consulting firm from Boston to explore the options for the college and their findings supported his conviction that the best economic solution for the college was to begin admitting men in the fall of 1991. When the consulting group's report backed Hellman's position, his arguments became highly convincing to members of the board, most of whom came to support his stance on the coed question. In a letter addressed to "Alumnae and Friends of Mills," Hellman and Metz explained their view: "The Board of Trustees weighed the risks and uncertainties involved in changing Mills' mission to become a coeducational college. They recognized that we will risk losing some students who particularly want to study at a women's college; but the Board also acknowledged that we will gain other students who wouldn't consider Mills because of its single-sex status. The Board believed that as the only selective, nonsectarian, liberal arts college between Portland, Oregon, and southern California, Mills would have a unique opportunity."

A few faculty believed the cards had been stacked by Hellman and the board when the Boston Consulting Group was hired. They were driven by "strategic planning" and the idea that Mills needed to better position itself if the school was to have any control over its future. Julie Batz was an organizational consultant herself and a 1985 graduate of Mills College. She played a key role in the eventual student strike and had strong thoughts about the Boston Consulting Group and how they managed their analysis. "I remember being really skeptical about their findings because their methodology and my methodology were so different. They develop a strategic plan by going to a school and analyzing a situation. Then they tell you what you should do as opposed to engaging actual people who live and breathe on the campus and saying, 'What do you think we should do.'" Batz preferred a more collaborative process whereby organizational consultants facilitate local input and generate solutions through dialogue with a group of involved participants. Such a process inherently is easier to sell to a campus community in that they are directly involved in the assessment and development of ideas. The lack of involvement and the unilateral approach of the consulting group contributed to the resistance arising among the students, faculty, and alumnae.

Edna Mitchell, a professor of education (later she became the director of the Women's Leadership Institute at Mills College), also disagreed with the strategies used by the Boston firm. Along with Theodore Thomas, dean of social sciences, she was to co-chair the task force looking into the coed option. Part of the task was collecting information on other colleges that had moved from all-women's to coeducational status. Dr. Mitchell commented, "We had a couple of advisors from the Boston Consulting Group helping us. At our first meeting it was very clear, it was stated explicitly, that the goal of the task force was to demonstrate, to build the case for Mills going coed. At first, I thought I had misunderstood what I heard." Mitchell was not supportive of altering the essential identity of Mills College. Nevertheless, she wanted to do what was best for Mills and so she agreed to serve on the task force to examine the coed question. "I was open to finding out what really might happen to Mills. Not building the case against going coed. Not building the case for going coed." However, when Mitchell realized that representatives of the consulting group, along with co-chair Thomas, were committed to developing the case for Mills as a coed college, she resigned from the committee.

Of the three strategies analyzed—expanding enrollments but remaining an all-women's college, going coed, and reducing institutional size—the faculty clearly favored an effort to increase enrollment while maintaining the college as a women's institution. Ken Burke, a professor in the drama department, commented: "It was very clear that the majority of the faculty thought we should stay single sex and that we should remain a liberal arts college." Burke was surprised that the announcement to admit men came without in his estimation much public debate on the matter. "Now, at that point, I certainly thought, and I believe a lot of other faculty members thought, that what would happen next would be some kind of more public debate from the trustees about the option." But there was to be no more debate of the matter. The board believed that enough discussion had already taken place. President Metz had spent the better part of the year visiting with alumnae around the country and discussing the options and the difficult decision Mills faced.

For much of the spring semester of 1990, students had organized rallies and marches to express their strong conviction on Mills remaining an all-women's institution.[12] In an opinion piece published in the *Mills College Weekly*, the college's newspaper, a student captured some of the sentiment of the day as women marched from the Tea Shop at the Student Union to Alderwood Hall, where the board of trustees was meeting to decide the fate of the college:

> As I marched along with my peers I truly believed that the songs we sang and the slogans that we chanted would be heard by the board of trustees and Warren Hellman and would influence them to keep Mills a women's college. I steadfastly held to my beliefs until I heard Warren Hellman utter six words that have led to my disillusionment in the governing body at Mills: "I feel like a Southern sheriff." Not only was his comment inappropriate, but it seems to me that it could have been interpreted as racist and sexist. After all, if he sees himself in the role of a Southern sheriff, which can be equated with power, then according to the binary model we women, faculty, and administration are the powerless, voiceless minority subject to the will of the power structure.[13]

A second student also provided an inkling about the depth of emotion students felt: "Tuesday's rally filled me with inspiration and a real sense of hope. The turnout was overwhelming. The sound of hundreds of women singing 'Remember' [a favorite traditional song of Mills College students] gave me shivers of exhilaration. You could feel the power in the air, it was sweet and shimmering like champagne. I was intoxicated by the strength of our voice."[14]

Throughout the weeks leading up to the official decision, students at the college made their positions known to the board and to the administration. Robyn Fisher was a twenty-one-year-old senior finishing up her year as student body president. Fisher was opposed to becoming a coeducational institution and expended a great deal of energy throughout the year trying to get the message out to students that admitting men was a real possibility. She, along with other representatives of student government, held numerous meetings with students to discuss the options. For whatever reason, the message was not getting across to them. Fisher spoke of the apprehension she and others in student government had at the time: "We were quite concerned very early on in the process and tried to alert the student body as much as we could. . . . We had a gut feeling that coed was the direction the board was heading." She went on to explain that in some way it seemed as though the students were in denial: "We tried to be proactive and get people involved. We tried roundtable discussions, town hall meetings where we invited the student body to begin to talk about the options. We wanted to start a student coalition to come up with our own options that had been well thought out and then take them to one of the committees. We tried working with the staff and the faculty very early on to come up with options, but we were not able to get the kind of student support that was needed. The student newspaper began to pick up on some of the discussions that were going on, but overall the reaction of the student body was pretty apathetic."

Sonja Piper, also a member of student government, shared Fisher's frustration: "We spent the whole year trying to convince the student body that coeducation was one of the options being discussed and under consideration by the administration and the trustees. We had a town meeting in the fall of 1989 and hardly anyone showed up. . . . People like Robyn Fisher, myself, and others involved in student government that year were really hurt and disillusioned because people actually thought that we had sat by idly while we allowed these events to unfold. But the thing is no one wanted to believe. People were in denial that coeducation could be a reality."

The Impending Announcement

At first, few believed the rumors that had surfaced in the fall of 1989. However, when the rumors turned to serious-minded press coverage in January of 1990, student concern grew. T-shirts popped up around campus with sayings such as "Mills College: Better Dead Than Coed." This had come to replace the official T-shirt: "Mills College: Not a girls' school without men, but a women's college without boys." Yet, many students still did not see coeducation on the horizon. They felt the whole idea of going coed had been downplayed. Elizabeth Bales graduated from Mills College in 1993 and in the spring of 1990 was finishing her first year at Mills. She spoke about the possibilities known to the students and of the impending announcement of May 3: "Everyone was afraid the announcement would be about going coed, but the board had downplayed it to us. There had been a big deal made about the fact that they had three or four different options and I honestly did not feel that they were completely straightforward with us, that going coed was their top option. We heard over and over, 'Oh, it's only one of the choices.' There were rallies and there were letters sent around by students before the decision was made but I think if everyone had realized how serious they were, that it was probably the top choice, there would have been a lot more noise made beforehand."

As a decision about the future of Mills approached, a sense of urgency fell on the student body. Students increased their efforts to make their position known to the trustees. A week before the scheduled board meeting to decide the fate of the college, students tied yellow ribbons around trees and demonstrated at the front gate of the campus. Rallies were held throughout the week, with the largest occurring on Wednesday, April 25. "The rallies are not for us," explained Lisa Kremer. "We're graduating. We're leaving. They're for future generations and women in general." Kremer went on to proclaim the benefits of being at an all-women's college. She talked about having developed the self-confidence to be able to speak her mind. "It doesn't happen the same way at coed schools." [15]

Lisa Kremer was a senior and a co-editor of the school's newspaper. She felt strongly about the school's tradition as an all-women's college: "The school has a history of commitment to women. A tradition that is older than most of the companies in this country. I think it's important to preserve those traditions. I think it's important to have an alternative education for women. I don't think women have to go to women's colleges but it should be an option for them. . . . It really widens your eyes as to how the world works. You understand better how women work together." Like Elizabeth Bales, Kremer also felt that the president and the board had played down the option of going coed. "At the newspaper we were quite worried about the possibility of coeducation but they repeatedly told us, 'Oh no, it's not that big of a deal.' They really tried to minimize the possibility of going coed."

The rally of April 25 attracted more than 350 students and alumnae. A number of those present signed cards pledging to recruit women to the college to help meet the school's financial burdens. Yellow ribbons were everywhere, tied to trees and to students' arms. They were worn as a sign of solidarity and unwavering commitment to the college's tradition. The faculty decided to take their own action and on Monday, April 23, voted 57 to 26 against admitting male undergraduates. In hearing of the faculty's decision, the trustees promised to take their position into account along with the clear message that students and alumnae had conveyed.

Prior to the 1989–90 academic year, President Metz had a grass mound built on the grounds of Toyon Meadow to provide an elevated section for speakers to stand and see out over their audience. It was the place where graduation and other such ceremonies were to be held. Toyon Meadow had long been the heart of the campus separating the main administration building, Mills Hall, from the Student Union. On the day of the impending announcement, students had collected facing the mound awaiting the administration's arrival. To their dismay, the college officials, including President Metz and Warren Hellman, exited the back door of Mills Hall and hastily set up their podium and microphone as they prepared to make their announcement on the opposite side of Toyon Meadow. The entire mass of students was surprised when they saw they had to turn around to face Hellman and Metz. After all, Mills Hall had been closed due to damages sustained during the 1989 earthquake and the mound was where most key presentations were made. Nonetheless, the eleventh hour had finally arrived and the future of Mills College would soon be revealed. Everything that Mills meant to the women flashed before them as history and tradition stood momentarily still.

The Magic of Mills

For Elizabeth Bales, the 1989–90 academic year was one of personal exploration. It was her first year at college and she had found the environment of Mills well suited for her. Several years later she reflected on her experience at Mills and why she viewed the college as a special place: "I'm not sure I can express it very well. In fact, as a freshman I didn't really have the words for it yet. Mills is not so much about escaping sexism. You can't ever escape sexism, you know. If you're a woman, you're a woman, and you don't get away from gender issues just because you go to a women's college. In a way they are more present than ever. But at Mills, you don't have to deal with whether you're male or female as much. In class, you're simply a student. Does that make sense?"

Bales went on to describe the competitive prep school she went to during her high school years and the sense of competition among students, competition for class standing, the highest SAT scores, grades, and so on. Mills was different: "I definitely didn't get a big sense of competition at Mills except the sense of challenging yourself to do the best you could. There's more a sense of support by faculty and other students and the staff. Rather than pushing people to think about doing better than their neighbors, they just pushed us to do the best we could." She went on to explain that in many ways the environment at Mills is very nurturing, then quickly added, "I'm almost hesitant to use that word because it's so stereotypical female." The fact that the percentage of women faculty at Mills was high was also significant to her. "You know, it was a lot easier to find a role model, especially if you were in the sciences or mathematics. The head of the computer science program is a woman. A great number of the science faculty are women and so instead of having to look around for someone to be a role model, there's someone right there."

Other former students also spoke fondly of the advantages of Mills. One alumna commented, "Mills provides a setting where women are more apt to take risks. They're more apt to speak out in class. They're more apt to take leadership roles. I just think that it really prepares women to go out in the world and do what they want to do. It's a four-year kind of haven. It's the same argument that you hear for Black colleges. I really believe they're parallel." This former student feels so strongly about Mills and its tradition that she has willed a portion of her estate to the college, but only if it remains an all-women's institution.

Another alumna and an active participant in the events of 1990 spoke in poetic terms about her experience at Mills: "It was like this incredibly protected time to unfold one's true beauty, whatever that may be for each individual. I was so used to achieving and trying to succeed and do better and better. I was caught in some sort of achievement paradigm. I don't know how I got caught up in that trap in the beginning, but it was there and it's throughout our society. At Mills there was this sort of divine pause. I mean, I just remember having this experience and actually feeling for the first time the sun on my skin. I could feel the heat of the sun . . . and I think it was like this for a lot of the women there." This student wrestled with whether to pursue a career in international relations or to follow her artistic inclinations revealed through her intense love for dance. For a while she tried to accomplish both. "Dance for me represented the choice of the heart, whereas international relations represented the choice of an outer world, the mind, and the need to succeed and prove something to society. In the end, I chose to dance because at Mills I found the space to experience life in that way. It was an environment that allowed pure creativity and innovation."

The preceding student found Mills to be a safe space in which to experiment with her creativity and her identity as a women. Elizabeth Bales found a similar space at Mills. Other students stressed how Mills offered them a chance to assume leadership roles. Lisa Kremer was a co-editor of the school newspaper. Robyn Fisher was the student body president in 1989–90. Sonja Piper served a key role on student government in charge of educational and social programs. Julie Batz attributed much of her success as an organizational consultant in charge of her own company to opportunities she had at Mills. All of these former students are talented and intelligent but may not have found the same kind of space to unleash their own sort of magic had they attended a coeducational college or university. As Fisher explained to a reporter in the spring of 1990, "I can do and be anything I want to here. I don't think I'd be given all those opportunities at a coed school."[16]

Decision Day

The stone bell tower known as El Campanile sits on the southeast corner of the campus near the mathematics and computer science building. It is one of several landmarks that add to the uniqueness and beauty of the campus. When the bell of El Campanile sounded on May 3, 1990, the women of Mills College could sense the historic circumstance awaiting them. As they made their way toward Toyon Meadow, an expectation of disappointment was in the air. With the bells echoing in their ears, more than a few students wondered if El Campanile soon would be draped in black.

The tolling of the bell of El Campanile pierced the students' hypnotic armor of denial and brought about a sense of panic, that something tragic was about to happen. Bales recalled the moment: "Everyone was tense and waiting for the bell to chime, waiting for the sound. I remember sitting in a class and waiting. Looking at the clock. We knew it was going to be right about a particular hour. I think it was three o'clock." When the bell sounded, Bales sensed that El Campanile tolled for the women of Mills. She was deeply saddened that Mills College as she had known it was about to be laid to rest.

Sonja Piper was on the grass of Toyon Meadow gathered near the mound waiting for President Metz and Warren Hellman to show up to make the announcement. Piper was surprised when she looked over toward Mills Hall on the other side of the lawn and saw Metz and Hellman gathering on the steps. "Some students shouted at them to meet us on our own ground. But the rest of us started walking over there. Warren Hellman started to speak as I was walking towards them and as he made the announcement I sort of froze in my tracks and there was this feeling of numbness and being stunned. All of a sudden someone grabbed me and started crying and it was Robyn Fisher." Piper described what she was feeling: "You just can't help but feel angry and betrayed and absolutely shocked and I too felt very emotional at that point. It was all that pent-up rage! And the way I expressed it was like many other women at Mills who were crying tears of frustration for a few minutes, then becoming very pissed off." Piper soon dried her tears, turned to her friends, and with deep conviction asked, "OK, what can we do at this point?" She was ready to take on the administration in response to what she saw as a grave injustice and a betrayal of the students and the school's deepest and most endearing tradition.

With the announcement, Mills College was directed down the same road that two hundred other all-women's institutions had followed during the past thirty years, thus leaving about ninety all-women's colleges across the country. Hellman struggled amid student obscenities and outcries as he tried to explain the board's rationale: "But one hard fact would not disappear," he said. "Mills needs at least one thousand undergraduates in order to secure a strong future." Hellman went on to explain that the change that made the most sense was to admit men as a means to increase enrollment. President Metz also spoke to the crowd, explaining that nearly everyone on the board wanted the school to remain an all-women's institution but that finances demanded that the college become coeducational.[17]

Piper was not the only angry voice piercing the normal serenity of Toyon Meadow. Many could be heard in large groups as they responded with cries of "No! No! No!" Others were speechless; their eyes told the story. Bales recalled her reaction to the announcement: "I think I was numb. Here I was this little eighteen-year-old. I hadn't even had my nineteenth birthday and I kind of went off reeling from the shock. I honestly think that I wandered around campus for a few days trying to figure out what had just happened to me. I don't think I was alone. I think there were a lot of women who were affected that way."

In a matter of minutes, Toyon Meadow was saturated with the saltwater of countless tears and the bitter anguish of the Mills College students and alumnae. A student described the actions that ensued: "I remember people yelling and screaming. . . . It was kind of like 'Strike! Strike! Strike!' And there was this kind of general sort of melee where people just couldn't stop crying and that sort of thing. People were just so emotional. I remember that one picture of the woman that went all around the world crying, sadly."

The picture to which the preceding student referred was that of Shannon McMackin and her reaction to the announcement. The picture was perhaps the most widely publicized image of the Mills strike and it left mixed feelings for many of the women. Students felt that the image of McMackin's anguish was exploited by the media, which used the picture to convey the hysteria of the Mills College women and thus reinforce traditional stereotypes of women. And although the initial reaction was one of profoundly felt pain, anguish, and frustration, what followed in the aftershock was hardly the image of the "hysterical woman." The picture of Shannon McMackin, which soon appeared in newspapers around the country, was the first taste the women of Mills College would get of the influence of the media. Although this perhaps was an instance in which the media got the upper hand, it would not take long for savvy to emerge among the strikers.

The Strike

Once the shock waves settled, the women of Mills College were far from hysterical. Within minutes students began to weigh their options. Silja Talvi, one of the few who had anticipated the board's decision, used her anger as a source of courage to aggressively forge ahead. Talvi challenged the students to take control of the situation and use the media as a tool for publicizing what they perceived as an unjust act that had dire consequences for the empowerment of women. Students were in awe of this young woman, whom many did not even know by name despite the small size of the campus community.

Some students comfortably find themselves leading groups of students through the organizational maze that is college life. They master the nuances of working with faculty and administrators and learn how to accommodate to their role models and mentors. These students tend to assume positions such as student government president, vice president, or perhaps resident assistant. They do not sell their souls simply because they learn to work within the system. Often, they are realists who have learned what it takes to get along in an organizational world. Silja Talvi is not one of these students.

Talvi described herself as a "communist anarchist." She explained, "Things don't always have to be top-down, hierarchical. . . . I don't believe in governing power structures. I don't believe that decisions can be made by a few for the many. I believe in community and in doing what's best for the community." For Talvi, participatory democracy in its truest sense is quite compatible with her vision as an anarchist. She recognizes that such a system is slow, cumbersome, and inefficient, but as she stated, "What's the alternative? My god, you have these horrible people making decisions for the rest of us. Look at how people suffer in our country. It's absurd." The decision of the Mills College board of trustees, and the role of Hellman and Metz, was one more example of a few ruling the many. Their decision was not one that Talvi could or would accept. At least not without a fight.

The evening following the announcement, the students organized a meeting in the Student Union to discuss what their reaction would be to the board's decision. An alumna who lived in the area and who was present during many of the student meetings described what happened and her feelings at the time: "It was just really emotional. Even talking about it now I get emotional. I was so excited to see the students so passionate about the issue. . . . I remember the meeting being very big. It was in the Student Union and there were tons of women there. It was very exciting to me. Seeing the women just really empowered and making decisions about what was going to happen next."

Silja Talvi was one of the most outspoken women at the meeting and she among several others called for a student strike to shut down the college. Again, the alumna recalled the tone of the meeting: "Essentially the students decided to strike and discussed what a strike might look like. Well, we were going to shut the college down. That's what it was gonna be. The college was gonna be shut down and how was that going to be accomplished? Who was gonna go where and what was gonna happen? And I remember people were just really kind of strung out, in the sense that emotions were running high. You kind of didn't really believe it was happening. It was sort of this almost surreal kind of experience. I just remember the sense of the karma and the strength that was coming out of the meeting. It was really awesome for me to see."

But few students actually knew how to carry out a strike and many doubted whether the administration would implement their decision anyway. Thus, while Silja Talvi explained the tactics of civil disobedience to women gathered at the meeting, she fought off apprehensions about whether the students would actually follow her lead: "There was a great deal of naiveté at the time. . . . and my experience at Mills was pretty isolated. I come from a very low-income background, a one-parent family and all that kind of stuff. So I was thrown into this milieu with more privileged students who basically believed things would always go their way. That's how they viewed life." Things rarely worked out for Talvi on their own. She had to make things happen. She had learned to be a fighter on the streets of Los Angeles and she brought a fighter's mentality to many of life's challenges. Talvi did not feel the same could be said about the students at Mills, whose attitudes suggested to her a certain outlook about life: "Things happen for me. The college won't go coed. That just couldn't happen to me." Thus, as she trained the students to lock arms with one another to avoid being easily arrested, and showed them how to lie on the ground to force the police to drag them off, in the back of her mind were serious doubts about whether her peers would have the courage to follow through. "The part that I wasn't sure about was were these women going to listen to me because I was a troublemaker on campus. I was seen as a freak or a misfit so I wasn't sure these people would give me the time of day."

Despite Talvi's reservations, her peers did come through and by seven the next morning the students had barricaded nearly every administrative entrance on campus. The task was made especially difficult since Mills Hall had been closed because of the earthquake and thus administrative offices were scattered around the campus. As a result, the strikers had to put up several barricades and develop a system of communicating from one location to the next. The students established their headquarters in the Student Union, which became known as "Runner's Headquarters," and communications moved from there to the barricades and back as they used bicycles and then walkie-talkies donated by alumnae to get information to and from remote locations. In the end, Talvi was surprised by the powerful reaction of her peers: "I was grateful for the presence of those women who embraced me and believed in me and in the larger political struggle for women's equality."

In the spring of 1990, Julie Batz was an organizational consultant running her own business in Washington, D.C. She was in the San Francisco area for a wedding at the time of the strike and learned of the board's decision from her parents as she picked up her luggage at the airport. Immediately, she raced to the campus to offer assistance. "I showed up at the campus and it looked like it was under siege. There were banners flying and posters. I remember one sign, MILLS COLLEGE CLOSED FOR REPAIRS. The students had taken over every building and had set up blockades." Batz recalled searching for students who looked like they might be in charge and giving them her name and a number where she could be reached. They looked somewhat skeptical but within a day or two they called Batz and asked her to facilitate the planning of a campus picnic and demonstration. "There was a group of students trying to organize a picnic . . . and I just started facilitating this meeting, and the picnic turned out to be very successful and there were speakers and music and all that stuff." Meanwhile, the students were holding meetings every night at their headquarters in the Student Union. They had a press and public relations team, a communications team, one for food, and a fundraising team, all of which gave reports on an ongoing basis. At the same time, the meetings involved a great deal of crisis management and planning. They talked about what had happened that day and how everybody was doing and what was going to be done the next day.

At times the meetings became shouting matches with various students and groups trying to be heard. Eventually, Batz was asked to help facilitate the everyday meetings as she had done for the picnic. "I ended up facilitating and consulting to the students for the next week or so." Batz decided to take an extended leave from her organizational consulting business and stay a while longer to serve as a facilitator. Her role essentially became helping the students to develop agendas for their meetings and then guiding group discussion and consensus building at those same meetings. She also advised the women as they struggled with the values they wanted to enact throughout the strike. For example, early on students were perplexed about how to run their meetings and resorted to *Robert's Rules of Order*. As Batz stated, "Some of the ways they went about things didn't support who they were and what they really wanted to accomplish." Part of her role became offering advice: "Look, you have options. If you don't like the way that your decisions are being made because a third of you are saying 'yes' and a third of you are saying 'no' and a third of you are abstaining from voting and you're wondering why you're not getting follow-through on decisions, then you can make decisions using a consensus process and this is what that is and here's how it works." Batz demonstrated how the meetings and the students could benefit from using visuals, writing down ideas and thoughts so everyone could reflect on them. She described the process employed: "I don't think that I was very directive at all with them. It was really much more of a kind of active listening and modeling facilitative behavior and every now and again kind of making an intervention and then stepping back. They were so open to those tools and it just felt very natural for them. In a matter of days they were the ones who were making the comments like 'Let's have one person talk at a time.' And, 'Is there a way we can divide our skills here and get more done.' They kind of just picked everything up."

As was the case for Chicano students and their multiracial allies at UCLA, the women of Mills College also turned to the past as a source of knowledge and guidance. In this case, it was the Women's Movement which offered sustenance as their personal agony over the future of Mills College was transformed into political agency. Like their predecessors, the women of Mills learned to turn their passion into something bigger than themselves, as the personal became the political. In her account of women's liberation, Sara Evans discussed the personal as political:

The women's liberation movement was initiated by women in the civil rights movement and the new left who dared to test the old assumptions and myths about female nature against their own experience and discovered that something was drastically wrong. And they dared because within these movements they had learned to respect themselves and to know their own strength. They could do so because the new left provided an egalitarian ideology, which stressed the personal nature of political action, the importance of community and cooperation, and the necessity to struggle for freedom for the oppressed.[18]

Few of the women at Mills likely would have labeled themselves as "oppressed," but when the decision about their school's future—and their "personal" futures—was made for them, they most assuredly felt the pain of disempowerment. Soon the personal became political and the strength of women organizing as womyn around the ideals of collaboration and egalitarianism was unleashed.

Elizabeth Bales, who served as a "runner" during the strike carrying information back and forth on her bicycle, commented, "There was a tremendous emphasis on building consensus. We wanted everyone to agree with what we were doing. We didn't want it to be a majority-vote type thing. We wanted everything to be a consensus decision so that all the actions we were taking were ones that the students could get behind." With the help of Batz, and the womynist commitments of students such as Silja Talvi, among others, the students worked hard to avoid the pitfalls of the organizational life represented by decisions such as the one made by the board, where a few powerful people write history for the many. They made every effort to resist turning to hierarchical structures and instead embraced feminist ideals of consensus and group decision making.[19] Once again, the legacy of the Women's Movement of the late 1960s and early 1970s blossomed on a little piece of land nestled among the Oakland Hills as freedom's web continued to be spun.

When the strike took place the hard work of the student government over the year was lost in the process and there was even finger-pointing directed at student representatives for not doing their part to inform students of the crisis. But as Robyn Fisher and Sonja Piper explained, they had tried but no one seemed to take them seriously. Seeing students suddenly alarmed and concerned was almost too much for Fisher and Piper to take: "Where was their alarm and concern when they had called town meetings and round tables to discuss the possibility of going coed?" Now students who Fisher and Piper had hardly known before were directing the student body and leading the strike. For them, the strike was bitter-sweet, in that it seemed that all their efforts over the past year were for naught.

Collegiate life can sometimes become fairly mundane, and the role of motivating or leading students through the everyday issues of student life often is not very stimulating or rewarding. In their leadership roles in student government, Fisher and Piper experienced the frustrations of having to motivate students to be concerned about the college's future. This is the reality of collegiate life, wherein apathy can be a difficult obstacle for student leaders to overcome. But, as was mentioned earlier, there are many facets to the collegiate experience and in certain contexts different organizational and leadership abilities may be needed. The idea of "situational leadership" comes to mind here, especially during a crisis. Silja Talvi, for example, learned the tactics of civil disobedience and in turn helped to train an entire campus of student strikers. Without her knowledge of protest, one can only guess what might have become of Mills College.

"We arrived with our sleeping bags and camped out on the first night," recalled Shannon McMackin. "We couldn't go anywhere to get food. We always had to stay at the barricades. We had actually learned at, I think maybe the second meeting, how to lock our arms, what to do if they tried to come, if the police came." McMackin and her peers blockaded administrative offices, jammed campus phone lines, and drove their cars around campus honking their horns. When the horns wore down, a local auto repair shop fixed them for free. Most students boycotted classes and several faculty, as a show of support for the strike, held classes outside. Other faculty canceled classes altogether and informed students through word of mouth that their grades would be based on what they had accomplished up to that point in the semester, which at the time of the strike was almost over. As part of their outcry over the board's decision, several of the students shaved their heads and taped their mouths shut to symbolize the lack of voice they had in making the final decision. Students donned T-shirts that read "Better Dead Than Coed." They decorated the entire campus with yellow ribbons and balloons symbolic of their solidarity and commitment to Mills. The students threatened to continue the strike through finals week and into graduation if the decision was not reversed.

Despite their passion and commitment to the strike, students nonetheless were frightened by what they found themselves in the middle of. Shannon McMackin commented: "There was a time when people didn't know what would happen if they participated in the strike. Some of us wondered if we would fail classes and so the early part of the strike was a key moment. It was most difficult I think for the movement because of the apprehension. That's when the professors stepped in and supported us. We all kind of went to our teachers and they said, 'Oh, you're fine. You just have to do what you think is right.'"

A couple of days into the strike the students gained additional support from the faculty when they voted to oppose the board's decision and offered to do extra work without pay to help ease the financial problems of the beleaguered institution. The faculty asked for a five-year delay in admitting men in order to give the college a chance to find alternative solutions. Professor Edna Mitchell recalled the faculty reaction: "We had a meeting right after the announcement. About an hour or so later we met in the faculty lounge and began putting together a petition that was circulated among the faculty. We then had a special meeting of the faculty the following day. Many of the faculty were not in favor of what we wanted, and so they didn't sign on. But most of the faculty signed on to make a commitment to trying to help the college increase its enrollment if we were to remain single sex." While the students welcomed faculty support, the board of trustees found the suggestions limited and requested greater detail and a more specific action plan that would ensure financial viability. Nonetheless, the reaction of the board provided a ray of opportunity.

A week into the strike progress appeared to be made as the board publicly announced it would reconsider its decision if it received detailed plans outlining alternative strategies. The key reason the executive committee of the board reopened the issue, as reported by President Metz, was a proposal from the Alumnae Association to increase the $72 million endowment by $10 million as well as to begin an intensive fund-raising campaign to nearly double the association's annual $450,000 gift to the college. The striking students saw the board's reticence as one more indicator that their strike was beginning to have an impact. While they were making headway, it was not the time to give in, and accordingly, the incoming student body president, Melissa Stevenson Dile, reiterated the students' stance that a formal reversal must be made before they would call an end to the strike.[20]

In the meantime, the peaceful resistance by the students had frayed some nerves and a shoving match had broken out at one location as a faculty member tried to gain access to his mail. "Teachers, staff and administrators are getting a little testier," reported one of the several hundred student strikers. Several administrators asked to be let into their offices but were refused and the jovial kidding witnessed on the first day of the boycott was replaced with angry stares from a few frustrated administrators.[21]

For the next few days, students, faculty, and staff met almost around the clock as they worked to develop concrete plans to save Mills College as an all-women's institution. The Alumnae Association continued its fund-raising efforts and much progress was made. As the end of the second week approached, optimism was like the morning dew hovering over the grass of Toyon Meadow.

The Role of the Media

Early on in the strike, the students recognized the need to use the media to get the word out nationally. They wanted the entire country to know that one of the last bastions of women's education was under attack and that action needed to be taken. Denise Beirnes, an alumna living in the area, recalled sitting at one of the barricades early in the strike when a student runner brought knowledge of a fait accompli: "We've got Donahue! We're gonna be on Donahue!" Denise was surprised: "People were really trying to get to the press to get the word out and I was just kind of really blown away by it all. Here's this woman who just sat in this room and got on the phone and got the Donahue Show that day." A few days later, several students from Mills College appeared on the nationally televised show, as support from around the country grew. There was also a great deal of negative reaction, in that many conservatives interpreted the women's efforts to keep men out of Mills College as similar to the efforts of military academies such as Virginia Military Institute (VMI) and the Citadel to keep women out. Of course, there were major differences. First, men had not faced years of oppression and educational inequities. And second, VMI and the Citadel both receive state and/or federal support and therefore are compelled to abide by equal opportunity guidelines. Mills College, on the other hand, was a private institution and had a right to adopt restrictive admissions practices.

Initially, the press had free rein to pull any students they wanted off the barricades for an interview. A few of the impromptu interviews were helpful, and others were not. Students felt media coverage was creating limited images of Mills College women. Some believed that women of color were not being given equal air time. Others felt that there was too much focus on the emotional outpouring that accompanied the two-week-long strike. Students certainly recognized the emotive quality of their struggle, but there were other aspects not being covered by the press. Courage, assertiveness, and strength of conviction were also evident. Why weren't these qualities being described? For example, when Warren Hellman first made the announcement of the board's decision, Silja Talvi raised both hands in the air and "flipped him off" while she yelled "Fuck you!" at the top of her lungs. Her actions were hardly those of a passive, fragile, disempowered individual, and yet, of course, such images never reached the public's awareness. Talvi expressed anger with the media's early coverage: "They tried to make us look like whiners and make us look really weak. And they tried to make us look like lesbians, which, of course, some of us were. They tried to do everything to undermine the strike. It's just the way the media works. It's the way they deal with stuff. It's sensationalism. It's obnoxious. It doesn't give credit where credit is due. I guess there's something threatening about a woman with her two middle fingers extended yelling at a rich man."

As the strike progressed, students sensed the need to gain a degree of control over the television and newspaper people gathered daily at the campus. The students decided to make their own decisions about when interviews would be permitted. Denise Beirnes recalled the evolution of the strike and discussions about the media: "I think as the strike progressed, we became smarter about the media. By about the second week of the strike, you went up to Mills and it was like you were in a different world because of all the satellite dishes that were there. . . . There was press from all over the world, and what had happened was people started to realize that they had to be careful in talking with the media. . . . People got kind of real smart and said, 'Okay, what we need to do is we're going to meet with the press at certain hours every day and that's gonna be it.'"

The important role of the media cannot be stressed enough. From early on, it was clear that the media would play a major part in the strike. As with other student movements, the greater the external support protestors can gain the better for their cause. The powers that be tend to respond to outside pressure, Beirnes surmised, and then added, "I think that if the press hadn't come, if there hadn't been that flow of information to the outside world, the strike might not have worked." Another student supported Beirnes's appraisal: "The media was the vehicle through which the pressure was created to force a reversal. By making it such an issue and putting it in the public's eye as much as we possibly could, it put the president, the board, and Warren Hellman in a really uncomfortable place. It was like a hot spot that they didn't necessarily want to be in."

As news about the strike reached other campuses, supporters of women's education and Mills alumnae sent faxes and letters, made phone calls, and even showed up on campus. The strikers realized the support they were gaining, and their resolve was strengthened exponentially. Perhaps they were right in seeing their struggle as much more than simply a matter of whether one small college admitted men or not. Maybe this *was* a battle about the place of women in the broader society and a vision of freedom for everyone.

A Change of Heart

As the second week of the strike progressed, optimism was high among the students.[22] They could see the lack of conviction in Metz, Hellman, and other board members as evidenced by their openness to considering alternative strategies. The strength of the alumnae support was crucial inasmuch as they not only offered to raise significant funds but also threatened to limit or end financial support if the decision was not reversed. In the end, between the public outcry, alumnae counterpunches, and the ever-present student strikers, it was too much for the board to face.

Two weeks after the students began their boycott of classes and their encampment of the administrative buildings, the strike was winding down. The mood was euphoric as students expressed confidence that the board, which was scheduled to meet on May 18, would reverse itself. About two hundred students gathered on the lawn of Toyon Meadow in anticipation of the victory. The laughter throughout the campus told of their relief. "We are victorious," proclaimed one of the student leaders, Anna Stravato, as she addressed the crowd. "We have made our point. This strike is a dam stemming the tide of closings of women's colleges across the country." Stravato closed by linking their actions to the larger struggle for women's rights and equal opportunity. "Our struggle will not end with this strike. It goes on into next week, next year and until all women of every kind are represented equally in this society."[23]

"We did it! We did it!" The students win! After two weeks of student protests the board of trustees finally reversed its decision. Warren Hellman delivered the announcement to the students. "All of you have had a lot of banners for us," a smiling Hellman stated to about three hundred students, faculty, and alumnae who gathered on the steps near the Student Union. "Here's one for you," he said as he unfurled a banner reading "Mills. For Women. Again."[24]

Hellman went on to say, "I think we have all won. Sometimes in your lifetime, you're involved in something that may not just change an institution, it may change the world. I think you've done it." He explained that the turning point had come when the alumnae association developed a strategy for raising the necessary revenue to help the school continue its commitment to women's education. Additionally, students and faculty devised ideas for increasing student enrollment: Students would do more recruiting and faculty would add an extra course to their teaching loads and would offer evening classes to attract more nontraditional students. "When the entire Mills community turned its strong commitment into solid action plans, new factors were introduced to completely change the equation," Hellman stated.[25]

President Metz also spoke to the crowd. "Our passion for women's education has made history—herstory!" And incoming student body president Melissa Stevenson Dile commented, "I believe we at Mills College have proved to ourselves and the rest of the world the inestimable value of women's education." She later noted that the new interest in Mills likely would not have been as strong without the dissension caused by the strike. "None of the constituencies of the college would have stretched as far as they have had we not gone through this cataclysmic experience."[26]

The students spent much of the rest of the day cleaning up after themselves in an effort to return the campus to its previous appearance. Nothing had been damaged and all the signs and slogans written on the sidewalks and streets around the campus had been done in erasable chalk. As a striking graduate student explained, "We're striking because we love Mills. We want to take care of it."[27]

Making Sense of It All

When it was all said and done, students and faculty gave a great deal of the credit to the Mills College alumnae, who spoke not only with their words but with their pocketbooks as well, the latter constituting a language easily understood by those who are held accountable for the financial viability of an institution. In one student's words, the alumnae essentially said, "Excuse us! Do you want our money or don't you? We're not giving our money to a coed Mills." Thus, not only did the alumnae threaten to limit their giving, they also made promises to increase giving if the board changed its mind about admitting men. This was no small vow to those with the power to reverse the decision. Of course, had it not been for the ruckus raised by the 1990 Mills College students, the alumnae likely would have never had the opportunity to organize the level of support necessary for a reversal.

Elizabeth Bales reflected on the keys to the strike: "Looking back now I can say that it was the students who sort of got the ball rolling and the alumnae were the big guns who came to stand with us and said, 'We're adding our support to the students.' The alumnae were wonderful. They brought the students food on the strike lines. They were tremendous." Bales went on to add, "I think it's a great demonstration that if you get enough people together who passionately believe in something and are, you know, damn-the-torpedoes determined, they will make it work. Then you can make tremendous things happen."

Only two days after college officials reversed their position and agreed not to admit male undergraduates, nearly four hundred students participated in graduation ceremonies and joined the proud alumnae of Mills College. Sharon Richardson Jones, director of outreach activities for the Oakland Athletics, called upon the graduating students to take what they had learned from the recent crisis as a means to "overcome obstacles" and "create your own opportunities." Jones, who graduated in 1976 from Mills, told the audience that 1990's graduation would mark a special place: "Today, the eyes of the nation—maybe even the world—are on you." The emotional outpouring was continued by graduating senior Shannon McMackin. "This is Mills College—for women. Again. We are strong. We are proud. We are Mills women."[28]

On Friday, June 22, 1990, Mills College announced the resignation of President Mary Metz. "Our new vision for Mills will require even greater effort and continuity of leadership for at least five years," stated Metz, who had been president for nine years. "With deep regret, I have concluded that I cannot make another uninterrupted five-year commitment." In the end, it was the president's willingness to introduce men to undergraduate life that cost her the support of the student body. Perhaps the most telling and disappointing experience for Metz took place during the first week of the strike. At one of the early rallies, the students insisted on Metz's publicly stating what her vote had been on the coed issue. When she informed them that she had voted to go coed, the students in unison turned their backs on Metz as an expression of feelings of betrayal. Melissa Stevenson Dile, who at the time of Metz's resignation had begun her tenure as student body president, commented, "Now that she has resigned, it might be possible for students to feel more comfortable about believing the administration will fully pursue the various plans to ensure Mills remains a women's college."[29]

In the new strategy for Mills, the board outlined several specific accomplishments that needed to be reached. They included the following:

increasing enrollment to nine hundred students by fall 1993 and one thousand by fall 1995, raising $10 million in new endowment by 1995, reducing the amount of tuition that goes for financial aid by 3 percent by fall 1995, increasing the alumnae association's annual unrestricted gift from $450,000 to $750,000, raising the faculty-student ratio to one-to-thirteen from one-to-ten, increasing the percentage of alumnae who donate to the college from 40 percent to 50 percent, and restructuring the curriculum and academic organization of the college.[30] Some results were achieved rather quickly. For example, Linda Kay, the executive director of the Mills College Alumnae Association, reported that after only one week of the telephone campaign her office had already collected more than $3 million worth of pledges. The alumnae association also had received $750,000 toward the $10 million goal of increasing the endowment.[31] And talk of admitting men had completely dissipated. "The issue of coeducation is dead at Mills," said Janet Holmgren McKay, the new president of the college. "In a simplistic way, the alumnae and students said, 'Don't sell us short.' Women really rallied."[32]

In the end, the publicity the college received led to unprecedented alumnae support. Forty-six percent of the alumnae wrote checks (up 7 percentage points from the previous year). The size of the average gift increased from $239 in 1988–89 to $380 in 1990–91, an astonishing 59 percent increase. An endowed chair was awarded to the women's studies department. Applications to the college rose as well. The extra money contributed to a decision by the board to freeze tuition at the college for two years, thus keeping tuition and room and board to around $20,000 through 1993. The hope was that holding tuition down might increase enrollment. Although the entering class following the strike year was almost exactly the same size as the preceding one, the next year's class was up by almost one hundred students.

The strike was a watershed event in the history of student culture at Mills. Not that student activism was a new brand of behavior: Some one hundred years earlier and in the middle of the school's main square a group of students burned a coffin with a picture of the school's president on it. Their actions reflected outrage over accusations that the male president "had taken a kiss unwillingly from one of the teachers," in the words of Marge Thomas, editor of the alumnae magazine, *Mills Quarterly*, and the college's unofficial historian.[33] More recently, during the late 1960s and 1970s students pressured the college to develop an ethnic studies program and to hire more faculty of color. In the late 1980s, students such as Silja Talvi became involved in a highly effective divestment movement at the college. Although Mills had a history of student activism, following the strike and the resignations of President Metz, students began to assert themselves in ways that previously were not evident. The attitude expressed by students was that they had bailed the institution out of its bind and therefore they should assume greater responsibility for the college.

Students increased their participation in a wide range of student activities. Orientation was one example. Incoming students were required to view a student-made film about the strike and the college's tradition as an all-female institution. The film conveyed the determination with which the students peacefully shut down campus operations and their jubilation when the trustees rescinded the original vote. New students indicated that the strike and publicity surrounding it had been a positive influence on their decision to attend Mills. They expressed a desire to study at a college where students have such a strong sense of commitment to their school and its traditions.

Upper-class students exhibited greater commitment to Big Sisters, a program designed to assist incoming students with their transition to college. As in many four-year institutions, student attrition had been a problem over the years at Mills, and students were more willing than ever to give of their time to enhance retention efforts. In addition to the Big Sisters program, students also increased their participation in outreach activities designed to attract prospective high school students and increased their involvement in fund-raising efforts, including a student telethon. With the renewed energy of a highly charged student body, the administration had to face ongoing questions about the place of women in the institution. The students' sense of trust in the administration had been shattered by the board's decision, and reestablishing that trust was a major challenge. Nonetheless, much optimism flowed throughout the college as a result of the strike and the spirit of empowerment that followed the students' victory.

The strike of 1990 went to the core of the college's identity as a women's institution. It forced administrators and faculty to think about what it means to be a women's college in the 1990s. Schools such as Mills offer opportunities that coeducational colleges and universities have not been able to provide. What do these different opportunities mean to women? How do women at colleges such as Mills see themselves and what might be learned from their experiences? And, can their experiences be used to inform coeducational institutions around the country? Although the preceding questions largely have been addressed throughout this chapter, they also were examined in an opinion piece published by Mary Hartman in the *Chronicle of Higher Education* in July of 1990. In reflecting on the Mills College episode, she explained,

> The women of Mills did much more than earn a reprieve for their college for women—in itself, no small thing. Equally significant was their readiness to educate a curious public about why they cared so much. They cheerfully conducted countless media forums, sparking widespread debate on the merits of single-sex education. Their spirited exchanges and passionate commitment showed the world that what they appreciate first about women's colleges is the empowerment they experience in institutions that place women students at the center of their educational mission.[34]

Hartman, dean of Douglass College in New Jersey, which is Rutgers University's version of an all-women's institution, went on to highlight the impressive record of women's colleges: graduates are twice as likely as female graduates of coeducational institutions to earn a doctorate; alumnae of women's colleges made up 42 percent of all women participating in the last Congress; they graduated one-third of the women identified as key corporate leaders in a *Business Week* article (despite the fact that graduates of all-women's colleges constitute only 5 percent of all college-educated women).

Hartman made an important point when she connected the success of the women at Mills College to the larger social struggle for gender equity, particularly within the walls of academe. She went on to write, "The message from Mills is not only about women's colleges: it is also a message about the state of women's education at the end of the 20th century. And it is not a reassuring one. . . . Simply opening the doors of our nation's colleges and universities to women has not insured equitable treatment."[35] In many ways, as Hartman eloquently pointed out, the events on the campus of Mills College in the spring of 1990 represented one victory in an ongoing struggle for educational and social equity for women.

But the actions of students at Mills were not only about the empowerment of women: They also acted as *students* with a desire to have a voice in shaping the future of their institution. In this sense, the Mills College strike was also an effort to forge a more participatory form of decision making at the college. Students such as Silja Talvi alluded to the problem of a few making decisions for the many and brought to life pages from another Mills—C. Wright Mills and his classic sociological work *The Power Elite*.[36] In their efforts to shape the school's future, the students took the only recourse available to them—protest—and in the spirit of participatory democracy that inspired the Port Huron Statement of 1962, in which C. Wright Mills's work played such a vital role, they wrote their own history. The popular slogan of the Students for a Democratic Society was once again relived: "Let the people decide."[37] And the people of Mills College did.

The Aftermath

While President Metz was seen in contemptuous terms as a result of her support of a coeducational Mills, and eventually was forced to leave, the students seemed to cast her in a different light as the years passed. Elizabeth Bales commented, "I think she was a scapegoat in a way. I think she did what she thought would be best for the college because she couldn't just think about what she wanted for the institution. College presidents have to think about what is going to insure the survival of their institution as a place for quality education." If President Metz made a mistake it was underestimating the meaning Mills College had for its past and present students. Or perhaps, she had little choice but to support Warren Hellman, one of the few at the top of the ladder who remained standing after the decision was overturned despite being hung by the students in effigy.

When it was over, it was time to reflect on what had been accomplished and why the strike had been so successful. For alums such as Julie Batz, the strike was a source of pride. She was proud of how the students had handled themselves. "I think there was a real congruence between the students' values and their actions and that's when they were the most effective. They had values about inclusion, about group decision making, and integrity, and it just showed in everything that they did." For students who graduated as part of the Mills class of 1990, the strike holds a special place in their memories as well. For Shannon McMackin, the strike was her last taste of innocence: "Near the end of the strike, I felt this powerful sense of optimism and bonding with other students and organizers. But in the back of my mind I knew it wasn't real. I wanted to believe that organizing and civil disobedience works. I thought that I was gonna leave Mills and there was going to be this revolution. But when I got in the real world, outside of Mills College where the Oakland police wouldn't carry me off, I realized that they will carry me off. There was a feeling of disillusionment I felt after I graduated." Today, McMackin is studying for her masters degree in urban studies and wants to improve the quality of life in inner cities. However, she realizes the process of change is slow, at times too slow for her to feel she is making a meaningful contribution.

Sonja Piper was a sophomore at Mills during the strike of 1990 and was actively involved in student government. She was the programming chair in charge of major social and educational events and served as a member of the student government executive board. As a member of the student government, Sonja had inside knowledge of some of the administration's discussions throughout the year about the status of Mills, but she had a hard time convincing herself that the administration could ever make such a decision. Six years later, as a film executive working for Disney Productions in Hollywood, she reflected on the positive experience that Mills provides for women but at the same time seemed saddened by the bottom-line mentality to which she believes the school will eventually succumb: "Ultimately, money speaks louder than idealism. I think the world operates on the almighty dollar. It doesn't matter if there's a situation in which a corporation or an educational institution does a good job helping people or empowering them, because if it isn't fiscally sound then it doesn't matter what kind of change they are making. Organizations are run by business people who all they see are dollars. They don't look at the idealistic side of things."

Following the strike, life at Mills did not return to the serene days of the past. For example, not long after the strike ended, student complaints and dissatisfaction with the racial atmosphere at Mills surfaced. A few years after the strike of 1990, Diane Chen, a 1985 graduate of Mills College and civil rights attorney in San Francisco, facilitated a town meeting to help the campus deal with racial issues, which had been present for years but seemed to become more obvious after the strike. While facilitating the meeting, Chen quoted Frederick Douglass: "If there is no struggle, then there is no progress." Mills had faced one struggle in the spring of 1990 and now had a different set of issues to confront. In many ways, the 1990 strike was about women having a voice in shaping the identity of the institution they held so dear. The racial tension that they currently faced was about women of color having the same opportunities to participate fully in campus life. As one woman in attendance stated, "There may not be an old-boys network here at Mills but there certainly is an old-girls network."

In the spring of 1996, students at Mills were once again involved in campus activism. They had set up tables outside the Student Union and were passing out information calling for greater diversity among the faculty. What was clear was the passion that had been stirred in the spring of 1990 still was evident to a degree as the women of Mills came to take on other important issues of identity and voice. A student commented on the current challenge to students: "Well it's ironic that the faculty doesn't recognize racism as a problem because the whole point of going to an all-women's college is so you can identify with your fellow under-represented and marginalized. Obviously students of color would want to have an educator who could relate to their lives, their perspectives. Granted, these are very intelligent professors who can teach and are sensitive to issues in a certain way, but it doesn't in any sort of way compare to having someone from the same racial background as yourself."

To a few in the administration, the current protests were the negative offspring of the success of the strike of 1990. A high-ranking official in the Mills College administration commented on the contemporary student protesters: "One of the fallouts of the strike that is not so great is the students got their way. They overturned the board's decision and now sometimes they say, 'We did it once and we can do it again.' They think they can get whatever they want. Protesting is a way they see to get what they want. What they don't understand is that during the strike they had the majority of the community behind them—faculty, alumnae, staff. They had huge majorities behind them. That's not true on every cause they have. . . . The protest over diversifying the faculty is very, very different. . . . They want more faculty of color. They want to have some kind of power over how the affirmative action statement is written." Clearly, this administrator believed that the students of Mills College in 1996 were more demanding than recent generations of students. They demonstrated when they believed a policy was unjust and they often made life miserable for certain faculty and administrators. As the decade of the 1990s progressed, student activism was alive and well, at least at Mills College.

Power and Pride

Sometimes students seize upon an issue and call forth an aspect of themselves that lies dormant in their souls because they lack a cause worthy of their passion. This was the case for Shannon McMackin: "But once this happened at Mills, I went, 'Ah, this is what I've been waiting for.' " Most people wait their entire lives for something powerful enough to stir their emotions. The opportunity to experience something meaningful enough to generate the kind of commitment most of us aspire to in one form or another rarely comes along. For the women of Mills College, the spring of 1990 presented such an opportunity to them and they reached out and grabbed hold with all their might. McMackin was asked to deliver the graduation speech that year at Mills and her comments spoke to the kind of emotion that often drives student demonstrators: "Emotion is not a weak quality. It's passion, and passion more than logic leads to change." For McMackin, passion for deeply held convictions can turn defeat into victory.

In a hidden cranny in a small courtyard near the Mills College Student Union stands a bronze sculpture of a woman standing straight and proud, head and arms raised to the sky. The seven-foot-tall statue is the work of Roberta Weir, a 1986 graduate of Mills. The sculpture captures the image of a proud woman at her moment of triumph. Weir's work became the symbol of the strike of 1990 and its image was often depicted by students along with the phrase "strong women, proud women." Like Weir's statue, the Mills College strike of 1990 is a monument to women's power and pride.

chapter five

"PROMISES MADE, PROMISES KEPT"

The Struggle of American Indians
at Michigan State

Columbus was lost; so is Engler," yelled a group of American Indian students gathered at the capitol building for a March 1995 rally in Lansing, Michigan.[1] On the eve of the Republican primary, a large contingent of college students, many of whom attended Michigan State University, had organized the demonstration to pressure Republican Governor John Engler to reconsider his plan to end the state's tuition program for American Indians. The Michigan Indian Tuition Waiver Program had evolved over the years from a long-standing agreement between the state and its Indian population, and students were not about to take his action sitting down. Cognizant of the waiver's history, students held signs which read "Give us the waiver or give us the land" and "Honor your commitment." As a few hundred demonstrators marched and chanted slogans along the sidewalk in front of the capitol, another group known as the "Tree Town Drummers" pounded out a relentless Native beat signifying to Governor Engler and anyone else within earshot that these students would not go silently into the night.

The March rally at the capitol was only part of a long struggle that would last throughout three consecutive academic years, from 1993 to 1996. The whole ordeal would leave Michigan State University students such as Lula Brewer and Hanna Windstorm[2] disillusioned about the possibility of improving the lives of their people. Brewer, who during the academic year 1994–95 was a sophomore majoring in studio art and English, fought off the tears as she talked about how much the waiver meant to her and her family: "Because I am the oldest grandchild in my family, my cousins look up to me. And the thing is that if they take the waiver away, my cousins will not have a way to go to college. . . . I think most people will just feel like college is not for them. College is too much trouble. They don't have the resources without the waiver." And Windstorm, a first-year student studying marketing, saw the tuition waiver as a key program for improving the educational attainment of American Indians. Without such programs, she believed, tribes throughout the state would continue to suffer economically. For Lula Brewer and Hanna Windstorm, Governor Engler's assault on the waiver program was one more example of legislative betrayal by people who make agreements and then forsake them at the state or federal government's convenience. The general feeling between Brewer and Windstorm was that if the government can break treaties[3] whenever they please, then they are not worth the paper they are written on.

Sammy Walker,[4] a junior, also discussed Engler's actions in terms of a language of government betrayal. "It showed once again that breaking treaties is something that has lasted for two hundred years in this nation. Everybody looks at it and says that violating treaties was something that was done in the past. That treaties were only broken back in the late nineteenth century. And that it doesn't happen today. But it does happen today. It happens all the time. It is happening right now and nothing has been done about it. . . . So most of what would be called 'liberal America' say they are outraged by the treatment of Native Americans and they speak about it as if it all happened in the past. It is happening right now and there is no outcry." To Walker, Engler's efforts represented just one more broken promise to pierce the hopes of his people.

Because of his position on the tuition waiver, Engler had clearly become the primary antagonist and the target of student outrage and counterattacks. Walker held little back in discussing the governor. "As far as I am concerned Engler is an evil, evil man. He is evil personified. He is a political animal." Walker felt that Engler simply wanted to take the money from the state's poorest—American Indians—and then give a tax break to the middle and upper classes. Because many Indians do not vote, Walker supposed that Engler knew little damage could be done to his political support. He imagined what Engler was thinking: "What are Natives to me? Do they vote? No, for the most part. They don't go out to the polls. So what do I have to lose? I have nothing to lose and I have everything to gain. I can gain [$3 million] for the budget. I don't lose anything politically. What do I care if it hurts somebody?"

As the 1995 spring semester came to a close, most of the more than one hundred MSU American Indian students headed home for the summer unsure of what their future held. After much debate and politicking between Governor Engler and members of the state legislature, the tuition payments for the 1994–95 year finally had been approved, but the governor was making no guarantees about the future. At the close of the school year, Paul Dearhouse was finishing up his next-to-last year of college and hoping to get his degree in material science and engineering the following year. He had been supported by the waiver program and was skeptical about what the future held for himself and others within the Native community at MSU. "I would say that the attitude was one of hopelessness. Because a lot of people, including myself, were feeling like 'What can we do that would influence their thinking in the capital?' You know. . . . What kind of contact do they have with students on a daily basis? What do they know about us? Why should they even care about the waiver program or our people's struggles?. . . There was a lot of despair. It's like 'Damn you Engler!' He is really coming after us. . . . So I assumed that he would just kill it off."

Lula Brewer, Hanna Windstorm, Sammy Walker, and Paul Dearhouse saw the academic year come to a depressing halt as they battled feelings of resentment, anger, and uncertainty. Contributing to their emotional state was an attitude among many of their fellow MSU students that American Indians did not deserve "special" treatment. Indian students found themselves quietly walking away from conversations so as not to stir more bitterness as they overheard negative comments from their peers. Maintaining positive relations was important, and confronting others about their lack of knowledge and understanding of the situation was difficult. But more than a few students were assertive enough to challenge others to learn the history of the waiver. "If they only knew why the waiver was created in the first place, then maybe they wouldn't be so quick to condemn it," said Angie Shinos, a sophomore in mathematics during the 1994–95 school year. She saw rallies and demonstrations as tools for educating other students about the tuition waiver and its significance to the Native population. Shinos explained that the key to their struggle would be to gain support from the people and from other MSU students. The only way this could be accomplished was by telling everybody about the program and its history: "Let everybody know. Educate them. . . . Once people find out what the real reason is—why we have the tuition waiver—they will support us."

In 1934, Governor William Comstock approved the transfer of lands from the federal Indian School at Mount Pleasant, a small community about fifty miles north of the state capital of Lansing. In exchange for the property, the state of Michigan was to provide free education for Native residents throughout the state. In a letter addressed to the Honorable Harold L. Ickes, Secretary of the Interior, Governor Comstock acknowledged the following: "As Governor of the State, in accepting this grant [the Indian School and property at Mount Pleasant], I acknowledge the condition that the State of Michigan will receive and care for (in state institutions) Indian residents within the state on entire equality with persons of other races and without cost to the federal government." The letter confirmed the responsibility of the state to "receive and care for" American Indian students.[5] At the time of Comstock's signing of the agreement, education for Native students simply meant providing free transportation from reservations to the nearest school. In the 1930s, few rural residents of Michigan, including Anglos, went much further than the eighth grade. Consequently, at that time the "free education" agreement was not applied to postsecondary education.

William LeBlanc, Executive Director on Indian Affairs with the state of Michigan, highlighted the recent history of what had come to be known as the Comstock Agreement. He explained that in 1964 Michigan Governor George Romney appointed a task force to study American Indians within the state. The task force presented a report on the "Indian problem" to the governor, which eventually led to the creation of the Michigan Commission on Indian Affairs in 1965. Governor Romney charged the commission with two concerns: to focus on the (1) health and (2) education needs of American Indians throughout the state. As part of the latter concern, the commission was to clarify the role of the state in supporting higher education for the Native population.

The commission eventually funded the Touche Ross Report, which sparked an interest in reevaluating the "free education" article within the Comstock Agreement. The Touche Ross Report revealed the abysmally low socioeconomic standing of the state's American Indians and noted that only 3 percent of urban and 2 percent of rural Indians had completed college.[6] Despite the state's having received federal funds over the years for the education of American Indians, it was quite apparent that that responsibility had not been taken seriously. As a consequence, in 1976, under the sponsorship of State Senator Jackie Vaughn III and with the support of Indians throughout the state, Republican Governor William Milliken signed into law Michigan Public Act 174, which recognized the state's historic obligation (due to the Comstock Agreement) to educate Native students. Two years later, greater clarity was provided as the state legislators passed Michigan Public Act No. 505, which reads as follows: "A public state community or public junior college, public college, or public university shall waive tuition for any North American Indian who qualifies for admission as a full-time, part-time, or summer school student, and is a legal resident of the state for not less than 12 consecutive months." The act went on to define a qualifying Indian as any person who is not less than one-quarter Indian as certified by the person's tribal association and verified by the Michigan Commission on Indian Affairs.[7] The act of 1976 and the revisions of 1978 are generally referred to as the Michigan Indian Tuition Waiver Program (MITWP).

From Governor Engler's perspective, the tuition waiver program is simply a legislative act subject to revision. Furthermore, like many conservatives around the state, Engler sees it as an entitlement program that should not exist. Opposing Engler are many liberals who see the program as falling in line with the philosophical ideals of affirmative action. However, both arguments anger many of the Native students at Michigan State who see the waiver neither as an entitlement nor as a part of the state's commitment to affirmative action. Simply stated, they view the waiver program as part of an official arrangement representing a legal and moral obligation of the state to its Native population. For them, the waiver program is legislatively rooted in the Comstock Agreement and therefore should not be restructured without serious discussion involving their input and approval. American Indian students complain that many citizens around the state fail to recognize the historic relevance of the exchange of property at Mount Pleasant. The land exchanged was permanently given up, and therefore what was offered in return should be just as permanent. Additionally, in claiming the site of the federal boarding school for Indians, the state assumed the responsibility for the education of American Indians in Michigan, a responsibility thus relinquished by the federal government. This meant an end to the federal practice of shipping Indians off to boarding schools.

For nearly twenty years, fifteen thousand students who were members of the Saginaw Chippewa Indian Tribe of Michigan, Sault Ste. Marie Tribe of Chippewa, Grand Traverse Band of Ottawa and Chippewa Indians, Keweenaw Bay Indian Community, Hannahville Indian Community, Lac Vieux Desert Indian Community, and Bay Mills Indian Community attended public colleges and universities throughout the state with the financial support of the tuition waiver. In 1993, for example, 2,390 students attended Michigan colleges under the tuition waiver program amounting to $2,605,289 of state funding. Northern Michigan University had the largest enrollment of American Indian students with 179. Lansing Community College was next with 160 students. Michigan State University, with 111 students enrolled in the program, had the seventh highest total.[8] Although these numbers are certainly not extremely large, they nonetheless would be cut significantly if the waiver program were eliminated.

The Pros and Cons

Native students at Michigan State and Lansing Community College and the other Michigan public colleges and universities survived Engler's 1994–95 attempt to end the waiver program, but in the fall of 1995 they returned to campus to face a renewed effort on the governor's part. In the summer of 1995, Governor Engler sent out a warning shot for those students returning to school: "As Michigan public colleges and universities begin the 1995–96 school year, they must understand that I will not support further appropriations to reimburse them for tuition waived for Native American students."[9] In fact, the 1996 Executive Budget proposed by Engler and submitted to the legislature in February of 1995 excluded the tuition waiver program entirely. Engler offered four reasons why he did not support the program. First, he argued that it discriminated against other minorities, such as African Americans, who are not eligible for the waiver. Engler's spokesperson, John Truscott, commented that Engler wants to end the program because he believes it is unfair. "There are a lot of minority groups that should have this kind of program. Why should Native Americans be singled out? He believes that everyone should be treated equally."[10] Maureen McNulty, press secretary for the Michigan Department of Management and Budget, supported Engler's position: "This isn't about keeping education away from American Indians. It's about giving equality to all students."[11]

A second reason Engler gave for not supporting the program is what he perceived as potential abuse of the program. Administration officials have expressed concern that the tuition waiver program is "the only state-funded scholarship program that has no limits on enrollment or expense, nor a means to limit funding to the most needy." State Representative

Timothy Walberg called the proposed cutting of the program long over-due because it operates "without any checks or balances. There was no way to ensure that the applicants really were Indians."[12]

A third reason often given was that the financial situation for American Indians had changed for the better as a result of extensive gambling revenue obtained from reservation casinos. And fourth, the governor believed that the most needy of the current recipients of the tuition waiver would be able to replace the waiver with other state scholarships which Engler had proposed be increased by almost 10 percent.

Once the semester resumed, MSU American Indian students, joined by faculty, staff, and community members, were quick to counter Engler's offensive. In a variety of public forums, the students pointed out that if the program were need based, it might only cover the very poorest Indians around the state, and the reality is that many people who do not qualify for financial aid (such as part-time students) still have a difficult time making it through college. For American Indians, who already have such low college attendance rates and high attrition rates, the added financial burden is just one more barrier. And besides, as many students were quick to point out, the waiver is not simply a legislative program—it is part of an agreement involving the exchange of land. A sign held at the demonstration at the capitol the previous spring stressed this point: "Give us the waiver or give us the land."

Pat Dyer-Deckrow, a part-time graduate student supported by the waiver, had strong feelings about the program: "Because it is an obligation that was supposed to be kept, we should never have had to take out student loans for any educational programs at all. It was supposed to be an exchange for the resources and not just the land itself. . . . My grandmother is ninety-two years old. She never had anything paid for by the state. No education. Nothing. So somebody paid for us, for our generation and others to follow so that we would have something."

Contemporary American Indian students see education as a solution to the economic woes of their communities, and the Michigan Indian Tuition Waiver Program is obviously part of that solution. Hanna Windstorm, for example, believes that education is one of the keys to solving tribal problems and conflicts. She argued that tribal politics often get in the way of forming a unified front to fight governmental efforts to end programs such as the tuition waiver: "Education is going to bring us out of . . . I don't want to say poverty, but it can change our economic status. It can help rework the tribal system. Like hiring people because they know what they are doing. People should not be hired because their family member knows somebody who knows somebody who will get them a job in the tribe. Education is going to change the whole workings of the tribal network. . . . I think if you just get really good people who know what they are doing and are dedicated to a cause, then things would change as far as tribes being able to work things out. People can see that we are trying to fight to keep the tuition waiver but they also see that we are always fighting each other."

The reality is that most American Indian students are nontraditional (twenty-five and older) and have limited access to other methods of paying for college. Loans are not a good option, as many plan to return to lower paying jobs in Indian communities or on reservations. Some students have access to federal grants, but primarily this option only works for full-time students, who are in the minority among MITWP recipients. Data compiled by the Native American Institute at MSU revealed the following characteristics about MITWP recipients. Sixty-seven percent of the students who use the tuition waiver are part-timers and thus are not eligible for most forms of financial aid. The 67 percent is twenty points higher than national data that reveal 47 percent of college students attend part-time. The average age of MITWP recipients is thirty years. And interestingly enough, among current recipients of the tuition waiver, approximately 70 percent are female.[13]

The preceding data, as well as the narratives of undergraduate students such as Lula Brewer and Paul Dearhouse and graduate students like Pat Dyer-Deckrow, provide insight into the unique struggles of American Indians at Michigan State University. But the problems these students highlight are not unique to a single university and in fact extend throughout much of American higher education.

American Indians in Higher Education

From the earliest days of higher education in North America, Indians were the targets of missionary strategies which sought to educate "savages" in the ways of Christianity. In the late 1700s, and following over a hundred years of missionary work, an Anglican educator commented that Indians possessed "an untameable savage spirit, which has refused to hear the voice of instruction."[14] The "untameable savage spirit" referred to in Gerald Goodwin's work became the title for an article later written by higher education historian Irvin "Bobby" Wright, himself a Cree from Montana, as he traced the cultural dilemma of American Indians and higher education:

> When we contemplate the historic mission of higher education, particularly in relation to American Indians, and, more importantly, when we view that mission from a native perspective, we discover the historic roots of cultural persistence that continue today to result in their rejection of the higher education enterprise. American Indians have adamantly refused to surrender to an institution which for centuries has sought to assimilate them, to remake them in the image of their European subjugators.[15]

The resistance described by Wright was mentioned by Pat Dyer-Deckrow as she discussed her own life and experiences in education: "I come from a very matriarchal family and my grandmother really pushed education. So a lot of my family members are very educated. And it has helped us to get out of poverty. But my grandmother also made sure that we knew our values and who we were as a people before we went off to college. I know some Native American families are afraid that if their children go to college to get a higher degree, when they come back they won't know them. They will be totally removed. They won't value their culture anymore."

Chad Waucaush was a junior majoring in parks and recreation during the academic year 1995–96. He was involved in the demonstrations to preserve the tuition waiver program. Waucaush had strong views on the education of American Indians and how their culture had been denigrated in the process: "The educational history of Native Americans compared to Anglo Americans is a lot different. Anglo Americans come from the perspective of learning by emphasizing writing. Like writing things down in a classroom. Teaching stuff like that. Native people come from more of an oral culture. They convey meanings through stories and stuff like that. . . . Everything has a reason or symbol behind it. A spiritual or cultural symbol is used to help get the message across to somebody. What I believe really damaged Native people's views toward education was [that] in the past, instead of using the abilities they already had and the concepts they had already learned, teachers tended to ignore all that the Native Americans already knew." The suspicion and contempt that some of his elders have toward a college education make perfect sense to Waucaush: "So when students go back to their Indian communities after being away at college, they do not know where to fit in. And so I have heard a lot of people, elders, say that it's kind of a 'pain in the bones' because there are so many other things that a college education is not teaching them. It is seen as taking away their identity. Taking away any kind of cultural ties through all these other motives that surround Anglo education."

Waucaush offered an example of Anglo American educators rejecting Native culture: "Anglo educators would use punishment if Indians used their Native language in the classroom. They would humiliate them. I have heard stories from elders. Teachers would put boards in their mouths in front of the classroom and use a lot of cruel ways to humiliate the person so that they wouldn't do it again. . . . Whenever you mention education, you hear stories from our elders about why our grandparents dropped out in fifth grade, eighth grade, or tenth grade. After so many generations of not getting hardly any education, it is hard to talk about today's kids going to college. That was not what was expected of me."

Native youth such as Chad Waucaush often adopt a different stance toward higher education than their elders and see a college education as necessary for survival in today's world. Sammy Walker also talked about the importance of getting an education: "The larger issue is that we need to be educated in order to effectively deal with the majority culture in the U.S. We have little choice but to have to play by their rules. If we have to play by the rules, then the best thing we can do is know the rules of the game as best we can. And going to college is one of the ways to learn the rules. And if you are not educated, then you are not on a level playing field. We are already disadvantaged as it is. The playing field is already slanted, so the best that we can do is to try to become educated."

As of the early 1990s, Bobby Wright was one of only a handful of scholars who had begun to address the unique problems of American Indians in higher education.[16] William Tierney was another scholar who explored some of the issues raised by Wright's research. Tierney conducted an extensive qualitative study of American Indians in higher education and challenged integrationist views of the role of higher education.[17] Specifically, he raised questions about the application of the work of Vincent Tinto, who had developed theories of student departure based on social and academic integration.[18] Essentially, Tinto argued that the key to student success, as measured by persistence, was for the student to develop a sense of connection to the institution.

Alexander Astin's "student involvement theory" parallels some of the assumptions undergirding Tinto's work in that Astin argued that increased institutional involvement on the part of the student lends oneself to better academic performance.[19] "What I mean by involvement," explained Astin, "is neither mysterious nor esoteric. Quite simply, student involvement refers to the amount of physical and psychological energy that the student devotes to the academic experience. A highly involved student is one who . . . devotes considerable energy to studying, spends a lot of time on campus, participates actively in student organizations, and interacts frequently with faculty members and other students."[20] Thus, while Tinto's work has been utilized primarily to examine student persistence, Astin's has been used to explore student achievement.

Based on the work of Tinto and Astin, higher education researchers have applied social integration models in order to explain the college student experience. In terms of examining the collegiate lives of minority students, most researchers have utilized these theories to identify variables that lead to greater levels of social integration and presumably enhanced performance and higher graduation rates (and transfer rates for community college students).[21] One should not be too surprised to learn that minority students tend to score lower in measures of social integration and reveal lower levels of success as defined by their higher rates of departure. The simple solution often suggested, based on social integration models, is that minority students need help in fitting in. The goal, in the case of culturally diverse students, is to develop institutional programs to assist them in becoming more fully integrated.

Logically, the work of Tinto and Astin makes perfect sense. There is, however, a problem of application with social integration models. In short, administrative practice based on social integration perspectives tends to envision minority students as being in some way "deficient" and therefore in need of intervention if they are to survive in college and university contexts. The strategy often followed is that minority students through a variety of support services must learn to adjust their behaviors, attitudes, values, beliefs, etcetera to better suit those of the mainstream culture of the institution, and thereby become more socially and academically connected. In adopting new cultural modes for surviving in Eurocentric institutions, what becomes of the cultural identities that diverse students bring to the institution? This is one of the points Tierney raises when he suggests that "researchers and organizational participants need to come to terms with how they will incorporate the different voices of American Indians into the organization."[22] By this, Tierney means that institutions ought to be reshaped around a multicultural perspective more reflective of the cultural diversity brought to the institution by diverse students. Instead of trying to help American Indian students fit a Eurocentrically conceived university, the institution would examine how its structures might be modified to better reflect the cultural identities of Indians as well as those of other culturally diverse students. For example, if some cultures favor more collaborative learning styles, then why not incorporate such options into pedagogical practice? Furthermore, if a large percentage of students at a particular institution have Spanish as their first language, why not at least hire some employees proficient in their language? Such considerations become part of the decision making in a multicultural organizational context.[23]

Tierney placed the need for change squarely on the shoulders of colleges and universities and not on the diverse students who often feel disempowered within mainstream educational settings. Kathryn Tijerina and Paul Biemer addressed this same concern when they wrote, "Creative thinking about how to successfully connect American Indian students to the university must be balanced with methods to make the university more responsive and welcoming to the Indian student."[24]

Pat Dyer-Deckrow spoke to the dilemma identified by Tierney, Tijerina, and Biemer, and other multicultural theorists: "For American Indians, this balancing of two worlds is a struggle. It doesn't matter what social class you are from. I think the Indian students who are truly, truly successful, materialistically speaking, a lot of times abandon their cultural roots. And then when they want to try to come back, to reclaim their Indian heritage, it is hard because we are mad at them because they gave up a lot of our culture in the process. And so the kid is really well off financially now, but how do you think he feels about having lost his family in the process of succeeding?" She also alluded to different values that may be at work for Indian students: "I think for a lot of Indian students it is hard to make decisions about college and about a major. It is hard to narrow down what you want to do for a career, because the main intent is not to try to be the richest, but rather it is more important to find out, as an elder once said to me, 'What is going to make you happy?' And sometimes this is a difficult question to answer." Dyer-Deckrow concluded her thoughts by pointing to a passage she had read from Bobby Wright's work: "For many, success in education means mastering white ways on one's own terms by maintaining some commitment to Indian values and tradition."[25]

Hanna Windstorm reinforced some of the points made by Dyer-Deckrow: "I think lots of students think that when they graduate they are going to work for the tribe. They are going to raise their family near the community. They are not looking to aspire to make more than $30,000. They are just trying to stay in their little place and have a comfortable spot." She also shared her thoughts on the cultural conflict that many American Indians have with regard to education. "It is a real funny thing because there is a conflict among Native Americans. There are people who are for education and there are people who are not. Some people see it as abandoning your culture. My feeling is that people look at it with mixed feelings because the whole thing of the last five hundred years has always been that education has been pushed on Native American people. So I think there is a lot of hostility towards education. I am trying to say that when you get a lot of education you are seen as pulling away from the community automatically because you are seeing different things besides what is just inside your reservation or your community at home."

For a variety of cultural and structural reasons, American Indians have the lowest high school and college completion rates of any racial or ethnic group. For example, most studies reveal that only about 6 percent of all American Indians go on to earn the baccalaureate. This contrasts to 23 percent for Anglo Americans, 12 percent for African Americans, and 7 percent for Hispanics.[26] With such figures in mind, it is imperative that programs such as the Michigan tuition waiver be continued as a means of contributing to educational achievement for American Indians. Also, programs with great flexibility such as MITWP are better suited for Native students, who because of cultural and tribal commitments may need to move into and out of college at varying points in their lives. Federal student loan and grant programs do not generally provide the kind of flexibility beneficial to these students. As already mentioned, the argument that the waiver program should be supported because of the limited educational attainment of Indians falls within the general philosophical parameters of affirmative action.[27] However, for many of the Indian students at Michigan State University such logic is seen to be dangerous, since affirmative action decisions are always open for debate and legislative whim, as evidenced by recent decisions in California regarding the passage of Proposition 209. Thus, the student activists who have organized resistance against Governor Engler have focused on the historic merits of the program and its ties to the Comstock Agreement of 1934. They do not think of themselves as receiving special treatment or minority entitlements.

Early Unrest

As early as the academic year 1993–94, Governor Engler had sent notice that the tuition waiver program was in trouble. Students in MSU's

North American Indian Student Organization (NAISO) were slow to respond at first, but soon they gathered momentum as the fall semester progressed. Two major protests were eventually planned and carried out during the academic year.

The first large-scale demonstration by American Indian students took place in the spring of 1994, after students got wind of the governor's desire to eliminate the program. The demonstration was a march from the "rock" through the main administration building and then on to the Student Union, where a series of speakers addressed educational concerns. The large rock that marked the gathering site for the protest is a famous MSU landmark that students paint, on nearly a weekly basis, as a means to promote or celebrate campus events. "Class of 1994," "Gay Pride," "Welcome Delta Epsilon Alums," or "Beat U of M" are just a few of the phrases that might appear on the rock, only to be covered over the next week with a new coat of paint and a new slogan. The rock is situated in the heart of the campus next to the Red Cedar River and is only a few buildings away from the main administration building where President Peter McPherson's office is located. Every MSU student understands the meaning of "Let's meet at the rock," and so it was an obvious place to begin the march.

The demonstration was designed to call attention to NAISO's concern about the threat to the tuition waiver and to foster support among fellow students and faculty. As Paul Dearhouse explained, "The march was designed to educate students and bring the issue out in the open. To get people thinking about or at least hearing about it." Dearhouse went on to describe what he saw as the students' role: "I kind of view the students' job, as far as the tuition waiver goes is to make our voice heard. When you hear student voices, or a group of students protesting, generally people pay attention to them."

About 150 demonstrators gathered at the rock with a collection of signs and banners reflecting their dissatisfaction with the governor. A group of students representing a Native dance group wore traditional clothing including such items as calico shirts with ribbons, feathers, and geometric designs hanging from them. Several women wore frocks, vests, and knee-high moccasins. Many carried hand drums and rattles as well as other traditional instruments. The first stop on the march was the main administration building, where the students proceeded to move through the building from the first floor to the fourth and then back down. They then made their way to the Student Union, where a series of speakers were set to address the protesters.

The march was composed of a respectful group of students who simply wanted what they believed was owed to them. Several of the students were not even sure they had the nerve to join the march. But with the support of Hanna Windstorm, Paul Dearhouse, Lula Brewer, and Pat Dyer-Deckrow, and many others, they took solace in walking peacefully with one another. How different this group of protesters was compared to the nearly three thousand highly agitated students who in the spring of 1970 stormed MSU President Clifton Wharton's office demanding that he pay tribute to the students killed at Kent State.[28] Many of the Indian students involved in the current demonstration were not even born until the mid-1970s and all the talk by their professors about the activism of the 1960s seemed to have little meaning to them. The events of "Freedom Summer"[29] may as well have been centuries away from these students, and yet the narrative of democracy's struggle was being reenacted. In the summer of 1964, over one thousand volunteers worked to register Black voters throughout the state of Mississippi, and now some thirty years later, close to a hundred American Indian students were engaged in freedom's march once again, this time in the state of Michigan. And although the words of Freedom Summer's anthem—"We Shall Overcome"—likely did not ring in the ears of these contemporary activists, its spirit surely did.

Like other Indian students around the state, Waucaush resented Engler and his fiscal conservatism that sought to eliminate budget items regardless of their social and moral implications. "There was a lot of hostility towards Engler. A lot of questioning because we thought it was a successful program. It affected our lives. We saw the lives of our families getting changed by it. We have had families that were never in school but now we have different relatives attending college. We were questioning, if it is such a successful program, then why do they want to do away with it?"

At times the whole ordeal became deeply frustrating for Hanna Windstorm. "I have mixed feelings about a lot of things. I see the good in protesting as far as bringing people together for a common cause, but thinking that you are going to have an effect on the people inside that building [the MSU administration building] or if you go to the capitol—I have mixed feelings about it because they are just doing their job. They are going to go forth and play whatever game they want and get the votes they want, and I don't really know if I can make a difference or not. . . . It is like we are protesting, but why? Are we just putting on a show? I have mixed feelings about it because I guess I am not very vocal, very loud." Windstorm was not convinced that students yelling "Let's rock Engler!"

or "Let's get him!" or "Engler is awful!" was the solution. She believed that Engler was just one man on the totem pole and if it were not he, it would be someone else trying to take what was rightfully theirs. "It is a bigger game than that. You can't [vent] all your anger at one person. It is the whole body of people making these decisions. . . . He is not the problem. The problem is the whole attitude of the state. You can't go about changing people with signs like 'Engler dies today!' Maybe focus on another issue besides a person. Focus on the issue. I think it is just hard for us to educate people."

Lula Brewer was another of the students with unanswered questions and who had played a key role in planning the spring 1994 march. She talked about her fellow students and the significance of terminating financial aid: "Most of the Indian students who are on the waiver are either first generation or maybe their parents went back to school after their kids grew up. For people to say that we have gotten somewhere and we don't need it anymore is totally wrong. . . . A lot of American Indians are first-generation students, and for them to be taking it away makes you look at things in a different way. How unfair things can be. Maybe people have good reason to get a little more cynical about the government after stuff like this."

Windstorm, Brewer, and Waucaush also were among the few hundred students and community members who rallied at the capitol in March one year later. The students described their efforts as fairly successful and cited some of the support they had won among state legislators, including many Republicans. At meetings of the House Higher Education Committee and the Appropriations Higher Education Sub-Committee taking place during the same week as the capitol demonstration, several representatives spoke out against Engler's efforts. For example, Representative Lingg Brewer, a Democrat, stated that the tuition waiver is part of a treaty and thus can only be dissolved if both sides are in agreement. "This looks highly unilateral. It looks like this is being done by the people in power." Representative Paul Tesanovich, a Democrat from Michigan's Upper Peninsula, stated, "I have two federally recognized tribes in my district, and I'm angry that this is even in jeopardy." Two Republican Representatives also spoke out in support, arguing that confusion about the waiver contributed to its opposition. "Some see this as a free ride all the way through college," explained Dan Gustafson. "But it's tuition-only. It doesn't include room and board or books." And Jim McBryde of Mount Pleasant, the site of the original Comstock Agreement, commented, "There is a misconception that you check a box on a form and that makes you eligible for the tuition waiver."[30]

In spite of the Republican governor's opposition, the waiver program continued to have bipartisan support, and as a result of legislative maneuvering in the spring of 1995, influenced by student and community direct action, attempts to cut the program from the budget were short-circuited. For the time being, the students had won the battle, but the war would persist into the 1995–96 school year.

Reluctant Warriors and Their Comrades

Lula Brewer, who like Hanna Windstorm eventually would serve a term as president of NAISO, originally was born in South Dakota and is officially affiliated with the Ovawella Dakota tribe. Because her mother is full Odawa Indian, Lula is considered half Odawa and half Ovawella Dakota. In the spring of 1994, Lula Brewer was working in the residence halls as a minority aide, a part-time position in which students provide peer support to other minority students. She recalled her reaction the first time she heard about Engler's proposal to cut the tuition waiver: "When I first heard about the tuition waiver issue the university did not have a Native American coordinator in the Office of Minority Student Affairs. So the night I heard about it I made a flyer and sent it around campus telling people about what was going on." Shortly after publicizing Engler's proposal, Brewer joined other members of NAISO and staff from the Native American Institute to begin planning the protest march from the rock to the Student Union. From that moment on, Brewer's entire college experience seemed to revolve around the battle with Engler. The last thing she wanted to have happen was to look back and say that the students did not try hard enough. "We want to at least do all that we can so that way if they ever take it away we couldn't say that we watched them do it."

American Indian students at MSU had begun battling Engler as far back as the fall of 1993 when they first learned of his opposition to the tuition waiver. Members of the Indian community, especially the older nontraditional students, started political work at that time. As the 1994–95 academic year progressed, the conflict continued and eventually active members of NAISO found themselves organizing letter-writing campaigns to legislators, recruiting speakers from the state's American Indian community, educating other students about the issues, and encouraging whatever support they could muster.

For traditional-age undergraduates in NAISO, the whole battle was daunting at times and they often turned to elders who worked at MSU. They found staff members such as George Cornell and Arnie Parish to be rich sources of knowledge on the history of the waiver. Students also lacked understanding of tribal politics, and once again staff and non-traditional students helped to explain the complexities of tribal issues, the debates about casino revenues, and the state's responsibility in the waiver matter. The whole resistance movement was for several students the most significant learning experience of their college years. They developed a deeper understanding of the cultural dilemmas of American Indians and the role of higher education. They came to understand the complexities of legislative processes, which to them often usurped the rights of Indians. Students also developed a more comprehensive view of Michigan State University and some of the political processes shaping the reactions of President McPherson and Provost Lou Anna Simon. For example, some of the students openly discussed the fact that they understood that President McPherson could only do so much since he had only recently obtained a significant budget increase from the legislature for technological advances at the university. To come out publicly against the governor and his stance on the tuition waiver could jeopardize the university's budgetary gains in other areas.

In addition to turning to elders, members of NAISO also got significant support from other students of color. In particular, leaders in NAISO learned some of their direct-action strategies from a comrade in arms—Ernesto Mireles of MEChA (Movimiento Estudiantil Chicano de Aztlan). Through Mireles, as well as others within the MSU community, NAISO discovered a variety of tactics for attracting publicity to their cause. Some of the tactics, such as an on-foot pursuit of the governor's car during a homecoming parade, reflected the kind of radical efforts often employed by Mireles, who was well known around the MSU campus for the role he played in leading the campus "Grape Boycott." He and other Chicanos/Latinos had been involved in demonstrations over the past few years to force the university to end the purchase of grapes for campus dining facilities because of a concern that pesticides were causing serious health problems among migrant workers. Mireles and other Mechistas (members of MEChA) believed that Michigan State University, as the pioneer land grant institution and as a major agricultural research center, could be influential if it were to support such a boycott. A significant chapter in the Grape Boycott came to a climax in the spring of 1996 after several students fasted for nearly a full week. In response to the fast, President McPherson supported a measure that would allow individual residence halls the authority to vote on whether they would support the boycott or not. Perhaps the most noteworthy incident in the MSU grape chronicles was when a group of MEChA students met with McPherson in his office. In the course of a heated debate about the university's position, one exuberant student poured a bag of grapes onto the president's conference table and proceeded to climb onto the table and squish them with his feet. President McPherson did not find the incident amusing. After all, this was certainly not the kind of wine and cheese mixer to which he had grown accustomed.

Whereas MEChA in general, and Ernesto Mireles in particular, tended to use aggressive direct-action tactics, many of the students in NAISO leaned toward more peaceful strategies. Sensationalizing their cause was against the cultural norms embraced by NAISO members, and the militancy of Mireles and of MEChA left students feeling embarrassed at times. For example, Angie Shinos had mixed feelings about the rallies and the role of public demonstration in applying pressure to politicians and educational leaders. She feared that many within the American Indian community as well as the Anglo community might look at protesters "as a bunch of radicals whining about their problems." She also expressed concern about the image that people might have of NAISO and worried that some at MSU might see the organization as a radical student organization. "I think the demonstrations could have had a negative effect on our student group because people might think that all we do is protest and rally. That all we do is just cause trouble."

Shinos expressed the general sentiments of other Indian students including Lula Brewer, who also feared NAISO members' being labeled as "radicals." "There were other students who didn't feel right about protesting," explained Brewer. She went on to recall the spring 1995 demonstration at the capitol: "I think when we had our rally this past spring the *State News* [MSU's student newspaper] painted the picture that we were radical. We had one speaker who was from MEChA [Ernesto Mireles] and he had some radical things to say. But all we were trying to do is educate people, and the *State News* painted it like all we were trying to do was cry a lot about being minorities. The newspaper totally missed the point. The point that we were tying to make was that it was a legal issue— that it wasn't about minority entitlements—and they painted that picture anyway." Despite anxious feelings such as those expressed by Shinos and Brewer, NAISO remained actively involved in political strategizing throughout the academic year 1994–95, at least until the spring semester drew near its end and summer vacation was in sight.

Once again, college life returned to a bit of normalcy as April arrived and finals loomed around the corner. NAISO students returned to their studies as some prepared for their last finals at Michigan State. It was an upsetting year for many, but they did not want to forget why they had made their way to college in the first place. Despite all the disruptions caused by their ongoing battle with Engler, the students were there to learn. As the last finals were taken and the campus emptied seemingly overnight, many of the American Indian students returned to their homes and communities for the summer. A few played softball with their buddies back home. Others made their way north across the expansive Mackinac Bridge and took positions at summer camps in Michigan's beautiful Upper Peninsula. Some took summer jobs working for small businesses in their local communities. And a few stayed in East Lansing and worked on campus or at local coffee shops, stores, or restaurants. The pace was slower than the hectic days during the semester. All the classes, part-time work, and the organizing with NAISO had taken its toll, and though they had won the battle of 1994–95, the war with Engler remained a fact of life for them.

Homecoming Weekend

As August came to an end, the students filtered back to campus and once again found themselves face-to-face with the tuition waiver issue. The governor had not relented in his efforts to end the program and members of NAISO went about the task of brainstorming ideas for campus demonstrations. During one of their September meetings, several students pushed the idea to disrupt homecoming weekend, and after a serious discussion, plans began to fall into place. Because Engler was named the parade marshal, the students saw the homecoming parade as an excellent opportunity to raise the waiver issue. After all, this was their institution and Engler was not supporting Indian students. "Why should he be in our homecoming parade?" was the question students raised. "Because of what Engler has done to the waiver, some of us might not be here next year," said an exasperated Lula Brewer. "It just seems very ironic that a governor who takes away financial aid from students is in MSU's Homecoming Parade."[31]

On Friday, October 6, 1995, a group of around seventy American

Indian students, joined by supporters from MEChA including Ernesto Mireles, marched alongside the motorcade escorting Governor Engler and MSU President Peter McPherson. They followed the motorcade from the Evergreen Grill in downtown East Lansing to Sparty, the statue of the Spartan warrior near the center of the MSU campus and close to the entrance to the football stadium (the distance the motorcade traveled was about half a mile). There Engler was supposed to stop and speak to the crowd, but the students carrying their signs, banging their drums, and chanting their slogans altered his plans. Brewer offered her recollection of the event: "Governor Engler just got scared. He never even came out of his car. . . . He had his children with him so I guess he felt it wasn't safe for them. . . . We shouted and we had our signs. It was loud."

Many of the spectators lined up along the parade's route were annoyed by the demonstrators who seemed intent on ruining homecoming. Some of them yelled at the student protestors, "You guys are always trying to ruin it for everybody!" They did not understand the need for a dramatic show of discontent. Homecoming is an event intended to celebrate the academic community—a time when people come together despite their differences. Why were these students being so self-serving?

From the perspective of the American Indian students, they had a right to interrupt the parade, and if it meant ruining a piece of homecoming weekend, so be it. Their college careers were in jeopardy. Eliminating the tuition waiver was not simply a gubernatorial or legislative act; it was a violation of a longstanding agreement between American Indians and the state. Both sides made the agreement, and both sides should have to agree to alter it. "Promises made, promises kept," was one of the phrases they chanted during the demonstration and at a rally a few days later as they protested Columbus Day. Engler's stance toward the tuition waiver was one more example of how Indians around the country had been forced to give up their land for virtually nothing in return, because invariably the agreements and treaties would be altered or ignored. The tuition waiver was not something they were going to stand by and watch disappear from the state's list of obligations to its Native population.

As was often the case, students expressed reservations about disrupting homecoming, and a few openly wondered if it was the right thing to do. In spite of the strong turnout, there was significant disagreement over the homecoming strategy that had first been mentioned by Mireles. "There were people within the organization who didn't think it was right," recalled Lula Brewer. The mood of some of the Indian students was that they "didn't want to let our issue be known that way," added

Brewer. She was afraid that the demonstration offended too many people and that they would not understand that NAISO was simply trying to make people aware of their problems with Engler. "I felt like I had to keep explaining that all we are trying to do is get attention to the issue and I think people didn't see it that way. We are not as extreme as we might have looked."

Like Brewer, Paul Dearhouse noted his concerns: "I can see it from both sides. Homecoming is a time for alumni to come to town and have a good time. Enjoy the homecoming parade and watch football. And then we had the protests for Engler." Dearhouse was reluctant to participate when he first learned of the plans to demonstrate during homecoming. However, his mind was quickly changed when he heard that Governor Engler, a former graduate of MSU, was going to be the parade's grand marshal. "I thought it was a bad joke. I was like 'No way.' I knew that a protest was being organized and so I was like 'Yeah, I will be there.' I knew it was going to be kind of hectic, maybe a little bit rougher atmosphere because people would be more hostile towards us for disrupting homecoming. We get dirty looks all the time but it could be a little worse this time." If Engler's being the grand marshal was not enough motivation for Dearhouse, an incident from a previous year was. He recalled how NAISO had participated in the homecoming parade by organizing a group of American Indians dressed in traditional clothes. They rode in the back of a pick-up truck and beat a drum as they passed by onlookers. What still hurts Dearhouse to this day is that as they passed by the spectators many of them placed their hands over their mouths and chanted, "Whoa. . . Whoa. . . Whoa. . . Whoa. . . Whoa. . . Whoa." He found their media-inspired response to be denigrating, and if he and others in NAISO were to ruin their precious homecoming parade, well then so be it. As for this year's parade, Dearhouse concluded, "We had a good turnout and people were sticking together. I thought it was an effective hit on Engler. For him to know personally that he can't come to his alma mater because the things he does downtown don't go unnoticed. It was a message to him that we were going to stand up for what we believe." For Dearhouse, homecoming was important but it was not as important as having college careers ruined over political gamesmanship on Engler's part.

Only six days after the homecoming demonstration, a group of about thirty students and staff, dressed in black, gathered once again around MSU's rock to "commiserate" Columbus Day. One by one the demonstrators spoke about the despair that the day had come to signify in their lives and the lives of other American Indians. Pat Dyer-Deckrow commented, "This is not a celebration day for us. We have always been here and we resent the idea of discovery and the myth of the virgin land." She went on to explain that it was offensive that the indigenous peoples of North America were misnamed "Indians." The proper name for her ancestry is "Anishinabe," meaning the "original people." The Anishinabe of Michigan essentially are comprised of three tribes of American Indians often described as "the Three Fires Confederacy," which are the Ojibwa, Potawotomi, and Odawa. Each tribe has separate cultural and symbolic significance. The Ojibwas are the "spiritual keepers." The Potawotomis are the "fire keepers." And the Odawas are the "traders." What angered so many gathered at the rock was that the history of Michigan Natives remains unknown to most students around the state and yet there is a national day of remembrance for Christopher Columbus's getting lost in North America. Michael Tunte, a senior majoring in landscape architecture, expressed what many were feeling: "The story of Columbus discovering the 'New World' looks all pretty from the outside—then, when you break the surface, there's so much more that people don't want to talk about."[32]

Living Dangerously

The struggle between American Indian students at Michigan State University and the governor of Michigan is a reenactment of a common cultural motif. It is what Kathryn Tijerina and Paul Biemer described as the "dance of Indian higher education," whereby students take "one step forward, two steps back."[33] Higher education opportunities have been improved for American Indians throughout the state as a result of the tuition waiver. "One step forward." However, if Governor Engler has his way, the waiver will be eliminated in the near future and opportunities will once again become dismal. "Two steps back."

The relationship between American Indians and European Americans has been a painful legacy for the indigenous peoples of North America and it has left many of today's Indian youth embittered about their lives and their relationship to the larger society. European Americans tend to turn away from their colonial legacy and seek solace in the myth of manifest destiny and an attitude of "he who rules is right." Recognition of the cultural and physical genocide of North American Indians is a bitter pill that requires a good dose of humility to swallow. It means challenging the ideology of Western superiority and American ingenuity. It means seeing other countries, cultures, and peoples as historically and culturally valued. Swallowing the bitter pill means rejecting a contaminated account of history and facing the kind of dangerous memories held by students such as Brewer, Dearhouse, and Windstorm, the kind of memories that provoke "the ability to hope in the face of continued defeat."[34] And finally, swallowing the bitter pill involves embracing a more critical account of history such as that discussed in the work of Beverly Harrison:

> We need to remember that those who exercise privilege and control in the present also control "official" history. "Official" history suppresses the stories of resistance and dissent against the status quo and presents the past either as the triumph of the deserving or as inevitable. Critical history breaks open the past, in its full complexity, and re-presents that past as bearing a story of human struggle against domination. Even failed resistance bears powerful evidence of human dignity and courage that informs our contemporary vocations. Our remembered forebears and colleagues in struggle energize our lives as we live through the pressures and risks that real resistance to oppression always involves.[35]

Living dangerously, as many of the student activists described throughout this chapter and book have learned, requires opening up one's mind to a new way of thinking about the world of identity, culture, and politics. As Henry Giroux argues, "Dominant cultural traditions once self-confidently secure in the modernist discourse of progress, universalism, and objectivism are now interrogated as ideological beachheads used to police and contain subordinate groups, oppositional discourses, and dissenting social movements."[36] A commitment to living dangerously was revealed in the following comments passionately offered by an American Indian student at MSU: "As far as I'm concerned, I was enslaved in 1776. My family was. . . . I have mixed feelings at times too because as much as we complain, I would hate to be in the Middle East or I'd hate to live any place else. . . . I guess maybe I'd be happier if this were a socialist country, and maybe, you know, that might be the next step. . . . Well in many ways American Indians were communists. . . . But I guess the thing that bothers me the most, and which is probably why I chose to study history, was that we were very self-sufficient economically, yet it was looked down upon like we were inferior, primitive. That was the richest time of our culture because we had all our needs taken care of. . . . It is Western civilization that has pushed us to where we are now. Western thinking does not question technology. Harmony is not the goal. Mastering one's environment is. And I think we should have learned by now that mastery doesn't necessarily make people happier." This student went on to point out the problem with land ownership, and what she sees as one of the greatest shortcomings of modern societies: "A belief that someone can own the land, can possess nature. I think that's one of the biggest cultural conflicts because I think our philosophy is more Eastern. . . . One of the biggest problems that we have is people come along and they buy up all the lake shore. In our culture, nobody has the right to own the land. It was for everyone. Now with progress, they buy it up and then nobody else can enjoy it but their family."

A number of the other students in this study shared their memories as they returned to the issue placed squarely before them by Governor Engler. "It is an old issue in a way because it is a treaty issue and I guess no one has kept their treaties," commented Lula Brewer. She went on to explain that in her opinion Engler is really trying to get at the sovereignty of Indians throughout the state: "The way that I see it is . . . that Engler wants to go after our sovereignty, us having our own government on the reservation, and that is the real issue." Brewer believes that because the casinos have begun to be quite successful and have produced a good deal of revenue, the state wants to have more say in it and claim a larger piece of the pie. To her, it's the same old story: Once American Indians start to make their own way, it is construed as a threat and must be put down. One step forward. Two steps back. "Something else must be taken away—like the tuition waiver. . . . Basically, we can only go so far. That is what I am trying to say."

Paul Dearhouse connected his battle with the governor to the larger struggle of American Indians and the constant defense of their own culture within educational contexts such as university life. He also spoke positively about the critical experiences he had during college that helped him to value his culture: "I know that in college you come of age and stand up more. . . . In college you start thinking more critically about the issues that are affecting your people. Like you start to realize why things are bad in your community. You start to see maybe an historical basis for it. Then you stop to realize and you start to stand up a little bit more. . . . I think that a lot of Native students our age are getting back more to their roots, as far as the language and the culture. . . . My parents and grandparents were forbidden to speak their language. Boarding schools were designed to take the Indian out of the Indian—and assimilate and things like that. . . . Today's generation of Indians is working to reclaim our roots, our heritage." Dearhouse went on to comment that he sees the fight with Engler as part of standing up for Indian culture and identity and that the climate in the mid 1900s up until maybe the 1960s was that Indians should all be assimilated. "So I kind of think that things are looking up for us as far as going back to traditional roots. . . . We need a foundation. Otherwise we are just kind of lost in American society. Half of us have no sense of our tradition. . . . We need to push to reclaim our heritage and our identity."

An interesting point that often came up was the cultural connection between American Indians and students such as Ernesto Mireles of MEChA. Many students noted the strong bond between Indians and Chicanos in particular. As Pat Dyer-Deckrow explained, "In some ways they are half us. . . . The border of Mexico has been changed by the United States. In fact, before there was ever a U.S. government, there were the aboriginal people of this continent—Mexicans and Indians. I guess that's probably why we are connected on so many of these issues. . . . The border was imposed on us and imposed on them." Paul Dearhouse also spoke of these connections: "It seems that as long as I have been here, we [American Indian students] have always done things with Chicano students. Like done stuff together, supported each other. Whatever the issue, we have always been there for one another. I guess we are like one and the same people. . . . We are indigenous peoples. Chicano students have their roots in Mexico, and the Spanish and the conquistadors came over and took over their land. We had the English to deal with. And in the north, the French came and took the land. In that respect, we are like the same people just from different regions."

The points made by Dyer-Deckrow and Dearhouse in part explain why so many American Indian and Chicano activists reject holidays such as the Fourth of July and Columbus Day. As Dyer-Deckrow explained, "It is not a day of independence for us. . . . Who's freedom is it anyway? It is not ours." Many European Americans find remarks such as the ones offered by Dyer-Deckrow and other American Indians and Chicanos to be offensive. They might ask people who make comments such as these why they stay in this country if it is so oppressive. More than a few might even resort to that standard American logic of "If you don't love it, then you can leave it." But such thinking fails to empathize with the pain and suffering of non-European Americans, many of whom have ancestral roots dating back long before the arrival of the earliest European settlers. Their dangerous memories are threatening to Whites in this country, many of whom seem unwilling to examine the cultural complexity of minority identities and the passion they bring to their cause.

Through this lack of empathy and understanding, racism and social inequality get recycled from generation to generation. And thus we relive many of the cultural wars of the past as the quest for freedom marches into the next century.

Recently, a judge in California rejected a charge of racial discrimination filed by a group of African American employees. In rendering his decision, the judge explained that the employees should keep in mind the real suffering that "our forefathers" experienced and the great courage they exhibited as they made their way as pioneers across this great continent. A little bit of suffering such as racial discrimination is good for the soul or so it seems. One of the plaintiffs reminded the judge that she was an African American and that her forefathers most likely had not crossed the plains in covered wagons but instead had likely been dragged to this country with guns pointed at their heads and shackles attached to their feet. Why was the history that was so vivid to these African American employees so distant from this judge's memory?

Cultural Matters

As a result of the unique cultural experiences of American Indians and the surrounding cultural context that is so heavily Eurocentric, students must in effect exist simultaneously in two separate worlds. This reality parallels the notion of "double-consciousness" first pointed out in the work of W. E. B. Du Bois when he discussed the lives of Blacks in the United States: "The Negro is a sort of seventh son, born with a veil, and gifted with second-sight in this American world, —a world which yields him no true self-consciousness, but only lets him see himself through the revelation of the other world. It is a peculiar sensation, this double-consciousness, this sense of always looking at one's self through the eyes of others, of measuring one's soul by the tape of a world that looks on in amused contempt and pity."[37] A student highlighted the sense of "double-consciousness" discussed by Du Bois when he related his experience as an American Indian in a predominantly White university: "I sort of feel like you lead two separate lives. I try to be involved with people who are Native as much as I can and a lot of my socializing goes on with fellow Natives. But at the same time, I have this whole other life that I have to lead within the university. . . . So it is sort of like I have a time when I can attend pow-wows and socialize with Natives and I have a life with Anglos. So it is kind of like leading a double life."

Often students try to avoid a double life by rejecting their American

Indian identity altogether. Chad Waucaush talked about his experience as a minority aide working in the residence halls. Part of his job involved contacting other American Indian students and helping them to establish social networks within organizations such as NAISO. What upset Waucaush was the number of Native students he met who wanted to have little to do with NAISO and the American Indian community. "In my work as a minority aide I have to go out and talk to other Indian students. I have met a lot of them who didn't want to associate with other Indians, even if they came from an Indian background. . . . I could tell in meeting them that they didn't really want anything to do with me and so I started questioning why did they have this shame? I know a lot of people, depending on how they were raised, are ashamed to be Indian. They want to keep it hidden. 'Don't tell anybody.' So when they get to college they don't want to be recognized as a minority or as an Indian." Thus some American Indian students go off to college and attempt to pass as Anglos and in effect try to suppress whatever sense of consciousness they have as Indians. The experiences of these students is reminiscent of those described by gay students, who often consider staying closeted as a way to avoid persecution as members of a group deemed "contemptuous and pitiful." This attitude conveyed by American Indians angers students such as Waucaush and others in NAISO who work to establish a sense of pride among Indian students: "They pass as Anglos except when it comes to admissions and stuff like that. Except for when it is beneficial. That may be crude to say but that is what I have experienced."

Although cultural differences certainly were prevalent among the students, there were also connective cultural threads running through the lives of the majority of the American Indian students. One recurring theme related to the students' attitudes toward campus demonstrations and the idea of activism. As was mentioned earlier, many of the students had mixed feelings about taking issue with Governor Engler and his position on the tuition waiver. There was a tendency for students to express doubts about any actions that might disrupt social harmony, even if inaction meant suffering on their part. A student offered an explanation for this tendency: "Because they tend to be a quiet people seeking harmony over conflict, Native Americans often suffer because of their inability or desire to raise a public ruckus over mistreatment. . . . For the most part, Natives don't say a lot anyway. They are not as vocal a minority as some other minorities." This student went on to conclude that when Indians do go so far as to protest about an issue, then it must be something that is quite compelling.

Stacey Tadgerson, a specialist at the Native American Institute at MSU and a former recipient of the tuition waiver, also addressed the quiet disposition that characterizes some American Indians and which may contribute to abuses by legislative or governmental actions. Such a disposition makes student involvement in direct action difficult to achieve at times: "I think that for some people it [demonstrating on campus] made them a little bit self-conscious. They weren't sure if they should bring attention to themselves. . . . It was kind of like they were scared of losing it [the tuition waiver] and they thought if they brought a lot of attention to this issue then maybe it would be taken away. . . . Just let things happen as they are going to happen." Tadgerson expressed fear that a snowball effect may already be gaining momentum around the country and that the tuition waiver program was only one more example of conservative policy-making designed to reverse whatever minor gains underrepresented peoples have attained. She felt it was important to challenge American Indian students to hold the governor and other legislators accountable. "They are representing you. It's just getting that message across so that Natives understand their individual rights as well as their tribal rights."

The quiet and respectful quality of many American Indians is played out during NAISO meetings where twenty to thirty students typically gather around a large table but only a few speak. Many sit quietly by and say nothing until someone specifically asks for their opinion or their vote on an important matter that the group must decide. One student explained that he attended meetings for over a year before he ever said a word. But other students are more outspoken and tend to assume leadership roles within NAISO. They have to be careful, though, because NAISO members often look on such behavior with suspicion. The group must come first and leaders have to be watched carefully to make sure they reflect the proper values.

A Story without End

Perhaps it was fortunate for NAISO that a few outspoken students such as Lula Brewer and Hanna Windstorm were around, for they acted as catalysts motivating others to take democracy into the streets and publicly protest the governor's actions. In many ways, the attitude among students who seemed willing to let the chips fall where they may reflected a kind of learned helplessness attributable to years of exploitation. There was much that these students had learned through the history of

North American Indians, and so it is hardly surprising that some might fail to see the point of resisting the action of legislative officials. There were so many examples of pain and suffering to which they could turn, all of which served to deflate one's willingness to fight against a large and powerful system like a state or federal bureaucracy.

When the great Creek leader Red Eagle was forced to surrender to General Andrew Jackson and essentially end Native involvement in the French-American War, the stage was set for the forced removal of Natives from their lands and decades of mistreatment through legislative acts such as that which the students at Michigan State faced. Gloria Jahoda discussed the significance of the 1814 meeting between Red Eagle and Jackson:

> With that handshake, the two principal architects of the ultimate fate of the American Indian had sealed a bargain. Red Eagle's leadership in war had angered America. It had also convinced Andrew Jackson that America's frontiers would always be frontiers while there were Indians to annoy the settlers. The Indians must go. They couldn't be exterminated wholesale because of world opinion. But they could be uprooted and packed off to some remote corner of the country where they wouldn't be in the way. The haven would belong to them, they would be told in the traditional language of American Indian treaties, "as long as the green grass grows and the water flows," provided they began hiking en masse with a military escort to get there. At the Horseshoe Bend of the Tallapoosa River in Alabama, Andrew Jackson silently pledged himself to the policy of Indian Removal which in his presidency was to become law. It would be a simple law: any Indian who remained on his ancestral lands affirming his Indian identity would be a criminal. It didn't matter that the Great Plains already had Indian inhabitants who could hardly be expected to welcome red refugees. . . . Oklahoma was Indian destiny before it graced a single map. Not an Indian alive, except those who already inhabited it, considered it Holy Ground. East of the Mississippi, Ecunchate was lost land, a lost dream, and the road that led out of it forever became known as the Trail of Tears.[38]

While the Trail of Tears came to symbolize the unwavering force of governmental policies enacted against American Indians, events taking place over a century and a half later at places such as Alcatraz Island, the Cornwall Bridge in northern New York, and Wounded Knee served as catalysts for forging Indian resistance and sealed their historical place within the broadening Civil Rights Movement of the 1960s. Thirty years later, the embers of the early Indian protest movement of the sixties lived on through the actions of Hanna Windstorm, Lula Brewer, and Chad Waucaush as they fought for their rightful place within a democratic, multicultural society.

In February of 1994, American Indian students at Michigan State University traveled a much shorter route than the Trail of Tears as they made their way from the banks of the Red Cedar River and the rock at the center of campus to the main administration building and then the Student Union, where they listened to the empowering and impassioned words of friends and allies. Chad Waucaush reflected on the culmination of the march that brought tears to his eyes and the eyes of other American Indians present. As Waucaush explained, the highlight was that the students expressed their feelings: We each spoke individually. A lot of students got up there and just kind of poured their hearts out and just talked about how they felt. . . . I started realizing how much of an impact you can have. How much your opinion can mean to other people. I learned that if you step out with your opinion, your view, you just might make someone stop and think. . . . I realized the influence you can have by the way you live your life. Activism is a part of me. . . . Living by example because that is the best way people learn and so you can change a lot." Waucaush had an epiphany as he listened to other students and community members speak about their experiences. He could be an activist and speak out about issues concerning his people. Perhaps he was meant to play a leadership role after all.

Two years later, Waucaush and other Native students wondered whether all the demonstrations, all the marches, all the speeches had done any good. Engler had not won as of yet. But neither had they, for it seemed as though the tuition waiver could vanish any day. What would the next group of American Indian students at MSU have to endure? In any case, Waucaush, Brewer, and Windstorm felt glad that they had invested in the struggle and they could look back fondly and say that at least they tried.

Lula Brewer believed the campus demonstrations had an impact because she heard students around campus talking about the concerns of American Indian students. In her mind, they had succeeded in raising student awareness and understanding of the tuition waiver and its history. Brewer also had good feelings about MSU. Provost Lou Anna Simon had told the students that regardless of whether the state reimburses the university for tuition expenses, the university was committed to creating opportunities for American Indian students and that it would find a way to provide the financial support. Brewer believed that Provost Simon saw through the governor's attack on the waiver: "They know that this is a political game that Engler is playing. They know that he is just trying to use us in this little game."

As for plans for future demonstrations, American Indian students at Michigan State were waiting to figure out what strategy Governor Engler would employ next in his effort to save the $3,000,000 that the program costs annually. Many students believed he would find a way to take the money from gaming revenues. This strategy angers tribal leaders, who counter that they have already paid the state nearly $40,000,000 in casino taxes between March of 1994 and December 31, 1995. Other students wondered if the governor would simply cut individual college and university budgets by the cost of the waiver program, and thus accomplish his goal by circumvention.

Thus, for most Indian students at Michigan State University the issue remained unresolved and they learned to live with the daily threat that their tuition might not be covered and they might have to leave school or amass significant debt. As Paul Dearhouse stated, "You hear all these kinds of things over and over again. Like over the last couple of years. And you just get tired of hearing it. Like 'Damn man.' Because it's like he is doing this on a daily basis. We are still students trying to keep our heads afloat, you know. It's hard to keep fighting for it. For myself, I just have to get some momentum to do it and so I need to take a break for a while. Like right now I'm just chillin' out and not involved with a lot of things. . . . It's a draining process and I just got tired of feeling for it. You know what I mean? It's like, damn, you get tired of hearing about it."

Although many students like Dearhouse felt the frustrations of the ongoing struggle to stay in school, others such as Brewer remained in a state of alert awaiting the next battle. "No one feels too relieved because at any point the state could do it again. They could take away the waiver." Plans for future demonstrations have been put on hold, but when the time comes, Brewer, like the relentless Atlantic tide that carried Europeans to her shore, most assuredly will rise again. With visible emotion in her eyes, Brewer resolutely proclaims, "I'm glad we still have our signs": "Promises made, promises kept."

chapter SIX

"WE'RE HERE. WE'RE QUEER.

GET USED TO IT."

Gay Liberation at Penn State

In March of 1993, a group of over a hundred students from Pennsylvania State University traveled to Washington, D.C., to join a march for lesbian, gay, and bisexual equal rights and liberation. They represented only a fraction of what amounted to somewhere in the neighborhood of two hundred thousand demonstrators. For many of the Penn State students, the trip was the culmination of several years of political and cultural work aimed at improving the campus climate for lesbian, gay, and bisexual people. These were the students who organized campus rallies, coming-out celebrations, teach-ins, and a variety of political and educational activities as part of their contribution to gay liberation. Several of them played major roles in what was perhaps the key struggle for equal rights when they challenged the administration to add a sexual orientation clause to its official statement of nondiscrimination. The effort these students put into creating campus change was draining at times, and a trip to Washington and a chance to participate in a national day of celebration was a much needed reprieve.[1]

The day was still young as the Penn State delegation relaxed on the mall across from the White House and awaited their turn to join the march. The students reflected on the positive changes they had achieved and the long struggle that lay before them. Timothy Jones,[2] a senior, talked about the hard work and energy he had given to winning the approval for the sexual orientation clause. He recalled the many meetings with members of the board of trustees and other key officials. The most draining thing for Jones had been all the time spent educating misinformed members of the academic community about "the gay life-style," as straights frequently described it. Those were painful words to Timothy. His identity as a gay man was not simply a matter of a choice of lifestyle. Being gay was a complex and central facet of his identity. "Why was it so difficult for them to understand that?"

Samuel Bennett, a junior, shared Timothy's frustrations. He too had been heavily involved in student activism as a means to transform the campus climate. He played a key role in the efforts to get the sexual orientation clause passed and more recently helped to form a new student organization committed to fighting discrimination within the Penn State ROTC program. With the passage of the clause, Samuel and others felt that the program was in violation because of its official stance toward "homosexual" students. He had planned a number of resistance activities, including an educational campaign to make people aware of ROTC's discriminatory practices. One of his ideas was the development of a poster encouraging Penn State students to violate campus policies—"just like ROTC." His recommendations on the banner included the following: ride bikes on the sidewalks, keep library books, pay someone to take your exams, smoke in your classes, drink beer in front of Old Main, have sex on the golf course, and plagiarize in papers. Although Samuel believed wholeheartedly in challenging ROTC, he also recognized that he was up against a powerful organization whose governmental connections made his provocative activities that much more serious. There was a touch of irony in Samuel's commitment, in that he had been raised in a military family and his dad was a high-ranking officer. Thus, for Samuel, the fight with ROTC was personal in many ways: "This issue is something that I felt I had to take on. It had to be addressed. I really feel that I am effective because of my family's background in the military. I feel that what I'm doing is the right thing."

The Penn State delegation was one of hundreds from their state scattered within a large section of the mall lawn. The march was organized by states, and Pennsylvania was not scheduled to join the procession until later in the day. Consequently, the students from Penn State had time to kill, and the sunny March day made for a warm and peaceful break from the hustle and bustle of a typical weekend spent catching up on school work.

Sitting on the grassy lawn, several students relaxed hand in hand. Some leaned their heads on the shoulders of the persons next to them, while others took turns rubbing one another's backs. A few couples shared a kiss from time to time, while new romances blossomed like the cherry trees they had passed along the Potomac. For some, it was the first time they had displayed affection in public. No wonder so many of the Penn State contingent described their day as empowering.

As the students waited their turn, many shared their thoughts, their emotions. The students sensed the contribution they were about to make to what many perceived as a momentous occasion. For Samuel, the march was a "moment in history" of which he could be a part. A second student offered a similar view but worried about the "conservative backlash" he believed the march would generate. The entire event was overwhelming for a third student: "It's almost beyond words. I have never seen this many queer people at one place in all my life. I just don't know what to say. When we came out of the subway it was like every single person was lesbian, gay, or bisexual. People were even cheering."

With his new boyfriend resting on the grass in front of him, Samuel took on a glow seldom seen back in State College. From time to time, his partner leaned back against Samuel's chest as Samuel draped his arms around him, as if holding on to time itself. The smiles they cast expressed their joy. "It's like a fantasy world where you don't have to be concerned about holding hands. It's like what the world should be like," commented Samuel. And his partner added, "I can be myself for a while. I can be who I am." Another student, who essentially was in the closet back at school, started to talk but then paused for a few seconds. He looked at the vastness of the crowd that surrounded him, and then simply said, "I feel proud here."

The atmosphere on the mall lawn was a stark contrast to earlier that same day when the students had gathered in front of the HUB (the student center) at Penn State for the trip to Washington. A defensive posture was the norm and they were careful about expressing open affection. Although Penn State was a great improvement from their high school days of near complete isolation and fear, the campus nonetheless had a conservative quality to it that made most gay students think twice about coming out. Once on the bus, however, students began to clasp hands and embrace one another. Kisses shared by a few couples might have given a casual observer the impression that this was a typical college field trip. The sense of relief revealed by their physical expressions was powerful.

The battle for gay liberation had been waged for years, and even the conservative campus of Penn State University had not been immune to student stirrings. The passengers on the bus knew the history of how lesbian, gay, and bisexual students had fought for acceptance within the university and the surrounding community of State College. There had been a long struggle simply to win approval for a gay student organization. And then came the fight to add the sexual orientation clause. For them it was difficult to imagine why others failed to see the need to protect the rights of lesbian, gay, and bisexual people. How could someone argue that such rights were "special rights" for gays? That kind of logic angered students like Samuel Bennett and Timothy Jones. They just wanted the same rights and protections enjoyed by others. They imagined walking out of a campus movie holding hands with their lovers without fear of getting harassed or beaten up. They dreamt of raising personal experiences in classes, like heterosexual students often did, without other students or the professor snickering. They envisioned going to college parties without fear for their lives. And they wondered what it would be like to sit on the HUB lawn on that first warm spring day and embrace like so many other Penn State lovers did. Why could they not share in these precious college experiences?

To achieve the equal rights they dreamt of having, many of the lesbian, gay, and bisexual students from Penn State knew they had to sacrifice. They had to work to transform the images people held of gay lives. This was the challenge they faced. From their perspective, participation in the march on Washington was one more step in the larger struggle to change people's views. Being out and proud, which is what the march symbolized to many, was part of an empowerment agenda that had become central to the movement at the university. Student leaders had given up on the quiet, less offensive strategies of the past that they believed had achieved limited success. Instead, a group of student leaders from the Lesbian, Gay, and Bisexual Student Alliance (LGBSA) had begun to embrace queer politics and were inspired to follow in the footsteps of their late 1980s predecessors, Queer Nation and ACT UP. Their efforts, however, remained forever linked to the legacy of an earlier generation when gay liberation had its first success at the university.

Homophiles of Penn State

Pennsylvania State University has a history of strained relationships with its lesbian, gay, and bisexual students. In 1972 Joseph Acanfora was removed from his student teaching assignment at Park Forest Junior High School in State College, Pennsylvania.[3] At the time it was not clear to Acanfora as to whether the university or the State College Area School District had made the decision. What was clear, however, was the motivation behind his removal: his involvement in the campus group Homophiles of Penn State (HOPS). Also clear was the fact that the university had found it necessary to inform the Park Forest school that Acanfora was a member of HOPS.[4] To understand the significance of Acanfora's relationship to HOPS, one must step back to one year earlier when the organization began its struggle for official recognition as a student group.

On April 21, 1971, a request from HOPS for a student charter was approved by Penn State's Undergraduate Student Government (USG) only to be suspended three weeks later by then acting vice president for student affairs Raymond Murphy. In a letter addressed to HOPS Vice President Diane Whitney, Murphy explained: "This is to notify you that the facilities of the University will not be available to your organization until such time as there has been a complete review of the legality of this organization by University Legal Counsel. Beyond legal matters, there may also be a question of educational policy with respect to this charter. At the time that a review has been made you will be notified of a final decision with respect to this matter." Some four months later, Murphy announced that the student charter for HOPS was denied on the grounds that it posed a threat to the educational policies of the university. Once again, in a letter addressed to HOPS, Murphy elaborated the university's position: "We are advised that based upon sound psychological and psychiatric opinion, the chartering of your organization would create a substantial conflict with the counseling and psychiatric services the University provides to its students and that such conflict would be harmful to the best interests of the students of the University."

After months of legal preparations, on February 11, 1972, HOPS filed a lawsuit against the university alleging that their First (right to free speech) and Fourteenth (right to equal protection) amendment rights had been violated. A student plaintiff named in the suit was one Joseph Acanfora.[5] Three days later, Acanfora was removed from his student teaching assignment.

Acanfora sought an injunction from Centre County Court Judge R. Paul Campbell, and on February 22 he was reinstated in his student teaching assignment at Park Forest Junior High. Following a very successful student teaching experience in which the vast majority of students rated his overall performance as "good" or "excellent," he faced another barrier: The university decided to hold a hearing as to whether or not Acanfora should get his Pennsylvania Teacher's Certificate. Traditionally, such hearings are held only when there is cause to deliberate on the moral character of a student. And typically, cause involves some kind of legal violation such as a student's being arrested for falsifying a driver's license (a common practice for students under twenty-one who seek to be served in local bars). Of course, in Acanfora's case, there was no cause except that he identified himself as a "homosexual." Among the questions he faced at the meeting of the six-member University Teacher Certification Council chaired by the dean of the college of education, Abram W. VanderMeer, were the following: "What homosexual acts do you prefer to engage in or are you willing to engage in?" and "Do you look for other males with which to have sex?" As Acanfora explained, "I [couldn't] believe they were serious. It was so insane. . . . You just can't put a person in a box and label it 'homosexual'. . . . Homosexuals are people, and you have to remember that."[6]

The council was split in its decision, with three supportive of Acanfora and three opposed. This meant that the case would be passed on to the state education secretary, John C. Pittenger, who ultimately approved the certification, stating, "There is no legal barrier to granting a certificate to Mr. Acanfora since he has not been convicted of any criminal violation."[7]

The fact that the University Teacher Certification Council was serious is what is so frightening about the whole Acanfora and HOPS episodes and what makes the efforts of contemporary lesbian, gay, and bisexual student activists at Penn State so important. Acanfora, who would face additional problems when hired as a teacher in the state of Maryland, eventually appeared on the CBS show "60 Minutes," where the problems he faced as a gay teacher were brought to the nation's attention. And HOPS, after an out-of-court settlement, received its charter as a student group and paved the way for the present-day Lesbian, Gay, and Bisexual Student Alliance.

But the Acanfora and HOPS episodes did not end discrimination and homophobia faced by students at the university, as separate studies conducted during the late 1980s and early 1990s revealed. In 1988 the Campus Environment Team examined acts of intolerance that had occurred during the spring semester 1988. In all, thirty acts of intolerance were reported with 70 percent directed against gay men or lesbians. In 1990, professor Anthony D'Augelli conducted a survey of 131 gay men, lesbians, and bisexuals and found that 73 percent had been verbally insulted because of their sexual orientation; 31 percent had been threatened with bodily injury, with actual physical violence occurring in at least fourteen cases. A 1991 committee on gay and lesbian concerns chaired by professor William Tierney took the preceding findings into account when they recommended to the university's president that a sexual orientation clause be added to the university's statement of nondiscrimination. Adding the clause was seen by the committee as a necessary step toward achieving equal rights and full protection for lesbian, gay, and bisexual students, faculty, and staff.

Passage of the Sexual Orientation Clause

In 1991, Penn State's new president, Joab Thomas, inherited the controversy over the sexual orientation clause from his predecessor, the recently retired Bryce Jordan. As part of their effort to influence campus politics, students from LGBSA held teach-ins (often referred to as "straight talks"), candlelight vigils, demonstrations, marches, and coming-out rallies. Their goal was to raise the consciousness of the campus community by making their lives and struggles known to all. Although less prominent in their tactics, faculty and staff also played key roles, often organizing behind the scenes and offering their support and guidance to students.

In the process of building liberal and progressive support, gay activists also solidified the opposition; conservatives in the community were antagonized by what they saw as the dominance of gay issues at campus events and discussions. At many of the rallies, conservative students, led by religious organizations such as the Alliance for Christian Fellowship and Intervarsity Christian Fellowship, offered counterdemonstrations that often were equal or greater in student turnout. Clearly, the campus was divided on the issue. Divisiveness was most apparent by the many letters to the editor published on an almost daily basis in the school's student-run newspaper, the *Daily Collegian*. Gay students were described as "sick" or "perverted" by conservative students, who also complained that gays were corrupting the American family and that the country's demise was caused by gays and other liberals who were undermining traditional values. Religious students often resorted to biblical passages and described lesbian, gay, and bisexual students as "sinners" whose behavior was "abominable in the eyes of God." A frequently used line was "Love the sinner, but hate the sin." Such comments incensed gay students and allies, who responded with their own letters pointing out that being gay was about much more than simply sleeping with someone of the same sex. A liberal campus ministry supported lesbian, gay, and bisexual students by posting a pamphlet on its bulletin board that read: "Everything that Christ had to say about homosexuality." Upon opening the brochure one discovered a blank page, which was intended to reflect the teachings of Christ on the subject. As one minister affiliated with this ministry explained, "Why is there so much fuss about an issue that had little relevance to Christ?" The same minister practically was run out of town when she appeared at a local gay pride rally carrying the following sign: "If Christ returned today she would be a bisexual woman of color."

In an effort to appease campus liberals, who supported adding a sexual orientation clause, and conservatives, led by several members of the board of trustees who opposed specific mention of "sexual orientation" in any official university document, President Thomas drafted the following nondiscrimination statement for approval by the faculty senate (the proposed amendment is in italics):

> The Pennsylvania State University, in compliance with federal and state laws, is committed to the policy that all persons shall have equal access to programs, admission, and employment without regard to race, religion, sex, national origin, handicap, age, or status as a disabled or Vietnam era veteran. *In addition, the Pennsylvania State University will take appropriate measures to protect all of its students and all of its employees from harassment, abuse, or assault; and bases all educational and employment decisions on an individual's abilities and qualifications without reference to personal characteristics that are not related to academic ability or job performance.*

In seeking guidance from the faculty, President Thomas hoped to achieve greater support before passing on the recommendation to the board of trustees, which, in the end, had to approve any changes to the official policy.

But the faculty were less than thrilled with Thomas's clever wording, which to them was designed to avoid the inclusion of "sexual orientation" and therefore compromised its intent. Consequently, the faculty found it insufficient for protecting members of the gay community. They called for the addition of "sexual orientation" as a protected class equivalent to other classes already mentioned within the nondiscrimination policy. The majority felt that anything less than the inclusion of the phrase "sexual orientation" was short of the university's professed commitment to diversity. They also made it clear that being added as a protected category in a statement of nondiscrimination was not the same as being included in affirmative action policies: Rights to equal protection are not the same as being identified as a group which historically has been denied equal employment or educational opportunity.

On February 7, 1991, the Special University Faculty Senate Committee held public hearings to solicit feedback on the president's addition as well as their own recommendation to add the phrase "sexual orientation" to the statement. Extended testimony was offered by many within the campus community. Most favored the addition of the phrase "sexual orientation." The University Student Advisory Board, representing some twenty student organizations including the Association of Residence Halls, the Black Caucus, the Graduate Student Association, and the Interfraternity Council, came out in support of the faculty senate's version. Other groups such as the Commission for Women and the Lesbian, Gay, and Bisexual Student Alliance also voiced their support. Faculty members spoke on behalf of adding "sexual orientation" and several gave impassioned testimony of evidence of discrimination that they either had experienced or had witnessed at the university.

Despite support for the clause, there was an equally impassioned (though not as large) oppositional voice. As expected, the Intervarsity Christian Fellowship offered its rationale for not supporting the addition of "sexual orientation."

> It may surprise some people to learn that God does not accept all kinds of activities, either in this life or the next. He separates himself from those who do not conform to his will as expressed in his holy word. Some people think it doesn't matter what one believes, or does—that tolerance and acceptance is a virtue in and of itself. However, this is not what the scriptures teach. 'Do you know that the wicked will not inherit the kingdom of God? Do not be deceived: Neither the sexually immoral nor idolaters nor adulterers nor male prostitutes nor homosexual offenders nor thieves nor the greedy nor drunkard nor slanderers nor swindlers will inherit the kingdom of God.'

But another Christian perspective was offered by the Reverend Ann Ard of United Campus Ministry, an organization serving Penn State students that traditionally affiliated with seven liberal to moderate denominations including the local Quaker and Mennonite churches, the United Church of Christ, and the Church of the Brethren. She spoke to the different interpretations of scripture among Christians:

> The disagreement you may hear today between people representing Christian groups is based on differing interpretations of the Bible and Christian teaching. Our various doctrinal and theological disagreements ought not to influence the decision-making process at a public university. It is not the responsibility of the university to make decisions

based on the religious feelings of some in the community. It is the responsibility of the university to protect the rights of members of its community, whether or not some might be offended by that protection. . . . I urge you to recommend to the President the inclusion of the words 'sexual orientation' in the University's policy. It is the courageous and right thing to do.

Ard brought a voice of reason to the religious differences that had moved to the forefront of the controversy surrounding lesbian, gay, and bisexual rights. Her testimony served as a reminder not only of the diversity within the Penn State community but of the diversity within the Christian community as well.

Additional testimony was heard in the voice of Lori Ginzberg, an assistant professor of history and women's studies, who spoke on her own behalf. She alluded to comparisons between being Jewish and being gay and how historically both groups had faced widespread oppression, with the most obvious example being the reign of Nazi Germany and the Holocaust:

There are many lessons which Jews and gay men and lesbians have learned from the Holocaust, not least of which is the urgency of defending the liberties of peoples other than one's own. These lessons relate directly to the question of including the words "sexual orientation" in Penn State's nondiscrimination policy. What we have learned, Jews and gay folks, is that our best defense against bigotry is visibility, our greatest hope for change is neither assimilation nor silence, but identifying ourselves as a people.

Ginzberg not only reminded those in attendance that silence and invisibility are indeed dangerous; she also provided some insight into why identity politics may be something far more significant than simply an effort to foster "self-esteem," as critics such as Dinesh D'Souza and Arthur Schlesinger sarcastically suggest.

Following the public hearing of February 7, the faculty senate passed a motion to recommend that President Thomas include "sexual orientation" in the statement of nondiscrimination. There was still, however, one more hurdle to overcome: Getting the conservative board of trustees to pass the measure would be difficult. Eventually, this too was accomplished, as a group of students from LGBSA threatened a takeover of the president's office. In a secret meeting with a key member of the board, several students detailed their plan of action in the event that the board were to fail to approve the rewritten Thomas amendment. The student sit-in would be carried out with one intent: to generate media attention and bring embarrassment to the university officials involved in rejecting equal protection for lesbian, gay, and bisexual people. In a university as image conscious as Penn State, a student takeover was not the kind of publicity deemed desirable. After all, the school was still recovering from a takeover at the hands of African American students who in the spring of 1989 commandeered the university's communications center as part of their effort to boost Penn State's commitment to students of color. The board of trustees certainly did not want that kind of debacle on their hands again. With the possibility of an intense student demonstration hanging over their heads, the board voted to add the sexual orientation clause to the university's statement of nondiscrimination. The passage of the clause was seen as a giant step toward creating an affirmative campus climate for members of the Penn State lesbian, gay, and bisexual community.

The statement from professor Ginzberg provided important insight about the need for lesbian, gay, and bisexual people to be visible and to build upon a collective sense of identity. This was one of the primary objectives of LGBSA, which continued its activism in the aftermath of the passage of the clause.

Visibility

In *Sister Outsider* Audre Lorde wrote, "I have come to believe over and over again that what is most important to me must be spoken, made verbal and shared, even at the risk of having it bruised or misunderstood."[8] For many gay college students, coming out is a way of giving voice to a silenced life. Coming out is a way of sharing something that because of its intense social scrutiny becomes a defining aspect of one's identity.[9]

Coming out is a process that involves disclosing one's sexual orientation. The act of coming out most often begins with self-acknowledgment and typically expands to various social networks as individuals share understandings of their sexual identity with others through a process described as "self-disclosure." Furthermore, because lesbians, gays, and bisexuals exist in a social world where the vast majority of people assume others to be heterosexual, coming out is a never-ending process; no matter how many people know about one's sexual identity, there will be others over time to whom that individual will have to come out.

For many college students, coming out is more than an individual act of identifying with one's same-sex attractions. Frequently, there is a communal aspect to the process, in that a sense of commitment to a larger group becomes an important part of the coming-out experience. As one student at Penn State explained, "When I first started to come out I put a lot of energy into it; I expected it all to be so difficult. I felt like I committed myself to much more of a struggle for personal validation and it seemed like it came too easy. 'OK, I'm out. No big deal.' I set myself up for this long struggle that didn't happen and my only recourse was to move it from a personal level to a political level. If I could do a greater good by serving the whole community, that would be great. I felt like I had already done it for myself." And a second student added, "When I was an undergraduate, which was before I was out and proud and fighting for my rights, I might have gone to a gay pride rally but only to watch or offer support. But now, instead of merely supporting other advocates, I have become one myself. I have become more of a fighter for my own rights as opposed to a supporter of others fighting for my rights. I do that for myself and for the community."

In addition to highlighting a group sense of gay identity, the preceding students raise two other points. First, coming out is a process of becoming visible, and as such a process it necessarily challenges the norms of heterosexuality and in this sense may be seen as a contribution to creating cultural change. Second, coming out, for some students, leads to increased involvement in political actions related to gay liberation, as the students at Penn State demonstrate. Thus visibility has become the defining issue of gay students at Penn State and serves as a political challenge to a rather conservative campus and local community. In what follows, queer identity as an expression of visibility is discussed in light of what may be termed the "politics of silencing"—the combination of heterosexism and homophobia, which together have the effect of silencing gay lives.

In Search of a Queer Identity

It was a cold autumn day when a large group of students gathered on the steps of Schwab Auditorium as part of a local rally to celebrate National Coming Out Day. Another two hundred students stood on the nearby sidewalk; they were there to offer support as their friends and peers delivered coming-out speeches. Those whose apprehension about taking that giant step into the public's view remained strong observed from the background. Colin Hoffman, a junior studying engineering, was one student reluctant to come out in front of so many people. Only recently, he had admitted to himself that he was bisexual and he certainly was not ready yet to face a large audience and discuss something that brought out such deep feelings. Later, Colin talked about the rally: "It was so exciting just to be in the crowd. The whole rally was very emotional, even just standing there watching." On this chilly day in 1992, Colin was content to be a silent voice, listening and offering support to others as they talked about what it was like to be queer and proud.

Queer identity connotes a sense of pride and openness about one's same-sex desires as well as a degree of hostility toward heterosexism. Among other characteristics, being queer involves an attitude about one's sexual identity. This attitude was expressed by Colin Hoffman some nine months after observing National Coming Out Day: "Sometimes I feel like being very out and telling people who have a problem with it to piss off!" Colin went on to explain the frustrations he has endured in his struggle to make sense of his same-sex attractions: "I say I'm bisexual, but others in the gay community would be upset. They expect everybody to define themselves as either straight or gay, but things aren't so black and white." He described an incident that left him feeling nervous about being visible but also helped him to see that he had to make a firm decision soon. He was visiting in the student union with a friend from high school when two students from LGBSA walked past. "They looked very gay and wore pink triangles on their T-shirts. They walked by us and said 'Hi Colin' and stopped to talk to me about signs up in the LGBSA office. I just kind of sat there wondering, 'What does my friend think?' I don't think I'm ready for that kind of scene yet." A few months later, however, Colin had become quite open about his sexual orientation and was getting involved in queer politics. In fact, he had been nominated for a position as an officer in LGBSA and seriously considered accepting the challenge.

In addition to Colin, other students also held views about what it meant to be queer. As one student explained, "To be queer is to be open about your sexual orientation. It means not being ashamed in any way." A second student argued that "to be queer means to be political" (in the sense of engaging in gay politics). Still others use the word *queer* rather loosely as a unifying term for all lesbian, gay, and bisexual people regardless of whether those individuals identify as queer or not. Samuel Bennett commented, "I use the term *queer* to make people aware that I'm not excluding bisexuals and lesbians. It's not even in vogue yet among some queers. It's more of an activist, assertive term. It connotes pride in being a homosexual or bisexual. *Gay* possibly used to imply the same thing. It's adopting a term that was used in a negative way and conveying a different message, a message of pride, happiness, celebration."

Multiple interpretations of queer identity exist, and by the early 1990s it had become a contentious term within the gay community. Frank Browning described queer as a form of empowerment in which lesbian, gay, and bisexual people offer a political and cultural statement by making their presence felt in public settings. He discussed activities such as "mall actions": "Gay men and lesbians, usually in a three-to-one male-to-female ratio, mount 'queer visibility' expeditions, walking hand in hand into stores, shopping a lot, buying a little, and engaging in exaggerated mimicry of the straights who surround them. Occasionally, there is a kiss-in. The look is punk, drag, leather, bleached hair, dyed hair, earrings, ear cuffs, nipple rings, nose pins, scarves, streamers, and balloons."[10] Browning viewed queerness as involving a degree of rage toward heterosexism that often was manifested through organized political activities.

Alexander Doty offered a less confined conception of queerness when he argued that queer identity should not limit cultural expression to a specific political agenda. He believed that any "queerer than thou" attitude founded on a certain political, stylistic, or sexual agenda would lose the open and flexible space that queer as an oppositional expression was born to signify. As soon as queer rigidifies into a narrowly defined identity, then its oppositional quality will be lost by the normalization that accompanies the known.[11]

Even if one adopts Doty's broader vision of queer identity, one cannot help but conclude that oppositional expressions enacted by lesbian, gay, and bisexual students take on the political quality suggested by Browning simply because of the context of gay struggle in the United States. This was a point that Timothy Jones made when he discussed gay identity. He argued that if you wake up in bed with someone of the same sex, then you are political. "That's the bottom line. Everything we do is political, whether we want it to be or not." Timothy's point is not that merely having sex with someone of the same sex represents a political act. Instead, what he highlighted is that in a society that relegates gays to the closet, a lesbian, gay, or bisexual person is automatically thrown into a political battle zone, whether he or she wants to be or not.

On National Coming Out Day in 1992, Colin Hoffman was content to take a first step and simply be seen at a gay pride rally. However, other students at Penn State were there to be heard. These lesbian, gay, and bisexual students would stay silent no longer. Jackie White took her turn at the podium: "I'm one of the co-directors for the department of Womyn's Concerns. I've come out to speak because lots of us are here and some of us are queer. Not to mention the fact that I've fucking had it up to here. There are people who feel justified in teaching and preaching the suppression of love. There is a lot of shit that goes on in our world; therefore we need all the love we can get. So, how do they justify it all? By calling this love bad love, sinful love, the wrong kind of love. To them I say that's a fucking oxymoron. There's no such thing as bad love. I speak for all of us, and I mean all of us everywhere, when I say that love feels good. As for those who say that queer love isn't love at all, you simply have no idea how very wrong you are."

After Jackie, a gay student stepped up to the podium. He told a story of having been beaten up over the summer by a couple of students and the subsequent scar the attack left on his forehead. His assailants did not appreciate his flamboyant mannerisms. "I'm a queen and I'm not ashamed. I wear this scar as a badge of freedom—freedom that no one will ever take away from me." Another student stepped through a make-shift door frame erected at the top of the steps. The structure symbolized the passage from the closet to a public identity. "I came out to my dad so he would stop asking me about girlfriends. I came out because I'm a gay man. I don't want anyone to accept me—I want them to respect me for who I am." Then Timothy Jones addressed the crowd: "When I was little I was attracted to boys, not to girls. I lived with this feeling for years, without anyone knowing, without knowing what to do about it. It wasn't until I came to college that I realized it was possible to live happily as a gay man. Lesbian, gay, and bisexual people have two choices—come out or stay in your closet and continue hating yourself. Coming out is better than hating yourself."

Following in the footsteps of queer activists like Timothy Jones and Jackie White, one by one other lesbian, gay, and bisexual students climbed the steps of Schwab Auditorium as they sought to leave the ghosts from their closets behind. With each step, their personal burdens seemed to grow lighter. However, the students at Schwab were not the only ones attracting attention on this autumn day. Background noise could be heard from across the sidewalk and lawn separating Schwab from one of the campus's main classroom buildings. Willard Hall had been the center of student activity at Penn State for years, mostly because of its central location. This was the site where the "Willard Preacher" regularly spread his conservative Christian views in an effort to convert students. Although the Willard Preacher was often criticized by other Christians, including fundamentalists who felt his methods were alienating many students, he nonetheless tended to solidify opposition to gay liberation. While some two hundred students stood around the steps of Schwab in support of gay students, a similar-sized crowd encircled the Willard Preacher.

The Willard crowd was loud and it was hard for the students gathered at Schwab to maintain a focus on the coming-out speeches. Nonetheless, the students tried to keep their eyes and ears directed toward the impassioned speakers. "I kind of hope I get through this without crying," continued one student. "I think there is going to be a lot of finger pointing and I hope no one takes this personally. But I have some things that need to be said." In preparation for what no doubt was to be an emotional outpouring, the student paused to catch his breath and steady himself. "This goes out to the queer community. To those who don't know where they are. . . . I am sick and tired of being good enough to be your friend at a nightclub on a Sunday evening but not good enough to be your friend anywhere else. I am sick and tired of being beat up and abused while you stand by and do nothing. I am sick and tired of those who are politically out but who forget where they came from not so long ago. I am sick and tired of being good enough for you to talk to but not being good enough to be a guest in your home. And most of all, I am sick and tired of being sick and tired."

This student's testimony calls attention to the politics of silencing, which weigh so heavily upon the lives of lesbian, gay, and bisexual students. The phrase "the politics of silencing" refers to the oppressive social and cultural contexts that are used to marginalize lesbian, gay, and bisexual people and in effect keep them in the closet. The Willard Preacher standing in a public space and using the Bible to condemn gay students is only one example.

The Politics of Silencing

Public expressions such as "kiss-ins" or "mall actions" are acts of visibility designed to challenge the politics of silencing. Like students at Penn State University who organize coming-out rallies, straight talks, and other high visibility events, lesbian, gay, and bisexual college students throughout the 1990s have been engaged in a struggle to claim their own place on campus and in public life.[12] "We're here. We're queer. Get used to it." is the Queer Nation slogan that applies to many of the visible and politically active students.

The struggle of queer activists at Penn State illustrates the sort of campus oppression students across the country continue to face. That oppressive campus environments exist has been well documented.[13] Although we know that many environments are hostile for lesbian, gay, and bisexual students, very little is known about the ways in which these students actually endure and, in some instances, challenge campus cultures through direct action. In fact, in an analysis of literature on or related to lesbian, gay, and bisexual college students, the vast majority of over two hundred pieces of research dating from 1970 to the mid 1990s focused on the campus environments with which gay students must contend. These studies shed little light on the everyday experiences of coping with a hostile campus culture. In fact, only a few studies actually explore the lived experiences of gay college students. What these studies and others largely reveal is the strong relationship between coming out and a positive sense of gay identity.[14] Another point is that while coming out may be beneficial in developmental ways, coming out often results in students' becoming the targets of homophobia and harassment. Listen to the following Penn State students discuss incidents that they experienced during their college years.

- One January I was walking out of this downtown nightclub and these five drunk guys were arguing about something. All of a sudden as I passed by they opened the door to Chumlies [the only gay bar in State College] and yelled in "You fuckin' faggots!" I stopped and said, "Did someone yell 'faggot'?" The guy that yelled and the four others got in my face and pushed me down to the sidewalk. One was getting ready to punch me in the face but another one stopped him and said, "You don't want to get any faggot blood on your hands."
- I went to the George Bush rally with a bunch of other lesbian and gay people. We held signs protesting Bush's policies. We were chanting slogans against him when these fraternity guys came up to us and called us faggots and dykes and started pushing us out of the way. One person got punched in the face. Another woman got knocked down and we had to form a circle around her to protect her. They were trying to take our signs away. It was really pretty scary.
- I was walking home with this guy I was seeing. We were in front of this pizza place downtown. I started to talk to these three guys, just shooting the breeze. I didn't think that I'd said anything that might offend someone, and I didn't think it was obvious that I was gay, but I might have acted a little flamboyant. As two of the guys turned to leave, the third guy started to follow them, but all of a sudden he

turned around and hit me with his fist right in the forehead. I was pretty drunk so everything was pretty much a blur until the guy hit me and then I remember everything. The police and an ambulance came. I had to get eighteen stitches.

– I was physically assaulted once walking by the frats late at night. There were four guys and at first they verbally assaulted me, then one of them shoved me. They thought I was gay because they kept calling me "fag." This one guy drew back to punch me. I hit him in the nose. It was a knee-jerk reaction. I think I probably broke his nose. I took off and they left me alone.

The preceding incidents all involved a high degree of physical violence. However, homophobia manifests itself through other forms of harassment and discrimination as well. For example, Theo Wilson was walking along the main street in State College one day with a few of his friends when two women stopped them and asked for change. They were "canning" for charity. Theo gave them a little pocket money and began to move along. He described what happened next: "These guys behind us knew the girls and stopped after we started to walk away. One of them said something like, 'Dude, you asked a bunch of faggots.'" One of Theo's friends, who is rather protective of him, got upset and was ready to fight. But Theo convinced his friend to "leave it alone." "That's kind of my attitude. I'm more of a passivist than a radical or someone who might fight back. Compared to Martin Luther King and Malcolm X, I'm definitely more like King."

Out lesbian, gay, and bisexual students who live in the residence halls frequently face forms of silencing. A student woke up one morning to find written on the bathroom mirror the following words: "Fag in 408. We don't like cock suckers on our hall." This student made a habit of posting information about gay issues on his door and every now and then the articles would get torn down, written on, or spit at. "One time I put my clothes in the dryer and this guy got real upset with me because I guess he was next in line or something and so he left a note on the machine 'Hey fag I was here first.'"

Students also face discrimination in the classroom. A student recalled taking an African American studies class on the life of Martin Luther King Jr. and the Civil Rights Movement. The professor was pointing out three weaknesses of one of King's key advisors, Bayard Rustin. First, Rustin was a suspected communist. When the professor talked about this aspect of Rustin's life no one in the class said anything. Two, Rustin avoided the draft. Again, not a word was so much as whispered. Three, Rustin was a homosexual. Everyone in the class gasped. "That was the one unforgivable thing—that he was gay."

Despite the harassment students face if they come out, most of the students who participated in this study saw coming out as worth the risk of physical abuse. The reality is that coming out is a process that most individuals with strong feelings of same-sex attraction must confront as they work to develop a positive sense of self. The idea of coming out as a process marking a transition to an emerging identity is what led Gilbert Herdt to describe it as a "rite of passage."[15] A student described the metamorphoses related to coming out: "Coming out involves taking all the negative things that you've heard about yourself, heard about 'those people,' and just saying to yourself that none of it matters as much as you do. It means opening up the door and letting out all the internalized hatred, fear, self-doubt, and self-worthlessness. I think it's the point of breaking. You either come out or you sort of die."

For individuals who think of themselves as queer, coming out is part of the process of engaging in cultural struggle against the politics of silencing. The political and cultural goal of queer students at Penn State is to create a public sphere free of heterosexism and homophobia. Samuel Bennett maintained that "heterosexual culture is very set on making gay and lesbian people invisible, whether they use physical violence or institutional violence. Coming out is a way of battling back." Another student added, "My ultimate goal would be for someone to be walking around and someone else call them a name like 'fag' or 'queer' and have it sound as silly as me calling someone straight."

Understanding heterosexism and homophobia as sources of oppression is important to making sense of queer struggle. Richard Friend defined heterosexism as "the belief that everyone is, or should be, heterosexual."[16] Friend went on to add, "Based on the assumption of universal heterosexuality . . . a systematic set of institutional and cultural arrangements exist that reward and privilege people for being or appearing to be heterosexual, and establish potential punishments or lack of privilege for being or appearing to be homosexual."[17] Likewise, Audre Lorde described heterosexism as "a belief in the inherent superiority of one pattern of loving over all others and thereby the right to dominance."[18] The dominance of heterosexist ideology and culture leads to homophobia.

"Terror surrounding feelings of love for members of the same sex and thereby a hatred of those feelings in others," is how Lorde described homophobia.[19] For Friend, homophobia was seen as "the fear and hatred of homosexuality in one's self and in others."[20] While heterosexism relates to a set of ideologies pervasive throughout a culture, homophobia is the acting out of heterosexist beliefs and attitudes. The coming-out process and the more general process of establishing a public personae are crucial to the political and cultural struggle to eliminate heterosexism and homophobia. As one student explained, "I think it is really important to become highly visible once you come out. You need to work hard at changing people's views."

For the leaders of LGBSA, becoming political has meant embracing queer activism. Once again, Samuel Bennett is helpful: "Queer to me is different than gay. Not just because it includes lesbians and gays but it's more of an attitude. There is a political aspect of being queer. You have to be political to be queer but you don't have to be political to be gay." Another student added, "For me queer means any gay, lesbian, or bisexual person who is out. If they're not out, then they are not queer. It has a political connotation."

Although for some individuals *queer* is understood as a negative expression used to oppress lesbian, gay, and bisexual people, the term was purposefully selected by gay activists. Many of the gay students at Penn State identify as queer in an effort to dismantle and then reconstruct their own meaning of a lesbian, gay, or bisexual identity. They have turned a weapon of their adversaries—*queer* used as a negative term—into a cultural tool to battle their own social confinement. The reclamation of the term *queer* is akin to Evelyn Brooks Higginbotham's discussion of how Black people have traditionally conceptualized the term race: "Black people endeavored . . . to dismantle and deconstruct the dominant society's deployment of race. Racial meanings were never internalized by blacks and whites in an identical way."[21] In making this argument, Higginbotham advanced the work of Mikhail Bakhtin, who wrote, "The word in language is half someone else's. It becomes 'one's own' only when the speaker populates it with his own intention, his own accent, when he appropriates the word, adapting it to his own semantic and expressive intention."[22] Higginbotham argued that Blacks took the term *race* and "empowered its language with their own meaning and intent."[23] In a similar sense, lesbian, gay, and bisexual student activists at Penn State have been involved in a cultural battle to expropriate the term *queer*. They desired to give it their own meaning, one that would have an affirming and positive value. Their attitude is that being queer is something to be celebrated, not scorned. The following comment from a queer student sheds light on this idea: "The other day I told my roommate about the queer dance we planned. I asked him if he wanted to go. I told him there would be a lot of straight supporters there. But he laughed when I used the word *queer* to refer to myself and other gays. Then I explained to him its different meaning and why some of us call ourselves queer and that we refuse to let others use this word against us. 'Yes, I'm queer and I'm proud of it.' It's that kind of thing."

Reclaiming the term *queer* as part of a political strategy to create empowering representations of lesbian, gay, and bisexual identity is a central tactic among members involved in Penn State's LGBSA. Students such as Samuel Bennett, Timothy Jones, Jackie White, and others mentioned throughout this chapter are by no means representative of the majority of lesbian, gay, and bisexual students at Penn State. The students discussed in this chapter reflect the most visible and politically active students within the gay student community. It is probably safe to say that few others at the university identify in such a manner or exhibit the degree of resistance these students offer to heterosexism. The students discussed here underscore the idea of a "cultural worker" struggling to claim an identity that differs from or even rejects the norms of a particular society or culture. Henry Giroux discusses cultural workers as individuals engaged in political and pedagogical activities designed to fundamentally alter representational practices, with the ultimate hope of alleviating oppression. Although Giroux speaks mostly of "people working in professions such as law, social work, architecture, medicine, theology, education, and literature,"[24] it makes sense to also include student activists as part of a broad effort to rewrite culture and identity. After all, such individuals often engage in meaningful efforts to create social and cultural change and yet are not typically classified as "professionals."

For Bennett, Jones, and White, identifying as queer captures a sense of pride and openness about one's same-sex desires as well as a degree of hostility toward heterosexism and homophobia. The contentiousness of their strategy highlights the role language and culture play in shaping individual and group identities. Culture in particular plays a vital role in identity processes. As Michel Foucault maintained, "The fundamental codes of culture—those governing its language, its schemas of perception, its exchanges, its techniques, its values, the hierarchy of its practices—establish for every man, from the very first, the empirical orders with which he will be dealing and within which he will be at home."[25] One such fundamental code is heterosexuality.

The norm of heterosexuality is a cultural code that has been passed from one generation to the next through social institutions such as the family and education. In general, this view is discussed as social reproduction.[26] Social reproduction theory relates to how dominant cultural patterns are continually reconstituted. As Pierre Bourdieu[27] argued, people who possess the "correct" cultural knowledge ("cultural capital") are rewarded, while those who lack privileged experience are penalized. Educational settings typically reward upper- and middle-class values, thus limiting the opportunities and successes of lower- and working-class students.

From critical studies of schooling, researchers have uncovered student resistance—attitudes and behaviors students exhibit that oppose the norms and values conveyed in schools.[28] Resistance is a response to cultural forces that attempt to reproduce, and, in effect, silence those who hold values and beliefs in opposition to that which is taught. When students engage in organized struggle and direct action to modify the educational setting, their resistance may be envisioned as a form of cultural work.[29] Organizing gay pride rallies and other high visibility events are examples of cultural work on the part of queer students at Penn State. Their actions are in opposition to a normalizing society that seeks to reinforce the closet.

The normalization of society produces attacks upon the body and soul of individuals who, for whatever reason, reject society's norms.[30] The attacks come not only from the state, in the form of legal authority; social control is also the result of a system of constraints and punishments evident throughout the entire social structure. From the perspective of Foucault, we, in effect, become "our brother's keeper" watching over one another, making sure that norms are not violated, that dominant beliefs and values are upheld. We develop languages and social practices that order, exclude, disperse, and limit characteristics or behaviors outside the mainstream. The term *queer*, as it has been applied in the past to insult lesbian, gay, and bisexual people, is an example of how language may be used to exclude a specific individual or group of people who do not fit a certain norm. Sometimes people may even act as vigilantes correcting wrongdoers, and, in their eyes, righting the social balance. Extensive violence against gays is an example.[31] The totality of these tactics, many of which are outside our own conscious awareness, make up what may be described as the politics of silencing. The tactics are political in that power lies at their center, naming or silencing various individuals, groups, or behaviors. It is in response to the politics of silencing that gay activists at Penn State have engaged in their own form of cultural work.

Students as Cultural Workers

The Gay Liberation Movement of the early 1990s, especially as it was manifested on American campuses, drew inspiration from Queer Nation, which in many ways epitomized lesbian, gay, and bisexual people who refused to be silenced by the normalization of heterosexuality. Anthony D'Augelli shed light on the significance of the queer student movement: "The first post-Stonewall generation has redeemed the term *queer* as a tool for unrepentant empowerment. Intergenerational tension in the lesbian/gay population has emerged, an inevitable consequence of the conflict between accommodative successes and impatient fury."[32] D'Augelli went on to point out that lesbian, gay, and bisexual college students of the 1990s *expect* a place on campus—"they see no reason for shame."[33]

Penn State University offers an example of the power of the queer student movement, and the Lesbian, Gay, and Bisexual Student Alliance forms the center of student resistance. The goal of LGBSA, and queer students such as Samuel Bennett and Timothy Jones, is to instill in all lesbian, gay, and bisexual people an attitude of pride and openness. Solidarity is a key, as there is strength in numbers. The adoption of the term *queer* is in this sense a political tactic intended to both unite lesbian, gay, and bisexual people as well as highlight the positive aspects of gay identities. For example, Bennett discussed *queer* as a term that signifies pride in one's gay identity. Jones often used the term to denote the political aspect of being gay in a culture that he characterized as "heterocentrist"—a belief system revolving around a view that everyone is or ought to be heterosexual.

Although queer students at Penn State rarely organized "queer visibility expeditions" to the local mall or "zapped" local businesses, they nonetheless were actively engaged in a struggle to re-create the institutional culture. The point is that queer students at Penn State have actively contested the closet, with the goal of creating a more just environment. Their strategies of visibility were designed to have both a political and a pedagogical objective.

Many queer students expressed the sentiment that it is largely the invisibility of lesbian, gay, and bisexual people within the general population that prevents them from assuming their rightful place within society's power structures. As one student commented: "One thing that really bothers me is that, as a queer person, I find it very frustrating that so few people are willing to be out and active." For this student, being visible implies *publicly* demonstrating one's sexual identity while also exhibiting a commitment to the larger struggle for gay liberation.

The ways that students choose to demonstrate their gay or bisexual identities are diverse. Several students talked about acting out certain stereotypes as a way of letting people know that they are queer. One student mentioned mannerisms such as "snapping," which involves moving one's hand in a Z-like fashion starting above the head and snapping the fingers at the end of each stroke. Another student described mannerisms he incorporated into his behavior: "Just some of the stereotypical things. Crossing your legs a lot, wearing bright colors, laughing really loud in public, in a higher pitch maybe." This student recognized that these behaviors all related to different stereotypes but at the same time acknowledged, "They come from somewhere. Acting out stereotypes I think is a way to identify to each other." Another student mentioned excessive use of the hands in talking as a clue that one might be gay.

"Camping" was a phrase that students mentioned and involved incorporating traditionally feminine mannerisms with a touch of flamboyancy into one's public personae. For several students, "camping it up" was one way they chose to be visible. One student in particular talked about "camp culture": "I have this attitude that gays are more refined, more cultured, more mature, more intelligent than straight people. I know it sounds a little condescending but sometimes I think it's true. I mean sarcasm and cynicism go right over most straight guys' heads. I had a blast this past year watching the Academy Awards with a bunch of gay men. Talk about camp culture at its best. Camp follows the rule that if we didn't laugh about it or make fun of something we would probably have to cry. It's a form of cynicism that allows us to kind of celebrate that we are different. If you look at these straight people and laugh at them, they can't hurt you. You know, like, 'Look at Barbra Streisand's hair. It's awful. Who is her hairdresser? And Whoopi, where did you get that horrendous dress? At the Salvation Army?' It's a way of making fun of straight people for a change. A step up on them for once." For this student, camp culture offers visible evidence to the straight world that gays exist.

But not all gay students at Penn State are into camp. For example, one student is completely turned off by camp culture. "Feminization" is the term he used in reference to gay and bisexual men who for whatever reason "somehow need to act like women." He elaborated, "Sometimes the 'flamers' feminize their behavior and it really bothers me. I mean, I sit around and watch hockey games and drink beer and I don't see anything wrong with that. I think there is a tendency to overcompensate because of the gender fuck. But it comes off as denying one's masculinity, which should have nothing to do with being gay." Another student elaborated on the meaning of "gender fuck": "It refers to someone who completely defies what it means to be a certain gender." Thus, for some gay and bisexual men, one way to resist mainstream sexual scripts is to adopt what traditionally have been defined as feminine characteristics. This is what some argue camp is all about.

Gender is a social construction linked to sex. Masculinity and femininity are the models typically assigned to males and females through their socialization. Men are supposed to be strong, logical, and in control. Women are often portrayed as weak, emotional, and vulnerable (recall how the women of Mills College felt betrayed by the media for portraying them in this manner). These are socially assigned traits that are reproduced from generation to generation through socialization. By accentuating feminine traits, camp is in a sense a rejection of a particular construction of gender and the traditional meanings of masculinity. Brian Pronger claims that in coming out men are forced in part to fit into the socially constructed category of homosexual or gay man. As a result, gay men go through a process of reinterpreting their social worlds. An important aspect of reinterpretation involves confronting masculine and feminine prescriptions. "Gay men can come to see that the power relations for which the semiotics of masculinity and femininity constitute a strategy have little to do with their lives. The meaning of masculinity, consequently, begins to change."[34] In this light, camp may be seen as a recognition on the part of some gay or queer men that traditional feminine and masculine traits are inappropriately used to coerce male and female behavior. Their rejection of traditional masculine characteristics may be understood as an act of resistance.

Another reading of camp relates to visibility; camping it up is a way of signifying to others one's gay identity. Stereotypes about gay men being more feminine than straight men have been advanced over the years. Unquestioned beliefs represented by the gender inversion myth (that gay men are really more like women than they are like men) have reinforced such views. Consequently, gay men may act out certain stereotypes in order to be visible to other members of the gay community. A student explained: "Anything that deviates from the norm of the heterosexual community can be seen as a sign that someone is gay. For me personally, I act very effeminate."

In addition to camp, there were many other ways that students chose to be visible. Several students talked about wearing certain clothes as a means of publicly identifying as gay or bisexual. For example, one student explained, "I wear queer stuff on practically every piece of clothing I have. Mainly I wear stuff to let other gay and straight people know that I am gay. There are so many straights who don't know we exist that you have to advertise. My favorite T-shirt is one that has two men kissing and says 'Read my lips.'" A second student discussed how he dresses: "One day during Pride Week I wore my 'love knows no gender' T-shirt all around campus. I never had so much bounce in my legs. I felt wonderful and proud to be gay. I was full of positive energy for a change. I was happy and people were looking at me like what is that? I didn't even feel nervous—it was unbelievable."

Several students emphasized direct confrontation rather than adopting specific mannerisms or styles of dress. One student commented that he makes a point of talking to his professors after class to let them know he is gay. "I let them know that I am going to be open about being gay and if they have a problem with that then we are going to have a problem. If they don't, then I'll be the perfect student." This student mentioned other visible behaviors, such as turning his head to look when a guy walks by him, or not lowering his voice when he talks about gay issues. This student tended to adopt more subtle clues related to his sexual identity. "I certainly don't go for the flaming behaviors that some like to display—that's not part of my personality."

Samuel Bennett occasionally wears special clothing, but for the most part he prefers confrontational tactics: "I wear T-shirts with queer statements on special days such as National Coming Out Day. That's the only time I really dress to make everyone know that I'm gay. I don't modify my behavior out of fear. If anything I do the opposite. I've become very confrontational, and if I hear anyone bad-mouthing gay or lesbian people I purposely act gay so they might confront me about it. Then I can give them a piece of my mind. It's a mission in my life to be as visible as possible."

To students who identify as queer, coming out is more than an individual process meant to claim a public space; coming out also is a political effort designed to create greater awareness and achieve increased rights and visibility for all lesbian, gay, and bisexual people. One student maintained that simply being out involves a certain degree of politics, in that out lesbian, gay, and bisexual people at the very minimum serve as reminders to a straight society that gay people exist. "That's why I wear clothing that might tell people that I'm queer, such as a T-shirt with some type of queer saying on it." Another student identified himself as a "gay man/political queer." He elaborated, "Political queer is a more blatant way of defining myself as part of the community. Anyone who questions society's gender roles can be defined as queer. It can include transsexuals." A third student also discussed a community sense of identity: "It's one thing to think about being gay and how that affects me, but I think that I've become much more aware of the impact of anyone being gay in society." The preceding student finds "the politics of being gay" fascinating. "It's almost a shame that it is so political and that people just can't be gay like if they were straight. But there are politics behind being gay, and I've become much more aware of it." He went on to point out that he has learned to recognize the connection between other forms of oppression: "I've become a lot more aware of oppression in general. For me, racism, sexism, and homophobia are all part of the big three as far as problems go."

There are several strategies queer students at Penn State have utilized to bring issues into campus discussion. Foremost, there are two annually scheduled events: National Coming Out Day (NCOD) and Pride Week. NCOD corresponds to a nationwide event and is celebrated in October of each year. As we have seen, at Penn State University, NCOD takes the form of a rally on the steps of the school auditorium next to Old Main, where students speak out about their experiences as lesbian, gay, and bisexual people. Pride Week, on the other hand, involves a week-long series of activities that occur during the spring semester. Prominent speakers, entertainers, and programs are planned and sponsored by LGBSA in conjunction with other organizations such as the Graduate Student Coalition (composed largely of lesbian, gay, and bisexual graduate students), ALLIES (made up of students who support gay liberation), and the Bisexual Womyn's Group.

Another pedagogical effort of queer students involves conducting "straight talks." Straight talks involve lesbian, gay, and bisexual students speaking to a class or a residence hall about their experiences. Straight talks typically follow a question-and-answer format. At times, they can become quite confrontational, especially in cases where students in the audience are hostile to gay students, but for the most part, straight talks are received in a friendly, polite manner in which student curiosity about gay lives tends to be the central theme.

Pedagogical efforts primarily serve to increase awareness of queer lives and to challenge heterosexist attitudes and norms. Other cultural work done by lesbian, gay, and bisexual students at Penn State had more specific goals in mind and sought to change particular aspects of the campus community. Although Penn State students exhibit a great deal of concern about societal issues, the local culture of the university and State College is that which touches them daily and thus forms much of the focus of their political efforts. Throughout the academic years 1991–92 and 1992–93, queer students engaged in several significant activities. They played an integral role in documenting campus homophobia and their finished product was a four-hundred-page report offered to faculty and administrators involved in the debate over adopting a sexual orientation clause. In addition to the report, students also were heavily involved in lobbying efforts and committee work focused on gaining support for the clause.

Another political activity was their involvement in promoting a fair housing ordinance in State College that included protection based on sexual orientation. After extensive letter writing and participation in town meetings, the amendment was adopted. A number of queer students committed 1992–93 to protests to force the university to remove the ROTC program from campus. Although this effort had not succeeded, many of these students, including Samuel Bennett, vowed to continue their efforts until graduation.

Making Sense of It All

Queer students at Penn State work to convince other lesbian, gay, and bisexual students to come out and join their struggle. There can be no queer community without a visible presence. And gay liberation will always be in peril without a community. The need for visibility highlights the importance of coming out. Michelangelo Signorile is helpful here: "Remember that all those in the closet, blinded by their own trauma, hurt themselves and all other queers. The invisibility they perpetuate harms us more than any of their good deeds might benefit us."[35] But we should also remember that not all lesbian, gay, and bisexual college students have the same degree of social support. Not everyone has the kinds of friends and families helpful to leaving one's closet behind.

Through their increased visibility, queer students at Penn State have staked a claim to power and have gained a voice in campus life. Their goal is to create a diverse academic community and society where lesbian, gay, and bisexual people are full participants in the democratic process. But "conflict is inevitable if the multiple voices of different groups are to be heard. The lack of conflict either means that particular groups have been silenced and made invisible or that a democratic [community] based on the acceptance of difference has not been reached."[36]

There has been much conflict at Penn State. As Samuel Bennett high-lighted, "The administration has been *forced* [author's emphasis] to do almost everything that has been positive for us. They wouldn't see any reason to change anything if we didn't always kick and scream." Conse-quently, many students see forming an alliance with other gay students as essential if they are to achieve equal rights and fair treatment. Obvi-ously, grounding one's identity in a larger group context is intended to do far more than simply raise one's self-esteem, as conservative crit-ics often fail to observe. In fact, the ethnic and identity politics that Arthur Schlesinger scornfully describes as the "cult of ethnicity" is clearly an attempt to advance democracy by including previously marginalized peoples, such as gays, as full participants in social and political life. For Schlesinger, efforts on the part of groups such as LGBSA at Penn State, Chicanos at UCLA, and American Indians at Michigan State, are anti-American and antidemocratic because they focus on group rights instead of individual rights. In Schlesinger's words, the cult of ethnicity poses a threat to "the historic theory of America as one people—the theory that has thus far managed to keep American society whole." He goes on to write,

> Instead of a transformative nation with an identity all its own, America
> in this new light is seen as preservative of diverse alien cultures. Instead
> of a nation composed of individuals making their own unhampered
> choices, America increasingly sees itself as composed of groups more
> or less ineradicable in their ethnic character. The multiethnic dogma
> abandons historic purposes, replacing assimilation by fragmentation,
> integration by separatism. It belittles *unum* and glorifies *pluribus*.[37]

How ironic that Schlesinger assails multiculturalism because it promotes group identities, which in his mind threaten the ultimate group identity of "America as one people." One is left to wonder who gets to define this conglomeration of "Americans" as a singular unified group. Addi-tionally, the reality of life as a minority (including sexual minorities) is that frequently it is only through forging a sense of solidarity that these "individuals" have enough clout to influence campus and societal poli-tics. How many lesbian, gay, and bisexual people as individuals have the opportunity to make "their own unhampered choices"? Who willingly chooses the closet over dignity and self-respect? The closet is a direct re-sult of how members of a certain social group—"homosexuals"—have been persecuted, and it may be only through organizing around one's identity as lesbian, gay, bisexual, or queer that social change will come.

One cannot help but wonder where gay liberation would be today if it were left to the sole province of individual decision makers to forge more progressive social policies.

In the forceful way queer students at Penn State have raised issues of freedom and equality, they have helped elevate the consciousness of an entire campus. These students exhibited a commitment to ending the oppression of lesbian, gay, and bisexual people on both a campus and societal level. As one student commented, "I would like to see less of a negative attitude toward gay people on this campus and throughout the rest of the world. I'd like for more people to understand what gay is—that it's not something evil, that some of their closest friends are gay." Similarly, Samuel Bennett dreamt of seeing "less of the idea of tolerance and more of the notion of celebration."

Queer student activists have refused to accept the definition of themselves offered by society. They have cast aside the limitations placed upon them by both the institutional and societal culture and have staged opposition through the use of language and by their refusal to remain silent. They have fought the politics of silencing through increased visibility as well as specific educational and political strategies aimed at both achieving power for themselves and altering the perception of others. The adoption of the term *queer* as a self-identifier symbolized the students' commitment to altering views of lesbian, gay, and bisexual people and reflected their battle to transform an oppressive culture into a truly participatory society where freedom's web extends to everyone.

"GENETIC, HEREDITARY

BACKGROUND"

African American Resistance at Rutgers

The Civil Rights Movement launched by Blacks during the 1950s primarily was centered upon the ideals of equality and justice for all. These philosophical and practical principles drove a movement determined to put an end to the Jim Crow laws and discriminatory social customs that had become so prevalent under American segregation policies. However, as the civil rights struggle advanced into the mid to late 1960s, a change began to take place within Black consciousness. Identity exploration and discovering one's roots as an African American became vital to the experiences of politically minded Blacks, as the teachings of Marcus Garvey in the 1920s, Elijah Muhammad in the 1950s, and Malcolm X and Stokely Carmichael in the 1960s gained influence and the seeds of racial pride and nationalism took root. For these individuals, "Black Power" had significant implications for the struggle of the American Negro: "It includes race pride, an interest in the history of the American Negro and his past in Africa, and a desire to educate the black American in the acceptance of black as something good, not bad; and beautiful, not something of which to be ashamed."[1]

A number of the African American civil rights activists of the 1960s were college students. Many of these individuals played a central role in the formation and growth of the Black Power movement, which became increasingly influential as the decade neared its end. "The Black Panther Party had been founded in November 1966 by a group of students (including Huey Newton and Bobby Seale) who were members of the Afro-American Student Union at Merritt Junior College in Oakland, California. . . . Further, with the exception of Malcolm X, the leaders in the growth of the new ideologies were almost all black students."[2]

Through the work of individuals such as Carmichael, Newton, and Seale, among countless others, the Civil Rights Movement found fertile soil at American colleges and universities. The 1968–69 academic year proved particularly eventful as scores of students protested institutional policies that reinforced educational inequities and the continued oppression of African Americans. In a very real sense, this movement, which became most prevalent at urban institutions such as Howard, Columbia, NYU, Temple, and Rutgers, was the beginning of the contemporary Multicultural Student Movement, for as Richard McCormick noted, "their common objective was to compel predominantly white institutions to change their policies and attitudes to accommodate to the needs of a multiracial society."[3] McCormick went on to reflect on the significance of the cultural and political changes demanded by African American student activists: "For African Americans, [their calls for change] meant not only broadening access to higher education; it meant as well the construction of an environment within which they could feel emotionally and physically secure and where their cultural values would be respected and legitimized. In the view of some participants, what was required was nothing short of a revolutionary restructuring of American higher education."[4] Thus, even as far back as the 1960s, students of color were moving toward a cultural model of educational justice, and demographic and representational concerns were beginning to be seen as symptoms and not as the underlying disease. The critique of monoculturalism and Eurocentrism was slowly gaining strength.

A growing concern of the Black Power movement was gaining control over the education of American Blacks and fostering a learning context where African American identity could be advanced. To a large degree, the student unrest at Howard University described in chapter 2 is a reflection of this movement. But the movement was powerful at other universities as well, and Rutgers University in New Brunswick, New Jersey, was one campus where Black pride found expression in the late 1960s.

Throughout the 1960s, Rutgers witnessed growing tension on its campuses located in New Brunswick, Camden, and Newark as Black students became increasingly discontent with the educational and racial climate at the university. On April 4, 1968, the powder keg that had become Rutgers was set off as word of the assassination of Martin Luther King Jr. spread throughout the academic community. McCormick assessed the significance that King's assassination held for the students at Rutgers: "King's death had an unprecedented impact on black students at Rutgers. Malcolm X had been killed, and now Dr. King. No comparable leader remained. The sense of loss was compounded by feelings of pain and anger." As a Rutgers student remarked, "We realized we would have to carry on the struggle without him, by ourselves. We were shocked into the discovery that we could not just be students anymore." And McCormick concluded, "This realization brought African American students together, regardless of previous differences. It inspired them with a sense of urgency; slow progress must give way to rapid, massive change. Their anger suddenly rose; some even spoke of violence."[5]

The sense of urgency felt by the students manifested itself in a mandate from a quickly formed coalition of Black student organizations: "We black people have reached a breaking point. We shall not tolerate this racism any longer. This system must be changed whether with white help or without it."[6] Demands for increased recruitment and support of African American students soon followed as debates were played out in the student newspaper the *Daily Targum*. Comments from White students added fuel to the fire as many resisted what they perceived as special treatment for Blacks. As one student wrote, "I'll help anyone who helps himself, and no one who demands a gift!"[7]

Ultimately, a new plan was formulated for enhancing the participation of African American students at the university. The tenor had been established at Rutgers, and the following year (1968–69) more serious demonstrations took place. Perhaps the most visible protests were at the Newark campus, where students took over Conklin Hall and once again demanded increased recruitment of and support for African American students, who in the fall of 1968 accounted for only about 3 percent of the university's student population. White students expressed hostility toward the demands as the conservative group Young Americans for Freedom (YAF'ers) held counter-demonstrations outside Conklin Hall, which by this time had been renamed "Liberation Hall" by the Black Organization of Students (BOS). One of the demands of BOS members was a more open admissions policy with less emphasis placed on SAT scores. The students felt that the vast majority of high school students from Newark (a large percentage of whom were Black) were excluded from attending Rutgers because of standardized measures. This issue eventually would be debated by the faculty, and academic standards as measured by tests such as the SAT would be an ongoing source of contention in decades to come.

For the next twenty-five years or more, Rutgers University struggled to improve the enrollment and support of African American students. Debates about admission standards were ongoing, inasmuch as an institutional philosophy about the role of Rutgers in serving educationally disadvantaged areas of the state, such as Camden and Newark, were never fully resolved. Student protests arose from time to time but the tension and angst of the late 1960s seemed lost forever.

By the late 1970s, Rutgers had increased its enrollment of African Americans to close to 14 percent, only to see it drop over the next fifteen years to around 10 percent in 1994.[8] At the same time, the school's overall minority student population had risen to around 30 percent, with African Americans and Asian/Pacific Islanders accounting for the largest percentages. The school also had enacted programs such as Africana studies, although the funding of such programs was still relatively small and they clearly existed on the margins of the university's curriculum. In terms of faculty hiring, little had changed over the past fifteen years, with African Americans accounting for only 6 percent of the faculty in 1977 and only 5.7 percent in 1993.[9] Thus, while some improvement occurred in the early 1970s, little seemed to have been accomplished during the next fifteen to twenty years, leaving many African American students and faculty disenchanted with the university's commitment to diversity.

Disenchantment turned to rage when three devastating words spoken by Rutgers President Francis Lawrence were made public. The stage was set for a significant blow to be delivered to African American racial pride. After thirty years of struggle to improve the educational climate at Rutgers, African Americans at the university found themselves confronted by racial denigration once again. The year was 1995 but it seemed more like 1965. It was a historic moment and students refused to let it pass them by. If ever there was a time for direct action, that time had come.

Frederick Douglass once said, "Power concedes nothing without a demand; it never has and it never will." For African American students at Rutgers, this simple assertion by Douglass could not have been etched any deeper into their consciousness than if Douglass had risen from his grave and walked across the Livingston campus and then right on up College Avenue to New Brunswick. If White power had been an underlying current in their educational experiences throughout their lives, it suddenly was a live wire exposing their vulnerability as a pervasive yet covert form of racism was unmasked.

Those Three Words

On November 11, 1994, Lawrence spoke before a group of about thirty faculty gathered on the Camden campus of Rutgers. The substance of his talk concerned academic standards, the role of the Scholastic Aptitude Test, and the university's commitment to recruiting African American students. Little did he know prior to his presentation that his remarks eventually would send much of the university community scrambling for explanations and demands for his resignation. The text of his presentation included the following remarks:"The average S.A.T.'s for African Americans is 750. Do we set standards in the future so we don't admit anybody? Or do we deal with a disadvantaged population that doesn't have that genetic, hereditary background to have a higher average?" None of the faculty in attendance was struck by the president's comments, and it was only after a tape of his presentation was replayed nearly three months later that people took offense. In fact, it was Tuesday, January 31, when the *Star-Ledger* of Newark published a front-page story detailing the comments of Lawrence. The American Association of University Professors had shared an audio tape of his fateful November speech with the newspaper, which quickly decided it was page-one material.[10]

Once word spread of his comments, African American students as well as other students and faculty at Rutgers immediately called for Lawrence's resignation. A number of Rutgers faculty spoke out on the matter. Some sounded apologetic and angry at the same time. Paul Tractenberg, a professor at Rutgers School of Law in Newark, remarked, "Most of his behavior is indicative of a support for minorities. In this country, it's very difficult not to have subterranean feelings about race. The comments, though, once they're out, they're very hard to reclaim." He went on to add, "Serious minded students' roles here have been jeopardized or undermined. African-American students are always aware of having to validate or justify their ability. And when the president of Rutgers University says this, it's debilitating."[11]

"Freedom is never voluntarily given up by the oppressor. It must be demanded by the oppressed," wrote Martin Luther King Jr. from behind the bars of the Birmingham Jail. Freedom is not simply the physical quality of not being restrained. Freedom is complex and involves opportunities to create oneself, to shape one's life. When Francis Lawrence defined African Americans as lacking in genetic intelligence he diminished the freedom of Blacks in this country to grow and learn in an atmosphere untainted by prejudice. Words can deny freedom and produce social constraint and denigration. But the oppressed can weave their own webs of liberty through the power of passion and protest.

Although there had been an activist spirit present among certain African American students at Rutgers, student organizers rarely were successful in getting the vast majority of their peers to support their efforts. This of course changed dramatically following the remarks by President Lawrence. Darryl Scippio, a sophomore studying political science and Africana studies, commented on the immediate outpouring that followed the release of the remarks: "Students were very ready to do something. People were emotionally charged because of the comments. . . . Emotions ran really high amongst African American students. People were ready to move." Scippio was actively involved in a student organization known as 100 Black Men, and he found the invigorated student body a positive change from the usual apathy he saw around campus: "Student activists had always been trying to get people to organize. But students didn't really see any reason. He [President Lawrence] gave people a reason to demonstrate and he made the job of student activists very easy. The day after he made the comments, the day they came out in the paper, there was a mass student meeting and about one thousand students showed up. And that's just from word of mouth. Now, you know, you can't even get a hundred people to a rally if you organize it and put out flyers two weeks in advance!"

Clarence Tokley, who like Scippio was finishing up his second year, saw organizing campuswide protests as a matter of doing what was right. "It was something seeing all those people pulling together no matter what might happen. We were there because we knew what we had to do. We had that feeling of being together. . . . We were going after what we knew was right and doing it no matter what. No matter whether he [President Lawrence] apologized or not. Or whether the faculty backed us or not. The students were together. When it came down to it, we had to do our work and we did it. And that's what sticks out in my mind. We actually had an influence on other people." Tokley bristled at comments from administrators and media figures who implied that the students were just looking for an issue around which they could create an uproar. He pointed out that he attended Rutgers University for the same reason as everyone else—to get an education. But when students such as Tokley and Scippio witness an injustice committed against African Americans, they cannot just sit back and ignore it. If they do, when will it ever end? As Tokley commented, "I don't want my kids to have to go to college and have to worry about organizing. Like when we were organizing and stuff the administration was like 'Y'all should just go to school.' Don't they understand that if all we had to do was go to school then everything would be great? That's what we came here for, to go to school and to get an education. So we gonna have to make sure that if we can't do that then somebody else will be able to do it. Because it's not like we just sit around planning to protest; like I'm sitting in my room and say, 'I feel like protesting today. Let's have a rally.' No, we don't do that; we sit here and we sit here and we try to do our work but when we see something wrong, we're not gonna be so apathetic that we just gonna let you continue doing wrong."

The Immediate Reaction

Jessica Applebaum was a student at Rutgers and the news editor for the *Daily Targum* at the time. She recalled the state of disbelief the entire campus experienced and the chaos the episode created at the newspaper: "At first no one could figure out what was actually said and those who had heard were in a state of disbelief. People were running around campus trying to get information. The *New York Times* was calling the campus newspaper trying to get information. There was a press conference on the afternoon of the 31st where Lawrence explained that the comments were pretty much taken out of context. . . . We were mailing out, and faxing out, about a hundred copies of our article and everybody just wanted to know what the *Targum* was doing. Everybody wanted to know what was going on at Rutgers. . . . We were getting calls from the *Washington Post* and *Newsweek*, from foreign newspapers, from papers in Virginia. It came to a point where we were sitting there trying to figure out what we were going to put on the front page and somebody from the *Washington Post* called and we said we'll have to call 'em back. You don't say you're going to call the *Washington Post* back! But, you know, it was just so crazy in here all the time so it was difficult to be a student and to be a reporter."

Applebaum commented on what she saw as the most radical stance ever in the *Daily Targum's* long history: "I think the most radical steps that I've seen here at the *Targum* and just in the history of our paper, and we're 128 years old this year, was that we put an editorial on the front page asking for the president's dismissal." After Applebaum and the rest of the newspaper staff came back from Lawrence's press conference they got together to discuss their strategy: "We came back here to the office and we had a few decisions to make. First, we had to decide what our editorial stance would be. Were we going to say, well, maybe he didn't really mean it or maybe his initiatives in other areas show that this isn't really what he meant? Or, were we going to take the route which we ultimately took and say, well, you know, what he said was totally inappropriate for the figurehead of a large undergraduate and graduate research institution that prides itself on diversity. If our president can say something like this, what does that say for our university? Should he be our president? We determined in the room that day that he should resign." The next day the newspaper published a front-page editorial calling for Lawrence's resignation. What follows are some excerpts:

GENETIC HEREDITARY BACKGROUND. These words have been called badly articulated, but the statement made by University President Francis L. Lawrence is much, much more than that—those words have made it impossible for him to function adequately as a spokesperson, figurehead and leader of New Jersey's largest and most diverse learning institution.

With those three words, the president of our University became a symbol of racism that can no longer represent the diversity and progressiveness of Rutgers. Yesterday, administrators stood behind the president, claiming his progressive record negates his comments, and the faculty union asked only for an apology; therefore, it will be left up to students to properly denounce the statements made by our president and accept no less than his resignation or removal from office.

The editorial concluded by urging students to act: "The worst that can happen now is nothing. Students must rise to the challenge and demand that Lawrence be removed if he does not resign from his post as University president."[12]

For the next several days, Lawrence tried to cleanse his statement and lighten the shadow cast on Rutgers. "The fact these deeply regretted, wounding words made national news is especially unfortunate in view of Rutgers' tradition of excellence in minority access and advancement." However, Lawrence was unable to adequately explain the remarks, which he maintained reflected the opposite of his deeply held convictions about racial equality. Those three words are an "absolute contradiction of everything I believe or everything I stand for and of everything that I have done throughout my life." Lawrence extended his offer to redress the problem he created: "I can apologize from the bottom of my heart and try to make up for it by redoubling my efforts for minorities and working even harder to confront and overcome all of the barriers to access that such false ideas create."[13]

Despite efforts to explain the words as antithetical to his beliefs, many students were not buying his explanation and instead saw his slip as a reflection of deeply held convictions that in today's society typically cannot be voiced. His explanation that it was all a "misunderstanding" simply could not explain away why such words were used in the first place. Hundreds of angry students refused to accept his apology with many demanding his resignation while countless others resigned themselves to yet another setback in the struggle for social and educational equality. Otis Rolley, a political science and Africana studies junior, and one of the most outspoken students at Rutgers, commented, "These are deeply inflicted wounds coming out. People are hurt. People are discouraged."[14]

A story published in the *New York Amsterdam News* rejected explanations offered by Lawrence. "After two weeks of listening to the cassette tape recorded by a member of the American Association of University Professors (AAUP) on November 11, 1994, at a Rutgers Camden faculty senate meeting, we have concluded that Lawrence could not have misspoken at the time. We also categorically reject his various public explanations for why he uttered those reprehensible words."[15] The article went on to point out that Lawrence at first denied he made the statement and then later suggested that the tape had been altered. Of course, eventually he conceded that the comments were his but were not reflective of his actual perception. Three responses thus were offered by Lawrence: (1) he did not realize he made the remarks, (2) he did not believe the remarks to be true or indicative of his beliefs, and (3) he was sorry for what he said. His supporters offered three additional explanations: (1) he was fatigued when he spoke to the Camden faculty, (2) it was a rambling presentation, and (3) the words were jumbled and actually he tried to convey the opposite idea. However, the *Amsterdam News* claimed that after careful analysis of the taped discussion there is little evidence of Lawrence being fatigued and thus rambling incoherently. Included was a discussion of the syntactic structure: "The sentence in question, jumbled in any sequence, still lends itself to negative interpretation because of the mere presence of three words—whether they were coupled with either 'does' or 'doesn't.' The mere presence of the sentence also implies the existence of a contrary condition that has no place in a discourse on intelligence, since most reputable scientists believe that intelligence is acquired socially—not genetically." The article concluded:

It is therefore difficult to accept belated apologies for such a negative comment when it was used in conjunction with other esoteric statistics to prove a point. How is it possible to summon all of one's faculties to cite one's own achievements, cite another's failures in the same breath, and then characterize as a misstatement the only statement mentioned without any prodding whatsoever from anyone at the meeting? Why deny culpability for one part of a statement and not the other when the statement was delivered with such great verbal clarity and forethought?

On February 1, Lawrence stated publicly: "The ideas that intelligence levels differ based on ethnicity and that minorities are genetically inferior are monstrously perverse, demonstrably false, and completely unacceptable. I cannot explain a remark that said precisely the opposite of my deeply held beliefs. I can only apologize from the bottom of my heart." In the article in which the preceding quotation from Lawrence appeared, Black journalist Carl Rowan came out in defense of Lawrence: "We live in a time of such polarization, such growing racial hostility, that most Black students, and even faculty members, may not believe Lawrence. But I now believe Lawrence. . . . I would trust Lawrence ahead of any of the professors who, protecting their own special tenure status, used a recorded misstatement of his views to stir up an ill-considered Black rebellion and try to get him fired." He concluded by writing, "These are perilous times when Black people had better be careful in determining who are their allies and who are their foes. In this case, I stand with President Lawrence."[16]

An African American faculty member was angered by Rowan and others who misrepresented the issues at Rutgers. This professor responded to questions about Rowan's support: "That's like saying Clarence Thomas supported it. That doesn't carry any weight with me. A lot of Black people, people of color, women, are in positions precisely because they're going to sing the establishment line and that's part of the formula for success. So, you know, I'm not really persuaded by what Carl Rowan said. I do not think that Francis Lawrence is a bigot or a racist any more than your average American. I do think our culture, however, is deeply racist and that the average American has a lot of racist attitudes, maybe even unconscious or subconscious." The problem, however, is that Lawrence is the president of a major university with one of the largest African American student populations in the country. "That's the point," this professor went on to emphasize. "He's not supposed to be evaluated by the usual standards. If he's a truck driver or perhaps even a professor, you know, he can have a slip of the tongue. He can't be speaking as the head of a university. . . . The issue is not whether or not he's a decent guy at heart. But somehow, the press and other people wanted to play this other theme that, you know, 'what is he really like. Is he a decent person?' It doesn't matter what his real feelings are. That's not the issue. People have responsibilities that they incur that may be greater than normal by virtue of the position they hold. They need to be judged by how they exercise those responsibilities."

Despite support from Rowan and other media figures such as Alan Dershowitz, Lawrence's comments set off immediate furor among African American students at Rutgers. Not long after Lawrence's press conference the students at Rutgers were already organizing a series of public demonstrations to counter his offensive comments, misspoken or not.

The Demonstrations

The first large-scale student demonstrations took place on February 1, the day after the *Star-Ledger* released its story, as over five hundred students marched down College Avenue demanding the president's resignation. As the students marched they chanted "Hell no, our genes ain't slow!" From time to time, the procession halted and various speakers used a megaphone to voice their views of the president's remarks and what should be done about it. At one point, the entire march stopped and students sat down for a moment of silence. Eventually, chants of "What do we want? Resignation! When do we want it? Now!" broke the calm as students rose up and continued their march. The students ended the demonstration in front of the president's office in the Old Queens building. The book *The Bell Curve* was shredded to pieces and thrown in the direction of the building.[17]

The same evening, students filled the multipurpose room at the Busch Campus Center as over seven hundred students gathered to voice their concerns and to discuss a strategy for ousting Lawrence. Otis Rolley read a list of demands to the crowd: make courses in women's, Africana, Puerto Rican, Hispanic, and Caribbean studies part of the general education requirements for all Rutgers students; initiate recruitment and retention programs for minorities; and eliminate the SAT as a consideration in admissions decisions. And, of course, the ultimate demand was for the president's immediate resignation. Planning for the contingency that their demands were not to be met, Rolley discussed a few of the tactics the students might employ, including a boycott of corporations and businesses associated with the board of governors (who had come out in support of Lawrence's remaining at the university) and a boycott of classes taught by faculty who supported Lawrence. Other speakers called for solidarity among all Rutgers students, regardless of racial background. "The only way we can beat Fran Lawrence, the board of governors and Governor Whitman is with 100 percent student solidarity," stated Manny Figueroa, a junior and member of the Rutgers College Governing Association. "We need all the races together. . . . We can't let this be a divided issue."[18]

Pleas for multiracial support did not go unheeded, and the demonstrations took on a multicultural character as Latino, Asian American, Puerto Rican, Caribbean, and White students soon took an active role in protesting alongside African American students, who most often took the lead. Applebaum felt that the multicultural quality of the movement represented an awareness among underrepresented minorities that dramatic changes were needed at the university. "What we saw in essence was that this touched off a series of issues that people had been thinking about but the comments by Lawrence gave them a huge forum to demand changes."

On February 2, President Lawrence held an open meeting in which over three hundred students participated. Held in the Neilson Dining Hall on the Cook Campus, the meeting lasted an hour and a half before a large contingent of students walked out and Lawrence ended the meeting. Lawrence commented on his plan to respond to his mistake: "It's something I'm going to have to live with. The most positive way to respond is to redouble my efforts and address issues of more minority administrators, faculty, and students. . . . I'm here to learn how we can use this as a learning experience and grow." But many students were less willing to move forward, at least with Lawrence at the helm. Otis Rolley pointedly stated, "You've apologized and I forgive you. Now you also have to answer to what the student body wants. . . . I formally request your immediate resignation as president of Rutgers University." Rolley went on to add, "This isn't a dialogue; this is propaganda. . . . Be a man about it. You got busted; you must leave." It was at this point that Rolley and about one-fourth of those in attendance walked out of the dining hall.[19]

While many students sought Lawrence's resignation, the university senate at Rutgers came out in support of the president and officially accepted his apology. The resolution passed unanimously by the executive committee stated, "Our knowledge of him and his outstanding record of promoting opportunities for minorities at Rutgers University gives us no reason to believe that he meant what was said, and much reason to believe that he does not." But many students and faculty were angered by the actions of the executive committee and some openly disagreed with the resolution. As University Senator Mike Ristorucci, a junior, commented, "Fran Lawrence cushions himself in the university senate with people who support him. . . . [I see the resolution] as very underhanded considering they didn't consult any of their members."[20]

Despite the support of the senate, a group of about four hundred students packed the Livingston Student Center on Monday, February 6, to present a list of demands. The event was held by the newly formed United Student Coalition (USC), which continued the call for Lawrence's resignation. Diabb Abdus-Salaam, president of 100 Black Men and a senior at Rutgers, was one of the students to present the demands. "The issue and the problem is that students have no power at this university," explained Abdus-Salaam. "Fran Lawrence did not come to us first; he came to us last. If Fran Lawrence goes tomorrow, will we have power? If he stays, will we have power? We need to be clear on what the issues are." In addition to the previous demands related to diversifying the campus, the students added another concern: a restructuring of the board of governors to make it more representative of the state's population. Also, plans for a student walk-out and a demonstration at the Brower Common dining hall on College Avenue the following day were announced.[21] What they did not announce is what would happen later that night at the basketball showdown of the nationally ranked University of Massachusetts Minutemen and the Scarlet Knights of Rutgers at the Louis Brown Athletic Center in Piscataway.

The Rutgers–U. Mass Basketball Game

The first half was hotly contested as the unranked Scarlet Knights battled to a two-point lead over the number-four-ranked team in the country. The game had been highly anticipated and was seen by Rutgers' fans as a chance to gain some national recognition if they could hold their own or perhaps upset the Minutemen. Jacqueline Williams, a junior studying to be a physician's assistant, arrived late to the game after missing her train in Newark. Upon her arrival, she was surprised to learn not only that Rutgers was winning, but more significantly to her, the student demonstration that had been planned had not taken place after all. The United Student Coalition was supposed to lead a major demonstration at the beginning of the game. The protest was to include members of the basketball team, as USC hoped to force the game's cancellation and draw a national audience to their cause. As Williams later learned, the players had been warned not to get involved or they would face the possible loss of their scholarships. Consequently, the protest never occurred.

Williams stood in the packed arena confused and perplexed at what amounted to a tremendous lost opportunity. It was an opportunity, however, that she would not allow to slip away. As Williams explained, "We were all supposed to show up at the game and eventually not let the game go on at all. The game was never supposed to start." Williams discussed what happened next: "I had missed my train and, by the time I got back, halftime was about to start, and when I saw that there was no demonstration going on I kinda got frustrated. So I decided to take it upon myself to just stop the game."

It was near the end of halftime that Williams decided to seize the moment: she walked onto the court and planted herself at the center court circle. At first, two officials from the university attempted to talk her into leaving. They were joined by others who surrounded Williams and tried to coax her into moving off the court. They explained to her that the game would be canceled and her team would lose if she did not get up and leave. She just looked at them kind of incredulously—"as if a basketball game was more significant than fighting racial hatred and bigotry." Her stocking cap, pulled down to just above her eyebrows, outlined the transfixed and concentrated expression Williams presented as she refused to budge. She recalled the questions they shot at her: "What is your name? Why are you doing this? Who are you? Where are you from? Are you a student at the school?" Then a man approached her and explained, "We know why you're doing this. You made your point. Why don't you just leave?" Williams kept herself together despite being the focal point of the hundreds of fans gathered for the game and the camera crews which had by now surrounded her. In a calm and collected voice the only words she uttered were these: "I will leave when President Lawrence leaves."

Several students in the stands held a sign which read: "How do we deal with an intellectually 'disadvantaged' pres? We fire him!" They were asked by security guards to remove the sign but instead they walked onto the court to join Williams.[22] Soon five or six more walked out. Then seven or eight additional students joined the delegation at center court. Before long there were nearly two hundred students sitting on the court and the game had to be rescheduled. Williams was surprised—no, shocked—that other students took so long to join her. The few minutes she sat alone at half-court were like hours. On the outside she appeared as cool as a cucumber, but on the inside she was stewing like a caldron of spicy soup. "I knew I was not the only one who was frustrated by the things that were said by President Lawrence and the type of treatment that we have been receiving throughout the university. . . . I just couldn't believe that I was the only person who would think to seize this moment, to let the whole world know that this is a very racist institution and the fact that President Lawrence was still here. . . . Nobody ever wants to fight against it and I couldn't believe how passive some people could be. We study Black history and all this other stuff from the past, the type of things and treatment that Black people went through like slavery, and the first thing that comes out of most people's mouths is 'Boy, if I lived during that time I would have fought back. I woulda did this. I woulda did that.' Well, I say now is your time. There's this big chance to fight back against that type of treatment but they hesitated to do it and I couldn't understand what was going through their minds."

Many in the audience eventually came to the support of Williams. Others, however, shouted and jeered: "We want hoops!" and "Get off the court!" could be heard throughout the arena. Racial epithets were also used as tempers boiled. Because Rutgers has a school policy that forbids forcefully removing students engaged in peaceful demonstrations, university officials were left with no option but to postpone the game. Thus, with the Scarlet Knights leading the number-four-ranked team in the country 31–29, Atlantic 10 commissioner Linda Bruno suspended play after a thirty-minute delay. The image of Jacqueline Williams seated at center court was soon transmitted around the country and students had succeeded in calling wide-scale attention to the inflammatory comments.

Williams believed that the basketball sit-in was a means to an end and not the final solution. It was one way to battle the pervasive racism she experienced every day growing up in Newark and then faced first during her attendance in public schools and then college where institutionalized racism was the norm. President Lawrence's comments were simply an example of the kind of institutionally supported bigotry that occasionally seeped out from under the lid of the so-called melting pot. The sit-in, to her, was more than simply a demonstration. It was a way of hitting the university in its wallet. She explained: "I see what goes on at home and in the streets. You just have to wonder about what you can do to try and change things. I know that protesting to me is not the answer. It's not the way to fight. Protesting is only a way to bring something to the attention of others. I think that's the mistake a lot of students make when they continuously protest. They see it as a way to fight against whatever it is they don't agree with. Especially when it comes to institutional racism, which is one of the reasons why I decided to do what I did, you know, to expose institutional racism. . . . Back in the sixties it was a way for them to fight. But here and now in the nineties they don't care what you do. You can protest all you want and as long as you don't do anything to affect them personally, then nothing is going to change." For Williams, cutting into the university's profits by disrupting the basketball game was a way to demonstrate the power of the Black student community. Once the administration saw the potential of student solidarity, perhaps they would consider the students' demands.

Although many around the country condemned the actions of Williams, as evident by the hate mail she received, others found inspiration in her courage. For example, in an article published in *Black Issues in Higher Education* Timothy Quinnan talked about the "cultural politics of hope" represented by Williams's lonely trek to center court. Quinnan argues that incidents such as this need to be interpreted from perspectives that help us to understand difference and the role that hope plays in our struggles to achieve equality. In his role as a student affairs professional he considers himself to be a "worker in the cultural politics of hope." Quinnan often relies on postmodern theories and their commitment to difference and multiculturalism to inform his work on his own campus and to guide interactions with students. As he explains, postmodernism "offers strategies for educators to adopt in fostering institution-wide dialogue and accommodation of divergent perspectives. Further, postmodernism instructs us that difference and dissent are critical components of learning, must be encouraged, and may be constructively managed in academic environments."[23] Quinnan reminds us all that the actions of students such as Jacqueline Williams must not be silenced. Peaceful student resistance must be embraced for the suffering it reveals, the potential organizational learning it offers, and the hope it inspires.

But not everyone at Rutgers saw the hope underlying the actions of the student sit-in. Instead, many at the institution responded with the instrumentality to be expected of contemporary bureaucrats. At a press conference the day after the demonstration, Lawrence responded to the sit-in and the disruption of the game: "It should come as no surprise that we cannot allow the action of one group to interfere with the rights of another. That is the message I want to come through loud and clear."[24] But one could argue that the actions of President Lawrence interfered with the rights of African American students. After all, when the president of a major university offers a representation of African Americans as genetically inferior—whether intentional or not—does not such a remark influence how others perceive and indeed interact with African Americans? Obviously, none of us lives in a vacuum and whatever actions we take cause a reaction from someone else. Thus, the question of whether someone's rights have been denied is one that must continually be answered by taking into account the social and political context. When a basketball game is postponed because of a student protest, is someone's right to attend such a game any more relevant than someone else's right to be treated with dignity and respect? Obviously, questions about rights and whose are violated under certain conditions are not so easily answered.

The Demonstrations Continue

The day after the sit-in at the basketball game, the United Student Coalition had its demonstration on the steps of the Brower Commons as it had planned. But this time instead of the six or seven hundred students that they had been drawing to various demonstrations, only about one hundred showed up. USC reiterated their earlier demands for restructuring the board of governors, improved recruitment and retention efforts for Black and Latino students (and faculty were mentioned as well), and a more diverse curriculum. By this time, mention of tuition rollbacks was also included in the list of demands.

Three days after the sit-in, students from New Brunswick were joined by students from the Newark and Piscataway campuses as they moved their protests to the meeting of the board of governors.[25] The Rutgers Association of Black Law Students (ABLS) continued to be adamant about Lawrence resigning. If Lawrence will not resign, ABLS stated, "we strongly urge the board of governors to immediately remove him from office and replace him with a president who recognizes his duties to enhance educational value for the students, to promote goodwill and to be socially responsible." Anthony Mulrain was one of five members of ABLS allowed to speak to the board. Mulrain believed Lawrence had seriously failed in his duties to represent Rutgers University and had done significant damage to the African American community. "His racist remarks are a punishing blow to every young African American who is trying to do something responsible." Marissa Cunningham, chair of the Rutgers-Newark ABLS also spoke at the meeting and highlighted the potential far-reaching impact of Lawrence's statement: "At first we were not quite sure if asking for his resignation would be the solution to the problem because we saw the problem simply as a Rutgers issue. We felt that if he stayed he would be in the best position to implement necessary changes within the administration. . . . We realized [however] that this is not solely a Rutgers issue. It is a national issue."[26]

Despite protests from ABLS, among others, the board gave a vote of confidence to Lawrence. Additionally, Christine Todd Whitman, governor of New Jersey, expressed her support for President Lawrence, describing him as a "strong proponent of encouraging diversity." Governor Whitman stated that the decision should be left to the board of governors and that she would not join the chorus calling for Lawrence's resignation.[27]

On February 15 President Lawrence and the administration, at the direction of the board of governors, met with student leaders to form a committee charged with improving the quality of life for students at the university. Members of the Association of Black Law Students complained that the impromptu meeting called by Lawrence excluded many of the African American students most concerned about campus life and they saw his actions as one more attempt to silence outcries from the African American community. According to ABLS, only one of the students involved in the meeting was Black. A representative of ABLS commented: "It is interesting, though, that the students who were present and who seemed to have been given a little bit more notice than we have been given were students who had either spoken out in support of Lawrence or who had remained neutral on the issue of his resignation." They went on to state, "We will not make any assumptions about the planning on the part of the administration, but we will say that the divisive intent that it implies will not be tolerated. We will not tolerate any attempts by the administration to stifle or punish certain groups for speaking out against Dr. Lawrence. We will also not tolerate any efforts to avoid the major issues by appeasing some students with unrelated concerns."[28]

As February wore on and as the committee formed by Lawrence gained a degree of legitimacy, the campus began to return to a state of normalcy. Random protests, however, continued to break out until the middle of April. For example, in early March two law students, Regis Ferguson and Nicole Davis, were arrested at the Newark campus as they attempted to obstruct entry to the S. I. Newhouse Center for Law and Justice, while other students carrying signs marched in front of the building. The two students were forcibly removed by police officers, who used pepper spray and handcuffs. Ferguson was charged with obstructing a public passage, aggravated assault on a police officer, and resisting arrest, while Davis faced charges of obstructing a public passage, hindering apprehension, and disorderly conduct.[29]

In April, more serious events took place as a bomb exploded early in the morning on Tuesday, April 4, in the lower level of the Mabel Smith Douglass Library. No one was injured but all thirteen libraries on the New Brunswick campus were evacuated later in the day.[30] The next day, two bomb threats targeting the Paul Robeson Library were reported, but no explosions occurred nor were any bombs found. Leslie Fehrenbach, assistant vice president for public safety, believed the latter incidents simply were cases of copycats following the actions that had taken place the previous day.[31] Then, on Friday, April 7, a bomb was discovered in the Douglass Library. The bomb was found in a hollowed-out book by a library worker shelving books. Agents from the Federal Bureau of Investigation, with the assistance of the Bureau of Alcohol, Tobacco, and Firearms, were heading up the investigations.[32] Jessica Applebaum of the *Daily Targum* commented on the bomb incidents, the first of which was set off on April 4 and coincided with the date of the assassination of Martin Luther King Jr.: "Nobody took responsibility for it but there is rumor, speculation. I think that the police and officials at the university tied it back to the same students who were protesting. . . . The FBI is still looking into it. There are signs up in the library that the FBI is still looking for suspects." The bombings were never resolved nor was it known in fact whether the occurrences were linked to the demonstrations resulting from Lawrence's comments.

On April 11, two students associated with the United Student Coalition held a press conference to announce that they were going on a hunger strike until President Lawrence resigned. It was also announced that a rally would be held the next day at the Old Queens building. While efforts on the part of these students and the demonstration at the Newhouse Center for Law and Justice in Newark represented a struggle that had become somewhat haphazard, the upcoming rally at Old Queens rejuvenated the movement, if only temporarily.

On Wednesday, April 12, a group of students blocked traffic at one of the major intersections between Piscataway and New Brunswick. They were part of a contingent of students who had moved from the main New Brunswick campus (from near the Old Queens building) to the intersection. One of the demonstrators explained that the intersection was selected because it serves as the connection between Route 27, Route 18, and the New Jersey Turnpike. "We picked it out as the center point where all those highways connected and we just blocked it off. We weren't trying to obstruct traffic. We were just trying to close Rutgers down. We were trying to keep the busses from going from one campus to another." Rutgers University is a collection of several colleges including Livingston, Douglass, Busch, and New Brunswick. Students can take classes at any of the Rutgers colleges, and the entire operation of the university depends on bus transportation to and from the various locations. Thus, targeting the nexus of major transportation routes made perfect sense to the student demonstrators.

Clarence Tokley described the day's events as "a day of confusions— a day of chaos." The plan was to collect on the lawn of the Old Queens building on College Avenue where the president's office is and then march through New Brunswick. As busloads of students got off at the College Avenue bus stop, many decided to join the demonstration and the crowd quickly swelled to some five hundred or more students. The group then proceeded toward New Brunswick, where police had already blockaded street access and rerouted traffic. As the students and their police escorts made their way toward downtown New Brunswick, spontaneity got the best of the protesters and they changed their plans. As Tokley explained, "We were heading into New Brunswick but when we got there we just said forget it and just went straight to Route 18. That's like a major highway. They knew about New Brunswick so they already had the roads blocked off. When we went to Route 18 that threw them off and there was nothing they could do 'cause we were on a major highway. And that's where we got into it with the Piscataway police."

The students made their way to the president's house, which is just off of Route 18. Once there, they were informed by a press representative of the president that he was out of town and that if they didn't leave they would be removed from the premises. The students held an impromptu rally on the president's lawn; various individuals briefly spoke and chants demanding Lawrence's resignation filled the air. Eventually, the group grew tired and, recognizing Lawrence's absence, they made their way back to College Avenue. By this time, they had already lost quite a few students who had headed home or elsewhere. Nonetheless, there were still some two hundred students as part of the continuing demonstration. Tokley described what happened next: "We started to head back to College Avenue, toward the main campus to have another rally. And then a whole bunch of people just decided that we were going to stay at the intersection and just block traffic. And we just formed a big circle and blocked off traffic." According to Tokley, it was around 4 P.M. and the traffic quickly backed up for miles. The intersection they blocked is one of the busiest in the area and thus it did not take long to get an official response as an estimated seventy-five police officers arrived at the scene.

Khai Harley, a sophomore and member of 100 Black Men, recalled the arrival of the police: "There was a group of sisters sittin' on the road, at the intersection actually, I wouldn't even say a group of sisters—there was a group of women, sittin' there and the police proceeded to try and pick them up, to move them out of the way without saying anything to anybody. And when they attempted to do so a group of people rushed over there to see what was goin' on. There they are liftin' these girls up . . . . Then as soon as they were approached they immediately put the sisters down, backed up and started sprayin' everybody with mace and pepper spray." Several of the brothers involved were also clubbed and "poked with billy clubs," stated Harley.

Students' descriptions of their treatment at the hands of the police were not very positive. "The police called us niggers, told us to suck their dicks and had time to get bats, mace, and riot gear," said Ayinde Brinkley, a visiting Morehouse student. "People are assaulted and they have to defend themselves for being assaulted," said Eunice Brinkley, mother of Ayinde. Brinkley reported that she was horrified when she watched TV and witnessed her son being maced and dragged by his hair.[33] A student who participated in the demonstration recalled her experience: "When we blocked off the highway, there was a lot of police brutality and they sprayed people with pepper spray. One girl got hit in the head, I believe, with one of the officers' clubs. It was such a shame because we had formed a circle . . . and we tried to reenact the scene at the basketball game. Several of the students had their backs to the police officers and they just came up from behind. Nobody even knew they were coming and they just started swinging all through the group. Why the brutality? Why would you come up from behind somebody and hit them?" This student could not help but think about all the revolutionary rhetoric that some Black organizations espouse. She was beginning to understand why so many groups called for more serious, perhaps even violent responses to the oppression experienced by African Americans. "It was an unbelievable sight and then right there at that moment, the one thing that I kept thinking about was how a lot of the Black revolutionaries constantly talk about how Black people need to get together and just have a revolutionary war or whatever you want to call it."

But the students at Rutgers were for the most part not militant revolutionaries, and the violence some of them experienced and that others soon learned of served as a wake-up call for many who retreated from the movement and returned to their studies. Jacqueline Williams believed that the suburban, middle-class Blacks who had joined USC and the larger movement were not used to this kind of a fight. "There's a difference between the Blacks who live in the suburbs and the Blacks who live in the city. I've been a fighter all my life. I had no choice but to be a fighter 'cause I was raised in the ghetto. When you have people that live in the suburbs, it's like they don't come in contact with the same types of things that we experience in the ghetto." Thus, while some of the students may have been prepared or perhaps expected violence, the majority of the students were eager to get back to their school work and end the demonstrations.

The observations by Williams about differences among Blacks are supported by the research of Patricia Gurin and Edgar Epps, who report that urban students were more likely to engage in civil rights demonstrations in the 1960s than were rural students.[34] And Robin Kelley[35] points out that Black resistance in the United States has long been tied to social position and class status. Therefore, it may come as no surprise to some that middle-class Blacks might be less willing than their working- and lower-class brothers and sisters to engage in political demonstration, especially when there is the potential for violence.

Based on a videotape of the incident, seven students were identified and later arrested. At the hearing that followed, one of the charged students stated to presiding judge William Gazi, "We had a message to get across and we thought we had a First Amendment right to do so." He added, "We were not informed by police verbally that we were doing anything legally wrong." Judge Gazi countered that their actions went beyond freedom of speech and that the students had no legal right to obstruct traffic. The judge handed down sixty hours of community service in Middlesex County and fines of $252 each (the NAACP contributed $415 to the students for shared legal fees). Judge Gazi stated, "You interrupted the flow of traffic and inconvenienced the public." As Steve Guzman, a Rutgers junior, explained, the prosecuted students felt they were singled out by the police: "They picked seven people out of a group," said Guzman. The students believed they were targeted because of their high profile on campus. Guzman was formerly student body president. Damian Santiago and Jamal Phillips were co-captains of the Rutgers basketball team. Trevor Phillips was a former president of 100 Black Men.

John Brinkley, Ayinde's father, commented about the episode: "I hope what they were trying to do, in bringing attention to Francis Lawrence's statements, doesn't get lost in legal proceedings. When you stand up there are consequences but sometimes it's worth it to change things."[36]

Media Coverage

Once again, as in the cases at Mills College and UCLA in particular, the media played a central role in bringing the students' causes and the issues they wished to raise before a larger audience. Without the attention garnered by the basketball sit-in, much of what became known about President Lawrence's remarks and the students' response may have remained only a regional news item. A professor at Rutgers talked about the media: "They got national attention through the media. In that sense, it had a great impact. It seems, however, since the 1960s, even though the media has the ability of exposing some of the problems of social life on college campuses, protest in the 1990s is not enough any more. It just doesn't seem to make the changes that are necessary. You know what I mean? Something else has to happen." This professor agreed with earlier comments offered by Jacqueline Williams when she said that student protest is only a means to a larger end and that more hard work on the part of students must follow if real change is to occur.

A couple of African American faculty openly wondered what the media coverage might have resembled had more of the reporters been Black. One professor followed the coverage quite closely and believed that White reporters described the entire episode differently from Black reporters. As he explained, the White reporters tended to portray Lawrence in a sympathetic manner: He was a good guy who simply made a slip of the tongue. Black reporters, he argued, were far more critical and raised serious-minded questions about the comments. "Could someone actually make such a slip? Could he have been searching for different words? And if so, what were the comparable phrases that he was trying to express?" A second faculty member also discussed the bias that he perceived existed in the media: "People in the media, and high-ranking officials and newspapers closed ranks and supported Lawrence. . . . There was this great desire to turn Lawrence into the victim. Somehow people were beating up on this decent guy. 'There those Blacks go again, being unreasonable, outrageous.' There was a closing of ranks. A sense that they had to stand together against the radicals out there. The establishment will not act in a way which concedes validity to Black American protests or that empowers Black Americans by acquiescing to their demands. There was a lot of that."

While media coverage may have been biased, it at the same time served as a vehicle for students to achieve national attention. However, the media coverage eventually subsided, with the exception of efforts by the *Daily Targum*, and as early as late February the movement appeared to be dying. Otis Rolley did not so much sense that student interest was dwindling as much as he felt that the media's interest was fading. As he argued, "If anything has died down it's the coverage, not the movement." Later he added, "A quiet storm is still a storm," and explained that USC was focused on educating students about the issues before they planned their next action.[37] But lack of coverage could kill the movement, and as protests wound down it was not always clear which came first, smaller crowds at demonstrations or the lack of presence of the media.

The arrests following the April 12 demonstrations on Route 18 in many ways brought a close to this chapter in the long history of racial struggle at Rutgers. Certainly, it would not end here, but the storm caused by the president's remarks was subsiding and all that was left was to make sense of what had happened. One thing was clear: The movement to oust Lawrence was not simply an issue of concern to African American students. Practically from the very start, the movement truly had been a multiracial struggle with Latino, Asian American, Puerto Rican, and White students all playing roles in the demonstrations. The painful comments were unifying in that they brought a sense of compulsion to nearly every minority student and progressive-minded White as they fought against a form of inequality that they felt undergirded the entire university. The kind of discourse put forth in books such as *The Bell Curve*, they felt, gave voice to what many Whites seemed to believe but refused to openly acknowledge. To students who formed the United Student Coalition, Lawrence simply had slipped and let down his guard.

Culture and Identity

For one African American professor at Rutgers, the comments of President Lawrence, along with the indictments of Black intelligence in the book *The Bell Curve*, were both troublesome: "*The Bell Curve* has caused a great deal of controversy in the academic world and there are too many painful things there for Blacks, for African Americans. Because of Black kids scoring lower on SAT's and Graduate Record Exams [GRE's]. For something like that, *The Bell Curve* is very painful, if it's even suggested. There are many reasons for the test scores and so on, and for someone to say, well, you know, we're genetically inferior, it means that no matter what you do nothing will change that. . . . There's nothing you can do, nothing in this world can change your posture as an inferior human being. . . . That's a terrible indictment, because of your birth."

The question of a genetic link to intelligence received widespread national attention late in 1993 after the publication of Richard Herrnstein and Charles Murray's controversial book. The book's central argument—that race and genetics shape intelligence—has been discredited by critics who have attacked the authors for clearly lacking an understanding of how cultural influences contribute to performance in standardized measures. In fact, the book itself and the surrounding controversy were blamed by Lawrence for what he claimed was a misrepresentation of what he truly believed: "It [*The Bell Curve*] was on my mind, no question about it."[38]

While some of the Rutgers students wanted to continue their battle despite the possibility of violence escalating after the demonstrations on Route 18, Jacqueline Williams was among a group of students who believed it was time for African Americans to show the university what they could do with their minds. "I tried to explain to some of the leaders of the United Student Coalition . . . that people know what Black people are capable of doing. They have seen us over the years through the 1960s and probably before that. They know we have the power in our fist. They know we can fight. We can stand up to the cops if we have to. We have had battles with police officers, shoot-outs, or whatever. But it's time to focus on the fact that we cannot only defeat them with the iron fist but we can now also defeat them with our intellect. We can use our brains for this. We don't always have to be violent in order to get what we want. You have to show them that we are intelligent enough to sit down and talk with them—where you can think out a thorough plan, an educational plan." Williams saw a need to move the struggle to a more institutional setting where collectively African American students could begin to negotiate significant change at the university. They had gained an ear, so to speak, and now was the time to converse but in a dialogue that those in power might be able to understand, removed from the threat of public demonstration or violence.

The educational vision embraced by Williams points out the reality that schooling for African Americans has been and continues to be circumscribed by racism and by people who fail to understand the interconnections between culture and identity. In their classic study of students' experiences at historically Black colleges, Gurin and Epps stress the interconnections between educational achievement and identity.[39] One of the problems that they point to is that achievement in the United States is most often defined in individualistic terms and yet for many Black Americans success has a collective quality to it. For members of a group marginalized within the larger society, a sense of collective consciousness becomes an important source of identification and action. And the actions related to group commitments are not necessarily the kinds of actions rewarded in an educational system framed by individualism. Thus, the sense of identity inspired by one's African heritage is at times incompatible with the mainstream culture of the United States, which so often is framed by Eurocentric norms and values rooted in the rugged individualist.

The cultural experiences of Blacks most recently have been highlighted by debates surrounding the role of Ebonics in school instruction. The inability of some to accept the legitimacy of a language spoken by many African Americans is akin to the same reluctance to recognize that subcultural experiences are in fact quite diverse. The fact that African Americans have unique cultural forms and yet must learn the cultural manifestations of White society raises the specter of Blacks having to exist in two separate social worlds which often pull them in opposite directions. This sense of dual identity or "double consciousness" makes the experiences of Blacks and other minorities significantly different from that of the White majority. As W. E. B. Du Bois wrote in *The Souls of Black Folk*,

> The history of the American Negro is the history of . . . longing to attain self-conscious manhood, to merge his double self into a better and truer self. In this merging he wishes neither of the older selves to be lost. He would not Africanize America, for America has too much to teach the world of Africa. He would not bleach his Negro soul in a flood of white Americanism, for he knows that Negro blood has a message for the world. He simply wishes to make it possible for a man to be both a Negro and an American, without being cursed and spit upon by his fellows, without having the doors of Opportunity closed roughly in his face.[40]

But not all Blacks experience the identity dilemma of trying to fit within a White society while struggling to claim the richness of one's African blood. Molefi Kete Asante always knew that he was not part of the White society.

When I got up in the mornings to go to the cotton and tobacco fields, little white children got up to go fishing in the lakes or to camp. I knew that much from seeing them at the swimming pool, at the lakes, and at the parks as I rode those trucks back and forth to work. That was the experience it seemed of the white children I either saw or heard about; however, certainly somewhere in Georgia there must have been other whites with work experiences similar to mine. The point, though, is that most of the labor in the South during that period was performed by Africans. There were and remain in this country dual societies, one white and richer, one black and poorer. Perhaps in a great number of Africans these societies and the "two warring souls" converge to create a caldron of psychological problems; this was not the case with me or my family.[41]

Asante thus sees little need for Africans living in the United States to seek integration between the complex identities formed through a heritage rooted in Africa and one forged in America. For him the answer to the contemporary dilemmas faced by Blacks is to embrace fully their African roots. His philosophy, known as Afrocentricity, has come to influence many African American student activists of today. "Afrocentricity is the belief in the centrality of Africans in post modern history. It is our history, our mythology, our creative motif, and our ethos exemplifying our collective will. On the basis of our story, we build upon the work of ancestors who gave signs toward our humanizing function."[42]

To many White Americans, the discourse of Asante is frightening and seems to resemble the early rhetoric of Malcolm X when he preached Black nationalism and the establishment of a separate African American nation. But within Asante's work is a passionate calling forth of the strength of Africa and a willingness to embrace his own "blackness," a quality made difficult by a society that makes the denigration of that which is "black" comforting to the White majority. The identity project engaged in by Asante is in part a struggle to represent Blacks on their own terms and necessarily reject the images and representations offered over time that have become so much a part of White cultural hegemony. It is akin to the struggle bell hooks spoke of when she wrote, "As a radical intervention we must develop revolutionary attitudes about race and representation. To do this we must be willing to think critically about images. We must be willing to take risks."[43]

Khai Harley saw the student protests at Rutgers connected to hope and a belief in the idealism of the 1960s. He also felt the movement attested to two basic groups within the African American community: "I have a theory that Blacks throughout America have an identity crisis. They're searching for an identity. They're in constant struggle to find out who it is they are. And generally you find two groups of people. You find a group of people who look to identify with their African heritage, you know, but have a problem doing so, because of the culture in America that has buried African heritage for so long and has prevented Black Americans from identifying with it. Or you have the population of people who seek to assimilate, accommodate themselves to American society. But they do so without realizing that America does not want them to be Americans." Harley went on to relate his theory to contemporary Black activists and their search for meaning: "I think student activists are searching to find an identity of their own. They're trying to forge their own identity, and the only form of comparison that they have is to look back toward the fifties, sixties, and seventies, to the protest movements of those time periods. . . . My parents talked to me about the sixties and about what went on. The unity and solidarity that Black people expressed during that period of time. And it's something that a lot of student activists don't see nowadays and it's something that they long for."

Students such as Jacqueline Williams, Otis Rolley, Clarence Tokley, Darryl Scippio, and Khai Harley took serious risks to offer their own interpretations of an empowered African American identity. The desire was to forge their own representations in a seemingly endless battle waged against denigrating cultural attacks such as that offered by President Lawrence. The image of Jacqueline Williams, firmly planted at the center of a basketball court, rupturing American hyper-fascination with the culture of sports, was as powerful an image as those of the Black Resistance Movement in the late 1960s. Williams still cannot believe how important the basketball game was to the people who tried to coax her off the court. "You are going to upset everyone who came to see the game," they said. Imagine that.

America has for years claimed to be a color-blind society that sees racial identity as irrelevant to one's ability and opportunity to succeed. Such thinking has led to conclusions by cultural individualists that African Americans must in some way be deficient. What they fail and perhaps refuse to recognize is that in no way have we created a color-blind society. In refusing to admit the racial construction of American life, individualists, conservatives, moderates, and even many liberals propagate a deeply entrenched racism. "The net effect of the color-blind theory is to institutionalize and stabilize the status quo of race relations for the twenty-first century: white privilege and black deprivation."[44] The African American students at Rutgers, as well as their multiracial allies, understand the myth of the color-blind society and have posed a challenge to American higher education to build truly multicultural institutions of higher learning.

Moving Forward with an Eye to the Past

The idea for Black History Month reflects the growing imperative that all Americans, not simply African Americans, understand the history and contributions Black Americans have made to the diversity of U.S. society. An ironic aspect to the Rutgers demonstrations was that they started on February 1, a day that marked the beginning of Black History Month. On the same day that the *Daily Targum* released its story about President Lawrence, they also published a small caption on the first page entitled "Black History Month 1995." Under the caption were comments from Richard Nurse, assistant vice president for undergraduate education at Rutgers, in which he offered his view of the importance of the yearly celebration: "Black History Month is an opportunity to celebrate the diversity and richness of the African American community and an opportunity to connect with heritage in the African Diaspora."

The early work of African American activists such as Stokely Carmichael, Bobby Seale, Angela Davis, and Huey Newton was a driving force for Black student activism in the late 1960s at institutions such as Rutgers. Other more prominent civil rights leaders such as Martin Luther King Jr. and Malcolm X also stirred the passion of the students of that period. Clearly, the students of the 1990s have been influenced by the work of previous generations of activists. And although today's students look to Malcolm X and King for inspiration, they in no way want to be confused with the generation of the sixties. As Clarence Tokley explained in complaining about media coverage of the events at Rutgers during the spring of 1995, "The media's not gonna give it to you. The only time you'll see it [student demonstrations] in the media is like in some novelty special about the retro or the past. They think it's something like with the sixties, and they'll say that too. Like they'll say these people are trying to relive the 1960s. And it's not the sixties. It's the nineties, going into 2000. And it's not that we're trying to relive it. It never stopped livin'. I'm just trying my best to get people to see that it never stopped livin'."

The Multicultural Student Movement of the 1990s is not about students trying to re-create the civil rights struggle of the 1960s. That struggle, as Clarence Tokley aptly noted, "never stopped livin'." Things may have quieted down for a few decades, but student unrest and commitment to creating a truly democratic and inclusive society continue to this day. Although African American students at Rutgers and their multiracial supporters exhibited a similar kind of passion and commitment to social transformation evident during the 1960s, their cause was clearly one for the nineties and served as a painful reminder of the stronghold racism continues to have over American society. For Khai Harley, it was a mistake to look back on the 1960s uncritically: "I feel it's unfortunate but today's students romanticize about the sixties and seventies. They romanticize about the mass protests, the rallies, the marches, and the riots and so forth. You know, instead of looking at it in a realistic context they look to reenact that period. But they are doomed to repeat the past, instead of adapting to what the environment is now."

A student reflected on the potential positive that could come from the remarks of President Lawrence: "We live in a society where you cannot express racism so it comes out every now and then in different symbolic and subconscious kinds of ways. I think that may be what happened to Lawrence and that some part of him really did believe that. And I think that it was kind of good that it happened at Rutgers because it symbolizes in many ways the place of African Americans in higher education. It's been a school that's had a long history of African American activism." Perhaps the struggle at Rutgers would have long-term implications and just maybe it would provide a ray of hope for Americans around the country who have yet to face their own racist assumptions about others. Unearthing racism certainly will lead to increased tension and conflict, as was evident at Rutgers University in the spring of 1995. However, without such efforts it is likely that racism will continue to eat at the collective soul of American society, and that colleges and universities will continue to enact racial inequality well into the twenty-first century.

chapter eight

COLLECTIVE

CONSCIOUSNESS

Toward an Activist Identity

In the preceding chapter, Khai Harley was introduced as one of the activists at Rutgers University who helped organize the student response to President Francis Lawrence. Harley hoped that the incidents at Rutgers would lead to the emergence of a national movement among college students to create social change. "I believe that the student protests, because they gained national exposure, may provide students across the country a sense of responsibility and a sense of hope. I believe it [the movement at Rutgers] may have encouraged a lot of students to stand up and do something about the situations that they're faced with. The level of emotion that existed at Rutgers during this whole event could spread across the entire country, to other campuses and other universities." Harley went on to add: "The average student doesn't realize the power and the impact that they have on the university and what they can get accomplished if they show a collective effort. . . . The comments by President Lawrence lent an immediate sense of unity and a sense of solidarity and strength."

Whether the actions of students at Rutgers and students at other schools such as Mills College and UCLA served as catalysts for increased student activism is unclear. What is clear, however, is that across the country the 1990s evidenced a renewed commitment by students to social justice and educational equity, at the same time that conservative forces won battles to eliminate programs such as affirmative action.

Arguably, it has been the force of conservatism throughout recent decades that created an environment in which progressive-minded students saw little choice but to join arms to launch a countermovement. The Divestment Movement provided a portrait of how a battle might be waged, and as the eighties gave way to the next decade, changes were taking place on the American college scene. The Multicultural Student Movement was thus a reasonable response to the influence that conservative politics had assumed at college and university campuses around the country.

No single day epitomizes the conviction of multicultural activists more than the annual celebration of the birthday of Martin Luther King Jr. In 1997, for example, students around the country organized events for January 20 to pay tribute to a man whose life and death had come to symbolize many of the ideals reflected by multiculturalism. Who can ever forget his dramatic and inspiring "I Have a Dream" speech delivered on August 28, 1963, in the shadows of the Lincoln Memorial as part of the historic march on Washington:

> I have a dream that one day this nation will rise up and live out the true meaning of its creed: "We hold these truths to be self-evident: that all men are created equal." I have a dream that one day on the red hills of Georgia the sons of former slaves and the sons of former slave owners will be able to sit down together at a table of brotherhood. I have a dream that one day even the state of Mississippi, a desert state, sweltering with the heat of injustice and oppression, will be transformed into an oasis of freedom and justice. I have a dream that my four children will one day live in a nation where they will not be judged by the color of their skin but by the content of their character.

In his speech, King was able to impugn the hatred and bigotry of an entire nation and offer an inspirational portrait of something better. He envisioned a world in which love formed the core of relationships with one another. The love King dreamt of knew no racial bounds: "I have a dream that one day the state of Alabama, whose governor's lips are presently dripping with the words of interposition and nullification, will be transformed into a situation where little black boys and black girls will be able to join hands with little white boys and white girls and walk together as sisters and brothers." His vision was powerful and the more than two hundred thousand freedom marchers gathered around him could feel his words reach into their souls and tug at their spiritual centers. King's life was about freedom and he extended the web of freedom to everyone. In concluding his speech, he challenged all of America, from east to west, north to south, to join freedom's march.

Let freedom ring from the snowcapped Rockies of Colorado! Let freedom ring from the curvaceous peaks of California! But not only that; let freedom ring from Stone Mountain of Georgia! Let freedom ring from Lookout Mountain of Tennessee! Let freedom ring from every hill and every molehill of Mississippi. From every mountainside, let freedom ring. When we let freedom ring, when we let it ring from every village and every hamlet, from every state and every city, we will be able to speed up that day when all of God's children, black men and white men, Jews and Gentiles, Protestants and Catholics, will be able to join hands and sing in the words of the old Negro spiritual, "Free at last! Free at last! Thank God Almighty, we are free at last!"

King's gift was his ability to bring people to a common vision. Unlike any leader in U.S. history, King could put to words what many had buried in their hearts, and he did it with such grace and passion that the differences which had served to divide one from another suddenly seemed surmountable, and a collective struggle possible.

On college campuses around the country, the significance of January 20, 1997, did not go unnoticed. For example, at Michigan State University the student association declared classes optional and various groups took advantage of the academic community's attentiveness as they raised issues at several of the campuswide celebrations. For example, Mark Torres, co-chair of the Culturas de las Razas Unidas, complained of the hypocrisy of a university administration that purports to support the ideals of King but then fails to stand behind a grape boycott to protect migrant workers.[1] A few months later, to mark the thirtieth anniversary of King's assassination, a group of more than forty students and faculty gathered around the MSU rock at the center of campus to celebrate what they defined as "A Day without Violence." As one of the student organizers, Chong-Anna Rumsey, explained, "Generation X does have a conscience. We are here not only because of Dr. King's death, but so we can speak about our own experiences." And journalism sophomore Victor Walker commented, "It's important for us to remember our past, and acknowledge it now. King spoke for me when I couldn't speak."[2]

On January 20 at Indiana University at Bloomington, an estimated five hundred students held a rally and a boycott of classes to protest what they described as the university's limited commitment to diverse students and faculty. The students introduced a list of demands to the administration that vividly expressed their commitment to multiculturalism. Their

"Declaration of Demands" included approval and implementation of a Latino studies department, the appointment of an Asian American advocacy dean, the creation of an Asian cultural center, the maintenance of the Office of Diversity Programs, funding for gay, lesbian, and bisexual student support services, and immediate arrangements for an increase in both non-White and women faculty.

The rally at Indiana University served as a reminder that, despite the celebratory quality of the King holiday, there was much political and cultural work still to do. Consequently, there was tension at many of the campus events and activities organized around the country. This was especially true at the State University of New York at Binghamton, where the day took on new meaning in light of the events that had occurred over the immediate academic year. In the fall of 1996, students of color, along with progressive Whites, formed a multiracial student group known as the Binghamton Coalition as a response to the election of conservative Anthony J. Bernardello to the post of student association president. Bernardello was a thirty-seven-year-old Desert Storm veteran who in the fall of 1996 was intent on storming SUNY Binghamton and the university's rampant "liberalism" that he believed discriminated against Whites. For Bernardello, like supporters of Proposition 209 in California, it was time to put an end to affirmative action and other policies that threatened the individualist traditions of U.S. society and gave support to liberals, whom Bernardello labeled as "White haters."

Early in his tenure, Bernardello called for the firing of professors who espoused liberal and leftist ideology. The greatest conflict, however, was created when Bernardello appointed six White males to the executive cabinet and then removed the lone minority, the vice president for multicultural affairs. According to Bernardello, the VP had been elected by the "cultural unions"—the Black Student Union, the Haitian Student Union, the Latin American Student Union, and the Gay Student Association—and consequently, Whites had been excluded from the process. What became crystal clear as the fall semester progressed was that Bernardello had the potential to set the university's multicultural initiatives back many years. In fact, he had warned the campus early on in his tenure that race relations would likely get worse.

In an effort to make their voice known, members of the Binghamton Coalition attempted to gain access to a Student Association meeting, a meeting which was normally open to the public but had come under restrictions because of previous student disruptions. Consequently, only thirty students were allowed to participate as observers. This did not sit well with the coalition, which wanted to put pressure on Bernardello and the executive cabinet as well as bring greater public awareness to the embattled president's positions. When a group of about seventy tried to enter the room where the Student Association meeting was held, they were blocked by campus police, some of whom used pepper spray in deterring members of the coalition. The students then conducted an impromptu sit-in occupying the lobby of the administration building. A few days after the preceding incidents, several hundred students took over the administration building to protest police brutality and the reign of terror provoked by Bernardello.

The president of SUNY Binghamton, Dr. Lois B. DeFleur, came under attack from a variety of fronts. To conservative students at Binghamton, the administration had catered too heavily to minorities and it was time to correct inequities that had been created over the years. For students of color and their White allies, DeFleur had not taken strong enough action against Bernardello and thus enabled him to practice what many saw as overt racism. Thus, for students of color at SUNY Binghamton, the year proved to be an eventful one, with many of them distracted to the point that their studies suffered. These students could relate to a comment made by an African American student activist at Rutgers University when he explained in a slightly exasperated tone that college would be a breeze if it were not for all the other distractions. In the end, the celebration of the King holiday brought both joy and frustration: the joy of what the Civil Rights Movement had accomplished and frustration with how much further there was to travel. The incidents at Binghamton also highlight how multicultural and multiracial organizing is often in response to the strength of conservative politics and its infringement on programmatic strategies for creating social and educational equity.

While schools such as Indiana University and SUNY Binghamton witnessed stirrings of the Multicultural Movement throughout the year (as well as reactions to it from students such as Bernardello), student activism as a response to conservative politics was hot and heavy in the state of California as Proposition 209 (misleadingly entitled the "California Civil Rights Initiative") was passed in the fall of 1996. At the state-wide MEChA conference at California State University at Northridge, sixteen hundred students rallied in protest of the legislation. Earlier, a group of about one thousand students at the University of California at Berkeley staged a protest as a smaller group of twenty students took over the Campanile to protest actions taken by the University of California and UC President Richard Atkinson. Their complaint with Atkinson was his support of the regents' efforts to end race, gender, and ethnicity as factors in admissions, hiring, and contract decisions. The occupants of the Campanile released a statement addressing their concerns:

> The Campanile Tower is a symbol representing the University, and the Ivory Tower of elitism and exclusionism. Our occupation defies the passage of Proposition 209. Our occupation is an act of resistance and reclamation. We will occupy the tower until our demands are met or otherwise. In addition to our occupation we have made a commitment to fast, in order to purify our bodies and strengthen our spirits. Representation of people of color on the UC campuses will decline by 50 to 70 percent as a result of Proposition 209 being implemented (figures from the UC Office of the President). If the University decides to comply with 209 they will essentially be locking us out. This occupation represents us taking back our right to education.

What agitated students the most was that UC complied with 209 prior to being forced to do so by a court order. To these students, university officials were overly zealous in their compliance, which to them indicated the racism underlying the UC system.

On November 11, 1996, only days after the passage of 209, twenty students from the Student Coalition for Justice were arrested at the University of California at Riverside for their participation in a sit-in at the administration building. Following the arrests, the UC Riverside Academic Senate met to discuss a resolution to drop charges against the students and to question rumors that UC officials had been warned by Governor Pete Wilson that student demonstrators should be prosecuted. Two students from MEChA spoke on behalf of those arrested, pointing out that the demonstration had been peaceful and was part of a larger struggle in support of diversity and educational equity. The faculty voted overwhelmingly in support of the resolution and another calling for the university to await the outcome of legal rulings on the bill. The legal rulings to which the faculty referred involved various challenges to 209 as liberal forces sought to limit its implementation through court action.

The xenophobia evidenced by support of Proposition 209 calls attention to the high levels of racism still existing in the United States. The kind of hatred spread by 209 was evidenced by a computer message at the University of California at Irvine when a former student sent a note in which he threatened to hunt down and kill Asian students at the campus. Irvine has one of the highest enrollments of Asian Americans, accounting for nearly half of the university's seventeen thousand students.

Progressive students responded by demanding that the university give greater attention to cultural diversity. They challenged the university to create programs designed to help students develop an understanding of cultural differences.

The struggle of Asian American students occurred elsewhere as well. Often labeled the "model minority" because of their high levels of educational attainment, it is not unusual for Asian Americans to be looked at as an example of how minority groups can be successful if they are willing to assimilate to mainstream culture. But the fact is that Asian Americans in many ways remain outsiders to a degree comparable to other underrepresented groups. Their educational success is more a reflection of differences associated with family/cultural traditions and economic background than the fact that they have fully embraced mainstream American cultural norms. Various campus initiatives support such a perspective. For example, in 1995 a group of students at the University of Maryland formed a new student group known as WAASP—Working for an Asian American Studies Program. Asian American students constituted roughly 15 percent of the student body, and the Asian American studies program represented the students' effort to redress the lack of adequate representation of Asian culture within the organizational and curricular structures of the university. The students eventually negotiated for $45,000 to establish the Asian American Studies Project. However, two years later the establishment of an academic program seemed no more likely than it had been back in 1995. Students grew angry in the spring of 1997 and argued that without a program it would be impossible for Asian American students to "understand their place in history and in the contemporary world." As leaders of the movement explained, they "need to make the unknown . . . known."

With little progress having been made, WAASP launched a vigorous campaign in the spring of 1997. One of its efforts involved forging an alliance with the Black Student Union, the Filipino Cultural Association, the Chinese Culture Club, the Indian Students Association, the Latino Student Union, the NAACP, the Asian Faculty/Staff/Graduate Student Association, the Jewish Student Union, the Women's Studies Department, and the Lesbian/Gay/Bisexual Association, as part of a large-scale campaign to establish programs of study reflective of a multicultural campus and society. Another action by WAASP was a boycott of the campus's "Take Another Look Fair," designed to promote the university's commitment to diversity. As part of their protest, representatives from WAASP occupied grounds outside of the student union (where the fair took place) and shared the following message: "Take Another Look: Is there really diversity here?" Their location outside the student union was intended to symbolize the ostracism of Asian Americans within the American college classroom. Later, a group of students representing the multigroup alliance forged by WAASP marched to President William Kirwan's office carrying signs and chanting "Asian American Studies Now!" The students demanded a meeting with the president in order that they discuss the implementation of the program. Like the Chicano student activists at UCLA, WAASP sought to restructure the university in a manner that included their own history and narratives. Targeting the curriculum and what ultimately is taught in the classroom made perfect sense to them, given the high priority that institutions such as UCLA and the University of Maryland place on the advancement of knowledge.

Student protests at the University of Massachusetts at Amherst and the New School for Social Research also included student demands for the creation of Asian American studies programs, among other concerns. These efforts reflected a key aspect of the Multicultural Student Movement which clearly sought to bring light to complex racial dynamics that moved beyond the simplistic portrayal of campus life as a "black and white" issue.

What is clear from many of the preceding examples, and the examples throughout this book, is the growing influence of multiculturalism in the way diverse students go about their collegiate lives. Perhaps what is helpful at this point is to explore some of the theoretical links and implications of the Multicultural Student Movement.

Theoretical Connections

An underlying premise to this book is that theory both reflects and informs social life. In other words, theories ought to be empirically linked and reflect lived experience to a degree. At the same time, it must be recognized that the way we think about the social world influences how we exist in it. The argument suggested here is that empiricism has dominated social science inquiry to such a degree that idealism has been relegated to marginal status. The work behind this book suggests that idealism needs to be incorporated along with empiricism if research is to contribute to the democratic vision. "The rational is real and the real is rational" is the famous principle explored by Hegel, who addressed the notion that what can be imagined or "idealized" ("Hegelian idealism") is as true and powerful as anything that might be observed empirically.[3] From this perspective, empiricism and idealism exist in a state of dialectical tension in which each informs the other.

Up to this point, the focus has primarily been on describing in an empirical manner a general movement among students of the 1990s. The argument presented thus far is that many of today's examples of campus unrest reflect a broad commitment to multicultural struggle and thus may be understood as the Multicultural Student Movement. But how can sociological theory about social movements be helpful in making sense of contemporary student activism? In other words, how can the imagined (the rational) inform our understanding of what has been observed (the empirical)? In making sense of the Multicultural Student Movement there is perhaps no sociological concept more helpful than the notion of "collective consciousness."

Herbert Blumer described social movements as "collective enterprises to establish a new order of life." He explains that "they have their inception in a condition of unrest, and derive their motive power on one hand from dissatisfaction with the current form of life, and on the other hand, from wishes and hopes for a new scheme or system of living."[4] Blumer went on to say that movements have their roots in a general shifting of the culture and reflect emerging conceptions people have of themselves, and of their rights and privileges. "Over a period of time many people may develop a new view of what they believe they are entitled to—a view largely made up of desires and hopes. It signifies the emergence of a new set of values, which influence people in the way in which they look upon their own lives."[5]

Blumer also talked about the importance an ideology plays in advancing a social movement. As part of the shifting cultural contexts, new ways of thinking about oneself in relation to the broader society emerge. The Multicultural Student Movement, for example, reflects an emerging view among diverse students and their allies that their identities as marginalized peoples must be fundamentally altered. Their changing visions of themselves are of course tied to a general ideology or utopian understanding of American public life and what it means to be an equal participant in a democratic society. Like shifts in culture, ideology and utopian visions also undergo changes over time,[6] and while equal opportunity and social justice may have meant one thing in the early 1960s (equal representation within institutional settings, for example), today such ideals may invoke different meanings. In the 1950s ending legalized segregation was seen as the end in the struggle to achieve equality for American Negroes. But only after such laws were erased was it possible to see that other forms of racial inequality still undergirded American society. Consequently, a new vision was needed that encompassed a more advanced version of equality and justice for all. Initially, the emerging vision was reflected in the ideals of "equal opportunity," and a number of social and legislative actions were taken to advance American society (affirmative action is one example). This new vision rested in a belief that equal participation within American institutions would lead to true equality. While this vision has yet to reach fruition (and may not under current strategies), another more complex utopian ideal has emerged in the form of multiculturalism. Multiculturalism is rooted in a vision in which equal participation is seen as part of a much deeper concern over the adequate inclusion and representation of diverse cultures within the social institutions which give shape to the larger society. Equal participation by minorities and women is part of a multicultural vision, but including important aspects of one's culture throughout organizational life is also part of the vision. Initiatives related to this latter concern are what many describe as identity politics.

The efforts of Chicano students at UCLA to situate their lives and histories as legitimate sources of knowledge by gaining departmental status for Chicano studies is an example of a changing vision of American public life in which a previously marginalized group has sought to alter the larger social landscape. Chicano struggle certainly was not new, but the goals of what constitutes equality and freedom for Chicanos has evolved over the years, just as it has for other oppressed groups such as women and African Americans. Where once having the opportunity to study at a college or university was seen as equality, a different vision has emerged over the last twenty to thirty years in which one's presence on campus is only part of the solution. Women offer an excellent example in that they now outnumber men in terms of their college participation rates and yet they face significant obstacles within academic contexts that limit their opportunities and their freedom. The Mills College strike was in large part a response to the ongoing inequities women face throughout the larger educational enterprise. For the Mills College women, preserving a woman-centered space was a way to provide an educational context where women could thrive.

In general, a utopian vision is a key component in the formation of a collective consciousness. Without a vision of how the world ought to be, it is unlikely that a concern for social transformation will have the depth and power necessary to forge ahead in spite of efforts to retain the status quo. But, of course, feelings of deep dissatisfaction, or what Marxist theorists have termed "alienation," also must exist to fuel the kind of political and cultural movements characterized by the 1960s and the present-day Multicultural Movement.[7] Thus, "we may define a student movement as a combination of students inspired by aims which they try to explicate in a political ideology, and moved by an emotional rebellion in which there is always present a disillusionment with and rejection of the values of the older generation."[8] Ideology and alienation may be seen as key aspects of a movement in which students "have a conviction that their generation has a special historical mission to fulfill where the older generation, other elites, and other classes have failed."[9]

Generational ties may be powerful, but we also must recognize that rarely are the actions of students completely owned by them alone. In many cases, the so-called elites, such as university professors, may actually be involved in guiding or promoting student unrest. For example, a number of faculty (supposedly from the "older" generation) played key roles in the cases of student protest discussed in this book. Many of these faculty protested during the 1960s and still maintain a degree of resistance to contemporary organizational life. Any suggestion that student uprisings largely reflect a generational phenomenon may be overly simplistic, given the intergenerational cooperation among students and faculty. Additionally, many of today's student activists are nontraditional students, and thus a number of student demonstrations may actually reflect a multigenerational movement (another aspect of multiculturalism). In fact, the mixing of generations among contemporary activists was noted by Zelda Gamson, director of the New England Center for Higher Education, as she attended a conference at MIT organized by Teachers for a Democratic Culture and the Center for Campus Organizing. Despite the mix, however, it was still clear that students were playing a leading role in contemporary campus activism, as Gamson noted: "What I loved most was that it was students activating faculty."[10]

While faculty often find themselves in the midst of political and cultural battles alongside students, it is also the case that their work itself may form a theoretical launching pad for student initiative. It was from the theoretical work of people such as W. E. B. Du Bois, Herbert Marcuse, C. Wright Mills, Malcolm X, and Georg Lukács, among others, that many of the most active student organizers of the 1960s drew their inspiration. In some cases, the influence of radical social theorists was quite direct, as when Tom Hayden in co-authoring the Port Huron Statement relied heavily upon C. Wright Mills for inspiration. Or when Angela Davis studied under Herbert Marcuse during her undergraduate days at Brandeis. The influence of Marcuse was strong enough that Davis eventually traveled to Germany to conduct her graduate studies at the Frankfurt School, where she worked with social philosophers Theodor Adorno and Jürgen Habermas, whose own work was deeply indebted to that of Karl Marx. The theories she studied under Marcuse and then later in Germany were not detached from her lived experience but instead helped Davis to make sense of the historic period in which she existed. Davis reflected on this time in her life and the dramatic political and cultural changes taking place during the 1960s:

> While I was hidden away in West Germany the Black Liberation Movement was undergoing decisive metamorphoses. The slogan "Black Power" sprang out of a march in Mississippi. Organizations were being transfigured—The Student Non-Violent Coordinating Committee, a leading civil rights organization, was becoming the foremost advocate of "Black Power." The Congress on Racial Equality was undergoing similar transformations. In Newark, a national Black Power Conference had been organized. In political groups, labor unions, churches, and other organizations, Black caucuses were being formed to defend the special interests of Black people. Everywhere there were upheavals.[11]

Davis captured the collective consciousness that was beginning to emerge around Black nationalism, a movement that increased in power as the 1960s progressed and as the struggle for civil rights took on greater fury.

From Marcuse in particular, Davis learned to integrate her life and philosophy of the world. In his theoretical attention to the progressive action of revolutionaries and revolutionary thinkers, she found ideas for bridging Black struggle and visions of a better life. Marcuse, for example, explicated Hegel's interpretations of the French Revolution and the basic principle that "thought ought to govern action." As Marcuse explained in deciphering Hegel's work, "The implications involved in this statement lead into the very center of his philosophy. Thought ought to govern reality. What men think to be true, right, and good ought to be realized in the actual organization of their societal and individual life."[12] Davis mixed the idealism of Hegel and the critical social theory of the Frankfurt philosophers such as Marcuse with her own rebel spirit and lived a life of a true revolutionary seeking social justice and equality for her people. But revolutionaries can pay a heavy price in the instrumentality of a modernist society where conflict is seen as a disruption to the functioning of economic machinery. Davis eventually would stand trial for charges of murder, kidnaping, and conspiracy as part of her affiliation with the Black Panther Party. Although she was found innocent of the charges, she nonetheless lost her faculty position at the University of California at Los Angeles, despite the support of a relatively young senior administrator named Charles Young.

The Black Panther Party, perhaps more than any Black political group of the age, characterized the power and pride of the African American movement, and the city of Oakland, California, became one of its key bases. Davis gave serious thought to the Black Panther Party while she studied in Germany:

> While I was reading philosophy in Frankfurt, and participating in the rearguard of S.D.S. [*Sozialistischer Deutscher Studentenbund*—the German Socialist Student League], there were young Black men in Oakland, California, who decided that they had to wield arms in order to protect the residents of Oakland's Black community from the indiscriminate police brutality ravaging the area. Huey Newton, Bobby Seale, li'l Bobby Hutton—those were some of the names that reached me. One day in Frankfurt I read about their entrance into the California Legislature in Sacramento with their weapons in order to safeguard their right (a right given to all whites) to carry them as instruments of self-defense.[13]

As Davis grew in her understanding of political and social change, Black Power began to make greater sense to her as a radical contribution to the civil rights struggle of African Americans. In time, she became deeply involved in the far left of the Civil Rights Movement. The evolution of her identity as a radical brings to mind Blumer's point that conceptions of the self and of others must form some kind of connection for joint action to be possible. The sense of connection between the self and the other may be understood in terms of the formation of a collective consciousness. Social movements thus must involve a degree of change in how individuals define themselves and eventually align themselves with others. As identity evolves, one seeks out others with whom this new sense of self can be shared.

For Georg Lukács, collective consciousness is more than simply a common understanding and sense of commitment to a particular political agenda: it involves a recognition of the historical role of the disempowered in creating fundamental social change. The change, as he and others such as Paulo Freire pointed out, must come from the development of a critical consciousness (*conscientization*), of the peasants in Freire's thinking, and from a sense of class consciousness among the proletariat in

Lukács' terms. Lukács explained, "Class consciousness is identical with neither the psychological consciousness of individual members of the proletariat, nor with the (mass-psychological) consciousness of the proletariat as a whole; but it is, on the contrary, *the sense, become conscious, of the historical role of the class.*"[14] And, as Freire argued, only the oppressed can lead to a "fuller humanity" and the quest for true freedom:

> To surmount the situation of oppression, men must first critically recognize its causes, so that through transforming action they can create a new situation, one which makes possible the pursuit of a fuller humanity. But the struggle to be more fully human has already begun in the authentic struggle to transform the situation. Although the situation of oppression is a dehumanized and dehumanizing totality affecting both the oppressors and those whom they oppress, it is the latter who must, from their stifled humanity, wage for both the struggle for a fuller humanity; the oppressor, who is himself dehumanized because he dehumanizes others, is unable to lead this struggle.[15]

Arguably, the movements of the 1960s failed to achieve the radical social change to which many students were committed. Lukács and Freire might argue that the kind of historical and critical sense of consciousness needed for radical transformation never fully emerged. Accordingly, one might ask—What happened to the revolutionary Black Power movement of the late 1960s and why did it fail to achieve the advances it sought for African Americans? One argument is that the power of a normalizing society (in Michel Foucault's terms) called upon its many tactics of oppression, tactics such as imprisonment (Bobby Seale and Huey Newton are examples), murder (Malcolm X), and media assassinations (Angela Davis). Another argument is offered by J. K. Obatala, a founding member of the Black Student Union at California State in Los Angeles and later chair of Black studies at Long Beach State University:

> A more realistic explanation would be that there simply never was a "black revolution." There was militancy, as well as anger, hate and racial frustration, but—except for radical rhetoric—never much of a genuine revolutionary conviction on the part of most black students. Ironically, if indeed there had been a meaningful degree of revolutionary commitment and understanding among the black student population, much of the chaos and confusion that was generated out of the black campus rebellion in its later stages might never have occurred. For the mature

revolutionary understands that real revolutions aren't made in a day and that violence is an important but not *all-important* part of revolutionary strategy; there comes a time in any protracted struggle when thought is much more important than action.[16]

Thus one could argue that the failure of the 1960s and in particular the Black revolution was its inability to effectively develop a critical and collective consciousness about the historical role of Blacks in the transformation of American society. A spirit of freedom and democracy was certainly ignited, but perhaps the development of a collective consciousness is years in the works and involves extended critical thought over the course of generations. Recall the comments of Jacqueline Williams, who played a key role in leading African American student resistance at Rutgers: "It's time to focus on the fact that we cannot only defeat them with the iron fist but we can now also defeat them with our intellect. We can use our brains for this. We don't always have to be violent in order to get what we want. You have to show them that we are intelligent enough to sit down and talk with them—where you can think out a thorough plan, an educational plan." Perhaps, the 1960s was simply a key point in the ongoing development of a collective sense of identity that must eventually fall to a new generation for its fulfillment. The student activists of the 1960s thus can be seen as early freedom fighters driven by the quest for a more democratic and participatory society. They certainly were not the first, though perhaps they were the most visible and most heralded. They take their place in the ongoing march toward a true multicultural society.

The democratic spirit that was revealed most dramatically during the 1960s has endured in the minds of countless college students since the May rebellions of 1970, and in the 1990s the collective consciousness of a decade of students committed to the broadest interpretation of democratic struggle inherent in the Civil Rights Movement continues to build. Sara Evans and Harry Boyte discuss the civil rights struggle and the 1960s as they affected the multicultural struggle thirty years later:

> Important as any changes in public law and formal code were the transformations in the life of communities themselves. Local protests began to generate a democratic movement culture. But the nature of the movement, for all its accomplishments, also imposed severe limitations on how fully it could realize its goals. On the broadest level, the civil rights revolt was intended, as Martin Luther King put it repeatedly, to 'make real the promise of democracy.' By democracy, those involved in

the movement meant not simply formal rights, like the right to vote, but participation and the transformation of power relationships which kept some in a dependent and inferior position.[17]

But the broad vision of King and others who saw the struggle of American Blacks as much deeper than simply equal rights was not necessarily the driving force of the movement. Again, Evans and Boyte are helpful: "Despite the broader vision of leaders such as King and Ella Baker and many of the rank and file, the civil rights movement was designed to address problems of legal segregation. Like the suffrage movement of women a half century earlier, it used a language of republicanism that stressed formal participation, not transformation of substantive relations of power."[18] Hence, the Civil Rights Movement of the 1960s with its focus on formalized democracy failed to achieve the more complex and far-reaching concerns of a participatory democracy, which involves much more than legalized opportunity. The Multicultural Student Movement of the 1990s, with its focus on full participation and cultural inclusiveness, thus may be seen as the emergence of a more sophisticated form of civil rights struggle centered upon restructuring power and identity.

The five cases that have been examined here call attention to the emergence of a collective consciousness around issues of democratic struggle. While these five movements were focused primarily on specific campuses, they all took on a multicultural tenor as a variety of groups came to the support of the students' cause. Recall that at UCLA a leading student group in challenging the administration was the Conscious Students of Color, a multiracial student group organized to advance Chicano studies. At Penn State, while the Lesbian, Gay, and Bisexual Student Alliance led the gay liberation efforts, they were also supported by the Black Caucus, the Graduate Student Association, the Interfraternity Council, and the Commission for Women. At Rutgers a multiracial coalition emerged in the form of the United Student Coalition. At Michigan State, American Indians and Chicano students entered into solidarity and together organized campus demonstrations. And the women of Mills College found supporters among fellow students and alumnae across racial and sexual-orientation lines. Within other campus movements, a collective identity organized around multiculturalism has also been evident. The efforts of Asian American students at the University of Maryland involved students from a variety of groups including African Americans, Jews, women, and gays. The Binghamton Coalition, organized in response to initiatives by the conservative student government president, was of a multiracial movement involving underrepresented minority students as well as progressive Whites. Demonstrations at Indiana University on the Martin Luther King Jr. holiday were led by a multiracial coalition. During demonstrations at the University of Massachusetts at Amherst in the spring of 1997, which included the takeover of the controller's office by three hundred students, protesters were joined by groups of students from Smith, Amherst, Hampshire, and Mount Holyoke colleges in what was a multiracial contingent seeking multicultural change.

Conservative criticism that identity politics has contributed to the fragmentation of the American college campus is not supported when one explores the various multicultural movements around the country, which, for the most part, are highly multiracial, multifarious, and multifaceted. The notion that African Americans, Chicanos, or gays for that matter are somehow isolating themselves from others as a result of their identity struggle does not hold up when put under close scrutiny.

Other movements during the 1990s have spanned not only interest groups and campuses but national and international borders. Student movements such as the Free Burma Coalition may be particularly valuable in understanding collective consciousness and its role in forging campus and social change as well as in understanding how contemporary students might make use of advanced technology for organizing purposes.

The Free Burma Coalition

The Free Burma Coalition (FBC) was formed in September of 1995 by a doctoral student at Wisconsin known to his supporters as Zarni. Through the use of the Internet, Zarni was able to spread word of the atrocities committed in Burma (Myanmar) by the military junta self-identified as the State Law and Order Restoration Council (SLORC), which took control of Burma in 1988. Thousands of college students and supporters of democracy were killed (Zarni believes that five to ten thousand people were murdered). SLORC was condemned in April of 1996 in a resolution from the United Nations Human Rights Commission for its atrocities including torture, forced labor, rape and sexual abuse of women, political imprisonments, forced population movements, and harassment of religious and ethnic minorities. FBC's hope was to force the SLORC to honor the 1990 elections wherein Burma's National League for Democracy, led by Aung San Suu Kyi, won by a landslide (60 percent of the vote and 82 percent of the legislative seats were won by the NLD).

However, the military refused to relinquish control and Aung San Suu Kyi, who went on to win a 1991 Nobel Peace Prize, was put under house arrest. As thousands of Burmese fled to Thailand, countless others were forced to labor for pennies on government work projects.

Through organizations such as the All Burmese Students' Democratic Front (ABSDF) and U.S. organizations such as Amnesty International, the FBC launched numerous economic boycotts and educational campaigns. In September of 1996, President Clinton agreed to conditional sanctions as part of an amendment to an appropriations bill sponsored by Senator Cohen (R-Maine) and Senator Feinstein (D-California). The amendment, which had bipartisan support, contained a proviso that would prohibit new investments in Burma if Suu Kyi were to be imprisoned or harmed or if any large-scale crackdowns on the pro-democracy movement were to follow.

Zarni was among those who fled his country in 1988. Eventually, he made his way to graduate school at the University of California at Davis, where he received his masters degree, and then he moved on to the University of Wisconsin, where in 1997 he was working on his Ph.D. in education. During his stay in California, he was hired to help work on the script for the film *Beyond Rangoon*, which he described as "a fictionalized version of what transpired in Burma during the late 1980s." Primarily through the use of the Internet, Zarni was able to form over 150 FBC groups at campuses in the United States and around the world. He also gained the support of organizations such as the Student Environment Action Committee (SEAC). The key moment in the organization's birth was in fact the 1995 conference of SEAC in Chapel Hill, North Carolina, where FBC was able to elicit SEAC's support and where they held their first demonstration, at a Chapel Hill Taco Bell. After the SEAC conference, FBC recruited hundreds of high school and college students from around the United States, who soon formed local FBC groups. Through the Internet, a close-knit community has emerged and members often refer to one another as fellow "Spiders." The Spiders and the work of FBC are guided by a clear mission statement:

> The Free Burma Coalition is the coordinating body for groups around the world working for freedom and democracy in Burma. Our mission is to build a grassroots movement inspired by and modeled after the anti-apartheid movement in South Africa. Our movement stands 100 percent behind the leadership of Daw Aung San Suu Kyi and the National League for Democracy, whom the people have recognized

as the sole legitimate leaders of Burma. Our objectives are twofold: to weaken the grip of the State Law and Order Restoration Council (SLORC) by cutting its substantial flow of foreign currency provided by multinational corporations such as Total, Unocal, Texaco, ARCO, and Pepsico among others; and to strengthen the position of the democratic forces within Burma by building up an international movement calling for the end of totalitarian rule under SLORC.

In a closing note attached to the organization's mission statement, Zarni returns to the Ethiopian proverb that symbolizes the movement's strength: "When spiders unite they can tie down a lion."

Like the other campus movements discussed in this book, much of contemporary student activism has its political roots in the 1960s. This is partially true of the Free Burma Coalition as well. Zarni explained, "The freedom movement in Burma started, I would say, in the early 1960s because the military took over the country in 1962 and they dynamited the historic student union building, which was very important for the national independence movement. They destroyed the building because they wanted to crush the spirit of the activism on campuses in Burma but obviously they have failed to do this. Each time a movement is crushed through violence, a new generation will pick up the banner and run with it."

During an interview Zarni talked about the strategy of the FBC and what inspired their movement: "We are inspired by our brothers and sisters who were active in the Divestment Movement of the past decade. So we use economic activism as the mainstay of our tactics. We are trying to get corporations out of Burma, trying to cut the financial support that the Burmese military regime is receiving from foreign multinational corporations. We're building on that. But we're also building an international solidarity movement, which we hope will lead to an international community of organizers and concerned citizens who are working on various campaigns to help support the democracy movement inside Burma."

A number of companies, including Liz Claiborne, Eddie Bauer, and Reebok, have withdrawn their investments from Burma as a result of FBC's economic pressure, and at least eight cities have launched boycotts of companies investing in Burma: Ann Arbor, Madison, Santa Monica, San Francisco, Oakland, Berkeley, Takoma Park, and Boulder. Also, the State of Massachusetts passed legislation barring state contracts with companies who do business in Burma. As a result of the Massachusetts legislation, Apple Computer terminated its relationship with distributors in the militarily controlled country.

Several student actions connected to FBC have taken place. For example, students at Stanford University collected over one thousand signatures urging the university to reject Taco Bell as a possible vendor in its student union. Taco Bell is a subsidiary of Pepsico (along with Kentucky Fried Chicken and Pizza Hut) and has been targeted at various schools around the country. At Penn State, which has a multimillion-dollar contract with Pepsi, students have asked the administration to publicly condemn Pepsi's involvement in Burma and apply pressure on the company to consider human rights violations in its investment policies. Students at Harvard pressured the university's food services to drop Pepsi in favor of Coca Cola, as did students at Colgate University. And the University of Wisconsin System has divested itself of Texaco Corporation stocks as a result of FBC activity.

In a move intended to pacify the FBCers, Pepsi sold its operations to its Burmese contractor, Thein Tun, but continued contracts with the company. The move was described by the FBC as simply a "shuffling of some papers" and was intended to mislead the anti-Pepsi campaign. Such a strategy did not fly with the FBC at the University of Arizona, which continued protests at the student union's Taco Bell. When the director of the union explained to the students that Pepsi had pulled out of Burma, the students clarified the strategy Pepsi actually had undertaken. Despite the attacks on Pepsi, Zarni and others within the FBC feel a degree of debt to the company. Zarni explained: "In a twisted way, we're thankful that Pepsi is there because, aside from the Internet, Pepsi is the second biggest factor that has helped the campaign grow. Because they arc so visible. If we didn't have such a visible company as a target I don't know if we would have grown the way we have. . . . It's a can't miss target. 'The choice of a new generation.' Just like freedom."

One of the factors that led to the emergence of the FBC was the shortcomings of *Beyond Rangoon*. When the movie failed to generate the kind of public outrage he had hoped for, Zarni decided it was time to turn to a different strategy. Along with other Spiders, Zarni developed possible tactics for raising public consciousness. One idea considered was a demonstration targeting Northwestern University, primarily because of a prominent faculty member in the business school who was on the board of Unocal Corporation. This idea fell through when several Spiders rejected the plan. Instead, the group planned a day of action for October 27, 1995.

During the early days of the FBC, Zarni relied on two friends for technical and political assistance. Alex Turner (the son of the famous anthropologist Victor Turner) provided Zarni with computer expertise and established the home page for FBC. The other key person was Zarni's political advisor, Todd Price, a community organizer. Armed with their own Web site and a list of interested students obtained during the SEAC conference in Chapel Hill, Zarni and the early Spiders followed their day of action with plans for a three-day, worldwide fast in the fall of 1996 (October 7 to 9). By using the Internet, FBC was able to reach hundreds of students around the country, who, in turn, informed hundreds more.

Soon, the web of FBC expanded and personal and political connections formed. Fifty-seven U.S. campuses participated in the three-day fast, including students at the University of Washington who set up a tent complete with information, legislators' addresses, photo displays, and handouts. Additionally, they had a running video monitor displaying various tapes describing conditions in Burma. Two typewriters were also present so that students could compose letters to state and federal legislators while they interacted with the Spiders. At Tennessee Tech, about twenty students participated in the fast and many others were involved in a series of events planned with the support of the International Student Organization, the Black Student Organization, the Chinese Student Association, and the Tennessee Young Democrats. Their activities included a showing of *Beyond Rangoon* and a protest at the university center over Tennessee Tech's contracts with Pepsi. A few weeks earlier, after hearing of the upcoming fast, Aung San Suu Kyi addressed the role of students in Burma's democratic struggle as she spoke to an audience in Rangoon:

> It is wonderful to learn that the students . . . across the United States
> and Canada will be taking part in the Free Burma Fast. Young people
> were the backbone of the public demonstrations of 1988 that swept
> away the rule of the Burma Socialist Program Party. The movement for
> democracy in Burma emerged from those demonstrations, in which
> many students lost their lives. It is then most fitting that students should
> be taking up the cause of the yet uncompleted democratic revolution in
> my country.

The FBC is one example of the power of the Internet to organize student resistance and to advance a collective sense of consciousness around democratic issues. The Center for Campus Organizing (CCO) in Cambridge, Massachusetts, also has recognized the power of the Internet and serves as an electronic clearinghouse for social justice activists around the United States. Through CANET, an Internet interest list, CCO has been able to link over two thousand student activists. The work of FBC and CCO offers insight into the power of electronic communication in fostering a collective commitment and the power held by seemingly insignificant masses when they unite around an important cause.

When Karl Marx argued that it would take a revolution of workers to overthrow totalitarianism he never could have imagined the advanced cultural forms that arguably would stymie such a vision. As many of the social theorists of the Frankfurt School in Germany have painstakingly pointed out, mass culture has produced a kind of hypnotic trance enabling the oppressive aspects of modernism to flourish. French postmodernists such as Jean Baudrillard also have called attention to the tranquilizing quality of contemporary life that contributes to social and political disengagement and a deepening dependence on the hyperreal world of television and the instant gratification of a technologically driven culture. The irony is that it was technology that first led Marx to be optimistic about the eventual proletariat uprising, in that he saw advances in travel and communication as key to the emergence of a collective consciousness.

> Now and then the workers are victorious, but only for a time. The real fruit of their battle lies, not in the immediate result, but in the ever expanding union of the workers. This union is helped on by the improved means of communication that are created by modern industry, and that place the workers of different localities in contact with one another. It was just this contact that was needed to centralise the numerous local struggles, all of the same character, into one national struggle between classes. But every class struggle is a political struggle. And that union, to attain which the burghers of the Middle Ages, with their miserable highways, required centuries, the modern proletarians, thanks to railways, achieve in a few years.[19]

Much has changed since the early writings of Marx, but the disempowerment and alienation that he described in the lives of laborers and peasants applies across a wide spectrum of the contemporary population. Indeed, the postmodern proletariat may include students, the marginalized, the perverse, and the disempowered, who through electronic communications may not be so disempowered any more. "Thanks," the postmodern proletarians say to the Internet for their ability to forge common understandings across the continent and around the world, something that until recently was the province of only the large multinational corporations and the most wealthy. The freedom and accessibility of the Internet may in part explain why so many forces are at work to gain control over it. Perhaps the Internet is freedom's response to the mass effect of political and cultural hypnosis.

Through the power of the Internet, FBC has been able to unite a community of activists concerned with human rights violations. Zarni is quick to point out that he did not create the community: "We did not form this community. The community emerged. We didn't set out to build a community of activists. After a while, people just started developing some kind of like friendship, or I guess some sense of solidarity. It was not something we planned. There was no intentionality. It just evolved." He went on to note how for many members of FBC their commitment to freedom has become essential to their identity. "It is something that takes up their leisure time. Something they share with their families at the dinner table and family gatherings. They recruit their big brother or little sister into the movement." Clearly, the Internet adds incredible power to the capacity to connect a community of activists and to foster a sense of collective identity.

Toward an Activist Identity

In the examples of student organizing discussed throughout this book, including the Free Burma Coalition, the importance of one's sense of identity and the connection one has to others has been fundamental. The emergence of a collective consciousness organized around a common aspect of one's identity is necessary for a social movement to gain strength. However, a collective identity and commitment does not necessarily mean that the cultural differences that are always a part of any social collectivity must be ignored or silenced. After all, the ultimate goal of multiculturalism is to create a society in which difference is embraced. Such a perspective reflects a vision of true participatory democracy. Multiculturalism, as a connective thread, reminds us that despite that which links one identity to another, there is much that makes us unique as well, and that one is never simply a Chicano, a woman, or a gay man. We all have multiple facets to our identities. This was most apparent in the Chicano studies movement at UCLA, which despite the strong commitment of the students involved, contained many sources of tension and division. It is a testament to the strength and conviction of the Chicano students involved that in the end their sense of solidarity pulled them through.

Although connections have been made across diverse groups on individual campuses, and student activists on some campuses have forged common understandings across geographic boundaries, the connections remain rather loose. Strengthening the multicultural webs, which in the 1990s began to bring students together, is the central challenge contemporary activists face in achieving the participatory democracy dreamt of by the likes of the authors of the Port Huron Statement and civil rights leaders such as Martin Luther King Jr. Otherwise, lesbian, gay, and bisexual students may take a step forward at one school, and lose ground at another. Underrepresented minorities move toward educational equity in one state, and then the rug is pulled out from under them elsewhere. American Indians take one step forward, then a few years later they may take two steps back. The norms of individualism keep the disenfranchised apart and in fact lead many to support legislation that limits their own educational and economic opportunities, as was the case in California when many minorities supported Propositions 187 and 209. Identity politics thus may serve a key role in organizing committed groups of students, but the groups themselves must remain open and flexible social spaces capable of building solidarity across cultural lines.

More than ever, cultural differences stretch the seams that once held communities together and provided individuals with a sense of commonality. Race, class, gender, sexual orientation, and age, among other characteristics, often prevent individuals from forging relationships with others. Despite the strains of the postmodern condition, connectedness is still an essential aspect of the self, which by its construction is a social self, and thus directly linked to understandings of the other. If we are to advance a sense of self bound to others, by sheer necessity we must find ways to align our actions, lest community and common struggle become an experience of the past.

There are many forces throughout society that stand to gain from the inability of the marginalized to form a collective consciousness capable of influencing social policies and practices. As some of the theorists introduced throughout this chapter have argued, serious thought must undergird the kind of collective consciousness necessary for social transformation. Such thought involves wrestling with ideologies and utopian visions. Committing oneself passionately to change is contingent on having a vision of *what ought to be* and experiencing that vision at the deepest levels of the self. The women of Mills College held to a vision of education as a safe and nurturing place for the development of women's identities. Likewise, Chicanos and Chicanas at UCLA, African Americans at Rutgers, gays at Penn State, and American Indians at Michigan

State all believed in a vision of an inclusive society where all people have opportunities to pursue higher education in a safe and affirming environment. For many of these student activists, participatory democracy and multiculturalism provide an ideological basis for making sense of their lives in these culturally diverse times.

It may come as a surprise that many of the multicultural activists discussed in this work are involved in the postmodern project when in fact few are likely to have had any academic exposure to this theoretical school of thought. And yet, theory derives in part from our understandings and interpretations of lived experience (mixed with imagination), and obviously one does not have to be a "postmodern theorist" to see the need for a more sophisticated understanding of cultural difference and its place in today's world. If there is a message coming across loud and clear from today's student activists it is perhaps this simple assertion: Our society needs more complex ways of organizing itself before it bursts at the seams.

We live in a society where police officers such as Mark Fuhrman on a daily basis make life and death decisions rooted in racial prejudice and hatred. It is a society where corporate leaders such as those at Texaco speak of African Americans as "black jelly beans" stuck to the bottom of the bag, where military leaders rape and sexually harass female recruits, and where lesbian, gay, and bisexual people cannot openly serve their country except in wartimes when such restrictions are conveniently ignored. It is a society where politicians design and citizens pass legislation to erase years of work to create equal opportunity for all people regardless of race or gender, as if the disease of hatred and bigotry suddenly has been cured. We live in a society in which the central governing bodies such as the Congress pass bills to deny same-sex couples the same rights as heterosexual couples and the president signs such legislation despite his counterbeliefs because it is the prudent thing to do in an election year. And sadly, so much of this is done in the name of justice, as phrases such as the California Civil Rights Initiative are tossed about with little critical reflection on what civil rights actually means in today's world. What has happened to serious-minded conceptions of freedom and social justice?

Perhaps it is not too surprising, then, that many of the oppressive aspects of our culture get played out on college campuses, where youthful exuberance has the strength and the innocence to envision something better. Indeed, students such as Silja Talvi, Marcos Aguilar, Timothy Jones, Jacqueline Williams, and Hannah Windstorm refuse to accept the inequities that many in our country have come to see as the reality of life. From their struggles, the views they espouse, and the strategies they enact, there is much evidence to suggest that the work of Chicanos, African Americans, American Indians, Asian Americans, gays, women, and progressive allies, among others, is part of a larger social movement the size and power of which remains to be seen. Perhaps the movement has already peaked. Or perhaps it is just now beginning to rise up and challenge the fabric of American social life.

Preface and Acknowledgments

1. Alexander W. Astin, Helen S. Astin, Alan E. Bayer, and Ann S. Bisconti, *The Power of Protest: A National Study of Student and Faculty Disruptions with Implications for the Future* (San Francisco: Jossey-Bass, 1975).
2. Mayer N. Zald and Michael A. Berger, "Social Movements in Organizations: Coup d'Etat, Insurgency, and Mass Movements," *American Journal of Sociology* 83, no. 4 (1978): 823–61.
3. Edmund Husserl, *The Crisis of European Sciences and the Transcendental Phenomenology*, trans. D. Carr (Evanston, Ill.: Northwestern University Press, 1970); Maurice Merleau-Ponty, *Phenomenology of Perception*, trans. C. Smith (New York: Humanities Press, 1962); Alfred Schutz, *Alfred Schutz on Phenomenology and Social Relations*, ed. H. R. Wagner (Chicago: University of Chicago Press, 1970).
4. Schutz, *Alfred Schutz on Phenomenology and Social Relations*, 56.
5. Ibid.
6. The one exception is the case study of the Free Burma Coalition. In this case, data were collected primarily by participating in Internet communications.
7. In Yvonna Lincoln and Egon Guba, *Naturalistic Inquiry* (Beverly Hills: Sage, 1985), the authors used several axioms to describe the naturalistic paradigm: (1) reality is multiplicitous and socially constructed and therefore must be examined holistically; (2) the researchers and the research subject interact to influence one another; hence, the knower and known are inseparable; (3) the aim of inquiry is to develop an interpretive understanding of social experience; (4) because social phenomena are highly interactive, cause and effect are difficult to ascertain; and (5) the various choices made by researchers reflect the values they hold.

8. Peter L. Berger and Thomas Luckmann, *The Social Construction of Reality: A Treatise in the Sociology of Knowledge* (New York: Anchor Books, 1966).

9. Lincoln and Guba, *Naturalistic Inquiry*.

chapter one: **Passion and Protest on Campus**

1. Doug McAdam, *Freedom Summer* (New York: Oxford University Press, 1988).

2. Ibid.

3. Joanne Grant, *Black Protest: History, Documents, and Analyses, 1619 to the Present* (Greenwich, Conn.: Fawcett Publications, 1968), 460.

4. Cherríe Moraga, *Loving in the War Years* (Boston: South End Press, 1983), 130.

5. Sara M. Evans, *Personal Politics: The Roots of Women's Liberation in the Civil Rights Movement and the New Left* (New York: Vintage Books, 1980); and Sara M. Evans and Harry C. Boyte, *Free Spaces: The Sources of Democratic Change in America* (New York: Harper & Row, 1986).

6. Maren Lockwood Carden, *The New Feminist Movement* (New York: Russell Sage Foundation, 1974), 64.

7. John D'Emilio, *Making Trouble: Essays on Gay History, Politics, and the University* (New York: Routledge, 1992).

8. Rodolfo Acuña, *Occupied America: A History of Chicanos*, 2nd ed. (New York: Harper & Row, 1981); Juan Gómez-Quiñones, *Chicano Politics: Reality and Promise, 1940–1990* (Albuquerque: University of New Mexico Press, 1990).

9. Scott L. Bills, ed., *Kent State/May 4: Echoes through a Decade* (Kent, Ohio: Kent State University Press, 1982), 76–77.

10. Ibid., 17.

11. Kenneth J. Heineman, *Campus Wars: The Peace Movement at American State Universities in the Vietnam Era* (New York: New York University Press, 1993); Seymour Martin Lipset, *Rebellion in the University* (Chicago: University of Chicago Press, 1976).

12. Arthur Levine, *When Dreams and Heroes Died* (San Francisco: Jossey-Bass, 1980).

13. Tony Vellela, *New Voices: Student Activism in the '80s and '90s* (Boston: South End Press, 1988).

14. Meta Mendel-Reyes, *Reclaiming Democracy: The Sixties in Politics and Memory* (New York: Routledge, 1995), xv.

15. Arthur Levine and Jeanette S. Cureton, *When Hope and Fear Collide: A Portrait of Today's College Students* (San Francisco: Jossey-Bass, 1998).

16. Mendel-Reyes, *Reclaiming Democracy*, 8–9.

17. Connie Leslie and Andrew Murr, "Martyrs for Multiculturalism: Courses that Students at UCLA Might Die For," *Newsweek*, 14 June 1993, 77.

18. See Richard Bernstein, *Dictatorship of Virtue: Multiculturalism and the Battle for America's Future* (New York: Knopf, 1994); Dinesh D'Souza, *Illiberal*

Education: The Politics of Race and Sex on Campus (New York: Free Press, 1991); Arthur M. Schlesinger Jr., *The Disuniting of America: Reflections on a Multicultural Society* (New York: Norton, 1992).

19. Ronald Takaki, *A Different Mirror: A History of Multicultural America* (Boston: Little, Brown, 1993), 427.

20. Eric L. Dey, Alexander W. Astin, and William S. Korn, *The American Freshman: Twenty-Five Year Trends, 1966–1990* (Los Angeles: Higher Education Research Institute, 1991), 10.

21. Ibid., 16.

22. Cheryl Clark, "18 Protesters Arrested after Rally at UCSD Demonstration," *San Diego Union Tribune,* 13 March 1996, sec. B, 1–2.

23. Donald E. Phillips, *Student Protest, 1960–1969: An Analysis of the Issues and Speeches* (Washington, D.C.: University Press of America, 1980), 103.

24. Richard P. McCormick, *The Black Student Protest Movement at Rutgers* (New Brunswick: Rutgers University Press, 1990), 24.

25. Gómez-Quiñones, *Chicano Politics,* 123.

26. C. Wright Mills, *The Power Elite* (New York: Oxford University Press, 1956).

27. James Miller, *Democracy Is in the Streets: From Port Huron to the Siege of Chicago* (Cambridge: Harvard University Press, 1994), 177.

28. Ibid., 13.

29. Tom Hayden, *Reunion: A Memoir* (New York: Random House, 1988), 97.

30. Ibid., 101–2.

31. D'Souza, *Illiberal Education.*

32. Alexander W. Astin, "Diversity and Multiculturalism on the Campus: How Are Students Affected?" *Change* 25, no. 1 (1993): 44–49.

33. Sylvia Hurtado, "The Campus Racial Climate: Contexts of Conflict," *Journal of Higher Education* 63, no. 5 (1992): 539–69.

34. Barry W. Sarchett, "What's All the Fuss about This Postmodern Stuff," in *Campus Wars: Multiculturalism and the Politics of Difference,* ed. John Arthur and Amy Shapiro (Boulder, Colo.: Westview Press, 1995), 19.

35. Audre Lorde, "Age, Race, Class, and Sex: Women Redefining Difference," in *Campus Wars: Multiculturalism and the Politics of Difference,* ed. John Arthur and Amy Shapiro (Boulder, Colo.: Westview Press, 1995), 191.

36. Todd Gitlin, *The Twilight of Common Dreams: Why America Is Wracked by Culture Wars* (New York: Henry Holt, 1995), 103.

37. Ibid., 164.

38. Takaki, *A Different Mirror,* 3.

39. Nathan Glazer, *We Are All Multiculturalists Now* (Cambridge: Harvard University Press, 1997).

40. Irving J. Spitzberg Jr. and Virginia V. Thorndike, *Creating Community on College Campuses* (Albany: SUNY Press, 1992).

41. Arthur Levine and Jeanette Cureton, "The Quiet Revolution: Eleven Facts about Multiculturalism and the Curriculum," *Change* 24, no. 1 (1992): 25–29.

42. John Dewey, *Democracy and Education* (New York: Macmillan, 1916).

43. See Andrew Barlow, "The Student Movement of the 1960s and the Politics of Race," *Journal of Ethnic Studies* 19, no. 3 (1991): 1–22.

44. Ruth Sidel, *Battling Bias: The Struggle for Identity and Community on College Campuses* (New York: Viking, 1994), 25.

45. Ronald G. Walters, *American Reformers, 1815–1860* (New York: Hill and Wang, 1978), 209.

46. Paul Rogat Loeb, *Generation at the Crossroads: Apathy and Action on the American Campus* (New Brunswick: Rutgers University Press, 1994), 362.

47. See Nicholas C. Burbules and Suzanne Rice, "Dialogue across Difference: Continuing the Conversation," *Harvard Educational Review* 61, no. 4 (1991): 393–416; Henry A. Giroux, *Border Crossings: Cultural Workers and the Politics of Education* (New York: Routledge, 1992); William G. Tierney, *Building Communities of Difference: Higher Education in the 21st Century* (Westport, Conn.: Bergin & Garvey, 1993); and Robert A. Rhoads, *Coming Out in College: The Struggle for a Queer Identity* (Westport, Conn.: Bergin & Garvey, 1994).

48. Sylvia Hurtado, Eric L. Dey, and Jesús G. Treviño, "Exclusion or Self-Segregation?: Interaction across Racial/Ethnic Groups on College Campuses" (paper presented at the annual meeting of the American Educational Research Association, New Orleans, La., April 1994); Hurtado, "The Campus Racial Climate."

49. Peter McLaren, *Critical Pedagogy and Predatory Culture* (New York: Routledge, 1995), 126.

50. Todd Gitlin, "The Anti-Political Populism of Cultural Studies," *Dissent* 44, no. 2 (1997): 77–82.

51. Edward E. Sampson, "Student Activism and the Decade of Protest," in *Student Activism and Protest: Alternatives for Social Change*, ed. Edward E. Sampson and Harold A. Korn (San Francisco: Jossey-Bass, 1970), 15.

52. Heineman, *Campus Wars.*

53. John R. Searle, *The Campus War: A Sympathetic Look at the University in Agony* (New York: World Publishing Company, 1971), 25.

54. Ibid., 25.

55. Jean Baudrillard, *Simulacra and Simulation*, trans. Sheila Faria Glaser (Ann Arbor: University of Michigan Press, 1994).

56. See Michel Foucault, *The Order of Things* (New York: Vintage Books, 1970); Michel Foucault, *The History of Sexuality*, Volume 1: *An Introduction*, trans. R. Hurley (New York: Vintage Books, 1978); Michel Foucault, *Discipline and Punish*, trans. A. Sheridan (New York: Vintage Books, 1979); and Michel Foucault, *Power/Knowledge*, trans. C. Gordan et al. (New York: Pantheon Books, 1980).

chapter two: **Historical Webs of Connection**

1. Scott L. Bills, ed., *Kent State/May 4: Echoes through a Decade* (Kent, Ohio: Kent State University Press, 1982), 98.

2. Ibid., 84.

3. Todd Gitlin, *The Sixties: Years of Hope, Days of Rage* (Toronto: Bantam Books, 1987), 7.

4. Laurence R. Veysey, *The Emergence of the American University* (Chicago: University of Chicago Press, 1965).

5. Seymour Martin Lipset, "Political Controversies at Harvard, 1636 to 1974," in *Education and Politics at Harvard*, ed. Seymour Martin Lipset and David Riesman (New York: McGraw-Hill, 1975), 18.

6. Kathryn McDaniel Moore, "Old Saints and Young Sinners: A Study of Student Discipline at Harvard College, 1636–1734" (Ph.D. diss., University of Wisconsin, 1972).

7. Dan A. Oren, *Joining the Club: A History of Jews and Yale* (New Haven, Conn.: Yale University Press, 1985).

8. Kathryn McDaniel Moore, "The War with the Tutors: Student-Faculty Conflict at Harvard and Yale, 1745–1771," *History of Education* 18, no. 2 (1978): 115–27.

9. Lyman H. Bagg, *Four Years at Yale* (New Haven, Conn.: Charles C. Chatfield, 1871), 702.

10. Christopher Jencks and David Riesman, *The Academic Revolution* (New York: Doubleday, 1968).

11. Stephen J. Novak, *The Rights of Youth: American Colleges and Student Revolt, 1798–1815* (Cambridge: Harvard University Press, 1977).

12. See Joseph R. DeMartini, "Student Culture as a Change Agent in American Higher Education: An Illustration from the Nineteenth Century," *Journal of Social History* 9, no. 4 (1976): 526–41; and Helen L. Horowitz, *Campus Life: Undergraduate Cultures from the End of the Eighteenth Century to the Present* (New York: Alfred A. Knopf, 1987).

13. Veysey, *The Emergence of the American University*, 37.

14. Oren, *Joining the Club*, 76.

15. For a discussion of student culture and the out-of-class experiences of American college students see George D. Kuh, "Assessing Student Culture," in *Assessing Academic Climates and Cultures*, New Directions for Institutional Research No. 68, ed. William G. Tierney (San Francisco: Jossey-Bass, 1990), 47–60; George D. Kuh, "In Their Own Words: What Students Learn outside the Classroom," *American Educational Research Journal* 30 (1993): 277–304; George D. Kuh, "The Other Curriculum: Out-of-Class Experiences Associated with Student Learning and Personal Development," *Journal of Higher Education* 66, no. 2 (1995): 123–55; and George D. Kuh and Elizabeth J. Whitt, *The Invisible Tapestry: Culture in American Colleges and Universities*, ASHE-ERIC Higher Education Research Report No. 1 (Washington, D.C.: Association for the Study of Higher Education, 1988).

16. Howard S. Becker, "Student Culture," in *The Study of Campus Cultures*, ed. Terry F. Lunsford (Boulder, Colo.: Westview Press, 1963), 12.

17. Ronald A. Smith, *Sports and Freedom: The Rise of Big-Time College Athletics* (New York: Oxford University Press, 1988), 68.

18. Ralph S. Brax, *The First Student Movement: Student Activism in the United States during the 1930s* (Port Washington, N.Y.: Kennikat Press, 1981).

19. Seymour Martin Lipset, *Rebellion in the University* (Chicago: University of Chicago Press, 1976).

20. Robert Cohen, *When the Old Left Was Young: Student Radicals and America's First Mass Student Movement, 1929–1941* (New York: Oxford University Press, 1993).

21. Ibid., 184.

22. Philip G. Altbach and Patti Peterson, "Before Berkeley: Historical Perspectives on American Student Activism," *Annals of the American Academy of Political and Social Science* 395 (1971): 1–14.

23. Franklin Delano Roosevelt, *Pearl Harbor: Speeches before and after Pearl Harbor* (New York: Shaman & Schlick Publishers, 1946), 77.

24. Richard Peterson, *The Scope of Organized Student Protest in 1964–1965* (Princeton, N.J.: Educational Testing Service, 1966), 7.

25. Seymour Martin Lipset and Philip Altbach, "Student Politics and Higher Education in the United States," in *Student Politics*, ed. Seymour Martin Lipset (New York: Basic Books, 1967), 199–252.

26. Ibid., 200.

27. Peterson, *The Scope of Organized Student Protest in 1964–1965.*

28. "Campus 1965: The College Generation Looks at Itself and the World Around It," *Newsweek*, 22 March 1965, 43–63.

29. Philip G. Altbach, "Perspectives on Student Political Activism," *Comparative Education* 25, no. 1 (1989): 97–110.

30. Leonard Baird, "Who Protests: A Study of Student Activists," in *Protest! Student Activism in America*, ed. Julian Foster and Durward Long (New York: William Morrow & Company, 1970), 123–33.

31. Arthur Levine and Deborah Hirsch, "Undergraduates in Transition: A New Wave of Activism on American College Campuses," *Higher Education* 22 (1991): 119–28.

32. Gregory B. Markus, Jeffrey P. F. Howard, and David C. King, "Integrating Community Service and Classroom Instruction Enhances Learning: Results from an Experiment," *Educational Evaluation and Policy Analysis* 15, no. 4 (1993): 410–19.

33. Levine and Hirsch, "Undergraduates in Transition," 126.

34. Julian Keniry, "Environmental Movement Booming on Campuses," *Change* 25 (1993): 42–49.

35. Paul Rogat Loeb, *Generation at the Crossroads: Apathy and Action on the American Campus* (New Brunswick, N.J.: Rutgers University Press, 1994).

36. Alexander W. Astin, *The American Freshman: National Norms for Fall 1989* (Cooperative Institutional Research Program: University of California at Los Angeles, 1990).

37. Alexander W. Astin, *The American Freshman: National Norms for Fall 1992* (Cooperative Institutional Research Program: University of California at Los Angeles, 1993).

38. Ibid.

39. Arthur Levine and Jeanette S. Cureton, *When Hope and Fear Collide: A Portrait of Today's College Students* (San Francisco: Jossey-Bass, 1998).

40. Frederick W. Obear, "Student Activism in the Sixties," in *Protest! Student Activism in America*, ed. Julian Foster and Durward Long (New York: William Morrow & Company, 1970), 15.

41. Doug McAdam, *Freedom Summer* (New York: Oxford University Press, 1988).

42. Irving Howe, *Student Activism* (Indianapolis: Bobbs-Merrill, 1967), 5.

43. Obear, "Student Activism in the Sixties," 24.

44. Lipset and Altbach, "Student Politics and Higher Education in the United States," 201.

45. Durward Long, "Black Protest," in *Protest! Student Activism in America*, ed. Julian Foster and Durward Long (New York: William Morrow, 1970), 459–82.

46. Joel Rosenthal, "Southern Black Student Activism: Assimilation vs. Nationalism," *Journal of Negro Education* 44 (1975): 113–29.

47. Long, "Black Protest," 460.

48. Howe, *Student Activism*, 5.

49. Joanne Grant, *Black Protest: History, Documents, and Analyses* (Greenwich, Conn.: Fawcett Publications, 1968), 460.

50. Long, "Black Protest," 464.

51. Lawrence B. de Graaf, "Howard: The Evolution of a Black Student Revolt," in *Protest! Student Activism in America*, ed. Julian Foster and Durward Long (New York: William Morrow, 1970), 319–44.

52. Ibid., 324–25.   53. Ibid., 326.

54. Ibid., 322.   55. Ibid., 341.

56. Long, "Black Protest," 459.

57. See Nathan Glazer, "What Happened at Berkeley," in *Student Activism*, ed. Irving Howe (Indianapolis: Bobbs-Merrill Company, 1967), 15–23; Seymour Martin Lipset and Sheldon S. Wolin, eds., *The Berkeley Student Revolts: Facts and Interpretations* (Garden City, N.Y.: Anchor Books, 1965); Seymour Martin Lipset, *Rebellion in the University*; and Philip Selznick, "Reply to Glazer," in *Student Activism*, ed. Irving Howe (Indianapolis: Bobbs-Merrill, 1967), 24–29.

58. Nathan Glazer, *Remembering the Answers: Essays on the American Student Revolt* (New York: Basic Books, 1970), 82.

59. Glazer, "What Happened at Berkeley," 16.

60. Ibid., 18.

61. Selznick, "Reply to Glazer," 27, 20.

62. Obear, "Student Activism in the Sixties," 18.

63. Ibid., 18.

64. Ibid., 20.

65. Durward Long, "Wisconsin: Changing Styles of Administrative Response," in *Protest! Student Activism in America*, ed. Julian Foster and Durward Long (New York: William Morrow & Company, 1970), 246–70.

66. Faculty Committee to Investigate the Dow Incident at Indiana Univer-

sity, "Indiana: The Anatomy of Violence," in *Protest! Student Activism in America*, ed. Julian Foster and Durward Long (New York: William Morrow & Company, 1970), 227–45.

67. Kenneth J. Heineman, *Campus Wars: The Peace Movement at American State Universities in the Vietnam Era* (New York: New York University Press, 1993), 201, 204.

68. Ibid., 190.

69. Ibid.

70. Ibid.

71. Jay Stevens, *Storming Heaven: LSD and the American Dream* (New York: Harper & Row, 1988), 320, 331.

72. Clark Kerr, "Student Dissent and Confrontation Politics," in *Protest! Student Activism in America*, ed. Julian Foster and Durward Long (New York: William Morrow & Company, 1970), 3–10.

73. Eric L. Dey, "Undergraduate Political Attitudes: Peer Influence in Changing Social Contexts, *Journal of Higher Education* 68, no. 4 (1997): 398–413.

74. Kenneth Keniston, "The Sources of Student Dissent," *Journal of Social Issues* 23, no. 3 (1967): 108–37.

75. Herbert Moller, "Youth as a Force in the Modern World," *Comparative Studies in Society and History* 10 (1968): 237–60.

76. See Robert Coles, *The Call of Service: A Witness to Idealism* (Boston: Houghton Mifflin, 1993); Erik H. Erikson, *Identity: Youth and Crisis* (New York: W. W. Norton & Company, 1968); and Robert A. Rhoads, *Community Service and Higher Learning: Explorations of the Caring Self* (Albany: State University of New York Press, 1997).

77. Edwin Diamond, "Class of '69: The Violent Years," in *Turmoil on the Campus*, ed. Edward J. Bander (New York: H. W. Wilson Company, 1970), 9–28.

78. Clark Kerr. *The Uses of the University* (Cambridge: Harvard University Press, 1963).

79. Harold Hodgkinson, "Student Protest—An Institutional and National Profile," *Teachers College Record* 71, no. 4 (1970): 537–55; and Lipset and Altbach, "Student Politics and Higher Education in the United States."

80. Lipset and Altbach, "Student Politics and Higher Education in the United States," 208.

81. Kerr, "Student Dissent and Confrontation Politics."

82. Talcott Parsons, *Toward a General Theory of Action* (Cambridge: Harvard University Press, 1951).

83. Peterson, *The Scope of Organized Student Protest in 1964–1965*.

84. C. Vann Woodward, "What Became of the 1960s? *New Republic*, 9 November 1974, 18–25.

85. Daniel A. Foss and Ralph W. Larkin, "From 'the Gates of Eden' to 'Day of the Locust': An Analysis of the Dissident Youth Movement of the 1960s and Its Heir of the Early 1970s—the Post-Movement Groups," *Theory and Society* 3 (1976): 1–44.

86. Glazer, *Remembering the Answers*, 193.

87. Arthur Levine, *When Dreams and Heroes Died* (San Francisco: Jossey-Bass, 1980), 27.

88. Ibid., 5.

89. Ralph H. Turner, "Campus Peace: Harmony or Uneasy Truce?" *Sociological and Social Research* 57, no. 1 (1972): 5–21.

90. For a detailed analysis of the Columbia University Divestment Movement see Eric L. Hirsch, "Sacrifice for the Cause: Group Processes, Recruitment, and Commitment in a Student Social Movement," *American Sociological Review* 55 (1990): 242–54.

91. Loeb, *Generation at the Crossroads*, 172.

92. Tony Vellela, *New Voices: Student Activism in the '80s and '90s* (Boston: South End Press, 1988).

93. Ibid.

94. Philip G. Altbach and Robert Cohen, "American Student Activism: The Post-Sixties Transformation," *Journal of Higher Education* 61, no. 1 (1990): 32–49.

95. Ibid.

96. Luke Tripp, "Race Consciousness among African-American Students, 1980s," *Western Journal of Black Studies* 15, no. 3 (1991): 159–68.

chapter three: **"Immigrants in Our Own Land"**

1. Bettijane Levine, "A UCLA Professor and 6 Students Have Gone Days without Food," *Los Angeles Times*, 1 June 1993, sec. E, p. 1.

2. For a discussion of multiculturalism in higher education see Estela M. Bensimon, ed., *Multicultural Teaching and Learning* (University Park, Penn.: National Center on Postsecondary Teaching, Learning, & Assessment, 1994); Robert A. Rhoads, "Critical Multiculturalism, Border Knowledge, and the Canon: Implications for General Education and the Academy," *Journal of General Education* 44, no. 4 (1995): 256–73; Robert A. Rhoads and Sylvia M. Solorzano, "Multiculturalism and the Community College: A Case Study of an Immigrant Education Program," *Community College Review* 23, no. 2 (1995): 3–16; Robert A. Rhoads and James R. Valadez, *Democracy, Multiculturalism, and the Community College: A Critical Perspective* (New York: Garland Publishing, 1996); William G. Tierney, "Cultural Politics and the Curriculum in Postsecondary Education," *Journal of Education* 171, no. 3 (1989): 72–88; and William G. Tierney, *Building Communities of Difference: Higher Education in the 21st Century* (Westport, Conn.: Bergin & Garvey, 1993).

3. Juan Gómez-Quiñones, *Mexican Students Por La Raza: The Chicano Student Movement in Southern California* (Santa Barbara, Calif.: Editorial La Causa, 1978).

4. Denise K. Magner, "Proposal to Revise Chicano Studies Divides UCLA," *Chronicle of Higher Education*, 1 May 1991, sec. A, p. 12.

5. Richard Vasquez, *Chicano* (Garden City, N.Y.: Doubleday, 1970), 374.

6. For a discussion of the history of Chicano struggle in the United States see

Rodolfo Acuña, *Occupied America: A History of Chicanos*, 2nd ed. (New York: Harper & Row, 1981); Ignacio M. García, *United We Win: The Rise and Fall of La Raza Unida Party* (Tucson: University of Arizona Press, 1989); Juan Gómez-Quiñones, *Roots of Chicano Politics, 1600–1940* (Albuquerque: University of New Mexico Press, 1994); Juan Gómez-Quiñones, *Chicano Politics: Reality and Promise, 1940–1990* (Albuquerque: University of New Mexico Press, 1990); Fred A. López III, "Reflections on the Chicano Movement," *Latin American Perspectives* 19, no. 4 (1992): 79–102; and Carlos Muñoz Jr., *Youth, Identity, Power: The Chicano Movement* (London: Verso, 1989).

7. Jimmy Santiago Baca, *Immigrants in Our Own Land* (Baton Rouge: Louisiana State University Press, 1979), 12–13.

8. Ernesto Galarzo, *Barrio Boy* (Notre Dame, Ind.: University of Notre Dame Press, 1971), 238.

9. Larry Gordan, "UCLA Rejects Plan for Chicano Studies Department," *Los Angeles Times*, 29 April 1993, sec. B, p. 1.

10. Ibid., 1.

11. Saul Sarabia, "Chicano Studies Fight Involves a Bigger Issue," *Los Angeles Times*, 30 May 1993, sec. M, p. 3.

12. Gordan, "UCLA Rejects Plan for Chicano Studies Department," 1.

13. Gómez-Quiñones, *Roots of Chicano Politics, 1600–1940*, 184.

14. Larry Gordan and Marina Dundjerski, "UCLA Has 2nd Day of Protest over Program," *Los Angeles Times*, 13 May 1993, sec. B, p. 1.

15. Tom Hayden, "Amid Cash Crisis, Hispanics Win a Historical Victory," *Chronicle of Higher Education*, 30 June 1993, sec. A, p. 40.

16. Larry Gordan and Marina Dundjerski, "Budget Threats on Chicano Studies Fail to Budge UCLA," *Los Angeles Times*, 15 May 1993, sec. B, p. 1.

17. "Chicano Studies Activists Begin Hunger Strike at UCLA," *Los Angeles Times*, 26 May 1993, sec. B, p. 4.

18. Levine, "A UCLA Professor and 6 Students Have Gone Days without Food," 1.

19. Chicano Coordinating Council, *El Plan de Santa Barbara* (Santa Barbara, Calif.: La Causa Publications, 1970), 9.

20. Ibid.

21. Ibid., 94.

22. Todd Gitlin, *The Twilight of Common Dreams: Why America Is Wracked by Culture Wars* (New York: Henry Holt and Company, 1995), 165.

23. Cherríe Moraga, *Loving in the War Years* (Boston: South End Press, 1983).

24. Larry Gordan, "UCLA Strikers End Fast," *Los Angeles Times*, 8 June 1993, sec. A, p. 1.

25. Ibid.

26. Ibid.

27. Ibid.

28. Ralph Frammolino, "A New Generation of Rebels: Latinos Are Demand-

ing Colleges Be More Responsive," *Los Angeles Times*, 20 November 1993, sec. A, p. 1.

29. Ibid.

30. Guadalupe San Miguel, "Actors Not Victims: Chicanas/os and the Struggle for Educational Equality," in *Chicanas/Chicanos at the Crossroads: Social, Economic, and Political Change*, ed. David R. Maciel and Isidro D. Ortiz (Tucson: University of Arizona Press, 1996), 165.

31. Gómez-Quiñones, *Chicano Politics*, 103–4.

32. Tom Hayden, *Reunion: A Memoir* (New York: Random House, 1988), 468.

33. Hayden, "Amid Cash Crisis," 40.

34. Refugio I. Rochín and Adaljiza Sosa-Riddell, "Chicano Studies in a Pluralistic Society: Contributing to Multiculturalism," *Bilingual Review* 17, no. 2 (1992): 132–42.

chapter four: **"Strong Women, Proud Women"**

1. Rosalind Keep, *Fourscore Years: A History of Mills College* (Oakland, Calif.: Mills College Press, 1931).

2. Rosalind Keep, *Fourscore and Ten Years: A History of Mills College* (Oakland, Calif.: Mills College Press, 1946), 15.

3. Ibid.

4. Katherine Bishop, "Women's College Struggles to Keep Its Identity," *New York Times*, 7 March 1990, sec. B, p. 5.

5. Roberta M. Hall and Bernice R. Sandler, "The Classroom Climate: A Chilly One for Women?" (research report sponsored by the Project on the Status and Education of Women, Washington, D.C.: Association of American Colleges, 1982), 3.

6. Dorothy C. Holland and Margaret A. Eisenhart, *Educated in Romance: Women, Achievement, and College* (Chicago: University of Chicago Press, 1990); Helen G. Koritz, "Women in Science: Changing the Climate," *Journal of College Science Teaching* 21 (1992): 260–61; Elaine Seymour, "Undergraduate Problems with Teaching and Advising in SME Majors—Explaining Gender Differences in Attrition Rates, *Journal of College Science Teaching* 21 (1992): 284–92; and Sheila Tobias, "Women *in* Science—Women *and* Science," *Journal of College Science Teaching* 21 (1992): 276–78.

7. Nancy Chodorow, "Family Structure and Feminine Personality," in *Woman, Culture, and Society*, ed. Michelle Rosaldo and Louise Lamphere (Stanford: Stanford University Press, 1974), 43–66; Nancy Chodorow, *The Reproduction of Mothering: Psychoanalysis and the Sociology of Gender* (Berkeley: University of California Press, 1978); Carol Gilligan, "Woman's Place in Man's Life Cycle," *Harvard Educational Review* 49, no. 4 (1979): 431–46; Carol Gilligan, *In a Different Voice: Psychological Theory and Women's Development* (Cambridge, Mass.: Harvard University Press, 1982); Janet Lever, "Sex Differences in the Games Children Play," *Social Problems* 23 (1976): 478–87; Marcia B. Baxter Magolda, *Knowing and Reasoning in College:*

Gender-Related Patterns in Students' Intellectual Development (San Francisco: Jossey-Bass, 1992); and Angela McRobbie, "Working Class Girls and the Culture of Femininity," in *Women Take Issue*, ed. Centre for Contemporary Cultural Studies (London: Routledge & Kegan Paul, 1978), 96–108.

8. Lawrence Kohlberg, "The Cognitive-Developmental Approach to Moral Education," *Phi Delta Kappan* 56 (1975): 670–77; Lawrence Kohlberg, "The Future of Liberalism as the Dominant Ideology of the West," in *Moral Development and Politics*, ed. Richard W. Wilson and Gordon J. Schochet (Westport, Conn.: Praeger, 1980), 55–68.

9. Mary F. Belenky, Blythe M. Clinchy, Nancy R. Goldberger, and Jill M. Tarule, *Women's Ways of Knowing: The Development of Self, Voice, and Mind* (New York: Basic Books, 1986); Ellen Messer-Davidow, "Knowers, Knowing, Knowledge: Feminist Theory and Education," *Journal of Thought* 20, no. 3 (1985): 8–24; and Iris M. Young, *Justice and the Politics of Difference* (Princeton, N.J.: Princeton University Press, 1990).

10. Diane Curtis, "Mills College Considers Going Coed," *San Francisco Chronicle*, 27 January 1990, sec. A, p. 3.

11. Ibid.

12. Mary Lane, "Rally Draws Students, Media," *Mills College Weekly*, 16 February 1990, p. 1; Mary Lane, "Faculty Endorses Single Sex," *Mills College Weekly*, 27 April 1990, pp. 1, 3; Sarah Ratcliff and Karen Lubisch, "Students Channel Energies," *Mills College Weekly*, 27 April 1990, pp. 1, 3; and Maria West, "Students Respond to Options, Comments, *Mills College Weekly*, 16 February 1990, p. 1.

13. Jeannine Miller, "Empowerment," *Mills College Weekly*, 16 February 1990, p. 2.

14. Nicole Yost, "Inspiration," *Mills College Weekly*, 16 February 1990, p. 2.

15. Diane Curtis, "Pressure on Mills College Not to Admit Male Students," *San Francisco Chronicle*, 25 April 1990, sec. A, p. 4.

16. Curtis, "Mills College Considers Going Coed," 3.

17. Diane Curtis, "Mills College to Go Coed: Trustees Vote to Admit Male Undergraduates," *San Francisco Chronicle*, 4 May 1990, sec. A, p. 1.

18. Sara M. Evans, *Personal Politics: The Roots of Women's Liberation in the Civil Rights Movement and the New Left* (New York: Vintage Books, 1980), 212–13.

19. For a discussion of organizational theorizing from a feminist perspective see Kathy E. Ferguson, *The Feminist Case against Bureaucracy* (Philadelphia: Temple University Press, 1984); Kathleen Iannello, *Decisions without Hierarchy: Feminist Interventions in Organization Theory and Practice* (New York: Routledge, 1992); and Marta B. Calás and Linda Smircich, "Re-writing Gender into Organizational Theorizing: Directions from Feminist Perspectives," in *Rethinking Organization: New Directions in Organizational Theory and Analysis*, ed. Michael Reed and Michael Hughes (London: Sage, 1992), 227–53.

20. Diane Curtis, "Mills College Board to Reconsider Vote: New Plans May

Allow It to Stay All-Women," *San Francisco Chronicle*, 11 May 1990, sec. A, p. 4.

21. Diane Curtis, "Faculty Backs Students' Position in Mills College Takeover," *San Francisco Chronicle*, 8 May 1990, sec. A, p. 3.
22. Mary Lane, "Board May Review Coed Decision Next Week," *Mills College Weekly*, 11 May 1990, p. 1.
23. Diane Curtis, "Mills College Students End Strike," *San Francisco Chronicle*, 18 May 1990, sec. A, p. 1.
24. Diane Curtis, "Mills Board Decides—Men Out: Trustees Decide to Keep College All Women," *San Francisco Chronicle*, 19 May 1990, sec. A, p. 1; Alisa Hicks, "Proposals Convince Trustees to Reverse Coed Decision," *Mills College Weekly*, 19 May 1990, pp. 1, 4; and Lisa Kremer, "Mills Womyn Celebrate," *Mills College Weekly*, 19 May 1990, pp. 1, 4.
25. Curtis, "Mills Board Decides—Men Out," 1.
26. Ibid.
27. Curtis, "Mills College Students End Strike," 1.
28. Dean Congbalay, "Graduates Drip with Jubilation at Mills College," *San Francisco Chronicle*, 21 May 1990, sec. A, p. 8.
29. Diane Curtis, "Mills President Quits—Target of Anger, She Backed Thwarted Plan to Admit Men," *San Francisco Chronicle*, 23 June 1990, sec. A, p. 4.
30. Jack McCurdy, "Trustees of Mills College Reverse Decision to Admit Undergraduate Men," *Chronicle of Higher Education*, 30 May 1990, sec. A, p. 2.
31. Curtis, "Mills Board Decides—Men Out," 1.
32. Michelle C. Quinn, "Mills Is Still Defiantly All-Women, But It'll Never Be the Same," *New York Times*, 1 September 1993, sec. B, p. 6.
33. Ibid.
34. Mary S. Hartman, "Mills Students Provided Eloquent Testimony to the Value of Women's Colleges," *Chronicle of Higher Education*, 5 July 1990, sec. A, p. 40.
35. Ibid.
36. C. Wright Mills, *The Power Elite* (New York: Oxford University Press, 1956).
37. James Miller, *Democracy Is in the Streets: From Port Huron to the Siege of Chicago* (Cambridge: Harvard University Press, 1994), 153.

chapter five: **"Promises Made, Promises Kept"**

1. Art Aisner, "Indian Tuition Plan Sparks Protest," *State News*, 13 March 1995, p. 3.
2. This student requested anonymity, so a pseudonym has been used.
3. The agreement made between the State of Michigan and its American Indian population technically was not a treaty, as treaties can only be made by the federal government.
4. This student requested anonymity, so a pseudonym has been used.

5. Michigan Federal Tribes Education Consortium, *The Michigan Indian Tuition Waiver: An Investment in the Future of Michigan's Original People* (Lansing, Mich.: Michigan Federal Tribes Education Consortium, 1996).

6. Arnie Parish, *A Descriptive Study of the Michigan Indian Tuition Waiver Program* (E. Lansing, Mich.: Native American Institute, 1996).

7. Michigan Federal Tribes Education Consortium, *The Michigan Indian Tuition Waiver*.

8. Parish, *A Descriptive Study of the Michigan Indian Tuition Waiver Program*.

9. Michigan Federal Tribes Education Consortium, *Michigan Indian Tuition Waiver*, 21.

10. Eleanor Templeton, "Indian Tuition Waiver," *State News*, 12 July 1995, 1–2.

11. Aisner, "Indian Tuition Plan Sparks Protest," 3.

12. Dawson Bell, "Governor Cuts Indian College Tuition Program," *Detroit Free Press*, 9 February 1996, Sec. A, p. 7.

13. Parish, *A Descriptive Study of the Michigan Indian Tuition Waiver Program*.

14. Gerald J. Goodwin, "Christianity, Civilization, and the Savage: The Anglican Mission to the American Indian," *Historical Magazine of the Protestant Episcopal Church* 42 (1973): 93–110.

15. Bobby Wright, "The 'Untameable Savage Spirit': American Indians in Colonial Colleges," *Review of Higher Education* 14, no. 4 (1991): 429–52.

16. See also the work of Elgin Badwound, "Leadership and American Indian Values: The Tribal College Dilemma" (Ph.D. diss., Pennsylvania State University, 1990); Judith E. Fries, *The American Indian in Higher Education, 1975–76 to 1984–85* (Washington, D.C.: Center for Education Statistics, 1987); Terry E. Huffman, Maurice L. Sill, and Martin Brokenleg, "College Achievement among Sioux and White South Dakota Students," *Journal of American Indian Education* 25, no. 2 (1986): 32–38; Richard Pottinger, "Disjunction to Higher Education: American Indian Students in the Southwest," *Journal of Navajo Education* 7, no. 2 (1990): 37–45; Richard Pottinger, "The Quest for Valued Futures: Steps on a Rainbow Journey," *Journal of Navajo Education* 6, no. 3 (1989): 2–11; Wilbur J. Scott, "Attachment to Indian Culture and the 'Difficult Situation': A Study of American Indian College Students," *Youth & Society* 17, no. 4 (1986): 381–95; and Kathryn Harris Tijerina and Paul Philip Biemer, "The Dance of Indian Higher Education: One Step Forward, Two Steps Back," *Educational Record* 68, no. 4 (1988): 86–93.

17. William G. Tierney, *Official Encouragement, Institutional Discouragement: Minorities in Academe—the Native American Experience* (Norwood, N.J.: Ablex, 1992); and William G. Tierney, "An Anthropological Analysis of Student Participation in College," *Journal of Higher Education* 63 (1992): 603–18.

18. Vincent Tinto, *Leaving College: Rethinking the Causes and Cures of Student Attrition*, 2nd ed. (Chicago: University of Chicago Press, 1993).

19. Alexander W. Astin, "Student Involvement: A Developmental Theory for Higher Education," *Journal of College Student Personnel* 25 (1984): 297–308.

20. Alexander W. Astin, *Achieving Educational Excellence* (San Francisco: Jossey-Bass, 1991), 134.

21. Lou C. Attinasi Jr., "Getting In: Mexican Americans' Perceptions of University Attendance and the Implications for Freshman Year Persistence," *Journal of Higher Education* 60 (1989): 247–77; Barbara A. Kraemer, "The Academic and Social Integration of Hispanic Students into College," *Review of Higher Education* 20, no. 2 (1997): 163–79; Michael T. Nettles, "Factors Related to Black and White Students' College Performance," in *Toward Black Undergraduate Student Equality in American Higher Education*, ed. Michael T. Nettles (New York: Greenwood Press, 1988), 17–34; Amaury Nora, "Determinants of Retention among Chicano College Students: A Structural Model," *Research in Higher Education* 26, no. 1 (1987): 31–58; Amaury Nora, "Campus-Based Aid Programs as Determinants of Retention among Hispanic Community College Students," *Journal of Higher Education* 61 (1990): 312–31; and Amaury Nora, "Two-Year Colleges and Minority Students' Educational Aspirations: Help or Hindrance?" in *Higher Education: Handbook of Theory and Research*, Volume 9, ed. John C. Smart (New York: Agathon Press, 1993), 212–47.

22. Tierney, *Official Encouragement, Institutional Discouragement*, 79.

23. See Estela M. Bensimon, ed., *Multicultural Teaching and Learning* (University Park, Penn.: National Center on Postsecondary Teaching, Learning, & Assessment, 1994); Robert A. Rhoads, "Critical Multiculturalism, Border Knowledge, and the Canon: Implications for General Education and the Academy," *Journal of General Education* 44, no. 4 (1995): 256–73; Robert A. Rhoads and Sylvia M. Solorzano, "Multiculturalism and the Community College: A Case Study of an Immigrant Education Program," *Community College Review* 23, no. 2 (1995): 3–16; Robert A. Rhoads and James R. Valadez, *Democracy, Multiculturalism, and the Community College: A Critical Perspective* (New York: Garland Publishing, 1996); Frances K. Stage and Kathleen Manning, *Enhancing the Multicultural Campus Environment: A Cultural Brokering Approach*, New Directions for Student Services No. 60 (San Francisco: Jossey-Bass, 1992); and William G. Tierney, *Building Communities of Difference: Higher Education in the 21st Century* (Westport, Conn.: Bergin & Garvey, 1993).

24. Tijerina and Biemer, "The Dance of Indian Higher Education," 93.

25. Wright, "The 'Untameable Savage Spirit,'" 448.

26. Bobby Wright, *American Indian and Alaska Native Higher Education: Toward a New Century of Academic Achievement and Cultural Integrity* (Washington, D.C.: Department of Education, Indian Nations at Risk Task Force, 1991).

27. For a recent discussion of affirmative action and higher education see Mildred García, ed., *Affirmative Action's Testament of Hope: Strategies for a New Era in Higher Education* (Albany: State University of New York, 1997).

28. Kenneth, J. Heineman, *Campus Wars: The Peace Movement at American*

State Universities in the Vietnam Era (New York: New York University Press, 1993).

29. Doug McAdam, *Freedom Summer* (New York: Oxford University Press, 1988); and Sally Belfrage, *Freedom Summer* (New York: Viking Press, 1965).

30. "Indian Tuition Waiver Fight Heats Up," *Lansing State Journal*, 3 March 1995, Sec. B, p. 3.

31. Amy Snow, "Angry Crowd Protests Engler at Pep Rally," *State News*, 9 October 1995, Sec. A, p. 1.

32. Sonja Madgevski, "Challenging Columbus," *State News*, 13 October 1995, pp. 1, 10.

33. Tijerina and Biemer, "The Dance of Indian Higher Education," 87.

34. Susan Welch, *A Feminist Ethic of Risk* (Minneapolis, Minn.: Fortress Press, 1989), 104.

35. Beverly Wildung Harrison, *Making the Connections: Essays in Feminist Social Ethics*, ed. Carol S. Robb (Boston: Beacon Press, 1985), 250.

36. Henry A. Giroux, *Living Dangerously: Multiculturalism and the Politics of Difference* (New York: Peter Lang, 1993), 90.

37. W. E. B. Du Bois, *The Souls of Black Folk* (New York: Dover Publications, 1903/1994), 3.

38. Gloria Jahoda, *The Trail of Tears* (New York: Holt, Rinehart & Winston, 1975), 17–18.

chapter six: **"We're Here. We're Queer. Get Used to It."**

1. The case study upon which this chapter is based is part of a larger ethnographic project focused primarily on gay and bisexual college males. For a more detailed analysis of the experiences of gay and bisexual college males, see Robert A. Rhoads, *Coming Out in College: The Struggle for a Queer Identity* (Westport, Conn.: Bergin & Garvey, 1994).

2. Throughout this chapter pseudonyms are used for the students who participated in the case study.

3. Barb Snyder, "HOPS Member Removed," *Daily Collegian*, 16 February 1972, p. 1.

4. Barb Snyder, "HOPS: 1 Year Old, But Learning Life Fast," *Daily Collegian*, 27 April 1972, p. 1.

5. Barb Snyder, "HOPS Sues University," *Daily Collegian*, 14 February 1972, p. 1.

6. Jeff DeBray and Rick Nelson, "Acanfora: The Struggle Continues," *Daily Collegian*, 27 February 1973, p. 1.

7. Ibid.

8. Audre Lorde, *Sister Outsider* (Freedom, Calif.: Crossing Press, 1984), 40.

9. For a classic sociological discussion of the role stigma plays in identity development, see Erving Goffman, *Stigma: Notes on the Management of Spoiled Identity* (Englewood Cliffs, N.J.: Prentice-Hall, 1963).

10. Frank Browning, *The Culture of Desire: Paradox and Perversity in Gay Lives Today* (New York: Crown Publishers, 1993), 33.

11. Alexander Doty, *Making Things Perfectly Queer* (Minneapolis: University of Minnesota Press, 1993).

12. See Wendy Dale and Darin Soler, "Class Acts," *The Advocate*, 7 September 1993, 45–47; and John D'Emilio, *Making Trouble: Essays on Gay History, Politics, and the University* (New York: Routledge, 1992).

13. See Anthony R. D'Augelli, "Homophobia in a University Community: Views of Prospective Resident Assistants," *Journal of College Student Development* 30 (1989): 546–52; Anthony R. D'Augelli, "Lesbians' and Gay Men's Experiences of Discrimination and Harassment in a University Community," *American Journal of Community Psychology* 17, no. 3 (1989): 317–21; Gregory M. Herek, "Documenting Prejudice against Lesbians and Gay Men on Campus: The Yale Sexual Orientation Survey," *Journal of Homosexuality* 25, no. 4 (1993): 15–30; Jane M. Low, "The Davis Social Environment: A Report of Student Opinions" (Student Affairs Research and Information, University of California at Davis, 1988); Randy Nelson and Harley Baker, "The Educational Climate for Gay, Lesbian, and Bisexual Students" (Student Services, University of California at Santa Cruz, 1990); Ronald A. Nieberding, "In Every Classroom: The Report of the President's Select Committee for Lesbian and Gay Concerns" (Office of Student Life Policy and Services, Rutgers University, 1989); C. F. Shepard, "Report on the Quality of Campus Life for Lesbian, Gay, and Bisexual Students" (Student Affairs Information and Research Office, University of California at Los Angeles, 1990); William G. Tierney et al., "Enhancing Diversity: Toward a Better Campus Climate" (Report of the Committee on Lesbian and Gay Concerns, Pennsylvania State University, 1992).

14. See Vivienne C. Cass, "Homosexual Identity Formation: A Theoretical Model," *Journal of Homosexuality* 4, no. 3 (1979): 219–35; Eli Coleman, "Developmental Stages of the Coming Out Process," in *Homosexuality and Psychotherapy: A Practitioner's Handbook of Affirmative Models*, ed. J. C. Gonsiorek (New York: Haworth Press, 1982), 31–44; Anthony R. D'Augelli, "Gay Men in College: Identity Processes and Adaptations," *Journal of College Student Development* 32 (1991): 140–46; Anthony R. D'Augelli, "Out on Campus: Dilemmas of Identity Development for Lesbian and Gay Young Adults" (paper presented at the annual meeting of the American Psychological Association, San Francisco, August 1991); Dana Finnegan and Emily McNally, *Dual Identities: Counseling Chemically Dependent Gay Men and Lesbians* (Center City, Minn.: Hazelden Foundation, 1987); Jeanne Miranda and Micheal Storms, "Psychological Adjustment of Lesbians and Gay Men," *Journal of Counseling & Development* 68 (1989): 41–45; Robert A. Rhoads, *Coming Out in College*; Robert A. Rhoads, "The Cultural Politics of Coming Out in College," *Review of Higher Education* 19, no. 1 (1995): 1–22; Robert A. Rhoads, "Learning from the Coming-Out Experiences of College Males,"

Journal of College Student Development 36, no. 1 (1995): 67–74; Richard R. Troiden, "Becoming Homosexual: A Model of Gay Identity Acquisition, *Psychiatry* 42 (1979): 362–73; and Richard R. Troiden, "The Formation of Homosexual Identities," *Journal of Homosexuality* 17, nos. 1/2 (1989): 43–73.

15. Gilbert Herdt, *Gay Culture in America: Essays from the Field* (Boston: Beacon, 1992).

16. Richard A. Friend, "Choices, Not Closets: Heterosexism and Homophobia in Schools," in *Beyond Silenced Voices: Class, Race, and Gender in United States Schools*, ed. Lois Weis and Michelle Fine (Albany: State University of New York Press, 1991), 211.

17. Ibid.

18. Audre Lorde, *I Am Your Sister: Black Women Organizing Across Sexualities* (Latham, N.Y.: Kitchen Table Press, 1985), 3.

19. Ibid., 3–4.

20. Friend, "Choices, Not Closets," 211.

21. Evelyn Brooks Higginbotham, "African-American Women's History and the Metalanguage of Race," *Signs: Journal of Women in Culture and Society* 17, no. 2 (1992): 251–74.

22. Mikhail M. Bakhtin, *The Dialogic Imagination: Four Essays*, ed. M. Holquist, trans. C. Emerson and M. Holquist (Austin: University of Texas Press, 1981), 293.

23. Higginbotham, "African-American Women's History and the Metalanguage of Race," 267.

24. Henry A. Giroux, *Border Crossings: Cultural Workers and the Politics of Education* (New York: Routledge, 1992), 5.

25. Michel Foucault, *The Order of Things* (New York: Vintage Books, 1970), xx.

26. Henry A. Giroux, "Theories of Reproduction and Resistance in the New Sociology of Education: A Critical Analysis," *Harvard Educational Review* 53, no. 3 (1983): 257–93; and Henry A. Giroux, *Theory and Resistance in Education* (South Hadley, Mass.: Bergin & Garvey, 1983).

27. Pierre Bourdieu, "The Forms of Capital," in *Handbook of Theory and Research in the Sociology of Education*, ed. J. G. Richardson (New York: Greenwood Press, 1986), 241–58.

28. See Penelope Eckert, *Jocks and Burnouts: Social Categories and Identity in the High School* (New York: Teachers College Press, 1989); Michelle Fine, "Why Urban Adolescents Drop into and out of Public High School," *Teachers College Record* 87, no. 3 (1986): 393–409; Michelle Fine, *Framing Dropouts: Notes on the Politics of an Urban High School* (Albany: State University of New York Press, 1991); Dorothy C. Holland and Margaret A. Eisenhart, *Educated in Romance: Women, Achievement, and College* (Chicago: University of Chicago Press, 1990); Jay MacLeod, *Ain't No Makin' It* (Boulder, Colo.: Westview Press, 1987); Peter McLaren, *Schooling as a Ritual Performance* (London: Routledge & Kegan Paul, 1986); Peter McLaren, *Life in Schools* (New York: Longman, 1989); Lois Weis, *Between Two Worlds* (Boston: Routledge &

Kegan Paul, 1985); and Paul E. Willis, *Learning to Labor* (Aldershot: Gower, 1977).

29. Giroux, *Border Crossings*.

30. Michel Foucault, *The History of Sexuality*, Volume 1: *An Introduction*, trans. R. Hurley (New York: Vintage Books, 1978); and Michel Foucault, *Discipline and Punish*, trans. A. Sheridan (New York: Vintage Books, 1979).

31. Gregory M. Herek, "Hate Crimes against Lesbians and Gay Men," *American Psychologist* 44, no. 6 (1989): 948–55.

32. D'Augelli, "Out on Campus," 5.

33. Ibid.

34. Brian Pronger, "Gay Jocks: A Phenomenology of Gay Men in Athletics," in *Rethinking Masculinity: Philosophical Explorations in Light of Feminism*," ed. L. May and R. A. Strikwerda (Lanham, Md.: Littlefield Adams, 1992), 45.

35. Michelangelo Signorile, *Queer in America: Sex, the Media, and the Closets of Power* (New York: Random House, 1993), 364.

36. William G. Tierney, *Building Communities of Difference: Higher Education in the 21st Century* (Westport, Conn.: Bergin & Garvey, 1993), 64.

37. Arthur M. Schlesinger Jr., *The Disuniting of America: Reflections on a Multicultural Society* (New York: W. W. Norton & Company, 1992), 16.

chapter seven: **"Genetic, Hereditary Background"**

1. Joanne Grant, *Black Protest: History, Documents, and Analyses, 1619 to the Present* (Greenwich, Conn.: Fawcett Publications, 1968), 426.

2. William H. Exum, *Paradoxes of Protest: Black Student Activism in a White University* (Philadelphia: Temple University Press, 1985), 24.

3. Richard P. McCormick, *The Black Student Protest Movement at Rutgers* (New Brunswick, N.J.: Rutgers University Press, 1990), 4.

4. Ibid.   5. Ibid., 24.

6. Ibid.   7. Ibid., 26.

8. Joyce Penfield, "Institutional Issues to Examine" (Report submitted to the Rutgers University Board of Governors, 1995), 5.

9. Ibid., 7.

10. Carrie Budoff and Jeannine Defoe, "Lawrence's Words Elicit Furor: President Defends Remarks on Role of Genetics, SAT," *Daily Targum*, 1 February 1995, pp. 1, 4.

11. Lisa Raff, "In Racism Fight at Rutgers, Jewish Students Claim Middle Ground," *Jewish Advocate*, 2 March 1995, p. 7.

12. "Editorial: A Call for Resignation," *Daily Targum*, 1 February 1995, pp. 1, 9.

13. J. Zamgba Browne, "Rutgers Students Escalate Calls for President's Ouster over Racist Remarks," *New York Amsterdam News*, 11 February 1995, p. 48.

14. "Rutgers' Students Reject University President's Apology for Racist Remark," *New York Voice Incorporated*, 22 February 1995, p. 1.

15. Dennis Mumbles, "Francis Lawrence Meant What He Said," *New York Amsterdam News*, 4 March 1995, p. 13.

16. Carl Rowan, "The Rowan Report: Black People Had Better Be Very Careful," *Indianapolis Recorder*, 4 March 1995, sec. A, p. 2.

17. Jeannine Defoe, "Students Take Unrest to Streets, Demand Action," *Daily Targum*, 2 February 1995, pp. 1, 5.

18. Jason Lynch and Francine Tardo, "Hundreds Voice Demands," *Daily Targum*, 2 February 1995, pp. 1, 5.

19. S. Mitra Kalita and Michelle Simonelli, "Students Walk Out after Meeting with President," *Daily Targum*, 3 February 1995, pp. 1, 4.

20. S. Mitra Kalita, "Senate Backs President: Executive Committee Passes Resolution Supporting Lawrence's Wednesday Apology," *Daily Targum*, 6 February 1995, pp. 1, 4.

21. S. Mitra Kalita, "Students Produce List of Demands," *Daily Targum*, 7 February 1995, pp. 1, 4.

22. S. Mitra Kalita, "Students Sit-In at RAC, Disrupt Game," *Daily Targum*, 8 February 1995, p. 1.

23. Timothy William Quinnan, "The Last Word: Culture, Theory, and Leadership," *Black Issues in Higher Education* 12, no. 2 (1995): 108.

24. "Rutgers' Students Reject University President's Apology for Racist Remark," p. 1.

25. "Rutgers Students Must Keep Protest Focused, *Philadelphia Tribune*, 3 March 1995, sec. A, p. 6.

26. Herb Boyd, "Black Rutgers Law Students View President's Remarks as a Symptom," *New York Amsterdam News*, 18 February 1995, p. 3.

27. "Rutgers' Students Reject University President's Apology for Racist Remark," p. 1.

28. William K. Egyir, "Rutgers President Angers Groups," *New York Amsterdam News*, 25 February 1995, p. 20.

29. S. Mitra Kalita, "Two Arrested in Take-Over," *Daily Targum*, 8 March 1995, pp. 1, 4.

30. S. Mitra Kalita, "Bomb Explodes in Douglass Library," *Daily Targum*, 5 April 1995, pp. 1, 4.

31. Michelle Simonelli, "Bomb Threats Spread," *Daily Targum*, 6 April 1995, pp. 1, 6.

32. S. Mitra Kalita, "Second Bomb Unnerves RU," *Daily Targum*, 10 April 1995, pp. 1, 6.

33. Annette M. Altson, "Seven Rutgers Students Plead Guilty in Anti-Racism Picket," *New York Amsterdam News*, 5 August 1995, p. 3.

34. Patricia Gurin and Edgar Epps, *Black Consciousness, Identity, and Achievement: A Study of Students in Historically Black Colleges* (New York: John Wiley & Sons, 1975).

35. Robin D. G. Kelley, *Race Rebels: Culture, Politics, and the Black Working Class* (New York: Free Press, 1994).

36. Altson, "Seven Rutgers Students Plead Guilty in Anti-Racism Picket," p. 3.

37. Michelle Simonelli, "Students Note Dwindling Activism Numbers," *Daily Targum*, 20 February 1995, pp. 1, 4.

38. "College Prez Blames 'Bell Curve,' " *Los Angeles Sentinel*, 15 February 1995, sec. A, p. 8.

39. Gurin and Epps, *Black Consciousness, Identity, and Achievement*.

40. W. E. B. Du Bois, *The Souls of Black Folk* (New York: Dover Publications, 1903/1994), 2–3.

41. Molefi Kete Asante, "Racism, Consciousness, and Afrocentricity," in *Lure and Loathing: Essays on Race, Identity, and the Ambivalence of Assimilation*, ed. Gerald Early (New York: Penguin Books, 1993), 127–43.

42. Molefi Kete Asante, *Afrocentricity* (Trenton, N.J.: Africa World Press, 1988), 6.

43. bell hooks, *Black Looks: Race and Representation* (Boston: South End Press, 1992), 7.

44. Robert Staples, "The Illusion of Racial Equality: The Black American Dilemma," in *Lure and Loathing: Essays on Race, Identity, and the Ambivalence of Assimilation*, ed. Gerald Early (New York: Penguin Books, 1993), 227–44.

chapter eight: **Collective Consciousness**

1. Jennifer Hrynik, "Speaker Recalls Slain Leader's Dedication," *State News*, 21 January 1997, p. 1.

2. Geoff Kimmerly, "Students Celebrate Legacy of King's Vision," *State News*, 7 April 1997, p. 1.

3. Siegfried Marck, "Dialectical Materialism," in *A History of Philosophical Systems*, edited by Vergilius Ferm (New York: Philosophical Library, 1950), 306–28.

4. Herbert Blumer, "Social Movements," in *Principles of Sociology*, 2nd ed., ed. Alfred McClung Lee (New York: Barnes & Noble, 1946), 199–220.

5. Ibid., 200.

6. For a classic sociological discussion of the historical and socially constructed context of ideology and utopian visions see Karl Mannheim, *Ideology and Utopia: An Introduction to the Sociology of Knowledge* (San Diego: Harcourt Brace Jovanovich, 1936).

7. For a discussion of the relationship between alienation and activism see Charles D. Bolton, "Alienation and Action: A Study of Peace-Group Members," *American Journal of Sociology* 78, no. 3 (1972): 537–61.

8. Lewis S. Feuer, *The Conflict of Generations: The Character and Significance of Student Movements* (New York: Basic Books, 1969), 11.

9. Ibid.

10. Scott Heller, "Educators on the Left Organize to Fight Attacks on Academe, Which They See as Part of a Bigger Effort to Divide Society," *Chronicle of Higher Education*, 11 October 1996, sec. A, p. 12.

11. Angela Davis, *Angela Davis—An Autobiography* (New York: Random House, 1974), 144.

12. Herbert Marcuse, *Reason and Revolution: Hegel and the Rise of Social Theory* (New York: Humanities Press, 1954), 6–7.

13. Davis, *Angela Davis—An Autobiography*, 144.

14. Georg Lukács, *History and Class Consciousness*, trans. Rodney Livingstone (Cambridge, Mass.: MIT Press, 1968), 73.

15. Paulo Freire, *Pedagogy of the Oppressed* (New York: Continuum, 1970), 31–32.

16. J. K. Obatala, "Where Did Their Revolution Go?" *The Nation*, 2 October 1972, 272–74.

17. Sara M. Evans and Harry C. Boyte, *Free Spaces: The Sources of Democratic Change in America* (New York: Harper & Row, 1986), 66.

18. Ibid., 67.

19. Karl Marx, *The Portable Karl Marx*, trans. and ed. Eugene Kamenka (New York: Penguin Books, 1983), 213–14.

Acuña, Rodolfo. *Occupied America: A History of Chicanos*. 2nd ed. New York: Harper & Row, 1981.

Aisner, Art. "Indian Tuition Plan Sparks Protest." *State News*, 13 March 1995, p. 3.

Altbach, Philip G. "Perspectives on Student Political Activism." *Comparative Education* 25, no. 1 (1989): 97–110.

Altbach, Philip G., and Robert Cohen. "American Student Activism: The Post-Sixties Transformation." *Journal of Higher Education* 61, no. 1 (1990): 32–49.

Altbach, Philip G., and Patti Peterson. "Before Berkeley: Historical Perspectives on American Student Activism." *Annals of the American Academy of Political and Social Science* 395 (1971): 1–14.

Altson, Annette M. "Seven Rutgers Students Plead Guilty in Anti-Racism Picket." *New York Amsterdam News*, 5 August 1995, p. 3.

Asante, Molefi Kete. *Afrocentricity*. Trenton, N.J.: Africa World Press, 1988.

———. "Racism, Consciousness, and Afrocentricity." In *Lure and Loathing: Essays on Race, Identity, and the Ambivalence of Assimilation*, edited by Gerald Early. New York: Penguin Books, 1993.

Astin, Alexander W. "Student Involvement: A Developmental Theory for Higher Education." *Journal of College Student Personnel* 25 (1984): 297–308.

———. *The American Freshman: National Norms for Fall 1989*. Cooperative Institutional Research Program: University of California at Los Angeles, 1990.

———. *Achieving Educational Excellence*. San Francisco: Jossey-Bass, 1991.

———. *The American Freshman: National Norms for Fall 1992*. Cooperative Institutional Research Program: University of California at Los Angeles, 1993.

———. "Diversity and Multiculturalism on the Campus: How Are Students Affected?" *Change* 25, no. 1 (1993): 44–49.

Astin, Alexander W., Helen S. Astin, Alan E. Bayer, and Ann S. Bisconti. *The Power of Protest: A National Study of Student and Faculty Disruptions with Implications for the Future*. San Francisco: Jossey-Bass, 1975.

Attinasi, Lou C., Jr. "Getting In: Mexican Americans' Perceptions of University Attendance and the Implications for Freshman Year Persistence." *Journal of Higher Education* 60 (1989): 247–77.

Baca, Jimmy Santiago. *Immigrants in Our Own Land*. Baton Rouge: Louisiana State University Press, 1979.

Badwound, Elgin. "Leadership and American Indian Values: The Tribal College Dilemma." Ph.D. diss., Pennsylvania State University, 1990.

Bagg, Lyman H. *Four Years at Yale*. New Haven, Conn.: Charles C. Chatfield, 1871.

Baird, Leonard. "Who Protests: A Study of Student Activists." In *Protest! Student Activism in America*, edited by Julian Foster and Durward Long. New York: William Morrow, 1970.

Bakhtin, Mikhail M. *The Dialogic Imagination: Four Essays*. Edited by M. Holquist, translated by C. Emerson and M. Holquist. Austin: University of Texas Press, 1981.

Barlow, Andrew. "The Student Movement of the 1960s and the Politics of Race." *Journal of Ethnic Studies* 19, no. 3 (1991): 1–22.

Baudrillard, Jean. *Simulacra and Simulation*. Translated by Sheila Faria Glaser. Ann Arbor: University of Michigan Press, 1994.

Becker, Howard S. "Student Culture." In *The Study of Campus Cultures*, edited by Terry F. Lunsford. Boulder, Colo.: Westview Press, 1963.

Belenky, Mary F., Blythe M. Clinchy, Nancy R. Goldberger, and Jill M. Tarule. *Women's Ways of Knowing: The Development of Self, Voice, and Mind*. New York: Basic Books, 1986.

Belfrage, Sally. *Freedom Summer*. New York: Viking Press, 1965.

Bell, Dawson. "Governor Cuts Indian College Tuition Program." *Detroit Free Press*, 9 February 1996, Sec. A, p. 7.

Bensimon, Estela M., ed. *Multicultural Teaching and Learning*. University Park, Pa.: National Center on Postsecondary Teaching, Learning, & Assessment, 1994.

Berger, Peter L., and Thomas Luckmann. *The Social Construction of Reality: A Treatise in the Sociology of Knowledge*. New York: Anchor Books, 1966.

Bernstein, Richard. *Dictatorship of Virtue: Multiculturalism and the Battle for America's Future*. New York: Knopf, 1994.

Bills, Scott L., ed. *Kent State/May 4: Echoes through a Decade*. Kent, Ohio: Kent State University Press, 1982.

Bishop, Katherine. "Women's College Struggles to Keep Its Identity." *New York Times*, 7 March 1990, sec. B, p. 5.

Blumer, Herbert. "Social Movements." In *Principles of Sociology*, 2nd ed. Edited by Alfred McClung Lee. New York: Barnes & Noble, 1946.

Bolton, Charles D. "Alienation and Action: A Study of Peace-Group Members." *American Journal of Sociology* 78, no. 3 (1972): 537–61.

Bourdieu, Pierre. "The Forms of Capital." In *Handbook of Theory and Research in the Sociology of Education*, edited by J. G. Richardson. New York: Greenwood Press, 1986.

Boyd, Herb. "Black Rutgers Law Students View President's Remarks as a Symptom." *New York Amsterdam News*, 18 February 1995, p. 3.

Brax, Ralph S. *The First Student Movement: Student Activism in the United States during the 1930s*. Port Washington, N.Y.: Kennikat Press, 1981.

Browne, J. Zamgba. "Rutgers Students Escalate Calls for President's Ouster over Racist Remarks." *New York Amsterdam News*, 11 February 1995, p. 48.

Browning, Frank. *The Culture of Desire: Paradox and Perversity in Gay Lives Today*. New York: Crown Publishers, 1993.

Budoff, Carrie, and Jeannine DeFoe. "Lawrence's Words Elicit Furor: President Defends Remarks on Role of Genetics, SAT." *Daily Targum*, 1 February 1995, pp. 1, 4.

Burbules, Nicholas C., and Suzanne Rice. "Dialogue across Difference: Continuing the Conversation." *Harvard Educational Review* 61, no. 4 (1991): 393–416.

Calás, Marta B., and Linda Smircich. "Re-writing Gender into Organizational Theorizing: Directions from Feminist Perspectives." In *Rethinking Organization: New Directions in Organizational Theory and Analysis*, edited by Michael Reed and Michael Hughes. London: Sage, 1992.

"Campus 1965: The College Generation Looks at Itself and the World Around It." *Newsweek*, 22 March 1965, 43–63.

Carden, Maren Lockwood. *The New Feminist Movement*. New York: Russell Sage Foundation, 1974.

Cass, Vivienne C. "Homosexual Identity Formation: A Theoretical Model." *Journal of Homosexuality* 4, no. 3 (1979): 219–35.

Chicano Coordinating Council. *El Plan de Santa Barbara*. Santa Barbara, Calif.: La Causa Publications, 1970.

"Chicano Studies Activists Begin Hunger Strike at UCLA." *Los Angeles Times*, 26 May 1993, sec. B, p. 4.

Chodorow, Nancy. "Family Structure and Feminine Personality." In *Woman, Culture, and Society*, edited by Michelle Rosaldo and Louise Lamphere. Stanford: Stanford University Press, 1974.

———. *The Reproduction of Mothering: Psychoanalysis and the Sociology of Gender*. Berkeley: University of California Press, 1978.

Clark, Cheryl. "18 Protesters Arrested after Rally at UCSD Demonstration." *San Diego Union Tribune*, 13 March 1996, sec. B, 1–2.

Cohen, Robert. *When the Old Left Was Young: Student Radicals and America's First Mass Student Movement, 1929–1941*. New York: Oxford University Press, 1993.

Coleman, Eli. "Developmental Stages of the Coming Out Process." In *Homosexuality and Psychotherapy: A Practitioner's Handbook of Affirmative Models*, edited by J. C. Gonsiorek. New York: Haworth Press, 1982.

Coles, Robert. *The Call of Service: A Witness to Idealism*. Boston: Houghton Mifflin, 1993.

"College Prez Blames 'Bell Curve.'" *Los Angeles Sentinel*, 15 February 1995, sec. A, p. 8.

Congbalay, Dean. "Graduates Drip with Jubilation at Mills College." *San Francisco Chronicle*, 21 May 1990, sec. A, p. 8.

Curtis, Diane. "Faculty Backs Students' Position in Mills College Takeover." *San Francisco Chronicle*, 8 May 1990, sec. A, p. 3.

———. "Mills Board Decides—Men Out: Trustees Decide to Keep College All Women." *San Francisco Chronicle*, 19 May 1990, sec. A, p. 1.

———. "Mills College Board to Reconsider Vote: New Plans May Allow It to Stay All-Women." *San Francisco Chronicle*, 11 May 1990, sec. A, p. 4.

———. "Mills College Considers Going Coed." *San Francisco Chronicle*, 27 January 1990, sec. A, p. 3.

———. "Mills College Students End Strike." *San Francisco Chronicle*, 18 May 1990, sec. A, p. 1.

———. "Mills College to Go Coed: Trustees Vote to Admit Male Undergraduates." *San Francisco Chronicle*, 4 May 1990, sec. A, p. 1.

———. "Mills President Quits—Target of Anger, She Backed Thwarted Plan to Admit Men." *San Francisco Chronicle*, 23 June 1990, sec. A, p. 4.

———. "Pressure on Mills College Not to Admit Male Students." *San Francisco Chronicle*, 25 April 1990, sec. A, p. 4.

Dabney, Michael, "Rutgers Students Continue Protest," *Philadelphia Tribune*, 10 February 1995, sec. A, p. 1.

Dale, Wendy, and Darin Soler. "Class Acts." *Advocate*, 7 September 1993, 45–47.

D'Augelli, Anthony R. "Homophobia in a University Community: Views of Prospective Resident Assistants." *Journal of College Student Development* 30 (1989): 546–52.

———. "Lesbians' and Gay Men's Experiences of Discrimination and Harassment in a University Community." *American Journal of Community Psychology* 17, no. 3 (1989): 317–21.

———. "Gay Men in College: Identity Processes and Adaptations." *Journal of College Student Development* 32 (1991): 140–46.

———. "Out on Campus: Dilemmas of Identity Development for Lesbian and Gay Young Adults." Paper presented at the annual meeting of the American Psychological Association, San Francisco, 1991.

Davis, Angela. *Angela Davis—An Autobiography*. New York: Random House, 1974.

DeBray, Jeff, and Rick Nelson. "Acanfora: The Struggle Continues." *Daily Collegian*, 27 February 1973, p. 1.

Defoe, Jeannine. "Students Take Unrest to Streets, Demand Action." *Daily Targum*, 2 February 1995, pp. 1, 5.

de Graaf, Lawrence B. "Howard: The Evolution of a Black Student Revolt." In *Protest! Student Activism in America*, edited by Julian Foster and Durward Long. New York: William Morrow, 1970.

Deloria, Vine, Jr. *Behind the Trail of Broken Treaties: An Indian Declaration of Independence*. New York: Descartes Press, 1974.

DeMartini, Joseph R. "Student Culture as a Change Agent in American Higher Education: An Illustration from the Nineteenth Century." *Journal of Social History* 9, no. 4 (1976): 526–41.

D'Emilio, John. *Making Trouble: Essays on Gay History, Politics, and the University*. New York: Routledge, 1992.

Dewey, John. *Democracy and Education*. New York: Macmillan, 1916.

Dey, Eric L. "Undergraduate Political Attitudes: Peer Influence in Changing Social Contexts. *Journal of Higher Education* 68, no. 4 (1997): 398–413.

Dey, Eric L., Alexander W. Astin, and William S. Korn. *The American Freshman: Twenty-Five Year Trends, 1966–1990*. Los Angeles: Higher Education Research Institute, 1991.

Diamond, Edwin. "Class of '69: The Violent Years." In *Turmoil on the Campus*, edited by Edward J. Bander. New York: H. W. Wilson, 1970.

Doty, Alexander. *Making Things Perfectly Queer*. Minneapolis: University of Minnesota Press, 1993.

D'Souza, Dinesh. *Illiberal Education: The Politics of Race and Sex on Campus*. New York: Free Press, 1991.

Du Bois, W. E. B. *The Souls of Black Folk*. New York: Dover Publications, 1903/1994.

Eckert, Penelope. *Jocks and Burnouts: Social Categories and Identity in the High School*. New York: Teachers College Press, 1989.

"Editorial: A Call for Resignation," *Daily Targum*, 1 February 1995, pp. 1, 9.

Egyir, William K. "Rutgers President Angers Groups." *New York Amsterdam News*, 25 February 1995, p. 20.

Erikson, Erik H. *Identity: Youth and Crisis*. New York: W. W. Norton, 1968

Evans, Sara M. *Personal Politics: The Roots of Women's Liberation in the Civil Rights Movement and the New Left*. New York: Vintage Books, 1980.

Evans, Sara M., and Harry C. Boyte. *Free Spaces: The Sources of Democratic Change in America*. New York: Harper & Row, 1986.

Exum, William H. *Paradoxes of Protest: Black Student Activism in a White University*. Philadelphia: Temple University Press, 1985.

Faculty Committee to Investigate the Dow Incident at Indiana University. "Indiana: The Anatomy of Violence." In *Protest! Student Activism in America*, edited by Julian Foster and Durward Long. New York: William Morrow, 1970.

Ferguson, Kathy E. *The Feminist Case against Bureaucracy*. Philadelphia: Temple University Press, 1984.

Feuer, Lewis S. *The Conflict of Generations: The Character and Significance of Student Movements*. New York: Basic Books, 1969.

Fine, Michelle. "Why Urban Adolescents Drop into and out of Public High School." *Teachers College Record* 87, no. 3 (1986): 393–409.

———. *Framing Dropouts: Notes on the Politics of an Urban High School*. Albany: State University of New York Press, 1991.

Finnegan, Dana, and Emily McNally. *Dual Identities: Counseling Chemically Dependent Gay Men and Lesbians*. Center City, Minn.: Hazelden Foundation, 1987.

Foss, Daniel A., and Ralph W. Larkin. "From 'the Gates of Eden' to 'Day of the Locust': An Analysis of the Dissident Youth Movement of the 1960s and Its Heir of the Early 1970s—the Post-Movement Groups." *Theory and Society* 3 (1976): 1–44.

Foucault, Michel. *The Order of Things*. New York: Vintage Books, 1970.

———. *The History of Sexuality*, Volume 1: *An Introduction* (trans. R. Hurley). New York: Vintage Books, 1978.

———. *Discipline and Punish*. Translated by A. Sheridan. New York: Vintage Books, 1979.

———. *Power/Knowledge*. Translated by C. Gordan et al. New York: Pantheon Books, 1980.

Frammolino, Ralph. "A New Generation of Rebels: Latinos Are Demanding Colleges Be More Responsive." *Los Angeles Times*, 20 November 1993, sec. A, p. 1.

Freire, Paulo. *Pedagogy of the Oppressed*. New York: Continuum, 1970.

Friend, Richard A. "Choices, Not Closets: Heterosexism and Homophobia in Schools." In *Beyond Silenced Voices: Class, Race, and Gender in United States Schools*, edited by Lois Weis and Michelle Fine. Albany: State University of New York Press, 1991.

Fries, Judith E. *The American Indian in Higher Education, 1975–76 to 1984–85*. Washington, D.C.: Center for Education Statistics, 1987.

Galarzo, Ernesto. *Barrio Boy*. Notre Dame, Ind.: University of Notre Dame Press, 1971.

García, Ignacio M. *United We Win: The Rise and Fall of La Raza Unida Party*. Tucson: University of Arizona Press, 1989.

García, Mildred, ed. *Affirmative Action's Testament of Hope: Strategies for a New Era in Higher Education*. Albany: State University of New York, 1997.

Gilligan, Carol. "Woman's Place in Man's Life Cycle." *Harvard Educational Review* 49, no. 4 (1979): 431–46.

———. *In a Different Voice: Psychological Theory and Women's Development*. Cambridge, Mass.: Harvard University Press, 1982.

Giroux, Henry A. "Theories of Reproduction and Resistance in the New Sociology of Education: A Critical Analysis." *Harvard Educational Review* 53, no. 3 (1983): 257–93.

———. *Theory and Resistance in Education*. South Hadley, Mass.: Bergin & Garvey, 1983.

———. *Border Crossings: Cultural Workers and the Politics of Education*. New York: Routledge, 1992.

———. *Living Dangerously: Multiculturalism and the Politics of Difference*. New York: Peter Lang, 1993.

Gitlin, Todd. *The Sixties: Years of Hope, Days of Rage*. Toronto: Bantam Books, 1987.

————. *The Twilight of Common Dreams: Why America Is Wracked by Culture Wars*. New York: Henry Holt, 1995.

————. "The Anti-Political Populism of Cultural Studies." *Dissent* 44, no. 2 (1997): 77–82.

Glazer, Nathan. "What Happened at Berkeley." In *Student Activism*, edited by Irving Howe. Indianapolis: Bobbs-Merrill, 1967.

————. *Remembering the Answers: Essays on the American Student Revolt*. New York: Basic Books, 1970.

————. *We Are All Multiculturalists Now*. Cambridge: Harvard University Press, 1997.

Goffman, Erving. *Stigma: Notes on the Management of Spoiled Identity*. Englewood Cliffs, N.J.: Prentice-Hall, 1963.

Gómez-Quiñones, Juan. *Mexican Students Por La Raza: The Chicano Student Movement in Southern California*. Santa Barbara, Calif.: Editorial La Causa, 1978.

————. *Chicano Politics: Reality and Promise, 1940–1990*. Albuquerque: University of New Mexico Press, 1990.

————. *Roots of Chicano Politics, 1600–1940*. Albuquerque: University of New Mexico Press, 1994.

Goodwin, Gerald J. "Christianity, Civilization, and the Savage: The Anglican Mission to the American Indian." *Historical Magazine of the Protestant Episcopal Church* 42 (1973): 93–110.

Gordan, Larry. "UCLA Rejects Plan for Chicano Studies Department." *Los Angeles Times*, 29 April 1993, sec. B, p. 1.

————. "UCLA Strikers End Fast." *Los Angeles Times*, 8 June 1993, sec. A, p. 1.

Gordan, Larry, and Marina Dundjerski. "Budget Threats on Chicano Studies Fail to Budge UCLA." *Los Angeles Times*, 15 May 1993, sec. B, p. 1.

————. "UCLA Has 2nd Day of Protest over Program." *Los Angeles Times*, 13 May 1993, sec B, p. 1.

Grant, Joanne. *Black Protest: History, Documents, and Analyses*. Greenwich, Conn.: Fawcett Publications, 1968.

Gurin, Patricia, and Edgar Epps. *Black Consciousness, Identity, and Achievement: A Study of Students in Historically Black Colleges*. New York: John Wiley & Sons, 1975.

Hall, Roberta M., and Bernice R. Sandler. "The Classroom Climate: A Chilly One for Women?" Research report sponsored by the Project on the Status and Education of Women. Washington, D.C.: Association of American Colleges, 1982.

Harrison, Beverly Wildung. *Making the Connections: Essays in Feminist Social Ethics,* edited by Carol S. Robb. Boston: Beacon Press, 1985.

Hartman, Mary S. "Mills Students Provided Eloquent Testimony to the Value of Women's Colleges." *Chronicle of Higher Education*, 5 July 1990, sec. A, p. 40.

Hayden, Tom. *Reunion: A Memoir*. New York: Random House, 1988.

————. "Amid Cash Crisis, Hispanics Win a Historical Victory." *Chronicle of Higher Education*, 30 June 1993, sec. A, p. 40.

Heineman, Kenneth J. *Campus Wars: The Peace Movement at American State Universities in the Vietnam Era*. New York: New York University Press, 1993.

Heller, Scott. "Educators on the Left Organize to Fight Attacks on Academe, Which They See as Part of a Bigger Effort to Divide Society." *Chronicle of Higher Education*, 11 October 1996, sec. A, p. 12.

Herdt, Gilbert. *Gay Culture in America: Essays from the Field*. Boston: Beacon, 1992.

Herek, Gregory M. "Hate Crimes against Lesbians and Gay Men." *American Psychologist* 44, no. 6 (1989): 948–55.

————. "Documenting Prejudice against Lesbians and Gay Men on Campus: The Yale Sexual Orientation Survey." *Journal of Homosexuality* 25, no. 4 (1993): 15–30.

Hicks, Alisa. "Proposals Convince Trustees to Reverse Coed Decision." *Mills College Weekly*, 19 May 1990, pp. 1, 4.

Higginbotham, Evelyn Brooks. "African-American Women's History and the Metalanguage of Race." *Signs: Journal of Women in Culture and Society* 17, no. 2 (1992): 251–74.

Hirsch, Eric L. "Sacrifice for the Cause: Group Processes, Recruitment, and Commitment in a Student Social Movement." *American Sociological Review* 55 (1990): 242–54.

Hodgkinson, Harold. "Student Protest—An Institutional and National Profile." *Teachers College Record* 71, no. 4 (1970): 537–55.

Holland, Dorothy C., and Margaret A. Eisenhart. *Educated in Romance: Women, Achievement, and College*. Chicago: University of Chicago Press, 1990.

hooks, bell. *Feminist Theory: From Margin to Center*. Boston: South End Press, 1984.

————. *Black Looks: Race and Representation*. Boston: South End Press, 1992.

Horowitz, Helen L. *Campus Life: Undergraduate Cultures from the End of the Eighteenth Century to the Present*. New York: Alfred A. Knopf, 1987.

Howe, Irving. *Student Activism*. Indianapolis: Bobbs-Merrill, 1967.

Hrynik, Jennifer. "Speaker Recalls Slain Leader's Dedication." *State News*, 21 January 1997, p. 1.

Huffman, Terry E., Maurice L. Sill, and Martin Brokenleg. "College Achievement among Sioux and White South Dakota Students." *Journal of American Indian Education* 25, no. 2 (1986): 32–38.

Hurtado, Sylvia. "The Campus Racial Climate: Contexts of Conflict." *Journal of Higher Education* 63, no. 5 (1992): 539–69.

Hurtado, Sylvia, Eric L. Dey, and Jesús G. Treviño. "Exclusion or Self-Segregation?: Interaction across Racial/Ethnic Groups on College Campuses." Paper presented at the annual meeting of the American Educational Research Association, April 1994, New Orleans.

Husserl, Edmund. *The Crisis of European Sciences and the Transcendental*

Phenomenology. Translated by D. Carr. Evanston, Ill.: Northwestern University Press, 1970.

Iannello, Kathleen. *Decisions without Hierarchy: Feminist Interventions in Organization Theory and Practice*. New York: Routledge, 1992.

"Indian Tuition Waiver Fight Heats Up." *Lansing State Journal*, 3 March 1995, Sec. B, p. 3.

Jahoda, Gloria. *The Trail of Tears*. New York: Holt, Rinehart and Winston, 1975.

Jencks, Christopher, and David Riesman. *The Academic Revolution*. New York: Doubleday, 1968.

Kalita, S. Mitra. "Bomb Explodes in Douglass Library." *Daily Targum*, 5 April 1995, pp. 1, 4.

———. "Second Bomb Unnerves RU." *Daily Targum*, 10 April 1995, pp. 1, 6.

———. "Senate Backs President: Executive Committee Passes Resolution Supporting Lawrence's Wednesday Apology." *Daily Targum*, 6 February 1995, pp. 1, 4.

———. "Students Produce List of Demands." *Daily Targum*, 7 February 1995, pp. 1, 4.

———. "Students Sit-In at RAC, Disrupt Game." *Daily Targum*, 8 February 1995, p. 1.

———. "Two Arrested in Take-Over." *Daily Targum*, 8 March 1995, pp. 1, 4.

Kalita, S. Mitra, and Michelle Simonelli. "Students Walk Out after Meeting with President." *Daily Targum*, 3 February 1995, pp. 1, 4.

Keep, Rosalind. *Fourscore Years: A History of Mills College*. Oakland, Calif.: Mills College Press, 1931.

———. *Fourscore and Ten Years: A History of Mills College*. Oakland, Calif.: Mills College Press, 1946.

Kelley, Robin D. G. *Race Rebels: Culture, Politics, and the Black Working Class*. New York: Free Press, 1994.

Keniry, Julian. "Environmental Movement Booming on Campuses." *Change* 25 (1993): 42–49.

Keniston, Kenneth. "The Sources of Student Dissent." *Journal of Social Issues* 23, no. 3 (1967): 108–37.

Kerr, Clark. *The Uses of the University*. Cambridge: Harvard University Press, 1963.

———. "Student Dissent and Confrontation Politics." In *Protest! Student Activism in America*, edited by Julian Foster and Durward Long. New York: William Morrow, 1970.

Kimmerly, Geoff. "Students Celebrate Legacy of King's Vision." *State News*, 7 April 1997, p. 1.

Kohlberg, Lawrence. "The Cognitive-Developmental Approach to Moral Education." *Phi Delta Kappan* 56 (1975): 670–77.

———. "The Future of Liberalism as the Dominant Ideology of the West." In *Moral Development and Politics*, edited by Richard W. Wilson and Gordon J. Schochet. Westport, Conn.: Praeger, 1980.

Koritz, Helen G. "Women in Science: Changing the Climate." *Journal of College Science Teaching* 21 (1992): 260–61.

Kraemer, Barbara A. "The Academic and Social Integration of Hispanic Students into College. *Review of Higher Education* 20, no. 2 (1997): 163–79.

Kremer, Lisa. "Mills Womyn Celebrate." *Mills College Weekly*, 19 May 1990, pp. 1, 4.

Kuh, George D. "Assessing Student Culture." In *Assessing Academic Climates and Cultures*, New Directions for Institutional Research No. 68, edited by William G. Tierney. San Francisco: Jossey-Bass, 1990.

———. "In Their Own Words: What Students Learn outside the Classroom." *American Educational Research Journal* 30 (1993): 277–304.

———. "The Other Curriculum: Out-of-Class Experiences Associated with Student Learning and Personal Development." *Journal of Higher Education* 66, no. 2 (1995): 123–55.

Kuh, George D., and Elizabeth J. Whitt. *The Invisible Tapestry: Culture in American Colleges and Universities*, ASHE-ERIC Higher Education Research Report No. 1. Washington, D.C.: Association for the Study of Higher Education, 1988.

Lane, Mary. "Board May Review Coed Decision Next Week." *Mills College Weekly*, 11 May 1990, p. 1.

———. "Faculty Endorses Single Sex." *Mills College Weekly*, 27 April 1990, pp. 1, 3.

———. "Rally Draws Students, Media." *Mills College Weekly*, 16 February 1990, p. 1.

Leslie, Connie, and Andrew Murr. "Martyrs for Multiculturalism: Courses that Students at UCLA Might Die For." *Newsweek* 14 June 1993, 77.

Lever, Janet. "Sex Differences in the Games Children Play." *Social Problems* 23 (1976): 478–87.

Levine, Arthur. *When Dreams and Heroes Died*. San Francisco: Jossey-Bass, 1980.

Levine, Arthur, and Jeanette Cureton. "The Quiet Revolution: Eleven Facts about Multiculturalism and the Curriculum." *Change* 24, no. 1 (1992): 25–29.

———. *When Hope and Fear Collide: A Portrait of Today's College Students*. San Francisco: Jossey-Bass, 1998.

Levine, Arthur, and Deborah Hirsch. "Undergraduates in Transition: A New Wave of Activism on American College Campuses." *Higher Education* 22 (1991): 119–28.

Levine, Bettijane. "A UCLA Professor and 6 Students Have Gone Days without Food." *Los Angeles Times*, 1 June 1993, sec. E, p. 1.

Lincoln, Yvonna, and Egon Guba. *Naturalistic Inquiry*. Beverly Hills: Sage, 1985.

Lipset, Seymour Martin. "Political Controversies at Harvard, 1636 to 1974." In *Education and Politics at Harvard*, edited by Seymour Martin Lipset and David Riesman. New York: McGraw-Hill, 1975.

———. *Rebellion in the University*. Chicago: University of Chicago Press, 1976.

Lipset, Seymour Martin, and Philip Altbach. "Student Politics and Higher Education in the United States." In *Student Politics*, edited by Seymour Martin Lipset. New York: Basic Books, 1967.

Lipset, Seymour Martin, and Sheldon S. Wolin, eds. *The Berkeley Student Revolts: Facts and Interpretations*. Garden City, N.Y.: Anchor Books, 1965.

Loeb, Paul Rogat. *Generation at the Crossroads: Apathy and Action on the American Campus*. New Brunswick: Rutgers University Press, 1994.

Long, Durward. "Black Protest." In *Protest! Student Activism in America*, edited by Julian Foster and Durward Long. New York: William Morrow, 1970.

———. "Wisconsin: Changing Styles of Administrative Response." In *Protest! Student Activism in America*, edited by Julian Foster and Durward Long. New York: William Morrow, 1970.

López, Fred A., III. "Reflections on the Chicano Movement." *Latin American Perspectives* 19, no. 4 (1992): 79–102.

Lorde, Audre. *Sister Outsider*. Freedom, Calif.: Crossing Press, 1984.

———. *I Am Your Sister: Black Women Organizing across Sexualities*. Latham, N.Y.: Kitchen Table Press, 1985.

———. "Age, Race, Class, and Sex: Women Redefining Difference." In *Campus Wars: Multiculturalism and the Politics of Difference*, edited by John Arthur and Amy Shapiro. Boulder, Colo.: Westview Press, 1995.

Low, Jane M. "The Davis Social Environment: A Report of Student Opinions." Student Affairs Research and Information, University of California at Davis, 1988.

Lukács, Georg. *History and Class Consciousness*. Translated by Rodney Livingstone. Cambridge: MIT Press, 1968.

Lynch, Jason, and Francine Tardo. "Hundreds Voice Demands." *Daily Targum*, 2 February 1995, pp. 1, 5.

MacLeod, Jay. *Ain't No Makin' It*. Boulder, Colo.: Westview Press, 1987.

Madgevski, Sonja. "Challenging Columbus." *State News*, 13 October 1995, pp. 1, 10.

Magner, Denise K. "Proposal to Revise Chicano Studies Divides UCLA." *Chronicle of Higher Education*, 1 May 1991, sec. A, p. 12.

Magolda, Marcia B. Baxter. *Knowing and Reasoning in College: Gender-Related Patterns in Students' Intellectual Development*. San Francisco: Jossey-Bass, 1992.

Mannheim, Karl. *Ideology and Utopia: An Introduction to the Sociology of Knowledge*. San Diego: Harcourt Brace Jovanovich, 1936.

Marck, Siegfried, "Dialectical Materialism." In *A History of Philosophical Systems*, edited by Vergilius Ferm. New York: Philosophical Library, 1950.

Marcuse, Herbert. *Reason and Revolution: Hegel and the Rise of Social Theory*. New York: Humanities Press, 1954.

Markus, Gregory B., Jeffrey P. F. Howard, and David C. King. "Integrating Community Service and Classroom Instruction Enhances Learning: Results from an Experiment." *Educational Evaluation and Policy Analysis* 15, no. 4 (1993): 410–19.

Marx, Karl. *The Portable Karl Marx*. Translated and edited by Eugene Kamenka. New York: Penguin Books, 1983.

McAdam, Doug. *Freedom Summer*. New York: Oxford University, 1988.

McCormick, Richard P. *The Black Student Protest Movement at Rutgers*. New Brunswick: Rutgers University Press, 1990.

McCurdy, Jack. "Trustees of Mills College Reverse Decision to Admit Undergraduate Men." *Chronicle of Higher Education*, 30 May 1990, sec. A, p. 2.

McLaren, Peter. *Schooling as a Ritual Performance*. London: Routledge & Kegan Paul, 1986.

———. *Life in Schools*. New York: Longman, 1989.

———. *Critical Pedagogy and Predatory Culture*. New York: Routledge, 1995.

McRobbie, Angela. "Working Class Girls and the Culture of Femininity." In *Women Take Issue*, edited by Centre for Contemporary Cultural Studies. London: Routledge & Kegan Paul, 1978.

Mendel-Reyes, Meta. *Reclaiming Democracy: The Sixties in Politics and Memory*. New York: Routledge, 1995.

Merleau-Ponty, Maurice. *Phenomenology of Perception*. Translated by C. Smith. New York: Humanities Press, 1962.

Messer-Davidow, Ellen. "Knowers, Knowing, Knowledge: Feminist Theory and Education." *Journal of Thought* 20, no. 3 (1985): 8–24.

Michigan Federal Tribes Education Consortium. *The Michigan Indian Tuition Waiver: An Investment in the Future of Michigan's Original People*. Lansing, Mich.: Michigan Federal Tribes Education Consortium, 1996.

Miller, James. *Democracy Is in the Streets: From Port Huron to the Siege of Chicago*. Cambridge: Harvard University Press, 1994.

Miller, Jeannine. "Empowerment." *Mills College Weekly*, 16 February 1990, p. 2.

Mills, C. Wright. *The Power Elite*. New York: Oxford University Press, 1956.

Miranda, Jeanne, and Micheal Storms. "Psychological Adjustment of Lesbians and Gay Men." *Journal of Counseling and Development* 68 (1989): 41–45.

Moller, Herbert. "Youth as a Force in the Modern World." *Comparative Studies in Society and History*, 10 (1968): 237–60.

Moore, Kathryn McDaniel. "Old Saints and Young Sinners: A Study of Student Discipline at Harvard College, 1636–1734." Ph.D. diss., University of Wisconsin, 1972.

———. "The War with the Tutors: Student-Faculty Conflict at Harvard and Yale, 1745–1771." *History of Education* 18, no. 2 (1978): 115–27.

Moraga, Cherríe. *Loving in the War Years*. Boston: South End Press, 1983.

Mumbles, Dennis. "Francis Lawrence Meant What He Said." *New York Amsterdam News*, 4 March 1995, p. 13.

Muñoz, Carlos, Jr. *Youth, Identity, Power: The Chicano Movement*. London: Verso, 1989.

Nelson, Randy, and Harley Baker. "The Educational Climate for Gay, Lesbian, and Bisexual Students." Student Services, University of California at Santa Cruz, 1990.

Nettles, Michael T. "Factors Related to Black and White Students' College Performance." In *Toward Black Undergraduate Student Equality in American Higher Education*, edited by Michael T. Nettles. New York: Greenwood Press, 1988.

Nieberding, Ronald A. "In Every Classroom: The Report of the President's Select Committee for Lesbian and Gay Concerns." Office of Student Life Policy and Services, Rutgers University, 1989.

Nora, Amaury. "Determinants of Retention among Chicano College Students: A Structural Model." *Research in Higher Education* 26, no. 1 (1987): 31–58.

———. "Campus-Based Aid Programs as Determinants of Retention among Hispanic Community College Students." *Journal of Higher Education* 61 (1990): 312–31.

———. "Two-Year Colleges and Minority Students' Educational Aspirations: Help or Hindrance?" In *Higher Education: Handbook of Theory and Research*, Volume 9, edited by John C. Smart. New York: Agathon Press, 1993.

Novak, Stephen J. *The Rights of Youth: American Colleges and Student Revolt, 1798–1815*. Cambridge: Harvard University Press, 1977.

Obatala, J. K. "Where Did Their Revolution Go?" *Nation*, 2 October 1972, 272–74.

Obear, Frederick W. "Student Activism in the Sixties." In *Protest! Student Activism in America*, edited by Julian Foster and Durward Long. New York: William Morrow, 1970.

Oren, Dan A. *Joining the Club: A History of Jews and Yale*. New Haven, Conn.: Yale University Press, 1985.

Parish, Arnie. *A Descriptive Study of the Michigan Indian Tuition Waiver Program*. E. Lansing, Mich.: Native American Institute, 1996.

Parsons, Talcott. *Toward a General Theory of Action*. Cambridge: Harvard University Press, 1951.

Penfield, Joyce. "Institutional Issues to Examine." Report submitted to the Rutgers University Board of Governors, 1995.

Peterson, Richard. *The Scope of Organized Student Protest in 1964–1965*. Princeton, N.J.: Educational Testing Service, 1966.

Phillips, Donald E. *Student Protest, 1960–1969: An Analysis of the Issues and Speeches*. Washington, D.C.: University Press of America, 1980.

Pottinger, Richard. "The Quest for Valued Futures: Steps on a Rainbow Journey." *Journal of Navajo Education* 6, no. 3 (1989): 2–11.

———. "Disjunction to Higher Education: American Indian Students in the Southwest." *Journal of Navajo Education* 7, no. 2 (1990): 37–45.

Pronger, Brian. "Gay Jocks: A Phenomenology of Gay Men in Athletics." In *Rethinking Masculinity: Philosophical Explorations in Light of Feminism*, edited by L. May and R. A. Strikwerda. Lanham, Md.: Littlefield Adams, 1992.

Quinn, Michelle C. "Mills Is Still Defiantly All-Women, But It'll Never Be the Same." *New York Times*, 1 September 1993, sec. B, p. 6.

Quinnan, Timothy William. "The Last Word: Culture, Theory, and Leadership." *Black Issues in Higher Education* 12, no. 2 (1995): 108.

Raff, Lisa. "In Racism Fight at Rutgers, Jewish Students Claim Middle Ground." *Jewish Advocate*, 2 March 1995, p. 7.

Ratcliff, Sarah, and Karen Lubisch. "Students Channel Energies." *Mills College Weekly*, 27 April 1990, pp. 1, 3.

Rhoads, Robert A. *Coming Out in College: The Struggle for a Queer Identity*. Westport, Conn.: Bergin & Garvey, 1994.

———. "Critical Multiculturalism, Border Knowledge, and the Canon: Implications for General Education and the Academy." *Journal of General Education* 44, no. 4 (1995): 256–73.

———. "The Cultural Politics of Coming Out in College: Experiences of Male Students." *Review of Higher Education* 19, no. 1 (1995): 1–22.

———. "Learning From the Coming-Out Experiences of College Males." *Journal of College Student Development* 36, no. 1 (1995): 67–74.

———. *Community Service and Higher Learning: Explorations of the Caring Self*. Albany: State University of New York Press, 1997.

Rhoads, Robert A., and Sylvia M. Solorzano. "Multiculturalism and the Community College: A Case Study of an Immigrant Education Program." *Community College Review* 23, no. 2 (1995): 3–16.

Rhoads, Robert A., and James R. Valadez. *Democracy, Multiculturalism, and the Community College: A Critical Perspective*. New York: Garland Publishing, 1996.

Rochín, Refugio I., and Adaljiza Sosa-Riddell. "Chicano Studies in a Pluralistic Society: Contributing to Multiculturalism." *Bilingual Review* 17, no. 2 (1992): 132–42.

Roosevelt, Franklin Delano. *Pearl Harbor: Speeches before and after Pearl Harbor*. New York: Shaman & Schlick, 1946.

Rosenthal, Joel. "Southern Black Student Activism: Assimilation vs. Nationalism." *Journal of Negro Education* 44 (1975): 113–29.

Rowan, Carl. "The Rowan Report: Black People Had Better Be Very Careful." *Indianapolis Recorder*, 4 March 1995, sec. A, p. 2.

"Rutgers Students Must Keep Protest Focused. *Philadelphia Tribune*, 3 March 1995, sec. A, p. 6.

"Rutgers' Students Reject University President's Apology for Racist Remark." *New York Voice Incorporated*, 22 February 1995, p. 1.

Sampson, Edward E. "Student Activism and the Decade of Protest." In *Student Activism and Protest: Alternatives for Social Change*, edited by Edward E. Sampson and Harold A. Korn. San Francisco: Jossey-Bass, 1970.

San Miguel, Guadalupe. "Actors Not Victims: Chicanas/os and the Struggle for Educational Equality." In *Chicanas/Chicanos at the Crossroads: Social, Economic, and Political Change*, edited by David R. Maciel and Isidro D. Ortiz. Tucson: University of Arizona Press, 1996.

Sarabia, Saul. "Chicano Studies Fight Involves a Bigger Issue." *Los Angeles Times*, 30 May 1993, sec. M, p. 3.

Sarchett, Barry W. "What's All the Fuss about This Postmodern Stuff." In

Campus Wars: Multiculturalism and the Politics of Difference, edited by John Arthur and Amy Shapiro. Boulder, Colo.: Westview Press, 1995.

Schlesinger, Arthur M., Jr. *The Disuniting of America: Reflections on a Multicultural Society*. New York: W. W. Norton, 1992.

Schutz, Alfred. *Alfred Schutz on Phenomenology and Social Relations*, edited by H. R. Wagner. Chicago: University of Chicago Press, 1970.

Scott, Wilbur J. "Attachment to Indian Culture and the 'Difficult Situation': A Study of American Indian College Students." *Youth & Society* 17, no. 4 (1986): 381–95.

Searle, John R. *The Campus War: A Sympathetic Look at the University in Agony*. New York: World Publishing, 1971.

Selznick, Philip. "Reply to Glazer." In *Student Activism*, edited by Irving Howe. Indianapolis: Bobbs-Merrill, 1967.

Seymour, Elaine. "Undergraduate Problems with Teaching and Advising in SME Majors—Explaining Gender Differences in Attrition Rates." *Journal of College Science Teaching* 21 (1992): 284–92.

Shepard, C. F. "Report on the Quality of Campus Life for Lesbian, Gay, and Bisexual Students." Student Affairs Information and Research Office, University of California at Los Angeles, 1990.

Sidel, Ruth. *Battling Bias: The Struggle for Identity and Community on College Campuses*. New York: Viking, 1994.

Signorile, Michelangelo. *Queer in America: Sex, the Media, and the Closets of Power*. New York: Random House, 1993.

Simonelli, Michelle. "Bomb Threats Spread." *Daily Targum*, 6 April 1995, pp. 1, 6.

———. "Students Note Dwindling Activism Numbers." *Daily Targum*, 20 February 1995, pp. 1, 4.

Smith, Ronald A. *Sports and Freedom: The Rise of Big-Time College Athletics*. New York: Oxford University Press, 1988.

Snow, Amy. "Angry Crowd Protests Engler at Pep Rally." *State News*, 9 October 1995, Sec. A, p. 1.

Snyder, Barb. "HOPS Member Removed." *Daily Collegian*, 16 February 1972, p. 1.

———. "HOPS: 1 Year Old, But Learning Life Fast." *Daily Collegian*, 27 April 1972, p. 1.

———. "HOPS Sues University." *Daily Collegian*, 14 February 1972, p. 1.

Spitzberg, Irving J., Jr., and Virginia V. Thorndike. *Creating Community on College Campuses*. Albany: SUNY Press, 1992.

Stage, Frances K., and Kathleen Manning. *Enhancing the Multicultural Campus Environment: A Cultural Brokering Approach*. New Directions for Student Services No. 60. San Francisco: Jossey-Bass, 1992.

Staples, Robert. "The Illusion of Racial Equality: The Black American Dilemma." In *Lure and Loathing: Essays on Race, Identity, and the Ambivalence of Assimilation*, edited by Gerald Early. New York: Penguin Books, 1993.

Stevens, Jay. *Storming Heaven: LSD and the American Dream*. New York: Harper & Row, 1988.

Takaki, Ronald. *A Different Mirror: A History of Multicultural America*. Boston: Little, Brown, 1993.

Templeton, Eleanor. "Indian Tuition Waiver." *State News*, 12 July 1995, 1–2.

Tierney, William G. "Cultural Politics and the Curriculum in Postsecondary Education." *Journal of Education* 171, no. 3 (1989): 72–88.

———. "An Anthropological Analysis of Student Participation in College." *Journal of Higher Education* 63 (1992): 603–18.

———. *Official Encouragement, Institutional Discouragement: Minorities in Academe—the Native American Experience*. Norwood, N.J.: Ablex, 1992.

———. *Building Communities of Difference: Higher Education in the 21st Century*. Westport, Conn.: Bergin & Garvey, 1993.

Tierney, William G., et al. "Enhancing Diversity: Toward a Better Campus Climate." Report of the Committee on Lesbian and Gay Concerns, Pennsylvania State University, 1992.

Tijerina, Kathryn Harris, and Paul Philip Biemer. "The Dance of Indian Higher Education: One Step Forward, Two Steps Back." *Educational Record* 68, no. 4 (1988): 86–93.

Tinto, Vincent. *Leaving College: Rethinking the Causes and Cures of Student Attrition*. 2nd ed. Chicago: University of Chicago Press, 1993.

Tobias, Sheila. "Women *in* Science—Women *and* Science." *Journal of College Science Teaching* 21 (1992): 276–78.

Tripp, Luke. "Race Consciousness Among African-American Students, 1980s." *Western Journal of Black Studies* 15, no. 3 (1991): 159–68.

Troiden, Richard R. "Becoming Homosexual: A Model of Gay Identity Acquisition." *Psychiatry* 42 (1979): 362–73.

———. "The Formation of Homosexual Identities." *Journal of Homosexuality* 17, nos. 1/2 (1989): 43–73.

Turner, Ralph H. "Campus Peace: Harmony or Uneasy Truce?" *Sociological and Social Research* 57, no. 1 (1972): 5–21.

Vasquez, Richard. *Chicano*. Garden City, N.Y.: Doubleday, 1970.

Vellela, Tony. *New Voices: Student Activism in the '80s and '90s*. Boston: South End Press, 1988.

Veysey, Laurence R. *The Emergence of the American University*. Chicago: University of Chicago Press, 1965.

Walters, Ronald G. *American Reformers, 1815–1860*. New York: Hill and Wang, 1978.

Weis, Lois. *Between Two Worlds*. Boston: Routledge & Kegan Paul, 1985.

Welch, Susan. *A Feminist Ethic of Risk*. Minneapolis, Minn.: Fortress Press, 1989.

West, Maria. "Students Respond to Options, Comments." *Mills College Weekly*, 16 February 1990, p. 1.

Willis, Paul E. *Learning to Labor*. Aldershot: Gower, 1977.

Woodward, C. Vann. "What Became of the 1960s?" *New Republic*, 9 November 1974, 18–25.

Wright, Bobby. *American Indian and Alaska Native Higher Education: Toward a New Century of Academic Achievement and Cultural Integrity*. Washington, D.C.: Department of Education, Indian Nations at Risk Task Force, 1991.

———. "The 'Untameable Savage Spirit': American Indians in Colonial Colleges." *Review of Higher Education* 14, no. 4 (1991): 429–52.

Yost, Nicole. "Inspiration." *Mills College Weekly*, 16 February 1990, p. 2.

Young, Iris M. *Justice and the Politics of Difference*. Princeton, N.J.: Princeton University Press, 1990.

Zald, Mayer N., and Michael A. Berger. "Social Movements in Organizations: Coup d'Etat, Insurgency, and Mass Movements." *American Journal of Sociology* 83, no. 4 (1978): 823–61.

Muhammad, Elijah, 189
Mujeres Latinas, 14
multiculturalism, 7, 8
Multicultural Student Movement, 20, 28, 30, 58–60, 189–218, 220, 227
multiversity, 51
Munoz, Carlos, 89
Myanmar. *See* Free Burma Coalition

NAACP, 210, 225
napalm, 48
National Coming Out Day, 9, 26, 184–85
National Day of Action, 12, 13, 17
National Guard, 4
National Guardian, The, 36
naturalistic inquiry, xi
Nazi Germany, 168
NBC, 26
New Deal, 34
New England Center for Higher Education, 229
New Left, 4, 6, 12, 17, 18, 19, 36
New School of Social Research, 226
Newton, Huey, 217, 232
Newsweek, 10
New York Amsterdam News, 197
New York Times, The, x, 195
New York University, 22
Nixon, President Richard, 49, 55
Nobel Peace Prize, 236
North American Indian Student Organization, 127–58
North Carolina Agricultural and Technical College, 41
North Carolina College, 41
Northern Michigan University, 132
Northwestern University, 238

Obatala, J. K., 232
Obear, Frederick, 40
Oberlin College, 1, 48, 95
Ohio National Guard, 4
Olmos, Edward James, 75
100 Black Men, 194, 201, 209, 210
One Stop Immigration, 65
Orangeburg Ultimatum, 43
On the Road, 50

Oregon Public Employees Union, 13
Oregon State University, 13, 14
Oren, Dan, 32
Organization Man, The, 50

Peace Movement, 5, 8, 47–50
Pennsylvania State University, viii, 10, 11, 17, 26, 48, 159–88, 234, 242
Peterson, Richard, 35, 36
phenomenology, ix, x
Polanco, Richard G., 67
Port Huron Statement, 19, 20, 72, 242
postmodernism, 240
Power Elite, The, 19, 122
Princeton University, 1, 33, 51
Progressive Student Alliance, 14, 15
Proposition 187, 7, 89, 242
Proposition 209, 89, 139, 223, 224, 242

qualitative research, xi
Queer Nation, 162, 174
Quinnan, Timothy, 204

Reagan, Ronald, 12
Reagan-Bush Years, 89
Reaganomics, 5
Reality Bites, 7
Reasoner, Harry, 26
Reclaiming Democracy, 7
Red Eagle, 156
Reed College, 1
Reisman, David, 32
Robert's Rules of Order, 111
Rodham, Hillary, 18
Romney, Governor George, 130
Roosevelt, Franklin Delano, 34
Roots of Chicano Politics, The, 69
ROTC, 10, 43, 160,
Rowan, Carl, 198–200
Roybal-Allard, Lucille, 67
Rustin, Bayard, 176
Rutgers University, xi, 18, 28, 29, 33, 122, 189–218, 219, 233, 234, 242; New Brunswick campus, 18

Saint Augustine College, 41
San Francisco State University, 46, 49

Library of Congress Cataloging-in-Publication Data
Rhoads, Robert A.
    Freedom's web : student activism in an age of cultural diversity /
    Robert A. Rhoads.
        p.   cm.
    Includes bibliographical references (p.   ) and index.
    ISBN 0-8018-5887-9 (alk. paper)
        1. Student movements—United States—Case studies.   2. College
    students—United States—Political activity—Case studies.   3. Multi-
    culturalism—United States—Case studies.   4. Multicultural education—
    United States—Case studies.   5. Minorities—Education (Higher)—
    United States—Case studies.   I. Title.
    LA229.R56   1998
    378.1'98'1—dc21   98-5004
                                                                        CIP